The Pursuit of Laughter

By

Diana Mosley

GIBSON SQUARE
London

First edition published in 2008 in the UK by Gibson Square

UK Tel: +44 (0)20 7096 1100
     Fax: +44 (0)20 7993 2214

US Tel: +1 646 216 9813
     Fax: +1 646 216 9488

Eire Tel: +353 (0)1 657 1057

     info@gibsonsquare.com
     www.gibsonsquare.com

     ISBN 9 7 8 1 9 0 6 1 4 2 1 0 0

The moral rights of The Estate of Diana Mosley, Deborah Devonshire, Martin Rynja to be identified as the author of this work has been asserted in accordance with the Copyright, Designs and Patents Act 1988.

Printed by Clays Ltd

Index

Editor's Note

Perhaps like everyone who only knew Diana from the media, I was not sure who she was. We first got in touch when in 2001 her sister Deborah Devonshire had kindly suggested I should ask Diana to write a foreword for a book on their sister Nancy Mitford. I had just started a publishing company and watched an entertaining documentary on Nancy. There was at that time nothing on her in print and I wanted to reissue the autobiography Harold Acton had edited from the letters Nancy had been collecting for this purpose before she died. Diana and I had only corresponded about the elegant and copy-perfect foreword that had rolled off the fax.

Now I was about to have lunch at her home in Paris. The interviews that I had read in advance made it sound as if being in the presence of Diana could be nerve-wracking on account of her at times strident political views—a very different person indeed from her Mitfordian autobiography *A Life of Contrasts* that I had also read.

I rang the doorbell next to the enormous *porte cochère* where she lived opposite the French Ministry of Defence, not at all sure what to expect. The concierge let me in and at the top of the stairs stood an attractive elderly lady with limpid blue eyes and striking white hair dressed in a well-tailored dove-gray dress. Although she moved deliberately, she seemed fit enough to run the Paris marathon. The first thing she said in the most extraordinarily elongated pre-War vowels was 'You must always shout at me, I am frightfully deaf.' The second, 'I was awfully worried, you are probably famished.' I had arrived by train from London but had forgotten about the one hour time difference and had been to embarrassed to tell Diana's maid on the phone the precise reason why I was delayed and had left it rather vague whether the general unreliability of public transport might have been to blame. But here I was an hour late, and she had been worried.

Exhausted by waiting for me, Diana retired for a while as I guiltily ate a perfectly cooked lunch—by her maid—in the dining room with fragrant white lilies, her favourite flower, while overlooking the large garden of the French Ministry of Defence where various functions were taking place in the dappled shade. When she re-emerged I had one of the most delightful afternoons I have ever had. The refreshing thing was that not for a second had I arrived at Mount Olympus—a feeling that one can get with those in the public eye born after the War. Evelyn Waugh, Lytton Strachey, John Betjeman, Churchills etc had all been close friends, but opposite me sat a gorgeous no-nonsense nineteen year old with a razor-sharp mind in a neat ninety year old body who enjoyed laughing about many subjects as well as batting away (with a number of home runs) questions on the 7 most controversial years of her long life. (Apart from A.N. Wilson's articles, Mark Steyn's column of his seduction, Valerie Grove's interview when Diana published an expanded edition her autobiography with me, and Duncan Fallowell's last interview, are probably the most true-to-life portraits—the photographs less often so as they seem to have been the ones from the end of a session with the photographer when Diana was getting tired.) At the same time, on her coffee table were tomes in German, English and French in various states of being read—if Britain liked intellectuals in the way France does, she might have wanted to be one.

After our meeting we became 'fax friends'—her joke. Over time arose the idea of this book—a collection of the diary she wrote from 1953 to 1958 and most of her journalism. Her last long-hand fax arrived two weeks before she died in the summer of 2003 when Paris was suffering under a prolonged heat wave. She did not want to move to an air-conditioned hotel and succumbed to the heat. I was deeply moved when her daughter-in-law Charlotte Mosley rang with the unexpected news. She was in the poignant words of A.N. Wilson 'a friend whose conversations and letters I already miss with aching sadness'.

The Mitfords: Letters between Six Sisters (2007) has brought a fresh interest in Diana as a writer and wickedly original observer of the twentieth century (including Oswald Mosley, the love of her life). It prompted me to resume editing the book that follows.

In many ways *The Pursuit of Laughter* is Diana's life in writings. Her teenage self was shaped by two women, her nanny who said on her wedding day 'don't worry no one will be looking at you', and her mother's childhood friend Violet Hammersley ('Mrs Ham') whose literary connections made the sisters feel like 'country bumpkins'. Diana quickly changed all that aged 19. At her burial next to her sisters, one of her Irish grandchildren—neither of us knew each other, though she looked exactly like Diana's photographs of the 30s—stopped me for a chat in the most likeably direct way, and I could see how Diana's friendships must have quickly multiplied away from home.

But the literary seeds only started in the 50s when the Mosleys moved from Wiltshire to Paris next to the Duke and Duchess of Windsor. Though no longer a supporter of the British Empire but an ardent European instead, Mosley decided not to mix in French domestic politics. There was also not much politicking left in Britain either as it was distant and hostile. He was banned from the British media for the time being, and so a publishing company was set up, Euphorion, after a character in Goethe's *Faust* sequel—released from jail Mosley had declared the death of fascism. Diana gave her loyal support—though she was never a politician like his first wife Cimmie Curzon, who stood as a prospective MP for Mosley's party. The idea was that Euphorion would publish his books while Diana would be free to commission a cultural list. She announced her translation of Goethe's first *Faust* with a modest volley of 3 orders (her 1985 translation of racing champion Nicki Lauda would dwarf Goethe), but she was more fortunate with

Stuka Pilot, a first-person account by the Luftwaffe's most decorated pilot. Though published without much hope as a list filler, British readers took to heart its anorak style and the author's expert thrashing of Allied forces; it became an instant bestseller.

More important however was the *European*, a cultural magazine with the same purpose. It circulated in a small number among an exclusive group of friends. From a standing start Diana edited from her home in Orsay a surprisingly professional monthly. At the age of 43, she was writing many of the light-hearted articles herself at the relentless pace required by a periodical. She wrote book reviews and a very witty diary for her readers to turn to when they received the latest edition. All are from her unexpectedly original point of view and in her distinctive Mitford style. Clearly in her element while 50s Paris was leading the world in fashion, ideas and literature, her articles are both waspishly funny, timeless and informed about anything from sex, to her friends, to sadism, to prison. They were completely separate from Mosley's ponderous pieces about the great issues of the day that appeared anonymously—the point of the magazine. It is said that Flaubert's punchy send-up of the French in his *Dictionaire des idées reçues* is untranslatable in English because the British have no 'received' ideas as such. But reading Diana's observations from France, she found a whole stock room of hypocrisy and nonsense. Having been jailed from the beginning of the war for being married to Mosley (Diana never knew the 2004 news that it was not Nancy but her father-in-law Lord Moyne, a former minister of agriculture, who ensured that she ended up in jail) she was less than persuaded by the certainties of British culture. She had an unerring eye for rubbish logic that her sisters must have learned to fear or shriek about with laughter. Surprisingly for the wife of a notorious politician, she also admits that she voted only once in her life (for a Liberal Democrat in today's political terms, it seems). Not previously freely accessible, this volume publishes the essays and diary for the first time.

More entertaining writing followed in her autobiography, *A Life of Contrasts*. Diana told me she was particularly proud of the Waughian portrait of her idiosyncratic mother-in-law Lady Evelyn Guinness (p. 58

below) which she had spent much time on to get right. Her nemesis Colonel Guinness (later Lord Moyne) receives a passing mention as she seems to have been put off by him—as minister of agriculture he was preoccupied with increasing Britain's beetroot production in 1928 (in 1944 he was blown up on his boat by Zionists when Churchill gave him the Middle East of the Empire). Later she wrote her best reviews for A.N. Wilson, literary editor from 1990 to 1997 of the *Evening Standard*. While being fair minded she sent up books in sentences that are as elegantly handled as a Chanel dress. Her review, for example, of saving the elephant—of which, as far as one knows, she had no knowledge—is a laugh and miles removed from being ill-informed, sour or grindingly Puritanical. Entirely a-religious, she dissects throughout her writings church tenets in a way that dispatches all cant in the most devastating and hilarious way.

This collection reveals much about Diana herself. She writes about her finding clever friends and observing that 'what they lack in good nature they make up for over and over again in the amusement and interest they provide.' It seems to have been a compass for her life. She wrote in another book about an incident when a few years before his death in 1980 Mosley disagreed in no uncertain terms with her. Mosley's biographer Robert Skidelsky, who was there, said after hearing him for a while, "'Oh, Kit [Mosley], *poor* Diana!" I turned to Robert: "Don't worry. One doesn't live with Kit for forty years and get upset by a few insults." Later on, when Kit came to say goodnight, he said, "It was *dreadful* of you to say that to Robert; he will imagine I am *rude* to you." When I laughed, he began to laugh too.' Perhaps no wonder her favourite book was *Wahlverwandschaften* [passions of choice], one of Goethe's most complex works—it is the jokes she said to me.

In many ways Diana belonged to the last of a literary type from previous centuries who had no concerns other than the irritation—in both directions—of their friends and relatives in politics. Reviewing Mrs Hammersley's translation of the prolific seventeenth-century letter-writer Mme de Sévigné, Diana says they 'could almost have been written yesterday. She walked in the woods, received her grand neighbours, chatted with the abbé, read a great many books, and never stopped assuring her correspondents that she was not in the least bored [p. 350].' This was a tease directed at Mrs Hammersley (who thought of herself as a poor exile in the Isle of Wight), but Diana shared an outlook that was identical to Mme de Sévigné. In the 30s Hitler had burst on the scene from nowhere—no one from the European ruling classes had ever heard of his family (even the name Hitler was made up). When asked by James Naughtie in 2002 on national radio what she would do if Hitler came through the door, she said without a pause 'I think you would be just like me and would ask him to tell a few things… He was a mystery person.' If her frank curiosity was a relic from the past, so was her *ancien-régime* incarceration in Holloway on the secret testimony of her former father-in-law who happened to have Churchill's ear— Churchill was also a relative through her mother. A healthy talent to annoy can be a risky thing in such circumstances. In previous centuries she herself would have written many entertaining letters from prison (she was only allowed two, plus one to parliament, every so often), but instead the cue to writing came later with the articles below.

This book seeks to show what those close to Diana saw in her, a delightful friend with a complex connection to modern history; a conundrum that tells us something about ourselves, too. Her brilliance lay in the art of conversation and friendship with many people, reflected in *The Pursuit of Laughter*.

Martin Rynja
November 2008

Deborah Devonshire

My sister Diana was the fourth child and third daughter of our parents, then David and Sydney Mitford. Three more daughters were born, so she was midway between the eldest (Nancy) and the youngest (myself).

An aura of beauty surrounded her, she was always the best looking woman at any gathering, without make-up or artifice, and often wearing clothes till they were threadbare. She was beautiful when she was born in 1910 and remained beautiful till her death aged 93. An acquaintance, who had not seen her for 50 years, was walking behind her in a Paris street and immediately recognised her, so distinctive was her walk.

It was Diana's beauty which made the first impression, but she had other qualities any one of which would have made her memorable.

Her 'education' was sketchy to say the least, depending on the talent (or lack of) of a single teacher, a governess, who had charge of all four energetic and opinionated children of varying ages, interests and abilities—none of them submissive or obedient. School, which Diana dreaded, was not a threat because my father did not allow it then.

When the childhood home of Batsford Park, Moreton-in-Marsh, was sold in 1919 my father bought Asthall Manor on the fringe of his estate near Burford. The ancient house had a barn nearby which he converted into a library for the Batsford books. The four elder children had bedrooms above, separate from the main house. My brother Tom's beloved piano was installed and there the teenagers could do as they pleased, uninterrupted by grown-ups, as long as they were punctual for meals and anything else which depended on my father's strict rules of punctuality. The books and Tom's music were their education.

Diana was 16 when we moved to Swinbrook House. This was a farmhouse a mile or so from the village, much enlarged by my father for his family, now seven with the arrival of three more girls.

The older ones lost their independence with the barn. They minded it more than my parents ever knew, nowhere now to themselves to sit, read, talk and play the piano, but they must share the drawing room with all who came or sit in their small bedrooms. The books were now in my father's study, where he was not to be disturbed.

Diana began to fret and longed to be grown up and away. She was sent to Paris to learn French and there she met the painter Paul César Helleu, a friend of our Bowles' grandfather, who had made several portraits of my mother and was an immediate admirer of Diana. He was the first of many who sat at her feet, spellbound.

She married Bryan Guinness when she was 18 and soon found that her natural friends were writers; Lytton Strachey, Harold Acton, Robert Byron, Henry Yorke, Evelyn Waugh, John Betjeman and many more became her companions.

The marriage did not last and in 1933 she moved with her two little Guinness sons to a house in Eaton Square where she could meet the man who from then on filled her entire life. Sir Oswald Mosley was married. There was no question of him leaving his wife for Diana, as politics was his passion and divorce would have ended his career. She accepted this state of affairs without question.

Diana's decision was shocking to my parents. Nearly 80 years ago moral standards were different and divorce carried a stigma. So deeply did they feel about it and the circumstances of her new life that my sister Jessica and I were not allowed to go to her house. It never occurred to us to question our parents' wishes and I did not get to know Diana well until after the war. It was not until after the unexpected death from peritonitis of Lady Cynthia Mosley that they were free to marry.

Diana and her next sister Unity often went to Germany in the 1930s where they met and made friends with Hitler and some of his intimates. Both Hitler and Goebbels (Frau Goebbels was a particular friend of Diana's) were present at Diana's secret wedding with Oswald Mosley in 1936. Our family knew nothing of it until much later.

I believe Diana was the only person to know Winston Churchill and Adolf Hitler well. Clementine Churchill was my father's first cousin and Diana and Tom Mitford were frequent guests at Chartwell; Diana Churchill being our Diana's greatest friend.

With the birth of two more sons, all her energies were now devoted to making a home for Mosley and supporting his ideas in politics.

Their long imprisonment without trial from spring 1940 to autumn 1943 denied her her four little boys. This must have had a deep effect on Diana though, such was her self discipline, it was never apparent to acquaintances.

She did not wish to be a public figure in her own right, to stand for Parliament or otherwise take part in staged events. She took the old fashioned role of total unfailing support of the husband she adored. A lesser person might have given up the unequal struggle against his unpopular views and a vehemently hostile press. After his death she leapt to his defence whenever the media produced an unfair or inaccurate picture of Mosley.

Diana's loyalty was proved once more in her efforts to see the ailing Duchess of Windsor during her prolonged and lonely final illness, 'her living death'. The Duchess's butler, Georges (afterwards decorated by The Queen for devoted service to the Duchess), had orders not to allow anyone in. Many times Diana took flowers, although she knew that a visit was forbidden.

She was always a great reader, hungry for literature and intellectually superior to her sisters. In her nineties she read and re-read German and French classics in the original, particularly Goethe and Proust.

Although she wrote brilliant letters all her life, Diana didn't start writing for publication until the 1950s. The words flowed easily. Like her sisters Nancy and Jessica, she was always very much herself—a debunker of pomposity and pretensions. She could conjure up a scene in a few words—describing Gerald Berners' house 'Faringdon, with a view of half England from its five drawing room windows', and Paul Mellon, whom she admired as a collector and philanthropist, 'sails through the eye of a needle with ease'.

Many of these reviews were for *Books and Bookmen* and the *Evening Standard*. She delighted in reviewing for the former, as she could decide the length of her piece. The newspaper was more widely read but was restrictive in length.

When she moved to a flat in Paris as a widow she was 89. It was near the office of Vogue magazine. Passing their window she was unconscious of the fact that the girls pressed their faces to the glass to see this elegant, upright great-granny to twenty-two walking by. She had become a legend.

During the move from their house at Orsay to the Paris flat her daughter-in-law, Charlotte (married to Alexander) was her prop and stay. She arranged everything and looked after Diana as if she were her own mother. Diana loved her deeply and this relationship was a joy in her last years.

In middle- and old-age her rare ability to make new and much younger friends was not so much an effort on her part as a necessity on theirs to hold onto her brilliant company and sympathetic nature. Those who worked for her felt the same affection.

It was interesting to see her with people who were prejudiced against her politically or in any other way. You could watch the hackles go down as the person slowly succumbed to the charm and intelligence he met so unexpectedly.

Her honesty floored her critics. They did not expect it and did not know how to deal with it.

In the memorable television interview with Russell Harty, her interrogator was several times at a loss as to what to ask next when her reply was truthful, with no hiding behind meaningless words in the style to which we have become accustomed when listening to our politicians.

At the end of the interview, the camera dwelt for a moment too long on Mr Harty, who gave a visible and audible 'Phew!' in thankfulness that it was over.

This book of her collected writing reflects her character. She was usually generous minded-of Cynthia Gladwyn, wife of an erstwhile ambassador in Paris, Diana wrote, 'I suppose I must declare an interest. She says in her diary that I am evil.' In spite of this strange statement Cynthia asked Diana to review her book on the British embassy in Paris and a favourable piece was published.

She could also be stingingly sarcastic, describing the old political adversaries Winston Churchill, Duff Cooper and the like. Of Churchill campaigning in the election of 1945 'with his cigar, his grin and his V sign'. Duff Cooper tells of 'praise of his own talents' and how his 'heart felt lighter than it had felt for a year' when he heard of the outbreak of war in 1939, and that night at the Savoy Grill he 'dealt very successfully with a cold grouse'. What would Diana have made of his diaries and boastings of female conquests, published recently?

Of a passage in Selina Hastings' Evelyn Waugh, which listed his misdoings, Diana wrote 'If Selina could have spent one single day with Evelyn, how enormously she would have appreciated the irresistible charm of the man, the cleverness, the sharply expressed and individual point of view, the wonderful jokes, the laughter!'.

Evelyn 'quarrelled with Henry Yorke and Randolph Churchill, both alcoholics like himself. All died in their late fifties or early sixties-their lives a sort of temperance tract.' Her perception of character was uncanny and this comes to light throughout her work.

Diana's political views and the opposite ones held by my sister Jessica were irrelevant to me from my apolitical stance. After years I still miss her letters and long to see her writing on the envelope with a French stamp. They were unique. Nothing can take their place. With her death so much in my life has disappeared for ever. But this volume reveals as much of her as it does of the people, books and places she describes. That is why I am so pleased to write this foreword.

The Pursuit of Laughter

The 30s and 40s

'Excuse me,' said a taxi driver as he deposited Lord Longford at his Chelsea flat, not long after the Copenhagen visit. 'I can never remember your other name. I know you're Lord Porn, of course, but your other name slips my memory.' Lord Longford likes publicity. He considers that even 'bad' or ridiculous publicity helps his good causes. He is an inveterate, untiring do-gooder, who needs must love the lowest when he sees it. 'Blessed are the poor in spirit'; the poorer in spirit the better, for him. If he has a fault (and I am not saying he has) it might be a grain of spiritual pride. As a prison visitor of renown he makes a bee-line for those convicted of the most horrible crimes. Possibly he likes sinners better than publicans, but he prefers either to the general run of hypocritical Pharisees.

Lord Longford is a clever man, the devoted husband of a brilliant wife and father of notable children. Ambitious, he has been a success in politics, several times holding high office, and also a success in the City as chairman of a bank. He is the author of an excellent book about de Valera and the Irish treaty, *Peace by Ordeal*. Mary Craig has discovered a great deal about his private life and his public life. She has written an enjoyable book, but it does not convey his charm; he emerges from her biography as an incorrigible oddity.

Apparently when Longford was given the Garter, Lord Mountbatten said it was an imaginative appointment, and Lord Longford was rather offended. After all, he complained, he was not a pop singer, but had been Leader of the House of Lords for years. I cannot help agreeing with Lord Mountbatten; it is very difficult indeed to think of Lord Longford as a knight, although he did once take part in a fight. This was in 1936 at a Mosley meeting in Oxford, where he got hurt and after which he changed his political allegiance from Conservative to Labour.

Frank Pakenham (as he then was) describes the scene:

I can still see Mosley standing there, black-shirted and black-trousered, looking like Wellington haranguing his troops before Waterloo… The socialists and revolutionary students had gone along to heckle: and I'd bought a two-and-sixpenny ticket just to see the fun. Someone shouted 'Red Front' and Mosley said 'The next person who shouts that will get thrown out.' Then Basil Murray, who was sitting just in front of me, stood up and said 'Red Front' very calmly, almost academically. Mosley ignored that, but when the next person shouted the slogan the Fascists came crashing down from the platform unbuckling their bicycle belts. Then the busmen joined in. They picked up the steel chairs from the hall and started using them as weapons. I was on the fringes of all this, but I decided I'd better join forces with the busmen, even though they were just as much in the wrong as the Fascists. So I started attacking the nearest blackshirts.

Christopher Mayhew (the Labour MP) was an eye-witness.

> I remember Frank distinctly that evening. He had a steel chair, one of those chairs with a back, and he was holding it over his head with both hands in order to do battle with the blackshirts. And two of them were hanging round his neck, bunny punching him.

'Unfortunately' (Frank goes on) 'I was fighting according to Queensberry rules, and they're not very effective against steel chairs and bicycle belts. So I got knocked to the ground, dragging some of the Fascists with me. Then someone stamped on my kidneys and put me out of action.'

What is a 'bicycle belt'? I have heard of a bicycle chain, but never of a bicycle belt. The blackshirts' leather belts had nothing to do with bicycles. When they were assailed by huge Frank and the steel chair he hoped to smash them with, they may have wished they too had a weapon, but they were a disciplined body of men, and they were fighting in full view of Mosley up on the platform. They were allowed to use only their bare hands when ejecting trouble-makers or resisting attack. I doubt whether Lord Queensberry, when he made his rules, would have permitted the bashing of opponents with a steel chair. And in some mysterious way the steel chair has changed hands as the story goes on; it is no longer Frank but the blackshirts who are using it, along with their mythical bicycle belts.

It so happens that I was also an eye-witness, and the Pakenham version is wide of the mark. Mosley paid no attention to sillies like Basil Murray saying Red Front. Undergraduates opened newspapers and pretended to read them, ostentatiously rustling them. Mosley said he was glad to see the young gentlemen were studying as he had heard they were backward with their lessons. This mild sarcasm was the signal for the undergraduates and what Frank calls the busmen to jump up, shouting, and seizing their steel chairs to attack the stewards. They had not come to 'heckle', they hoped to break up the meeting; but they were quickly put out of the hall, and then Mosley spoke to a large audience for an hour, and answered questions as usual. Another eye-witness was the Chief Constable of Oxford. When Maurice Bowra, who had not been present, wrote a Pakenham-like account of the meeting in his memoirs, the Chief Constable sent him a letter saying he had been unfair; Sir Oswald was very patient with interrupters until members of the audience started shouting, he wrote.

About the change of political allegiance, Lord Longford has said: 'Short of a change of sex, my life could hardly have been altered more radically.'

Faith, hope and charity, the greatest of these is charity. Longford is charitable. He does not give a fig for any of the things that make life worth living here below; art and music pass him by; even to good food he is indifferent. 'Feeding him,' says a friend, 'is like filling up a car with petrol.' He was once asked whether he saw himself as a success or a failure; his thoughts flew to St Peter. 'Of course, the question of success or failure in the worldly sense will not be the crucial one in front of St Peter. Nor will it be totally irrelevant. He will surely want to know how far we have used the talents given to us.' I suppose we can guess

St Peter's verdict. But what will Frank find to do up there? No more porn, no more prisons, no more injustice. Heaven knows, is the safest answer.

Another Christian socialist is Dr Mervyn Stockwood, the Bishop of Southwark. *The Cross and the Sickle* is a provocative title, but on the whole he wants what we all want: decent housing, less violence in the streets, a better life for everyone. How to get these things, that is the question. Perhaps he was carrying charity too far in allowing the Foreign Secretary to write a foreword. Short as it is, Dr Owen can only manage a sort of pidgin English. 'He identifies [sic] that they have no value-oriented philosophy…' Oh dear. Maybe his first language is Welsh.

Both Lord Longford and the Bishop of Southwark are now doing their utmost to help the victims of crime. Since in the past their charity has inclined them to hate the sin and love the sinner, rather forgetting the sinned against, this is important. Violent crime is one of the few growth industries in socialist Britain, and they are Christian socialists, both great favourites with the newspapers as well as members of the House of Lords. I hope this clever and charming pair will continue to struggle against crime, and porn, for many years to come, until St Peter takes them over.

Longford: a Biography, Craig, M., *Books and Bookmen* (1978)

Style and Laughter

Reading this memoir of my sister Nancy a thousand memories came flooding in of childhood, youth and age; of the fun, the oddities, the loves and quarrels which I suppose every big family knows. Ours was a babel of voices, arguments and laughter, and most of the laughter originated in my father who was to become Nancy's best 'character' as Uncle Matthew.

Do people change as they grow older, and if they do, which of their selves should the memorialist concentrate upon in order to distil the essence of the personality and bring it before those who never knew and never can know from their own experience? Perhaps Nancy changed rather little, less than most people; only the circumstances of her life changed. Harold Acton has wonderfully succeeded in finding the essential Nancy. He has understood her motives. He has understood that 'laughter was the golden key to Nancy's heart', as he says. She could never resist a joke, and she could never resist a tease. Other temptations she resisted. Money, for example, which she needed, greatly loved and successfully earned, and which rightly occupies a large place in this book, she could resist. She was offered immense sums to go to Hollywood for six months, and she refused. It should be added that having earned some money she gave it away with both hands to friends and relations.

Teasing gave her intense pleasure. Like many of the English she loved France and Paris; French food, French clothes, the beauties of the French eighteenth century. But simply to love was not enough, for nobody would be surprised, let alone put out, by that. She wanted people to gasp and stretch their eyes, therefore every other country without exception must be written down in order that France should take its rightful place, hardly upon earth but in a special paradise. Her fantasies and exaggerations where anything French was concerned were limitless. I have heard her describe a very ordinary, if pleasant, Paris flat as though it were both Trianons and half a dozen English stately homes complete with their art collections rolled into one. Rome, on the other hand, was according to her a village with a vicarage called the Vatican. Thus she managed to use her predilection for France as an all-purpose, hard-wearing tease.

If there is such a thing as objective truth Nancy never bothered about it. If she caught one half-laughing at some observation she knew one knew to be hardly in accordance with the facts, she would as a rule laugh too.

She sometimes went too far in her teasing, but she never minded the counter-attack. She was delighted with a letter from an Irishman after her quaint article on Ireland was published. 'Dear Miss Mitford, Hell would be a more fitting place for you than Ireland.' Evelyn Waugh, friend of a lifetime, teased her unkindly in a silly book they both contributed to, *Noblesse Oblige*. But Harold Acton is undoubtedly right when he says this was because of her socialism. Evelyn could hardly forgive her when, in common with a majority of her countrymen, she voted Labour in 1945. It was as if, unaided, she had brought socialism to power in England, and then had promptly gone away to live in France. When the result of the election was declared Nancy was still in London working in the bookshop. Osbert Sitwell flew in, seized the till, and ran out in the street with it shouting 'Labour has begun!'

In France, a dedicated Gaullist, she could see no fault in anything that happened during the General's years in office. She remained blind to the ruin of beautiful vistas within Paris due to the savage building of tower blocks exactly where they should not have been. One even heard her say apropos of tower blocks in other cities: 'That would never be allowed in Paris.'

All this mixture of teasing, loyalty and wildest fantasy was Nancy the romancer, the novelist. As historian she was scrupulously accurate and took great pains to check facts. Naturally, like every historian under the sun, she chose among the facts what it suited her to choose; but she did not invent. As the years went by she wrote better and better; her very last book, *Frederick the Great*, is a little masterpiece.

The best of companions, with a talent to amuse, Nancy had a real talent for friendship. One of her friends, Violet Trefusis, heroine of the Harold Nicolsons' ideal marriage, was a great trial to her. She was overjoyed when Violet, perhaps jealous of the successes as a writer she herself had never attained, sent her a furiously rude letter. Telling me of it she said 'Isn't it perfect, now I need never see Violet again.' A few years later Violet wanted to make up, and telephoned: 'I'm sorry if I gave offence.' Nancy: 'You didn't give offence, but you did give me an excuse.' The ideal rejoinder.

After the war Nancy was staying in the Isle of Wight with 'the Wid', our great friend Mrs Hammersley, an old lady always swathed in black scarves and shawls. Meat was rationed. 'We went to the butcher and Wid performed the dance of the seven veils before him and he gave us a cutlet' she wrote to me. Harold Acton has quoted extensively from her letters, so that one hears her own voice. He has linked them with a clever and perceptive commentary. He is the dreamt-of biographer, for he was beloved and admired by Nancy for almost fifty years. So unlucky in many ways, her luck in the world of books has held and her biography is exactly right.

What would she herself have thought of this amusing lively book, full of her stories and inventions, her jokes and loves and triumphs, and ending so sadly with cruel pain and illness? I can picture her expression and hear her laugh at her own extravagancies, reproduced by Harold. Like me, she would be deeply touched by his sympathy and affection, and she would shed a tear over her own suffering. After a lifetime of perfect health a rare kind of cancer attacked her. She, who did not like doctors, went from one to another in a vain search for her vanished well-being. Paying one of these doctors his bill she wrote: 'If I were as bad at writing as you are at curing people I should starve.' Until the very end, she never lost her love of a sharp joke.

Nancy Mitford: A Memoir, Acton, H, *Books and Bookmen* (1975)

Frivolous Rage

According to Nancy herself, at the age of three she suffered an appalling tragedy, the birth of my sister Pamela. Hitherto queen of the nursery, and the adored plaything of my parents, little Nancy found herself relegated to second place, the first being accorded to 'a screaming orange in a black wig', as she later described the baby. The nanny had no idea of the frightful trauma suffered by the three-year-old, and our parents still loved her best, blissfully unaware that she was inwardly boiling with rage.

One day they were walking in the street when she began to scream.

They were embarrassed and begged her to stop. Passers-by gave them angry glances, as if to accuse them of torturing the clear little curly-haired girl who was making such a noise. A sharp smack might have been a good idea, but my parents would have been incapable of such behaviour. All of a sudden she stopped, stood still and said: 'The houses are all laughing at me.' 'Yes, and can you wonder,' said her mother. Sydney, 'so much noise about nothing.' This was by no means Nancy's last tantrum, but she had resolved in future to get the laugh in first.

However, her troubles were only just beginning. Next year, and the year after, two more babies appeared: they were my brother Toni and myself. Our nursery was small, the house hardly more than a doll's house. The 'pram in the hall' (as the writer Cyril Connolly used to describe a baby in the house) became 'the prams in the passage'. The house is still there: Number One, Graham Terrace, London. Four children squeezed into the doll's house couldn't have been very comfortable for anybody.

Fortunately, two changes made Nancy's life happier. When she was six, a nanny who had been unkind to her was sent away, and our beloved Nanny, Laura Dicks, described by Nancy in *The Water Beetle*, came and stayed until she died years later. At the same time, Nancy was allowed to go to school, the Frances Holland school in our street, in Belgravia. A clever child, she shone at lessons and liked the company of her contemporaries as much as she disliked the babies at home.

School, for her, was synonymous with paradise, and home with purgatory. She prayed every night to be made, in some mysterious way she preferred not to think about, an only child. In case this was too difficult even for God, she had a second prayer. My mother had a rich friend who bought us expensive toys. Nancy prayed that this lady would adopt her.

In 1914, when the Great War began, another baby, Unity, appeared. However, we had by now moved to the country where my father, David, had inherited a large house, Batsford Park in Gloucestershire, from our grandfather, Bertie. Many of the 50 or so rooms were in dust sheets. Any of us who wished to read could choose a room to be alone and undisturbed. I was six, and we were all taught by a French governess we loved and a rather severe English governess. Nancy missed school, but the war was to blame. My father went to the Front, and it all seemed perfectly normal to us, as things do, to children.

Not far away was a military hospital. and the wounded soldiers came to tea, 30 or 40 of them at a time. They were dressed in soft blue clothes with a red cross on an armband. We played cards and puzzles, sang soldier's songs taught us by our nursery maid.

> Oh! The moon shines bright on Charlie Chaplin,
> His boots are crackin' for Want of blackin'
> And his little baggy trousers they want rnendin'
> Afore we send 'im, to the Dardenelles

The idea of a film actor at the Dardenelles was considered very comic by the wounded soldiers. Other songs mentioned place names such as Tennessee and Tipperary-we had no idea they were real places you could find on the map. Towards the and of the war, new countries began to be written about in the papers. We thought the name Czechoslovakia incredibly funny, and Nancy pretended to be a Czech lady with a strong foreign accent. We played this Czech game for years; she was a doctor, or perhaps even a surgeon, and tortured our brother by digging her sharp little knuckles into his ribs. I've no idea why it amused us so much, but it did.

When Nancy was about 12 an aunt, Lady Blanche Hozier, a great favourite of ours, had taken her up the hill to my grandfather's wild garden at Batsford. From this eminence, one could see all Gloucestershire and much of Oxfordshire. My aunt waved her arm and said dramatically, 'All this belongs to you.' Nancy rushed to tell our mother the good news. 'Oh, what utter rubbish,' she said. '*Nothing* belongs to you.' Nancy told me she was rather relieved. What could she have done with all those fields?

After the war she was allowed to go to a boarding school, which predictably she loved, and then she was grown up. I think Nancy herself began the legend of having been a tease, almost a bully, to us all. She probably was quite horrid to Pam, but my brother and I had nothing to complain about as children. She was very good company, very funny, rather spiteful perhaps. Her novels abound in wit and jokes, and are enjoyed today as much as 50 years ago. They are Nancy's gift to humanity.

When she died in 1973, our friend Harold Acton suggested writing a memoir. They had been friends for 40 years and nobody could have done it better. He was the cleverest of our friends, who had been an enormous influence on what has been called the *Brideshead* Generation at Oxford. Like Nancy herself, he was reserved. In his memoir, he refers to her love affairs in his own way. They were not happy, and he preferred to leave them to a future biographer; he would never have been able, or willing, to do the research. She therefore comes to life in *A Memoir* as the amusing, rather frivolous person she more or less pretended to be, and, to a great extent, really was.

Nancy Mitford: A Memoir, Acton, H, *Daily Mail* (2001)

Building Sights

If I have got an 'old home', I suppose it is Asthall. Our family lived there from when I was nine until I was 16, all my schoolroom years. No longer in the nursery when we arrived, I was almost grown up when we left.

Asthall is very far from being a stately home. There is no park, no drive, no view in any direction. It is a charming old manor house, with gables and leaded windows, roofed with Cotswold stone tiles, such as you find in most Cotswold villages. It lies between a hill and the churchyard, the ancient church only yards from the drawing-room windows.

It was rather strange that we lived there so long, since in my father's eyes it was a temporary dwelling. During the First World War he had inherited a large house with a good deal of land in Gloucestershire. Even we children knew it was to be sold at the end of the war, as we were too poor to live there. And sold it duly was. My father's dream was to build his own house, on a hill above Swinbrook in Oxfordshire. The village and land belonged to him, and the coverts and shooting he loved were nearby.

Meantime, while the building was going on, we were to live at Asthall, which adjoined his land and was conveniently on the market. Although we were six children, and soon to be seven, we could perfectly well have squeezed into Asthall for a couple of years. But no sooner were we installed than he began to build at Asthall. He built stables, garages, kennels. He built 'cloisters' that joined it to the old house. He put more bedrooms there. He made a great barn in the garden into a library and music room. This large room, furnished with hundreds of old books, a grand piano and sofas, with high windows looking south and east, was all the world to my brother Tom and me at Asthall. He played all day, Bach, Mozart, Beethoven, Brahms, and I lay on a sofa, reading and listening. The room was far enough away to disturb nobody. We were allowed to read anything, provided we put the book back where it belonged.

The chief beauty of Asthall was a long, panelled hall with windows on both sides and a fire at each end. We were sheltered from draughts by Chinese screens, black lacquer with enormous white lacquer characters, very old and beautiful. In the dining room were seventeenth-century Japanese screens depicting eagles and other birds of prey on palest gold background. These treasures had been brought from the Far East by my grandfather.

The other end of the hall led to my mother's drawing room, with my father's business room beyond. We often sat with him listening to his gramophone.

Our schoolroom was at the bottom of the oak staircase; it faced south, but was always cold. We had an English governess in the term and a French one in the holidays. In the evenings our governess read us one of the *Waverley* novels, or *Bleak House*, or *The Mill on the Floss*.

The nursery was upstairs; it was a haven, with our darling Nanny and beloved little sisters. My worst dread was that I might be sent to school, away from ponies, dogs, guinea pigs; above all away from the nursery and its denizens, but I never was.

In the holidays we were supposed to speak French, which resulted in a perhaps not unwelcome silence in the dining room. Visiting children considered us a noisy family, there was no question of being seen and not heard. We argued, teased, screamed with laughter at family jokes, the funniest my father's.

Sometimes gloom and quiet descended for a while, when my father used to tell us he was ruined. We wondered anxiously where the next loaf of bread would come from. He lost a lot of money trying to farm, but during the Asthall years he also made many disastrous investments, generally the result of talking to some brilliantly clever cove at the Marlborough Club, his London resort. Building was his expensive hobby.

'You realise you children will have to earn your own livings don't you?' he would say. 'I can't give you anything.' This made our blood run cold. We couldn't imagine that anyone would wish to employ us. For one thing, we did everything badly. We rode every day, but we didn't ride well. We played tennis, and went to tennis parties given by children in the neighbourhood, but they played far better than we did. We had music lessons in Oxford, and we went to a dancing class, with mediocre results. Could we even type.

When me father said he could give us nothing, my mother always said: 'Of course not. Girls don't expect it.'

It was my mother who made Asthall perfectly lovely inside, she who defended us from my father's vagaries. He usually disliked our friends, but she was welcoming.

On Sundays my father liked us to go with him to matins at Swinbrook, we preferred evensong at Asthall. Mr Ward, the Asthall vicar, once preached a sermon scolding my father: 'People who run shouting with their dogs through God's holy acre,' he said crossly. (We went coursing on Sundays and fetched the dogs from the kennels; the churchyard was a short cut). We told my father about the sermon but he only laughed.

When I was about 14 the organist left the village and Mr Ward asked me to play the organ. It was a very old organ; a village boy pumped the air into it, and if he stopped no sound came. I knew the service by heart; the little tunes of hymns and canticles were simple, and I knew just when to give Mr Ward his note and how to play the responses accompanying Mrs Ward's powerful contralto. Occasionally the organ seemed to come alive and emitted squeaks and groans, but I knew it would have to stay quiet when it ran out of air. I used two stops, one for noise, one for pathos.

The manor sthall was on the edge of the Heythrop country; we were allowed to hunt accompanied by the groom, but only if we rode sidesaddle. My habit, made in Cirencester, was probably not very elegant. I hacked to the meet, almost everyone did in those days.

The years went by, the slow years of childhood. We became very fond of the old house, and wondered if my father had forgotten about his dream. He loved fishing for trout in the Windrush, which flowed by the bottom of our garden. But he spent most of his time in the coverts, shooting in winter and watching the baby pheasants in spring, with his favourite keeper, Steele who, during the rearing season, lived in an old railway carriage in the wood, tending his broody hens.

But my father had another hobby: motorcars. He spent hours at Cowley with William Morris. As he had nothing much to do, it seems a pity, looking back, that he didn't earn his living by joining this immensely successful firm. It never occurred either to him or Morris, later Lord Nuffield, that his expertise might be turned to gold.

The dream persisted. My father sold Asthall and began to build again. Not just a house; he built cottages, stables, garages, all over again. As though at a loss as to what to build next, he even built a squash court, although none of us played.

How much did we mind leaving Asthall? Speaking for myself, not desperately. We had the same village life, the same Christmas parties for all the children from Asthall and Swinbrook and, although my parents saw no neighbours, there were some we liked. In any case, I was nearly grown up, life was about to begin, real life not dreams in a cold schoolroom. Being so incompetent, so 'bad' at everything, no longer seemed to matter.

'Families, I hate you!' said André Gide.

We never again had real family life after we left Asthall. We grew up, married; Tom no longer came for endless holidays. We saw each other constantly, but there was no longer the daunting, rather stifling feeling that you knew whom you would see, eat with, quarrel with, ride with, bore and be bored by, laugh with, day after day, week after week. Yet I did miss Asthall, its aged beauty, its terrifying pitch darkness at night, the odd sounds and fresh smells.

Nearly 20 years later my sister Nancy wrote her best-selling novels *The Pursuit of Love* and *Love in a Cold Climate*. Her masterpiece was her lifelike portrait of my father as Uncle Matthew. An old refugee from eastern Europe came into Heywood Hill's bookshop where she worked, to congratulate her. 'Onkel Matthew!' he said. 'He woz my father!' Rather surprised, she told this to Evelyn Waugh. 'Uncle Matthew is everybody's father,' was his reply.

My father was at his most Uncle-Matthew-like at Asthall. Angry, funny, affectionate, furious, uproarious by turns, and always totally unpredictable. At Swinbrook his gaiety seemed to diminish, and he became almost, if never quite, grown up.

Sunday Times (1997)

Friends and Fauna

Malicious, witty, sometimes affectionate, mercilessly teasing each other, Nancy Mitford and Evelyn Waugh corresponded for twenty years until his death. Having both sides more than doubles the fun of these letters.

They began to write regularly when she went to live in France. In

1945 Nancy told everyone she had voted Labour, and Evelyn pretended to think she alone was responsible for the grey and dreary England of the late 40s. At the end of the war he had written *Brideshead Revisited*; it made a lot of money which was snatched away from him by the tax gatherer. Rations became smaller. It was all her fault, and then she deserted the country she had ruined.

The War itself had been a disillusion. He had wished to look upon it as a crusade, but it ended with half Europe ruled by godless communists, while France and Italy seethed with barely hidden civil war.

Nancy was on the crest of the wave. She was in love with a Frenchman, 'the Colonel', and she too had written a bestseller, *The Pursuit of Love*, so that she was rich enough to follow him to Paris. Her marriage to Peter Rodd was on the rocks. She pretended to be living in a land flowing with cream and caviar, and shut her eyes to the shortages of Liberation. Evelyn rebuked her for saying 'Heavenly 1948', the blackest year in world history since 1793, according to him. The Colonel was as slippery as an eel, but she shut her eyes to that too. It is all so long ago that shafts of bitter humour, once deleted for fear of libel, can now illumine the scene. The actors are all dead.

Both writers were wildly funny, and the result is an irresistible book. The victims of their unkind jokes are mostly well-known, so that the letters will delight and possibly horrify nearly everybody.

Nancy and Evelyn earned their living by writing; money is a constant theme and worry. Evelyn had a large family to educate; Nancy's only extravagance was Dior. She implored Evelyn to come to France, but when he did it was seldom a success. He quarrelled with Duff Cooper at Chantilly, and generally made himself objectionable, as only he knew how.

Nancy found this quite difficult to deal with, and their friendship was really based on the letters. They made each other scream with laughter, the shadows were light. All the same, they lengthened: Nancy's love affair did not prosper, and Evelyn began to feel his Church under threat.

The advent of Pope John XXIII was a sorrow to Evelyn. The

reforms of the Vatican Council knocked him flat. He was only 62, and he dreaded the possibility of having to live with these reforms another twenty years. Strangely enough, his desperately sad last letters, in March 1966, were to me. I had asked him a question. He wrote: 'There is nowhere I want to go, nothing I want to do.' He died on Easter Day 1966.

The letters are impeccably edited by Charlotte Mosley, an expert on the period and its fauna; she has cleverly solved every puzzle.

The Letters of Nancy Mitford and Evelyn Waugh, ed. Mosley, C., *The Times* (1996)

A Monster Greatly Missed

'He was one of the great prose stylists of the twentieth century' but 'as a man he was a monster'. These are the two premises upon which, Selina Hastings says, Evelyn Waugh's reputation rests. No mention of the wittiest and funniest writer of our time. She has depicted an authentic monster, more monstrous by far than the Evelyn of previous biographers. Drunken, snobbish, insultingly rude; a neglectful son, a bullying father, a quarrelsome friends, and impossible man. Her source is Evelyn himself, who would have readily have admitted to this catalogue of sins of commission and omission.

She sees him as a great artist and admirable craftsman, but with a character so flawed by rage and cruelty and so overlaid with deep and selfish boredom that nobody in their senses would want to spend much time with him, however admiringly they read his books. Her biography is beautifully written and fascinatingly told, but something is missing.

If Selina Hastings could have spent one single day with Evelyn Waugh, how enormously she would have appreciated the irresistible charm of the man, the cleverness, the sharply expressed and individual point of view, the wonderful jokes, the laughter!

To take his sins listed above: drunkenness yes, when young, and more drink than was good for him all his life. Rudeness, yes, if people were rude or annoying to him. But the neglectful son had from earliest childhood known that his elder brother Alec was the adored favourite; and the bullying father was moody but often too, the originator of family jokes.

As to the quarrelsome friend, he quarrelled with Henry Yorke and with Randolph Churchill, both alcoholics like himself. All three became prematurely old, decrepit and furiously miserable; bored, literally, to death. All died in their late fifties or early sixties, their lives a sort of temperance tract. His other friends were devoted and life-long.

Naturally the rage and cruelty that were part of his character were exacerbated by drink. At Oxford he was drunk for days on end, which was devastating for his finances, his university work and, ultimately for his health. Yet all his disasters, all his quirks were put to use by him; nothing was wasted.

His failures at Oxford were distressing to the good old father, who paid his debts but had hoped for a brilliant degree to be followed by a steady publishing job in his firm. He bored and irritated Evelyn, who in order to get away became a private schoolmaster, which produced the hilarious *Decline and Fall*. His Oxford friendships, much later, were the origin of *Brideshead*.

Waugh's raffish London life and failed first marriage went into *Vile Bodies* and *A Handful of Dust*; his travels as a newspaper reporter made *Scoop* and *Black Mischief*. Even his distressing breakdown, the result of sleeping pills mixed with alcohol, became the brilliant *Ordeal of Gilbert Pinfold*. And so on throughout life with the war and his appalling disillusions producing his masterpiece, *Sword of Honour*. His novels are autobiographical, embellished with his uniquely comic genius.

Selina Hastings is perceptive about his religion, to him all important, The final tragedy for Evelyn, far more terrible than the Common Man whose Age he so disliked, was when the foundations of his faith were shaken by the upheavals in the Church caused by the Vatican Council and Pope John XXIII. The common man with a guitar performing in the aisle was more than he could bear.

His quarrel with Randolph Churchill was triggered by their forced intimacy during their mission to Tito during the war. This famous episode is told here to perfection, and is one of the funniest things in a fundamentally sad book: the history of a monster. But such a charming, witty, clever, amusing monster as never was; quite simply the best company on earth.

It is impossible not to think how greatly the author of this brilliant book and her subject would have appreciated one another, and to regret they were not contemporaries.

When Evelyn Waugh died, Nancy Mitford wrote to a friend: 'I see he is one of the people I have loved most in my life.' Are monsters so deeply mourned?

Evelyn Waugh, Hastings, S., *Evening Standard* (1994)

❋

The Order of the Boot

When W.F. Deedes was not yet Lord Deedes, the doyen of Fleet Street, when he was Mr Deedes, aged 22, he was sent by his paper, *The Morning Post*, to cover the war in Abyssinia. Advised about what equipment he would need in that faraway country, of which he knew nothing, by enthusiastic shops such as Austin Reed and the Army and Navy Stores, he bought so many things that his luggage weighed a quarter of a ton. Everything was paid for by *The Morning Post*.

He travelled by train to Marseilles and then by sea in a French boat to East Africa. The Suez Canal was full of Italian ships conveying soldiers to fight and conquer Abyssinia. Deedes took the train from the coast to Addis Ababa, a train reminiscent of English trains today, rather uncertain as to timetable.

He experienced all the usual frustrations of life in a Third World country, but, with his mountain of luggage, he arrived at his destination.

Needless to say, the place was full of journalists, falling over each other to use the primitive means of communication to provide their newspapers with news, but there never was any news. They were not allowed to leave Addis Ababa to go to 'the front' and see some fighting, and were far from sure there was any fighting.

The Italians dropped a few bombs here and there, destroyed a few ramshackle houses and killed a few people. The League of Nations was outraged; everybody was outraged.

There are many parallels with the recent Iraq war; the UN was outraged, millions of people took to the streets in protest in England, France, Germany and Italy, but the Americans, like the Italians in 1935, paid no attention to public opinion and quickly and easily won the war.

The Italians wanted Abyssinia for no particular reason. Unlike Iraq, it was not oil-rich, the Emperor Haile Selassie, the Lion of Judah, went into exile.

I believe he lived at Bath. After the Second World War he was sent back to Addis Ababa, where he was murdered and buried in a deep hole under his bathroom.

The hole was covered in concrete, but eventually his body was recovered, and who should go to his ceremonial-burial but Lord Deedes, who seems to love going to Abyssinia. We may be sure none of his visits was quite as enjoyable as his first.

Among the journalists when Deedes was 22 was Evelyn Waugh, aged 32.

He was, at that time, the most perfect companion imaginable. Lord Deedes says he was a real help, as an old Africa hand, and praises his efficiency, although he missed the one and only scoop by being away when it was achieved.

He doesn't mention the scintillating wit, the wonderfully original point of view of the Evelyn Waugh of those days. He detects the monster, but not, seemingly, the genius.

If, however, his small book about the adversities of being a reporter with nothing much to report sends people back to Evelyn Waugh's novel, *Scoop*, it will have been well worth writing, because *Scoop* is one of the best novels of the twentieth century.

Deedes says he has been identified with Boot, the Candide-like hero of *Scoop*, but that all they had in common was mountains of luggage. He is surely right about this.

At War with Waugh: the Real Story of Scoop, Deedes, W.F., Evening Standard (2003)

Harold Acton as a Young Man

When I met Harold Acton in 1928, I was 18 and he 24. His fame among our generation was already great; at Oxford he had been the undisputed leader of the cleverest undergraduates, a well-known apparition disapproved by many, with side-whiskers and huge trousers. A self-proclaimed aesthete, he defended his attitude with clever, malicious wit, as well as the exquisite courtesy which characterized him all his life.

By 1928 there was no longer sartorial oddity, he was tall and dark and soberly dressed, wearing a wide-brimmed black hat. We were guests of John Sutro at a little restaurant near the Strand, Rules. John Sutro brought out the fantastic best in Harold, we talked and laughed for hours. Harold was the cleverest, wittiest, most outrageous person on earth in those days. His voice, his accent, never changed. They made even quite ordinary observations seem unusual, and his wicked malice irresistibly funny. We never stopped laughing when Harold was there, and perhaps such an appreciative audience encouraged him to perform.

At that time he and his brother William had taken a large house in Lancaster Gate; William wanted to deal in furniture, and as his taste ran to vast rococo objects the house had to be big in order to display his wares. Harold was busy writing *The Last Medici*. He had also written a novel.

William was a dreadful worry to Harold. At Christ Church, having swallowed some drug, he had fallen out of a window in Peckwater Quad, hurting himself badly. His parents' favourite, they ordered

Harold to look after him, which he was quite unable to do. The Actons lived at La Pietra near Florence; very fond of his mother, Harold heartily disliked his father.

My brother Tom loved Harold as much as I did; they had not coincided at Eton, but as they dislike games both had been wet-bobs there, which meant that a boy could spend his summer afternoons on the river, reading or flirting and pretending to row. Harold told us that his little boat had inadvertently been swept over the weir, 'and my whiff was shattered to atoms'. Tom loved hearing this over and over again. 'What happened to your whiff, Harold?' 'My deear, it was shuttered to uttoms', said Harold.

He often dined with us, and sometimes a fellow guest was Lytton Strachey, who wrote to Carrington (28 May 1930): 'Once more Harold Acton figured—I felt myself falling under his sway little by little.' Nearly everyone fell under his sway.

Harold was the only person who succeeded in being friends with Nancy Cunard without forfeiting the friendship of her mother, Emerald. Nancy and her black lover were often to be seen at Lancaster Gate when visiting London, but if Emerald knew of it she never allowed it to affect relations with Harold, an ornament of her luncheons at Grosvenor Square. As a rule she waited until her guests were assembled before rushing in herself, but one day we were all, including Emerald, waiting for a late comer. When David Cecil was shown into a room where perhaps a dozen people were chatting, there was a moment's silence while he crept awkwardly towards his hostess, broken by Harold's slowly enunciated words: 'The Stricken Deer'. David Cecil had just published a biography of Cowper thus entitled.

Although at his English schools Harold, with his cosmopolitan background, Italianate accent and refusal to join in anything childish, must have seemed a strange phenomenon, he was apparently never bullied or harried. He must have had a very strong character, which in some unusual way kept him entirely immune. We were told that even at his private school barbarity did not prevail, and he recited his poems to astonished children of ten or eleven, provoking a rude reaction.

Perhaps his sharp tongue made them a little afraid of him, and his extreme politeness disarmed. He was always ready with a harsh but courteous snub if somebody tried to be rude. A hostile, rather mannish woman whose car had broken down near the house where we were all dining, said to him aggressively: 'You're not the kind of young man one can imagine doing things under a car!' Harold, slowly rolling his eyes, replied 'It all depends who with'.

In 1920 his novel, *Hum Drum*, came out. It was a grave disappointment to his admirers. By a piece of bad luck it appeared at the same time as Evelyn Waugh's brilliant *Decline and Fall*. They were reviewed together; nobody praised *Hum Drum*. As Harold and Evelyn had been at Oxford together, very much in the position of master and disciple, it was a painful episode. As if to underline it, Evelyn had dedicated his novel to Harold. On and off for the rest of his life Harold wrote fiction, but his talent lay elsewhere. His genius was in the brilliant charm and radiance of his personality, unequalled in his generation.

Although *The Last Medici* had a succès d'estime, Harold was deeply hurt, and decided to withdraw from London and go to live in China, the land of his dreams. He had become a notable figure in London, as he had been at Oxford. His departure was mourned by his many friends, and it was probably hastened by anxieties about William. He took him home to his parents in Florence, a nightmare journey with William threatening suicide.

Harold came back to England in the war and joined the Air Force. He resumed his friendships, and once went for a journey with Evelyn Waugh, 'our irascible friend' as he described him in a letter to me. But he found him too difficult, too rude. He himself never changed. He stayed with me in France, and I with him at La Pietra. It is for others to describe him there; I am one of the few who remember the fantastic and admirable Harold of long ago.

Evening Standard (1994)

38

Conversation Piece

When the Prince and Princess of Wales visited Harold Acton, the Princess was reported as having said she had never in her life met anyone like him. She was absolutely right. The only person remotely like Harold was his brother William, who died long ago.

Harold was a brilliant talker, whose idiosyncratic voice, with Italian inflections, amused the listener, quite apart from his inspired and malicious wit. William had the same voice. Harold wrote many books, but for some reason they never came up to the expectation of those who had been held in thrall by his conversation.

His memoir of my sister Nancy must be reckoned one of his best books. They had been friends for more than 40 years, ever since he left Oxford. He was born in 1904, and he and his brothers were educated at Eton and Christ Church, but they always seemed Florentine to us. Towards the end of his life he was host at his beautiful villa, La Pietra, to all the world. Everyone visiting Florence expected to be invited by him, and he angelically submitted to being one of the 'sights' on no account to be missed.

At school and at Oxford Harold was a poet, and dressed rather extravagantly; his contemporaries looked up to him as a perfectly civilised cosmopolitan paragon. To his friends he was, and remained for his whole life, a source of endless amusement and laughter, as well as a connoisseur of art and literature.

After Harold left Oxford, he and William lived for a time in a huge, ugly house in Lancaster Gate, where William bought and sold rococo furniture. Harold settled down to his writing. At the age of 24, he was already a shining fixed star in the London literary and social world, an ornament of Emerald Cunard's luncheons in Grosvenor Square, where his presence ensured fireworks and clever repartee such as Emerald loved to orchestrate.

Unluckily, the publication of Harold's novel *Hum Drum* coincided with that of Evelyn Waugh's first novel, *Decline and Fall*. This was a disaster for Harold, the critics hailing Evelyn. Harold went away to

Peking, William to Florence. They left a very sad gap.

Years later, in his *Memoirs of an Aesthete*, Harold wrote spitefully about Evelyn Waugh, Brian Howard, Robert Byron and Cyril Connolly. He pictures himself as having been the only civilised man among a bunch of backward and boorish Englishmen. Nobody seems to have minded; the attack never reached its target. Harold once described Evelyn Waugh in a letter to me as 'our irascible friend'. Which is fair enough, because he did become irascible as years went by.

It is a great mystery why Harold Acton, so witty and with such a penetrating understanding, was never able to get his talents down on paper, but it is a fact. In Peking he felt completely at home. He loved everything Chinese and translated Chinese plays, hoping they would be a success on the London stage, which they never were.

He came back to England for the war, and once when I asked him if he would ever return to his eastern paradise, he said no, every one of his friends there was dead. All were mandarins, killed by the communists.

In his *Memoirs of an Aesthete* Harold pays tribute to William and his talent for painting and drawing. He did vast portraits of his friends, all wonderfully like them, but in an old-fashioned style that ensured the portraits were underrated. His method of painting was to ask his model to allow her head to be photographed from every angle. Then William made rather beautiful pencil drawings, the studies for his paintings. The only other painter I knew who used photographers was Sickert; the results were very different. But fashion is all-powerful, and doubtless William's amazing facility was a disadvantage. His pictures are not works of art, but they are a faithful record of a whole generation of English women.

The last time I saw William was in the summer of 1940. France was falling, the British army had made its way home via the Channel ports, gloom was on every face. I ran into William by chance in Piccadilly, and we sat for a few moments to talk. 'What are you doing now?' I asked. 'I'm learning Urdu,' was his reply. He lived in a world of his own, and so, in a way, did Harold.

After the war Harold inherited La Pietra, and a new phase of his life began. He wrote well-received histories of the Bourbons of Naples, he was revered as an historian, as well as as a host and a wit. He and Nancy shared old friends, as well as an old enemy, Violet Trefusis. Their enmity was a great link: Violet was Harold's neighbour in Florence, and Nancy's in Paris. In his memoir there is a delightful photograph of her.

Harold changed nothing at La Pietra. The walls were covered with his father's collection of Italian pictures. Except for them and the villa itself, everything was redolent of 1900, red velvet armchairs with antimacassars. His mother's bedroom, the size of a large ballroom, where I slept when I stayed with him, had 18 oil paintings of the Madonna and Child on the walls, as well as a large Della Robbia china representation of the same subject.

A great joy for the last 20 years of Harold's life was that Lord Lambton became a neighbour. They were made for each other, with the same malicious sense of humour. There were screams of laughter from Harold's dining-room when this fantastically amusing man was a guest. It is sad that conversation is so ephemeral, and brilliant talk so rare. Never can two wits have been more closely attuned, more uninhibited, than they. Both were bibliophiles, art connoisseurs and gardeners.

Harold Acton never changed. I first met him in 1928, and saw him on and off until a couple of years before he died. He never seemed young or old; simply himself. He made a few television appearances, and was an instant star: the beauty of his surroundings, his exquisite courtesy to one and all, and his verbal dexterity.

Harold had no heir, and he hoped to bequeath his estate in Florence to Christ Church or to Eton. Both refused to accept it, incredible as it may seem. He therefore left it to an American university, whose fortunate undergraduates go to La Pietra to study Italian art.

Spectator 2001

❋

The Lady and the Tramps

'Poor old Ott, her wits have gone the way of her bladder.' Did these cruel and quite untrue words occur in a letter from Lytton Strachey to Virginia Woolf, or to his brother James, or are they apocryphal? If the latter, they not unfairly sum up the way he wrote about Lady Ottoline, his great friend and benefactress. He could never resist a joke, he loved to imagine his correspondent's scream of laughter, and probably he never thought his letters would be published.

Miranda Seymour's book is the perfect riposte to the spiteful accounts of Ottoline, which, along with her truncated memoirs 'edited' after her death by Philip Morrell, are all the public has been vouchsafed hitherto.

She describes a wonderful, extraordinary woman, who held the love of the cleverest man of her time, Bertrand Russell, to the very end of her life, and the friendship of three generations of writers and painters.

Russell wrote her 2000 letters, many of them passionate love letters, but she refused to leave Morrell. Russell married several times while remaining a great friend.

She had extravagant looks, huge features, 'a face like a horse', and she wore what can only be described as fancy dress. Feathered hats were pink, scarlet and orange; silks, chiffons and brocades were made into fantastic clothes. She was six foot tall, and struck everyone with amazement.

As a child I sometimes caught a glimpse of this gorgeous apparition in Oxford, driving her pony cart through streets full of drab undergraduates on bicycles, or choosing stuffs in Ellaston and Cavell. She was an unforgettable vision.

I knew her name, and that her country house had been a refuge for conscientious objectors in the Great War, and this in itself made her a heroine for me.

The intellectual friends Lady Ottoline collected at Garsington were monumentally disloyal, ungrateful and illmannered, not just

42

Lytton Strachey. He at least never 'put her in a book', as all the novelists did—notably D.H. Lawrence and Aldous Huxley—and she was wounded every single time, though she generally forgave in the end. Huxley's novel, in the window of Blackwell's, was bought by the Garsington vicar who had met him at the manor. He found a sermon he had injudiciously printed reproduced verbatim as a great joke.

Miranda Seymour shows that Ottoline's generosity and hospitality were far from easy for her. The Morrells were not rich, and the farm lost money. No wonder, as they who were supposed to work it lay under hedges discussing poetry and philosophy.

Is there another side to all this? Miranda Seymour is right hardly to hint at such a thing, so false was the picture Bloomsbury left. Nevertheless, Lady Ottoline did probe for everyone's secrets, she did question people closely about their loves and hates. She had powerful charm, and probably her guests often wished they had disclosed less.

I was once told that one Christmas at Garsington they clubbed together to give her a steaming outfit. They never felt their letters were quite safe when she was about. She was so deeply interested in them, she longed to know everything about everyone, and to interfere.

But when all is said, she was a great and unique person, generous, loving, appreciative of art, nature and human oddity, recognizing genius, admiring and fostering talent. She had wretched health and admirable courage, both physical and moral. She herself was a living work of art.

Her daughter, Julian Vinogradov, who suffered from the caricature of her mother in book after book down the years, told me she thought David Cecil's introduction to a photograph album the best description of her. It is sad that Julian died before this excellent definitive biography was finished.

Ottoline Morrell: Life on the Grand Scale, Seymour, M., *Evening Standard* (1992)

✻

Wonderful Arms

If I could have my way, I should go out to dinner every night, and then to a party or an opera, and then I should have a champagne supper, and then I should go to bed in some wonderful person's arms.

Who wrote that? Lytton Strachey, to Virginia Woolf. Strangely enough, the first time I ever met him part of the fantasy had come true. It was twenty years after, and he had become a literary lion who could have gone out to dinner as often as he chose.

We had been to the opera, and Lady Cunard gave a supper party afterwards for about forty people at a huge table in her upstairs drawing room at 7 Grosvenor Square: I suppose we were too many for the dining room. It was very gay and glittering. Lytton Strachey came and sat next to me, old and mysterious behind his beard and spectacles. I was 18, and not long married. I thought how wonderful and amusing and fascinating he was, and was amazed at my luck and at his condescension in honouring Lady Cunard with his presence at her party and me with his proximity. Writers and painters and composers seemed to me then the princes of mankind; they do still, but I realise now, as I did not in those days, that *Uebermenschen* can love gaiety and pleasure just as much as ordinary people.

But Lytton's periodic excursions into the *monde* were not always a success. 'Garsington was terribly trying' he wrote on one occasion after a visit to Lady Ottoline Morrell. 'I was often on the point of screaming from sheer despair.'

Many of these letters are bitter complaints about the small miseries of life. Lytton Strachey was delicate and always felt cold; cold during damp English summers, freezing in the winter time. The Bloomsburies had a genius for making themselves uncomfortable. This was not the result of dire poverty; the poorest peasant in central Europe would refuse to put up with such discomfort as they did—he would get himself a stove and keep it burning night and day When I knew Lytton he was quite rich and had a pretty country house, but I remember how cold it was staying with him.

The Bloomsbury revolt against Victorian values extended to other spheres besides literature and philosophy. No blazing fires or heavy nourishing meals for them; no scrubbed kitchens, shining door-knobs or starched linen. Lord Berners told a story about one of the group whose name I cannot mention because he is still alive.[*] This Bloomsbury was his host at dinner.

'Do you like oysters?' he asked.

'Yes, very much,' said Berners unsuspectingly.

'That's splendid, because I've bought some oysters from a *dirty* little shop round the corner.'

Leonard Woolf and James Strachey, who have edited the letters, leave dots here and there to spare feelings. This is very tantalising. They have obliged with some footnotes, but probably many people who knew already that Rumpelmayer was a pastrycook might care to be told who Carrington was: dear, faithful friend of Lytton Strachey, whose death killed her with sorrow.

[*] Clive Bell.

Virginia Woolf & Lytton Strachey: Letters (1956)

A Bloomsbury Echo

'What is to become of all these diaries I asked myself yesterday? If 1 died, what would Leo make of them? He would be disinclined to burn them; he could not publish them. Well, he should make up a book from them, I think, and then burn the body,' wrote Virginia Woolf. Leonard Woolf, thirteen years after her death, has made up the book from them; let us hope he has not burnt the body. After three hundred and sixty pages we could do *with* three hundred and sixty more—no doubt there are fierce things in them about the living, as here about the dead, but if Mr Woolf waits another few years could not a great deal more be published?

As it stands, the book is deeply interesting, the diary of a remarkable and gifted woman; written partly, no doubt, as a safety valve her highly nervous temperament and partly to remind herself of facts and figures connected with her writings, but also to note her thoughts on friends and acquaintances, books and poems journeys and everyday happenings. One is never conscious or its having been written with an eye to future publication, as one is for example in the *Journal* of André Gide. She never appears to worry about hurt feelings, or libel; never troubles to pose for an audience. Her judgments are completely honest and candid, and have the freshness and vigour of truth. (Read what she has to say about Lady Colefax, or on a slightly higher level about Lady Ottoline Morrell or Lady Cunard, compare it with the rubbish some other writers have felt obliged to churn out as *quid pro quo* for hospitality received. She pins them down, drab moths and gay butterflies alike.) She was gifted with the seeing eye; her descriptions are exactly right, there is never a wasted word. Her friends were the cleverest and most gifted of her contemporaries; it was their opinion of her writing that she cared about, even though she could be momentarily cast down by a bad review.

The diary abounds in examples of her talents as critic. After reading Katherine Mansfield's *Bliss:* '... her mind is a very thin soil, laid an inch or two deep upon very barren rock' (this in 1918, when Katherine Mansfield was being hailed as a new Chekov). Of Byron: 'The truth may be that if you are charged at such high voltage you can't fit any of the ordinary human feelings; must pose; must rhapsodise; don't fit in. He wrote in the Fun Album that his age was one hundred. And this is true, measuring life by feeling.' Of *Paradise Lost:* 'I can conceive that even Shakespeare after this would seem a little troubled, personal, hot and imperfect. I can conceive that this is the essence of which almost all other poetry is the dilution. The inexpressible fineness of the style, in which shade after shade is perceptible, would alone keep one gazing into it, long after the surface business in progress has been dispatched. Deep down one catches still further combinations, rejections, felicities and masteries.'

The art of writing was her chief passion; but the following shows her close observation, and curiously aloof sympathy: 'Saw and heard the Salvation Army making Christianity gay for the people; a great deal of nudging and joking on the part of very unattractive young men and women; making it lively, I suppose; and yet, to be truthful, when I watch them I never laugh or criticise but only feel how strange and interesting this is; wonder what they mean by 'Come to the Lord'. I daresay exhibitionism accounts for some of it; the applause of the gallery; this lures boys to sing hymns; and kindles shop boys to announce in a loud voice that they are saved. It is what writing for the *Evening Standard* is for...'

The Woolfs owned the Hogarth Press; they were offered *Ulysses* and refused it—a curious parallel to Gide's refusal, for the NRF, of *Du Côté de chez Swann*.

Most of the chief Bloomsbury figures are dead. Virginia Woolf, Lytton Strachey, Roger Fry, Maynard Keynes—they did not live to a great age, they never reached the *Grand Old* stage of an earlier generation. But some of the younger ones are still alive, and here is the first volume of David Garnett's autobiography. In it he describes his upbringing, with the typical background of the future Bloomsbury; the intellectual parents (Constance Garnett, a translator of genius, was his mother); the liberal, rationalist opinions; the famous friends; the cranky food; the sofa propped up with books; the solid discomfort. Excellent writer that he is, readers of *The Golden Echo* will eagerly look forward to the next installment; hoping, meanwhile, for a new novel after too many silent years.

Were the Bloomsburies as parochial as the name suggests? Roger Fry proclaiming the merits of post-impressionism to Edwardian London was an interpreter; Lytton Strachey, E.M. Foster, Virginia Woolf and David Garnett are artists, whose books will be read as long as there is anyone left to enjoy the 'combinations, rejections, felicities and masteries' of the English language which they all know how to employ.

A Writer's Diary, Woolf, V.; *The Golden Echo*, Garnett, D. (1953)

Nervous Endings

The second volume of Mr Garnett's autobiography is a less polished success than *The Golden Echo*; in places it reads almost like notes for somebody's memoirs rather than the finished product. Nevertheless the book has virtues, of which the chief is that the author tells tales and anecdotes about his clever friends and contemporaries the Bloomsburies which marvellously bring them to life. If, at times, the narrative seems jerky instead of running on ball bearings, it may be that it cost him a good deal to write about the war years which must, in some ways, have been a disagreeable time for him.

Unless he is buoyed up by particularly strong political or religious beliefs there is no doubt that, for a healthy man in the twenties, the position of conscientious objector in war time is a difficult one, even if he belongs to a group of clever and like-minded friends which forms a cushion between himself and the outside world. (Mr Garnett spent part of the 1914 war with Frankie Birrell working behind the lines in France among Quakers, and the rest with Duncan Grant as a labourer on a Sussex farm, where he stayed with Vanessa Bell). That simple people may suspect him of cowardice is the very least of the complicated feelings which he must have about himself and about the attitude of others towards him. Keynes, for example, the only member of the circle to take part in the world of action, faithfully gave evidence for all the Bloomsburies of military age at their Tribunals, and was obviously a great help in getting them exempted from fighting. Yet there was a 'painful scene' at 46, Gordon Square when 'the conversation turned on conscientious objection and Maynard declared that he did not believe anyone had a genuine conscientious objection. If he said this to exasperate Vanessa and Norton he certainly succeeded.'

In Mr Garnett's case the result of these tensions seems to have been that he suffered from nerves and *angst*. Not until a few years after the war, when success came to him did he become once again the delightful person he was in *The Golden Echo*.

Many of the best Bloomsbury sagas are told. There is the Garsington peacock, named Argus by Aldous Huxley, which got carbuncles and conveniently died in December 1917 and was roasted for Christmas dinner; when the guests were violently sick. Lady Ottoline said it was an appendicitis epidemic. And Lytton Strachey's evidence when he came before the Tribunal for conscientious objectors, where he was accompanied by his whole family:

> The Military Representative was inspired with a flight of fancy and asked: 'What would you do, Mr. Strachey, if you saw an Uhlan attempting to rape your sister?' Lytton looked at his sisters in turn, as though trying to visualise the scene, and gravely replied in his high voice: 'I should try to interpose my own body.'

The Flowers of the Forest, Garnett, D. (1955)

Past Notes from a Spirited Puritan

In her nineties, the last of the Bloomsbury group, Frances Partridge, has produced a delightful book, full of indiscreet gossip, amusing stories and fascinating journeys. There is something for everyone in these diaries, far and away the best she has bestowed upon the public.

Sharply observant, she gives a lyrical description of restored Warsaw and St Petersburg, enjoying every moment despite the bitter cold. Then there is a calm visit to David Garnett in his French cottage with its pastoral setting, walks in woods, hunting for wild flowers, talking about the past.

In Italy she goes on a rather frenzied tour with Dadie Rylands and

Raymond Mortimer, visiting cities, palaces, cathedrals and museums, almost too much beauty; Raymond is rather tiresome with his school-master-like comments forced upon his companions. For her journeys abroad she chose her companions well on the whole, not as easy as it sounds. Spain was perhaps her favourite country.

Back in England life was very different. Strikes galore, rubbish in the streets, electric fires sadistically fading during 'cuts', torch batteries and candles unobtainable: London in the early 1970s became almost as uncomfortable as it had been in the war.

All Frances Partridge's friends were ill, some desperately so. She herself is a widow mourning her clever husband as well as their only son, who died in his twenties, yet she flies to comfort her ailing con-temporaries. Her greatest friend Julia Strachey, always neurotic, at this time goes completely mad. The account of the descent into hell of the charming, intelligent Julia is frightful and sad as only the truth can be. It is a relief when Julia herself insists upon enmity where once had been deep friendship. Frances was getting to the end of her fund of sympathy when she was forced to abandon the terrible task to others.

There is a close-up view of many a broken marriage, when she is called to help in a situation where there is never much hope. There are also happy marriages, Heywood and Ann Hill for example, and visits to the Hills and Anne's eccentric brothers for the Aldeburgh Music Festival.

Two snowy Christmases she stayed with the David Cecils, another happy pair. David Cecil talked himself and everyone else into a stupor, and when Frances retired to her room she heard the Cecil voices rising uninterruptedly through the floorboards.

Very naturally, she dreads the Bloomsbury-hounds, and the cinema and television absurdities, pretending to tell the 'truth' about her famous friends and making a hash of it. But these talented and articulate people are not really at risk.

Frances Partridge reveals herself, as diarists always do, from Pepys to Chips, from André Gide to Alan Clark and James Lees-Milne. She is a puritan who responds to beauty. She hates war, cruelty, stupidity.

But she also hates luxury, grandeur, and even, almost, comfort. She fails to see the superb beauty of Houghton, within and without. Or if she sees it, she cannot approve. She says aristocrats are arrogant, picking on one lady, Kathleen Stanley, who was the kindest of women.

Her Puritanism just occasionally shows the tip of its ear, as the French say. Perhaps it is one of her virtues. Be that as it may, her book deserves the success which it will surely have.

The Diaries of Frances Partridge: 1963-66, Partridge, F., *Sunday Times* (1998)

Lifelong Fit of Giggles

Here are the scrapings of the barrel, more or less everything left behind by Henry Yorke (for that was Henry Green's real name) when he died. Much of it is well worth preserving: interviews, unperformed television plays, chapters of unfinished novels, scenes of family life half-truth half-caricature written in the merciless and sardonic way he had. Henry Green's grandson has edited these literary remains, putting them in chronological order. It is easy to see influences—Kafka, Henry James—but from the beginning Green's was such a distinctive voice that only he could have written these pages.

Greatly admired in his lifetime by other writers, Waugh, Auden, Isherwood, V.S. Pritchett for example, there will probably never be a school of Henry Green. As he himself said of Joyce, his style, his jokes, his marvellous dialogue were his alone.

He might have echoed Gide's cry: *'Familles! Je vous hais!'* There is bitterness in the way he describes a boring family evening, father and mother bickering and two sulky sons leaving them to it. There is a fantasy about a giant who appears in the park at Petworth. Henry Green's eccentric Wyndham uncles and aunts see him out of the window and are half terrified, half outraged. How to get rid of him? The butler is sent out, but is blown into the lake. Finally the giant goes, but not before bellowing that he had come there hoping to hear the family engaged in intellectual conversation.

There is a biographical chapter by Sebastian Yorke, Henry's son. He describes his father's delight in minor disasters and how amused he was when things went wrong. He may have looked upon life itself as one long sick joke. Yet for his friends he was one of the most delightful men of his talented generation.

Surviving, ed. Yorke, M., *Evening Standard* (1994)

Fluttering Wings

'Dearest Maud, dearest Primavera! I do not know what primavera means, or if I have spelt it sufficiently for you to recognize the word. It means Spring, doesn't it? It means joy, the joy of green leaves with the flutter of wings among the leaves. And you, dearest, mean all these things to me, for you are not, I am, convinced. a mere passing woman but an incarnation of an idea… You are at once the poet and the poem, and you create yourself not with silks and pearls, though these things are beautiful upon you. but by your intense desire of beauty and life.'

'I gave you all the love I was capable of. I never cease to think of you…'

The first passage quoted above was written by George Moore when he was 52 and had been in love with Lady [Emerald] Cunard for ten years. The second he wrote twenty five years later. His love for her lasted from their first meeting until his death forty years after. She destroyed most of his letters; all that remain are in this volume.

Lady Cunard was a great admirer of George Moore's books; he was a fervent admirer of her astonishing personality. 'To Maud Cunard,' he wrote, 'a woman of genius. Her genius is manifest in her conversation, and like Jesus and Socrates, she has refrained from the other arts.'

The audience for this marvellous, intelligent, inconsequent conversation was formed by her luncheon and dinner guests, and although she invited clever men to her house some of the company was not as amusing as it was fashionable. 'There are people about that are of no interest to me, as little intelligent they seem as squeaking dolls,' complained George Moore.

None of Lady Cunard's letters to her faithful admirer have been found, yet her portrait is clearly seen in his to her, from her marble eyes and gold hair, to her worldliness, her love of music, her brilliance. She would descend unexpectedly upon the old writer in Ebury Street, like a bright humming-bird, then rush away leaving a purple orchid for him to treasure.

She was everything that he could never be, and as he sat year after year writing and re-writing and revising his books, there is no doubt that she, brought him something uniquely precious. He was naturally, a little bit jealous. 'I was glad to see you brightening as usual the lives of dull people,' he once wrote, with a nip of sarcasm.

Letters to Lady Cunard 1895-1933, Moore, G. (1957)

❋

Beauty Betrayed

If Mary Pickford was the world's sweetheart, Greta Garbo was the world's goddess. She had perfect beauty and a rare acting talent, and unlike any other actress before or since she hated publicity in private life, refused to be photographed and evaded fans, autograph hunters and the Press.

Cecil Beaton was in every way her opposite. He loved and courted publicity, made his fortune from it, and kept endless scrapbooks into which he pasted every passing reference to himself in the English or American papers. He longed to meet Garbo, and having met her he longed to marry her. It would have been the all-time publicity coup.

Years later, he proposed. She wisely refused; both were homosexual, and in any case she would have loathed his social life, climbing (in his own opinion) ever higher, loving the lighted candle, luxury, success, people. She stayed with him in Wiltshire and told him he was hag-ridden; the hags were his mother, too fond of the bottle, and his lesbian secretary Maud Nelson. He noted in his diary every detail of their friendship and their intimacies, and finally betrayed her by publishing it in her lifetime. It was a dreadful thing to do by any standards, and strangely enough he realized this himself, but his desire to be known to the world as lover of the most beautiful woman in the world was too strong to be resisted. Diana Souhami describes how as publication draw near he suffered a sort of agony; at that very moment, absurdly enough, he was given a knighthood, and the pleasure he got from being a Sir was blighted by his apprehension about Garbo and his diary.

Some years previously Greta Garbo's lesbian friend Mercedes de Acosta had similarly betrayed the star. Badly needing money, she wrote memoirs and described a mountain holiday she had with Greta, six weeks when nobody knew where they were, the address a secret. It was this episode which sold the book and made Mercedes de Acosta a little money. She was never forgiven. Even when she was dying, in hospital, Greta Garbo refused to visit her.

Cecil Beaton, on the other hand, she did visit, grown old and bald and half paralysed by a stroke. Made furious by the diary, years had passed, and she went down to Wiltshire to say goodbye to her tiresome old friend. There were probably two reasons for this somewhat uncharacteristic behaviour. First, Garbo knew Cecil Beaton so well that she cannot have been surprised by what happened. Where his narcissism was concerned, he had no sensitivity, or even good manners. But secondly (something missing in this fascinating book) Cecil's redeeming feature was laughter. 'Give me the bonus of laughter' wrote John Betjeman in a poem at the end of his life. It was impossible to be with Cecil for half an hour, let alone half a life time, and not be convulsed with laughter. A look came into his face and he would say something in his drawling, braying voice which was inexpressibly funny. It is an important part of the man, who should not be remembered as the rather villainous creature depicted here. Among the illustrations in 'Greta and Cecil' Garbo is seen laughing with Cecil. There cannot have been many of these perfect moments in her Hollywood or her New

York life. Perhaps she forgave his disgraceful behaviour because he had amused her so much. The best possible reason.

Greta and Cecil, Souhami, D., *Evening Standard* (1994)

Impotent Comforts

Gerald Brenan lived to a great age; he was a prolific correspondent to friends and relations, who kept his letters. Very tempting to a biographer. Jonathan Gathorne-Hardy has not resisted, his book (although fascinating) is too long.

Many of the letters are full of what Cyril Connolly called Brenan's 'naïve sexual boasting', which embarrassed those who did not realize the agonies of a sensitive man to whom 'doing what comes naturally' was a near impossibility. He was often impotent.

Born in 1894, he hated his father and his barbarous boarding schools, and they are blamed for his complexes. At 18 his one idea was to escape, and free himself from his constricting background. With a bohemian friend, Hope Johnstone, he planned to walk to China. Telling a few lies, and with a few pounds, he ran off.

He met Hope in Paris, and found happiness, discomfort, hunger and danger. They slept in barns, or inns where the beds were alive with bugs, stole vegetables to eat and could well have died of hunger and cold when winter came. Hope gave up at Venice, but Brenan pressed on, until 'one dark evening in a snowstorm on a Bosnian mountain, I turned back'.

By letter, he bargained with his father for freedom to live in his own way. The parents were by then longing to compromise; he went home. He was 20 in 1914; he became a brave soldier, and at the front made friends with Ralph Partridge. It was a stormy friendship, because the love of Brenan's life, the painter Dora Carrington, married Partridge. But the most important thing that happened after the war was his long visit to Spain, chosen for its cheapness. All his best books are about

Spain, *South From Granada* a classic. He suffered from jealousy over Carrington, but she, Lytton Strachey and various writers stayed with him in his primitive cottage in the sierra.

He married an American poet, had endless unsatisfactory affairs with hippies and nymphets, and read enormously. The Spanish civil war and Second World War he spent in England, then back to Spain for the rest of his life, his writing at last beginning to sell. Fortunately his wife Gamel shared his love of discomfort; they had no bath or lavatory and on their travels stayed in flea-ridden inns.

The Spanish Labyrinth is his great book on Spain, and Gathorne-Hardy's chapter about it is, next to his account of the walk, the best thing in this enormous biography. There are several harrowing cancer deathbeds, that of Brenan's wife beyond bearing. All are culled from frightful descriptions in letters to long-suffering friends.

His own death—when, after a short spell in an English old people's home, the Spanish claimed him as their own and took him back to Andalusia—was at the age of 92.

When Strachey was dying, in 1932, Carrington seemed intent on suicide, and Ralph Partridge sent for two of her lovers, Gerald Brenan and Tommy Tomlin, hoping in vain they might induce her to live.

Probably not many people now alive knew the brilliant Stephen Tomlin, a sculptor married to Julia Strachey.

Strange that in this 'stupendous mass of paper' even his actual name should be omitted. True, he was known as Tommy, but Stephen Tomlin was a considerable artist and personality.

The Interior Castle: A Life of Gerald Brenan, Gathorne-Hardy, J., *Evening Standard* (1992)

A Sponge for All Seasons

Evelyn Waugh, his chief tormentor, called Cyril Connolly 'a droll old sponge', and that he certainly was. This excellent biography brings him wonderfully to life. His grotesque appearance, his velvet voice, the successes as a schoolboy that won him all the prizes at Eton, making Oxford drab by comparison, the knockabout turn of his marriages, the sloth and greed which gave him permanent angst but which he lacked the will to curb. It is not a sad life nor a wasted life, even if authorship of a masterpiece eluded him; he will be remembered as a brilliant critic, editor and personality.

The Unquiet Grave was no more than a commonplace book containing his nostalgic thoughts about Paris and the Mediterranean when war immobilized him in London; flawed by much that was rather absurd and irritating, it nevertheless echoed the feelings of his generation at that time.

All his life he was surrounded by adoring women, and never more so than when, financed by Peter Watson, he edited *Horizon* during the war. Lovely and devoted girls did the hard work of producing the magazine, ministering to him they fed him with honeydew.

He was capable of imaginative sympathy. Meeting a boy who had like him been a King's Scholar at Eton and was doing his military service soon after the war, the description of his basic training so horrified Cyril that he told him to write it all down, and published it in *Horizon*. Balm for the unwilling soldier. Connolly was dogged by poverty. His first wife, Jean, had some money, but the other wives had none. He and Jean were perfectly suited, her income was enough for their bohemian way of life. Dining with them was hazardous because of their pets; ferrets cannot be house-trained. When she left him because he was 'impossible', he mourned her loss on and off for the rest of his life.

His wit and clever conversation made Connolly a welcome guest, but he was not always asked twice by fastidious people. One host complained that he marked his place in borrowed books with bacon rind. He wrote brilliant reviews for the *Observer* until he quarrelled with the priggish owner, and subsequently for many years the *Sunday Times*, an excellent paper in those days. He promised endless books to eager publishers, but rarely wrote them.

Towards the end of his life he was invited to Austin, Texas, for an exhibition based on his '100 Best Books'. Expenses paid and a large fee, it was a recognition by America of his eminence as man of letters. Austin has an unrivalled collection of modern English books and MSS, he was happy to accept and was enjoying every moment until the cataloguer of Evelyn Waugh's library, a recent acquisition, asked him to solve some conundrums of place and identity. Connolly's eye lit upon Waugh's copy of *The Unquiet Grave*, and he could not resist looking inside to see what had been written in the margins. The brutal rudeness and dismissive jokes he found ruined his visit. 'For the rest of my stay in Texas I remained obsessed with Evelyn', he wrote. Waugh teased him even from the grave.

Connolly died, as he had lived, beyond his means. He left a huge overdraft at the bank; his rich friends generously paid up.

The photographs illustrating this delightful book are so badly reproduced that one succeeds in making the attractive Jean look uglier than Cyril himself, while Railway Club members seem to be hardly human.

Cyril Connolly: A Nostalgic Life, Fisher, C., *Evening Standard* (1995)

Enormous Huts

In July 1928 I went accompanied by Nanny, to stay at Bailiffscourt. This was a piece of country by the sea in Sussex which the Guinnesses [future in-laws] had bought a couple of years before; they had saved it from speculators who had planned to ruin the entire coast.

Bailiffscourt itself was a small farm-house at Climping, notorious as the home of Colonel Barker, a woman who pretended she was a man and married a Brighton girl. We loved this story which had filled the newspapers and I was considered very lucky to be going to see the place formerly hallowed by the presence of Colonel Barker. I soon discovered, however, that one must not mention Colonel Barker at Bailiffscourt; her name was taboo and Lady Evelyn preferred to forget that she had ever existed.

Lady Evelyn Guinness, her children, their Willoughby cousins, and two nurses lived in the Huts. These really were huts, made of pitch pine and set on brick foundations. They smelt deliciously of raw wood and salty air. They were planted down in the middle of a cornfield, and at the bottom of the field was the sea. There was a quite exceptional glare in summer outside the Huts; the flat treeless landscape, the enormous sky, the ripe corn and the sea reflecting back the light of the sun almost blinded one.

Lady Evelyn, like Farve, was a builder. She was going to build a very strange house; already her mind was full of her plans for it, but meantime the family put up in the Huts. Bryan and I wandered about the fields or sat on the beach. Sometimes we all went for a picnic on the Downs. When we reached the chosen spot the drivers of the cars unpacked a huge tea, a frying pan, a pat of butter, and eggs. 'Diana's so clever, Mummy, she can cook,' said Bryan, bursting with pride.

'I've never *heard* of such a thing, it's *too* clever,' said Lady Evelyn in her whispery little voice.

'I can't really. Only fried eggs. Anybody can do fried eggs,' I said modestly, but Lady Evelyn and the nurses took up the refrain. To cook! It was too wonderful.

At that time she was in her early forties; a very pretty, slight, fair-haired and blue-eyed person with a very tiny voice. Her voice was not exactly soft; it was more like a miniature hard voice, scarcely audible. She never raised it. She had a ferocious collie called Lady which bit men visitors. 'Lady! Lady! What do I see you doing?' Rather naturally, Lady never noticed this reproof, what with her own growls and the exclamations of her victim.

Lady Evelyn loved wild flowers growing among the corn and did her best to encourage them. Not only in the fields near the Huts were poppy and cornflower seeds strewn in profusion; all the way down in the train from Victoria to Arundel she would lean out of her carriage window in springtime, scattering weeds and seeds as she went. 'I'm afraid Walter doesn't quite approve,' she told me. Walter, Bryan's father, was Minister of Agriculture.

Lady Evelyn was on our side, but said she could not write to Muv and Farve. 'I shouldn't dare,' she whispered. While Parliament was in recess Bryan's father was away on his yacht—far away. He did not go to the Mediterranean, but to distant, savage lands.

In September he was expected back. Lady Evelyn and the children left the Huts and went to Heath House, Hampstead. 'I wish we could stay on at Bailiffscourt,' she said. 'Such beautiful weather. But I must go at once because of Christmas.'

'*Christmas*, Lady Evelyn?' I cried. 'But that's three months off!'

'Oh yes,' said Bryan, 'but it takes Mummy a good three months to do her Christmas. In fact she's really at it the whole year.'

This astonished me so much that I asked Rosalie and Pink McDonnell about it one day. 'Aunt Evelyn's Christmas is terrific,' said Rosalie. 'In fact Uncle Walter can't stand it. He always leaves England the moment Parliament rises because of the Grosvenor Place Christmas.'

Colonel Guinness, who turned up eventually, had a long talk with Bryan. I was invited to stay at Heath House; Bryan met me at Paddington and drove me to Hampstead. When we arrived his mother was gardening. She was walking along a path with a watering can, watering it here and there, if that is the word, with milk. 'Mummy's encouraging the moss', explained Bryan.

The garden was quite big by Hampstead standards; it looked rather sad. Ugly tufts of murky, un-tended grass and weeds sprouted everywhere, there were over-grown hedges with holes and gaps in them, and not a flower was to be seen except the odd dandelion and thistle. 'Mummy can't bear garden flowers,' Bryan told me. 'She only likes wild ones, and of course they don't do very well in London.'

Lady Evelyn pointed vaguely here and there. 'You can't imagine what a perfectly ghastly pergola there used to be,' she said, adding in a horrified whisper, 'And there were hideous roses—in beds.'

Inside, Heath House had also been transformed to Lady Evelyn's taste, and one saw what Bailiffscourt would eventually become.

Colonel Guinness seemed not to notice either the garden or the house. He talked about politics, people and health.

'*What!* No vitamins?' he said when I refused some raw carrot. The food was excellent; we ate it off a worm-eaten refectory table. I felt very shy of Bryan's father. He was kind but distant to me; but he had promised Bryan to write to Farve.

Every evening we dined early and went to a play. In the mornings Lady Evelyn did her Christmas shopping, and in the afternoon she scattered milk over the grim garden.

Farve gave in and we were officially engaged. I spent my time between Swinbrook and Grosvenor Place, where the Guinnesses returned in October. Lady Evelyn shopped all day now, as there were only about seventy shopping days till Christmas.

Grosvenor Place was like Heath House only much, much more so. When you approached the great, ugly Victorian imitation of a French château and walked up the steps the door opened at once. This was the work of George, the door man, who sat all day watching the entrance from a little window in the porch. He was by way of being clumsy. 'Did George knock you down?' was Lady Evelyn's first question when one arrived. George led the way across a dark hall with stripped pine panelling to the lift, which looked like a tiny mediaeval closet. The lift whizzed up several floors and was opened by a nursery-maid. Tea, and in fact most of life, was spent in Grania's nursery. Lady Evelyn herself slept in one of the night nurseries. The day nursery was a large cheerful white room with a bright fire, plenty of toys and books, and sofas covered in chintz. While the rest of the house was almost pitch dark, lights blazed in the nursery. Lady growled and made little dashes, but she only bit men guests; Raymond and Edward Greene, great friends of Lady Evelyn, always came to Grosvenor Place wearing riding boots because of the collie.

If one arrived for luncheon or dinner George handed one over to the head parlourmaid and the full oddity of Grosvenor Place was unfolded. The downstairs rooms were lined—panelled is not the word—with rough, blackened wood. The fires were encouraged to smoke and smoulder, because the effect Lady Evelyn wished to create was that of a house so 'early' that chimneys had not been invented. The furniture, besides refectory tables black with age—or with simulated age—one did not always quite believe in the Grosvenor Place furniture—consisted of dozens of Spanish chairs, of various sizes but similar design, a strip of dark, hard leather for the back, another for the seat, with many a rusty nail to catch a stocking here and there in the crumbling wooden frame. The lamps were made of bent pieces of iron holding sham yellow candles with yellow bulbs of about five watts shaded in thick old parchment—tallow, not wax, was the note.

On the tables were pewter pots containing bunches of grasses and wild flowers, and there were polished pewter plates and dishes to eat off. The forks had two prongs. The pewter things were made by Day, the head chauffeur, in a garage. He had given up driving and spent his whole time making more and more pewter plates, because Colonel Guinness liked to have dinner parties of over a hundred people. Lady Evelyn thought entertaining a tiresome bore, but she did it for his sake, only insisting that there must be enough pewter for everybody. To have had to fall back on silver or china would have been too humiliating.

On the day of a dinner party the cars went out of London at dawn, crowded with maids; when they got to the country they filled baskets with cow parsley, grasses and buttercups and then hurried back to London and changed into their medieval gowns made of stuff with a pattern of wild flowers on it, to be ready by the time the guests began to arrive.

The guests behaved rather badly; they all pretended to get hay-fever from the floral decorations. I sat next to Philip Sassoon at one of these dinners; he was quite furious because Lady Evelyn could just as well have had orchids everywhere instead of cow parsley and moon daisies, and gold rather than pewter. He loudly disapproved of her eccentricity.

Grosvenor Place had two of everything because it was numbers 10 and 11 knocked into one house. One of the big staircases was entirely taken up by Murtogh's slide. After a visit to a fair he had said to his mother: 'Why can't we have a slide from the top of the house to the bottom?' and immediately a beautiful, polished wooden slide was built and fitted on the staircase. Everybody, not only Murtogh, played on the slide. It was a marvellous idea perfectly executed.

Lady Evelyn's father was still alive. His only son, Uncle Ronny, was a bachelor of about fifty. He was charming and rather eccentric; he believed in the Hidden Hand and the Jewish World Plot. Colonel Guinness had no patience with Uncle Ronny's pet theories, but as he was a member of the government Uncle Ronny deluged him with literature about them which went straight into the waste-paper basket.

As soon as our engagement appeared in *The Times*, wedding presents began to pour in. When the presents were all arranged Lady Evelyn looked at them reflectively.

'The glass will be the easiest,' she said. 'It only needs a good kick.' She said silver was much more of a problem. 'Walter and I had such luck, all ours was stolen while we were on our honeymoon.'

All I remember of the marriage service is that Tom had got hold of a wonderful trumpeter who filled the church with triumphant sound when the choir sang Handel's 'Let the bright seraphim in burning row', and that the clergyman pressed his hand on my head so hard that the rickety wreath and veil arrangement almost fell over my eyes.

Lady Evelyn was a vision in cream velvet trimmed with sables. Just as we were going away Bryan rushed over to where she was standing and threw his arms round her. 'Good gracious, Bryan!' she said, in the little voice usually reserved for Lady.

From *A Life of Contrasts*, Mosley, D. (1977, 2002)

Blenheim's Eccentric Duchess

Gladys Deacon, whose classic face is carved in stone on a sphinx at Blenheim, was an American child living with her parents and sisters in Europe when an appalling drama struck the family. Mr Deacon had long been jealous of his wife's friendship with a certain Emile Abeille, and convinced that the two of them were locked-in together in her room at the Splendide Hotel at Cannes, he got the hotel secretary as witness and they broke open the door. Mrs Deacon, despite a bed which had clearly had two people in it, pretended she was alone; but Mr Deacon, candle in one hand and revolver in the other, saw a shadow in the adjoining sitting room and shot through a little canapé, mortally wounding the unfortunate Abeille, who was crouched behind it. The trial was at Nice, and Deacon was sentenced to one year in prison, of which he served a month. It was one of the most sensational *crimes passionelles* of the nineteenth century.

Mr Deacon went back to America and Mrs Deacon reverted to her maiden name of Baldwin, but everyone knew who she was, and the little girls could never appear without somebody whispering the dreadful tale. They grew up with it. Gladys was eleven in 1892 when her father shot her mother's lover.

Mrs Baldwin was soon installed at Caprarola, a palace near Rome, by her lover Prince Doria; but neither Roman nor Parisian society would receive her. As they grew up the girls were so beautiful and clever that they proved irresistible. Their mother longed for them to make 'good' marriages. Gladys in particular was brilliant, and Marcel Proust said of her: 'I never saw a girl with such beauty.' Her friends were writers and artists and intelligent people, many of whom were more intrigued than shocked by the old scandal.

When she was 40, after his marriage with Consuelo Vanderbilt had been annulled in Rome, Gladys married her lover of many years, Sunny, ninth Duke of Marlborough. What did she see in him? He was unprepossessing. The answer must be 'a duke'. Thenceforward a slow, steady decline began for Gladys. She had a disastrous face-lift; it left her with mouth awry and a chin which looked like a collapsed balloon. She was extraordinarily brave about this, in fact she behaved as if she had never looked in the mirror. She never referred to it, even obliquely.

In her first years at Blenheim she continued to see Paris friends as well as English friends. Daphne Fielding has used pages from the Blenheim visitors' book as end papers; in 1921 Sunny and Gladys' guests were Etienne de Beaumont, Princesse Winnie de Polignac, Mrs Keppel, Professor Lindemann, Lord Berners, the Duke's first cousin Winston Churchill, Princess Marina and her parents, and many more. Yet inexorably the sky darkened. Was Gladys a little mad when she gave her clergymen's luncheon, to which all the incumbents of the Duke's livings were tactlessly invited together? It was the talk of the neighbourhood. Gladys was not well looked upon, nor was the annulment of the Duke's first marriage.

Gladys had a French accent and she rolled her R's. 'Have you rrread' 'Thrrree Weeks?' she asked my father. 'I haven't read a book for three years,' he replied in Uncle Matthew vein. Lady Ottoline Morrell, not far off at Garsington, declared that Gladys was 'the most interesting character in Oxfordshire'.

As time went on she showed signs of becoming more eccentric, and the Duke began a series of friendships with ladies young and old; he loved dancing, which exasperated her. She indulged her passion for Blenheim spaniels in such a way as to wreck carpets and floors in the palace. She and the Duke parted company in bitter anger, not long before he died. Gladys retired to a farm in the Midlands; she called herself Mrs Spencer. Journalists who sought her there got a douche of cold water poured over them from an upper window.

A long night began for Gladys. She preferred not to see friends. Soon after the war the local police, worried by the strange old hermit she had become, made her relations come from abroad to visit her. She was certified insane. Daphne Fielding, a friend from former days, visited her many times in the hospital. She gives a touching account of Gladys; the ravaged chin and mouth had become normal, so that once again she had 'the face on the sphinx'. A beauty, whose unusual intelligence changed to madness, she lived on into extreme old age; pathos personified.

When she died last year aged 96 her possessions were sold for more than seven hundred thousand pounds; there were pictures by Toulouse Lautrec and Degas, her portrait by Boldini, beautiful jewelry, all relics of her youth and now immensely valuable. Knowing her as I did, I do not think she would have been either surprised nor particularly pleased by this financial tribute to her taste. She knew she was 'wonderful', and cared nothing for the world's opinion. But she would like Daphne Fielding's book, which ensures she will not be forgotten, and tells so well the story of her mother's drama, a drama that marked Gladys's life.

The book is splendidly illustrated; the photograph of the tenth Duke in his coronation robes is alone worth a fiver. He looks like a giant Dutch doll with a cigar in its mouth and a coronet on its head.

The Face on the Sphinx, Fielding, D., *Books and Bookmen* (1979)

And the Rich Filed in Two by Two

Edith Chaplin always thought of herself as a child of the Highlands, says Anne de Courcy. Perhaps she did, but this fey side of her nature was under control, and everyone else thought her the epitome of worldliness. She was the very image of aristocratic magnificence as she stood, with her somewhat Dutch doll-type solid good looks, smothered in jewels from head to foot, to receive the Tory faithful at the top of the stairs at Londonderry House. A nabob ancestor had brought enormous diamonds from India, 'given' by a maharaja.

The Londonderrys were both 21 when they married; the extremely attractive husband was the love of her life; the best thing about her was her absolute loyalty to him, despite his innumerable infidelities.

Tremendously rich, beneath his land were vast coal mines. The great coal owners in England were the Arabs of the nineteenth century, with the same love of display, and of horses and racing.

Lady Londonderry was an organiser of outstanding ability, getting cohorts of women to do war work in both wars. She was a noted gardener at Mount Stewart in Ireland, and she hunted several days a week in the shires. Lord Londonderry loved hunting and shooting, but he loved politics more. What with women, sport and Parliament, she saw little of him, and her biographer has a mass of letters to draw upon. It was Ramsay MacDonald, her great friend, who gave Lord Londonderry office in the National Government, Tory in all but name. For MacDonald, Lady Londonderry was glamour personified and he adored her. She was quite fond of him, for all his whining self-pity and embarrassing compliments, until the day he ceased to be prime minister, when the boredom became too much for her and the gorse at Lossiemouth lost its charm.

To his great credit, Lord Londonderry was one of the few who realised an airforce might be vital to Britain's survival. At the same time he did all he could to foster Anglo-German friendship, visiting Germany and inviting Goering to stay at Londonderry House for the coronation in 1937. Goering refused.

The Londonderrys had one son and four daughters. There were fusses over weddings, two of the girls marrying in register offices: one bridegroom was divorced and the other of Jewish faith. Lady Londonderry wanted a church, preferably Westminster Abbey.

Her clever son Robin had enormous sympathy with the miners, who had been treated abominably by the government in 1926 after the strike, and who provided the family's bottomless purse. He married a lovely girl who died tragically of cancer not long after the Second World War. Robin also died, several years before Lady Londonderry.

These deaths are not mentioned in the book, a strange oversight, since they must have touched the mother.

What about Circe? Lady Londonderry had an 'ark' of celebrities, given silly names, invited to Londonderry House for childish games and champagne. She should have been Mrs Noah, but Circe was preferred. A mystery for she turned none of her guests into swine. Anne de Courcy has written a very interesting book about how things were for the very rich in the first half of the century, including a clear if rather biased précis of the politics of those days.

Circe: The Life of Edith Marchioness of Londonderry, de Courcy, A., *Evening Standard* (1992)

Diana Mosley

Catty Musings of a Living Doll

Gift shops sell little dolls dressed in crinolines, covered in white lace with a rosebud here and there; they have white silk hair, rosy cheeks, ruby lips and black eyelashes. They are bought by misguided people to hide their telephones. Cynthia Gladwyn was one of these dolls to the life, with plenty of crinolines in her wardrobe. Her hair was silvery white while she was still quite young; she was very pretty in her doll-like way.

I suppose I must declare an interest. She says in her diary that I am evil. Is this libellous? Is it true? There is a saying: the greater the truth, the greater the libel, which is rather tempting, because it takes the wind out of the sails of the defence, were I to sue.

Cynthia herself was as good as gold and far from stupid, despite her insipid appearance.

For years her husband, Gladwyn Jebb, was our ambassador in Paris, and Cynthia really loved the splendid embassy and appreciated her enjoyable life there. She wrote a book about the house and strangely enough asked me to review it in *Books and Bookmen*; it was very well done.

She is endlessly gushing in her diaries: 'Quite the most exquisite… quite the loveliest… quite the kindest… quite the cleverest….' On the other hand she can, on occasion, be fairly catty. My sister, Nancy Mitford, loved clothes; she is described as wearing a dress not only too expensive, but also as coming to pieces, an unfortunate combination.

There are some interesting pages about the 1956 Suez fiasco because Anthony Eden and Selwyn Lloyd, when Prime Minster and Foreign Secretary, stayed with the Jebbs in order to cook up with their French counterparts their bright idea: that the Israelis should invade Egypt, and then the peace-loving English and French should separate the antagonists, while Nasser fell from power. Jebb was not invited to these mad plottings, as he should have been. He could have introduced common sense and have warned that essential secrecy would never have been possible with Fourth Republic French politicians. Needless to say, all was 'leaked'. Described by Cynthia Jebb from the sidelines, the whole affair, including Eden's and Lloyd's lies to the House of Commons, is described in all its pristine oddity. These were bad times for England; and for Europe, with Hungary bashed by the Russians.

The diary is full of that evergreen favourite of gossip writers, the Royal Family. The author likes and admires all the right royal ladies and gentlemen, and is cold and disapproving about the duds, never putting a foot wrong or hazarding an original view about any of them.

She is essentially naïve, and quite unconscious when England's wittiest man, Lord Lambton, is sending her up. She may recognize evil, but doesn't always see a joke.

The diary ends in 1971, with the Gladwyns keen Liberals who are beginning to wonder whether their leader, Jeremy Thorpe, is truly in the Gladstone mould.

Their son, Miles Jebb, has edited the diary, and described his mother's old age in a preface.

The Diaries of Cynthia Gladwyn, ed. Jebb, M., *Evening Standard* (1995)

He Achieved a Rare Perfection

'Envious dry blankets who did not know him, and those who read of his luxury and the world of beauty with which he could afford to protect himself… can think what they like, the dreary form-fillers… they cannot be expected to understand the pleasure and thankfulness those people feel who had the privilege of his friendship,' wrote John Betjeman in *The Listener* when Gerald Berners died in 1950. He was the funniest, cleverest friend anyone could wish for, and the most loyal and sensitive. David Cecil said he was the best-read man he ever knew.

As Mark Amory makes clear, he was never an intimate friend: reserved, shy, buttoned up. The only child of a dull, foxhunting mother and a clever, sarcastic father who was seldom at home, he was born in 1883 with a gift for music. Nobody sympathized; occasionally a guest played the piano and his first passion was for Chopin. His mother and his schoolmaster actively discouraged his music, hoping he might take to sport and games. At Eton he became ill, and these hated activities were forbidden by the doctor.

His Dame allowed him to play the piano, and go out sketching. He loved the beauty of Eton, and after he read a synopsis of *The Ring* and acquired the score, he lived in a fantastic world of gods, dwarfs and heroes.

A profession loomed. Diplomacy was chosen and Gerald was delighted to go abroad. He loved France, and in Dresden was taught how to write down his music. In his memoirs he describes a wonderful Christmas at Weimar, with glühwein, paper caps and the singing of Stille Nacht. Mark Amory has discovered he never spent Christmas in Germany; therefore much of what we think we know about his youth is fantasy, written when he was old. Perhaps his mother was not as dim as he pretends—it was she who bought Faringdon—the perfect small eighteenth-century house with a view of half England from its five drawing room windows.

Gerald failed the Foreign Office exam, a blessing. Instead of being sent to some outlandish place he spent happy years in Rome as honorary attaché at our Embassy. He adored Italy and made friends with avant-garde artists in Rome and Paris. In the 20s he inherited Faringdon, but he kept a house in Rome.

In about 1933 he met the Mad Boy, Robert Heber-Percy. Some said he first saw him swinging on a chandelier in a Munich hotel. Gerald was not fifty, a well-known composer from whom Diaghilev had commissioned ballets; his music was admired by Stravinsky. He invited Robert to bring his horses to Faringdon; Robert hunted, and efficiently ran Gerald's farms. He was no longer lonely in the country; the Mad Boy was sometimes outrageous, but never dull.

One year in Rome Gerald wrote a story about a girls' school, *The Girls of Radcliffe Hall*. He was headmaster, the 'girls' were Cecil Beaton, Oliver Messel, Peter Watson, and Robert, the heroine. The book has not worn well. It depended on the 'girls' crushes and jealousies, comic at the time.

At Faringdon he painted, wrote memoirs and composed *The Wedding Bouquet*, with words by Gertrude Stein and choreography by Frederick Ashton. It was produced at Covent Garden, with Constant Lambert conducting. The war came, and made him sad. Europe, his paradise, tore itself to pieces. Music cannot be bombed, but everything else was at risk. He shut Faringdon and went to live in Oxford. His depression deepened, he had some sort of breakdown. He wrote *Far From the Madding War*, very funny but a biting satire.

Back at Faringdon once more he almost recovered, and lived for several years sharing delicious food and the beauty of his surroundings with many friends. In those days of rationing people such as Cyril Connolly, who lived in London, thought of nothing but food. Gerald and Faringdon achieved a rare perfection.

Mark Amory has cleverly captured the essence of Gerald Berners: his professionalism in music, his generosity and genius for friendship, his teases and jokes and sure sense of values. He was broadminded about everything except pomposity.

Lord Berners the Last Eccentric, Amory, M., *Sunday Times* (1998)

Battling for Beauty

Are diaries 'true'? Jim Lees-Milne's are a long and fascinating novel, of which he is the charming, companionable and unpretentious hero. As he gives his characters their real names, and is as frank as he is observant, the diaries have probably wounded quite a few readers. They are sometimes true and sometimes invented, just as novels are. This sensitive man seems never to have imagined anyone might mind his strictures and jokes.

Here he is in his late sixties, thinking death is just round the corner. So many friends died, hardly a week without a painful loss. Yet he had 20 years to live. Although fond of them, he never spared his old friends, freely expressing his horror at what age had done to them. Some were shrunken and bent, some immensely fat like collapsed puddings, nearly all smelt rather horrid. He resolved to be very clean, an antidote to inevitable change and decay. He himself remained an elegant figure, and when he was over 80 my sister Pamela, seeing him stride across a field, said, 'Doesn't Jim look just like an undergraduate when he walks!'

As a young man, working for the National Trust, he did more to save England's beautiful country houses than anyone else has ever done. He deserved every honour England has to bestow, but, needless to say, he was neglected. Deeply religious, he was a Roman Catholic convert, but returned to the Church of England after Vatican II and because the Pope forbade birth control, as he here explains.

Those who knew him well are aware that he left huge chunks of his life out of his diaries; they are highly selective, like all novels. Pepys wrote his diary in shorthand so that 'my wife, poor wretch' should not know what he did with barmaids. Tolstoy hid his in his boot, he was taken ill, his boots were pulled off, Countess Tolstoy found it and read it and the fat was in the fire. Jim could have left his diary anywhere. If Alvilde had read it she would have found only eulogies and affection, all perfectly genuine. Theirs was a happy marriage; they liked the same things and, almost always, the same people.

All through his diaries Jim relates jokes and oddities, and in this volume is a comic masterpiece: his journey to Mount Athos with Derek Hill. After the usual Greek buses and rocking boats stuffed with peasants and their livestock, there were customs and form-filling, Derek telephoning an important monk to little avail. Once on the magic mount the horror of the expedition became clear. Carrying heavy knapsacks, they struggled up steep rocky paths to the monasteries. They slept in dormitories with other pilgrims, in iron beds with dirty, hairy rugs. They washed in a trickle of cold water in a filthy basin with no plug. The lavatories were so terrible that Jim remained constipated. The refectories produced beans floating in oil and hunks of dry bread; no butter or eggs because cows and hens are forbidden on the sexist mountain. The few decrepit monks prayed all night, the churches were too dark for a glimpse of Byzantine treasures, and they were not allowed to see Mary Magdalen's left hand, though an icon which had come on a beam from Palestine, taking 300 years, they did see. Tourists were few, and the beauty of Greek mountains and sea and ruins was like living in a Claude. But they squeezed themselves with alacrity into a jeep full of monks, to avoid a tiring climb. Sharp turns and bumps made the monks fall in heaps, losing their tall hats, their buns of hair coming down; it sounds worse than a vaporetto in the Venice rush hour. One monastery offered lumps of delicious Turkish delight: Derek took two. Jim liked the pious atmosphere, unchanged since the sixth century. But what about the jeep and the telephone? Robert Byron loved it 70 years ago despite fleas, but he was in his twenties.

In November Jim came for a last visit to me in France with my sister Debo. We had a delightful evening, but next day he felt deathly ill and they had to rush home; he died a few weeks later. He was brave to come. He was nearly 90, and we had been friends since he was 11.

Jim was a pessimist. He predicts here that we shall be living in a Marxist hell within ten years. There will be no more hawthorn in May, no hedgerows, the farmers will have bulldozed them. All the trees will have died, not just elms but oaks, beeches, sycamores. Twenty years on, none of these disasters has happened. But he lived for beauty, and his whole life was dedicated to saving what is left.

Through Wood and Vale, Lees-Milne, J., *Sunday Times* (1998)

High enough on the Ladder

A gossip writer's job is an intensely disagreeable one. He is abused either by his friends and acquaintances for betraying confidences, or else by the newspaper which employs him for failing to betray them. In this tricky school Mr Driberg learnt his métier, and his book about Lord Beaverbrook is a perfect illustration of the gossip writer's dilemma. This time it is his readers who may complain that not enough is told, while it appears that the victim feels he has told too much—'a hostile biography'. Over all hangs the threatening cloud of the English law of libel, which as usual spoils the fun.

The two most interesting things in Lord Beaverbrook's life are (1) how he became a millionaire before he was 30 and (2) how he built up his group of newspapers and made another vast fortune with them. Mr Driberg deals briefly with these matters, but at great length with his former employer's pursuit of political power. Three times in his life Lord Beaverbrook enjoyed a modicum of power: when he was active in the intrigues which made Bonar Law leader of the Conservative Party in 1911 and replaced Asquith with Lloyd George in 1916, and again in 1940 when Churchill harnessed his energy (for he is a human dynamo) to aircraft production. During the remainder of his career he has been on the outskirts of politics, and while the autocratic rule he exercised over his newspaper empire was real enough, the power it conferred was illusory.

For like Hearst in America, it was power he wanted, and, also like him, he apparently thought he could reach his objective through his newspapers. Both men imagined that X-million readers represented X-million supporters in the struggle for political influence. They were wrong. American politicians were terrified of Hearst's support, which invariably proved fatal to them. Possibly at this moment Sir Anthony Eden would welcome a return to the time when he was daily abused in the Beaverbrook press. The more frenziedly the *Daily Express* shouts an opinion the more decisively (it sometimes seems) do its readers reject that opinion.

Between the wars Lord Beaverbrook's ambition soared. His invariably successful opponent in the Tory party was Mr Baldwin, who was neither so rich, nor so clever, nor so energetic as he, and who owned no newspapers. What had Baldwin got that Beaverbrook lacked? He was an educated man; but Lord Beaverbrook's enemy of later years,

Ernest Bevin, had probably less education than the press lord himself. Presumably the answer is that Baldwin's character and principles were acceptable to the public, and that Lord Beaverbrook's (even had he not hobbled himself with a peerage) were not.

Many people, reading this book, will be amazed to learn that he ever for one moment set his hopes so high. Nevertheless, looking back over the years, it is no wonder if he feels surprised at the extent to which political influence eluded him. Possibly he even now imagines that his newspapers guide their readers' thoughts and actions. Yet the fact remains that however good the racing tips, however witty the Osbert Lancaster drawing, however exciting the strips, however unconsciously funny Mr John Gordon may be, the readers of these delightful features pay no attention when they are ordered to vote for X, Y and Z, and are very apt instead to vote for A, B and C. As to the proprietor's vendettas, his likes and dislikes and policies, they are so kaleidoscopic and unpredictable that the public, though much entertained by his newspapers, does not take them seriously.

Mr Driberg's book would probably have been more successful had it been less thoroughly bowdlerised. As it is, though cattiness pervades it, the scratches are slight. If (as is possible) he had the power and the desire to wound, he has been frustrated; thus the title of his book has a double meaning.

Beaverbrook: A Study in Power and Frustration, Driberg, T. (1653)

Fellow Travellers

Evidently Mr Tom Driberg finds poor fat grubby chain-smoking communist Guy Burgess a more sympathetic subject for biography than he found rich energetic transatlantic bossy buccaneering Lord Beaverbrook. Nothing could exceed his tender regard for the former unless it be his spiteful resentment of the latter. Guy Burgess, of course, is not a man calculated to arouse either envy or malice; he is too far down the ladder.

Mr Driberg relates of him that he so much dislikes violence and cruelty that he ostentatiously turned his back when a boy was beaten school. It may seem strange that someone so sensitive about the barbarous practices of his own countrymen should be so insensitive to the vast organised cruelties of Soviet Russia; but perhaps he simply turns his back again. The child father to the man?

Burgess appears to have disclosed little or nothing that we did not now already from Cyril Connolly's book, from Petrov, and from the reluctant Foreign Office White Paper, about the case of the 'missing diplomats'. It is curious that the *Daily Mail* should consider extracts from Mr Driberg's book the scoop of the decade, or of the century, I cannot remember which it was supposed to be. Surely not on account of Burgess's sentimental and amateurish little sketch of a night view of Eton College chapel from Luxmoore's garden—likely, no doubt, to evoke tender memories in some of *Daily Mail's* Etonian readers, but of small interest to those educated at other schools?

As to his visit to Sir Winston Churchill at Chartwell during the Munich crisis, we do not require to be told by Mr Guy Burgess what Sir Winston thought about war with Germany. It will come as a surprise to nobody. 'I hope to be employed again,' he is quoted as saying, and Mr Driberg comments: 'it has been forgotten how completely down and out politically, Churchill at that time seemed.'

'You know, Tom, living in a socialist country *does* have a therapeutic effect on one,' says Mr Burgess, and he goes on: 'In London I was lonely for the important things—I was lonely for Socialism.'

I hope Mr Driberg's bad luck in having his little whitewashing effort published just now (he could not have been expected to guess what his Russian socialist friends would be about)* will not put him off trying to get another scoop next time he spends his summer holidays in Moscow. Maclean's story might be interesting, if he would tell it. But perhaps he is not seedy enough, or silly enough, to arouse Mr Driberg's sympathetic interest.

* Guy Burgess and Donald Maclean emerged in Moscow in 1956 after vanishing 5 years earlier.

Burgess: A Portrait with Background, Driberg, T. (1956)

Inches Apart

In the 20s it was fashionable to attack modern youth (the grandparents of today). Whenever news was scarce, journalists filled up their paper with articles about short hair, long hair, short skirts, outsize trousers— all, according to them, symbols of decadence and immorality. Undergraduates outraged the older generation by having their trousers made several inches wider than had hitherto been thought modish for men, and this was supposed to be the outward and visible sign of their unmanliness, irresponsibility and laziness. What a contrast, said the journalists, with their elder brothers and uncles who had fought in the war a few years before.

Christian Scientists have a theory that to speak of illness, or of pain, brings it about by 'making a reality' of it; similarly, believers in magic are careful not to mention undesirable phenomena for fear of attracting them, of the word becoming flesh. Perhaps these ideas are not so fanciful after all. Certain it is, that modern youth in the 30s made a reality of the reputation which had been given to the post-war generation; though strangely enough they were not much attacked for it, the newspapers were bored with the subject by the time they arrived on the scene.

Mr Toynbee, in his memoir of two friends both of whom were killed in the Second World War, makes the period 1934-40 (so near in time, so different in essence, to the 50s) live again. *Friends Apart* is a text-book for parent-baiters; but it was not only their parents and respectable acquaintances who were exasperated by the uninhibited anti-social behaviour of Mr Toynbee and Esmond Romilly. The highly disciplined Communist party, to which they naturally turned in their revolt from bourgeois society, also failed to make them conform and found them intractable material, useless for its own purposes.

Perhaps they did not become Communists because of any positive ideological agreement with Communist political theory, but for the same reason that they stole dozens of top hats from Eton boys while they were in chapel. *He only does it to annoy, because he knows it teases....*

Years have passed since then; the Toynbee parents' ugly duckling has grown into a swan. He writes so well, remembers so accurately, is so Rousseau-esque in his candour that his book is, in its way, a minor work of art. The two friends are dead; Esmond Romilly was only 22 when he was killed, Jasper Ridley not much more. Who can say what would have become of them, how they would have developed? The child is father to the man, and neither can be judged by the years of *Sturm and Drang* which link them.

Friends Apart, Toynbee, P. (1954)

❃

Such Dessicated Old Chestnuts

The Macmillan family of publishers came from a croft on Arran Island, as Harold Macmillan, prime minister, allowed nobody to forget. Humble origins are quite common, but there is something special about an island in the Hebrides. Life was so very primitive and uncomfortable, to exist at all such a tough business, the surroundings so dramatically beautiful, that it is quite in order to boast about it for one hundred and eighty years.

In 1816, when their son Daniel was three, the Hebridean ancestors moved. He and his brother Alexander, through apprenticeships and hard work, were the founders of the firm. Their favourite motto: 'Except ye repent, ye shall all likewise perish.' Religion, work, love of books and all the Scotch puritan virtues made their success. Daniel died of TB aged 44, his brother and partner lived until 1896 and became rich. Daniel was grandfather of Harold Macmillan.

The account of this persevering though delicate family's rise is well done, but the half of the book devoted to Harold Macmillan is very disappointing. It is a twice-told tale and the addition of vulgarities cannot disguise the fact that we know it too well. Huge biographies and autobiographies have left no gaps. Davenport-Hines says in his preface that private papers were denied him. He therefore resorts here and there to guesswork. He guesses that Harold Macmillan disliked his bossy American mother, though Macmillan says he owed everything to her.

When Macmillan marries Lady Dorothy Cavendish the book takes off and becomes an extended gossip column. Again, no surprises. Stories about the eighth Duke of Devonshire can hardly be said to have much to do with Macmillan, or even with Lady Dorothy, who was only his great-niece. Yet here they are, the most desiccated of chestnuts.

As we all know, Lady Dorothy fell in love with Macmillan's contemporary and fellow MP Bob Boothby. Her youngest child, who died long ago aged 40, was by him. This well-documented affair may have fuelled Macmillan's ambition, and he got to the top of the greasy pole. 'Suez' in 1956 was misconceived; once a vital British interest as gateway to India, it had not been so since Indian independence in 1947. For our secret ally Israel, Egypt was highly important. Macmillan was belligerent, then backed down. He and Selwyn Lloyed lied blue to the House of Commons about something supremely unimportant, Macmillan almost choked with indignation. He was a great actor.

He lived to an immense age, for twenty years a widower. His hobby was talking; he talked and talked. Anne Fleming wrote he was 'a crashing bore'. But he did not bare his teeth aggressively, as Davenport-Hines says he did. When he bared his teeth he was trying to smile. It was just that they stuck out too far.

The Macmillans, Davenport-Hines, R., *Evening Standard* (1992)

Seizing the Passing Day

Why do people keep diaries? Because they enjoy doing it, most likely; the theory that they hope thereby to achieve immortality is a bit far-fetched. No need to ask why people read them, for they are irresistible; and this applies just as much to diaries obviously written with publication in view as to those like Samuel Pepys's, written in code, which give at any rate the illusion of being strictly private. A person must be a quite exceptional bore if having faithfully recorded his life day by day he nevertheless cannot amuse his descendant who chances upon the neglected manuscript gathering dust in an old trunk, even though a stranger might put it on the fire for being too dull.

For family peace it is as well that diaries, like wine, should be allowed to mature. The Tolstoys were inveterate diarists, and Countess Tolstoy, whenever she could find it, always read her husband's diary and never liked his references to her or his descriptions of their quarrels, so that bitter resentments developed. In order to preserve it from her prying Tolstoy took to hiding it in his boot. One day he had a heart attack and she lovingly put him to bed and pulled off his boots. Out fell the diary. She pounced upon it and one of their worst rows followed. Tolstoy should, like Pepys, have invented a secret code.

Most modern French writers keep diaries and publish them from time to time, and very entertaining (and doubtless profitable) they are. Gide's *Journal* wears better than his novels; Julien Green confesses himself to his diary and his readers never tire of his spiritual odyssey; Montherlant's *Carnets* display his pessimistic view of human baseness and also the random thoughts of a remarkable mind; the Mauriacs, father and son, are also among the many who have given their diaries to the world in their own lifetime; both are readable, François Mauriac extremely so. As to Eckermann, it is hardly fair to include him among favourite diarists. On every page of his *Conversations with Goethe* there are marvels of imagination and perception which make his book one of the great books of the world, but that is because Goethe is a genius of the first water.

At the other end of the scale was a lady's diary read out in court a few years ago at a public enquiry concerned with a damaging leak of secret information which had occurred in the financial world. Doubt was cast upon entries like 'Went to the hairdresser'. It was suggested this must really mean something rather sinister, but in the end the judge accepted that it was the echo of an empty mind.

In *Dear Diary* Brian Dobbs confines himself to English diarists, describing and giving snippets from a rich variety beginning with Pepys and Evelyn down to recent times with Lady Cynthia Asquith, 'Chips' Channon and Harold Nicolson. His book whets the appetite and reminds one that the literary executors of both Lady Cynthia Asquith and Virginia Woolf must be persuaded to vouchsafe further thrilling instalments. So far tantalisingly little of either has been published. Mrs Woolf was extremely spiteful about her friends and enemies, but the few remaining Bloomsburies must be hardened to instults, since the two great biographers of Bloomsbury, Michael Holroyd and Quentin Bell, have neither of them troubled to pull any punches, and one more battering could not matter much.

Evelyn Waugh's diaries are in a different category. Presumably if he had not meant them to be published he would have destroyed them; nevertheless they give a totally false picture of this brilliant writer, who in real life was so dearly loved by his friends. However much these friends may be bruised by his bludgeon, it is Evelyn himself who comes off badly.

Of Mrs Sidney Webb and her amusing diary of political gossip Brian Dobbs says: 'there seems to be a modern tendency to sneer at her', and for this he blames her nephew Malcolm Muggeridge. This is unfair. Mr Muggeridge in his dazzlingly brilliant autobiography described Mrs Webb sitting on Mr Webb's lap. It must have been an unforgettable sight-she tall and handsome, he 'at once repulsive and ridiculous. His tiny tadpole body, unhealthy skin…' (not Malcolm Muggeridge's description of Sidney Webb, but Mrs Sidney Webb's own). Not only has Mrs Muggeridge published an excellent life of her aunt, but Mr Muggeridge gives the wonderful old pair high marks for worthiness. It is just no good pretending they had not also got a comic side; it is one of their charms.

When Harold Nicolson was writing his life of George V he was given permission to read the king's diary. He hurried to Windsor in a fever of excitement only to find that the whole subject matter concerned the weather, temperature and rainfall. When one considers the stirring times King George had lived in, it puts one in mind of Louis XVI's entry for 14 July, 1789: '*Rien.*' However it would not do for royal personages to write Tolstoyan diaries about family rows, or even to divulge their deep thoughts about their ministers, or give their true opinion of a Command Performance at the Palladium, and perhaps '*rien*', or 'scattered showers heavy at times' are the ideal diary entries for monarchs.

Mr Dobbs's book is very enjoyable, beautifully printed and cheap. There are one or two odd things in it. Why should Lord Ponsonby be turned into a bogus-sounding foreign nobleman by being called Baron Ponsonby? And why is the expression 'getting to the top of the greasy pole' in politics attributed to 'one Conservative ex-minister'? Why not say Disraeli?

Dear Diary: Some Sketches in Self-Interest, ed. Dobbs, B., *Books and Bookmen* (1974)

Vita's Fruity Climbing Disaster

There are several V. Sackville-Wests. There is the galumphing land girl of the First World War who felt free because she was wearing breeches. There is the ferocious sapphist who ran away with Violet Trefusis, described in *Portrait of a Marriage*, the funniest book since *The Diary of a Nobody*, with the delightful farce of the two husbands turning up at a hotel in Amiens where the ladies were hiding, to tear their wives apart and force them back to hearth and home.

Then there is the breathless snob, staggered by her noble origins and the grandeur of Knole in *The Edwardians*, and the middle-aged lady, still in breeches, making a beautiful garden and writing garden notes for the *Observer* fifty years ago, telling how to grow lilies from seed and other useful hints. The notes are gathered into this book. Far the nicest Miss Sackville-West, but is she reliable?

Not altogether. She told *Observer* readers they should plant climbing roses to run up all fruit trees no longer bearing fruit. I had four such trees, two apples, a pear and a peach. I planted as advised and within two years all four trees had fallen leaving the roses without support. An orchard disaster.

In Your Garden, Sackville-West, V., *Evening Standard* (1996)

The White Linen Brigade

The heroine goes mad in white satin and the confidante goes mad in white linen. That's life. Ladies in waiting on the whole belong to the white linen brigade, even if they cannot always be dignified by the name of confidante. The duller the Court the plainer the attire and the more tedious the role.

For hundreds of years it was well worth while to be as near the Monarch as you could possibly get. Power and patronage resided in the person of the King or Queen; there was endless opportunity for intrigue, for lining your pocket and for contriving the advancement of your relations. The game was dangerous. 'Off with her head!' frequently brought a promising career to a premature and bloody close. This was naturally the case when the lady had royal blood and could be a rival who might attract a following in the country.

The greatest Queen, Elizabeth, the virgin queen, wished all her ladies to be virgins too. She vetoed many a marriage and was furiously angry when nature took its course and her attendants produced illegitimate offspring.

In good King Charles's golden days the Court resembled, on a poorer scale, that of his cousin Louis XIV. Many of the court ladies were his mistresses and the mothers of newly-created dukes.

His niece Queen Anne accorded real political power to her adored

Sarah Churchill, as well as riches. But Sarah happened to be married to a genius, quite rightly created Duke of Marlborough. Put not your trust in princes; Sarah was ousted from royal favour, the Duke was stripped of his commands and even the building of Blenheim Palace was stopped. It was only finished after Queen Anne died and George I came to the throne. There was a sort of poetic justice in the fall from grace of the Marlboroughs due to the whim of a silly queen, for John Churchill who had hitherto owed everything to James II changed sides on the eve of James's battle with his son-in-law William III. James, in exile at St Germain, would have witnessed the altered fortunes of the Churchills owing to his daughter's vagaries with grim satisfaction, had he lived a few years longer.

As it was considered essential for royalty to marry royalty there were always quarrels and troubles at Court between the English and the French, Spanish or Portuguese ladies brought over by the consorts of our kings. In the eighteenth century the ladies were German, because henceforward Germany furnished consorts of both kings and queens, who were obliged to marry Protestants. More and more ladies in waiting were English, which removed a source of infinite annoyance from the Court. The Duke of Windsor remembered that when he was a child the moment the English courtiers had gone out of the room the royal family comfortably relaxed and spoke German.

Queen Mary was the last queen of royal birth, and even she started life as a Serene and not a Royal Highness. Queen Victoria was as sensible about this lapse from tradition as she was about so much else.

Although they now get virtually nothing, no profitable monopolies or other perquisites, let alone any political influence, there is never a lack of ladies ready and willing to sit up half the night answering letters, or stand for hours during ceremonial occasions, or leave their husbands and children for months at a time, in order to attend the Queen and other royal ladies. Explain it how you will it is a fact, and they become completely devoted as time goes by.

During the Great War George V allowed no wine or spirits at Court, which did little to enliven the atmosphere. His son George VI thought of another way to mortify the flesh during World War II. I was in prison at the time; there was an exceptionally dirty, primitive and degraded bathroom. I was surprised when one day two men appeared with paint and brushes; badly as the bathroom needed painting it seemed somehow out of character that it should occur to anyone to embellish or clean the prison in any way. The men took out a tape measure and exactly five inches from the bottom of the bath they carefully painted a thick green line on the chipped enamel. This was called King George's Line. The idea was that nobody should use more than five inches of water to bath in. I cannot remember why; water, with our nice English rainfall, was one of the rare commodities in plentiful supply, and it did not have to be imported. Whether courtiers respected King George's Line we shall never know, possibly they locked the bathroom door and disloyally wallowed. In any case it was a gesture, so important in times of national emergency, and doubtless the cost of paint and labour was minimal.

Which would you rather be, one of Queen Elizabeth's ladies in waiting beaten by her employer with such fury that a finger was broken, or her modern equivalent who walks behind the Queen loaded with flowers, sweets and cuddly toys bestowed by the adoring public?

It is by no means only the English who adore the royal family. The French never tire of reading about them, and invent thrilling stories. There is a magazine, read by every concierge in the land as well as most of the dukes, devoted exclusively to royalty, and even distant cousins of Belgian or Scandinavian royal personages are good for a mention.

Being a lady in waiting is not all beer and skittles. Somebody I knew was in waiting to Queen Mary in the war and nearly died of cold. Fires in bedrooms were forbidden. She asked if she might collect a few dry twigs and make one in her freezing room, but was told she could not. It speaks volumes for something or other that she did not resign. She helped Queen Mary with her war work, they collected ploughs and harrows left conveniently under hedges by the local farmers and dragged them triumphantly to a heap they made of scrap metal. The farmers rescued their tools as soon as the Queen had gone in to her tea.

Anne Somerset's book is well-written, well-researched and well-produced. The terrible story of Lady Flora Hastings, accused by Queen Victoria and others of bearing an illegitimate child when in reality she was mortally ill with cancer of the stomach is excellently told.

Tittle tattle about Court life inevitably comes from diarists: Pepys, Evelyn, Saint Simon, Lord Hervey, Fanny Burney, some near the events they describe, others relying on gossip. Perhaps we are too ready to believe everything they say. When one thinks of modern diarists, for example Harold Nicolson and the nonsense he wrote, possibly too much credence is accorded to their predecessors.

It is a pity that ladies in waiting do not, like the confidante, wear white linen; how chic it would be! The modern ideal is to fade gracefully and unobtrusively into the bus queue.

Cocktails and Laughter is a photograph album. For people over sixty it is like the old song 'Thanks for the memory... How lovely it was!' As with all snapshots a little imagination must be used if anyone is to be convinced that it really was lovely; they are almost as untrue to life as Cecil Beaton's cellophane and balloons or modern photographs featuring broken blood vessels and dirty wrinkles. Hugo Vickers is a perfect choice for writer of the preface. He is so kind, so indulgent to OAPs that he makes us out to be positively human. Loelia Duchess of Westminster, Lady Lindsay, is the daughter and granddaughter of courtiers; her father wrote a book about his years at Court which is brilliantly funny.

Proofreading of the captions is very poor. Verda for Verdura, Morosoni for Morosini, Princess Jane di San Faustino, most American of Americans, a 'smart Italian' and there is no such person as Lady Venetia Stanley. Not that it greatly matters. The theory that people now live almost for ever gets a bashing in *Cocktails and Laughter*, only a handful survive who might grumble at such trifles. Even if the young don't think it looks as lovely as all that, I notice they are glued to this book, gazing rapt at their grannies and gaffers; it will therefore have a great success.

Ladies in Waiting, Somerset, A. (1984)

Cocktails and Laughter; Photograph Albums, Lindsay, L., ed. Vickers, H. (1983)

✳

Acres of Roses

Since Lord Drogheda is my exact contemporary and we have a number of friends and acquaintances in common, and because he has been so closely associated with two institutions from which I have derived immense enjoyment and profit, the *Financial Times* and Covent Garden, it has been a pleasure to read his memoirs. He quite obviously has a perfect genius for getting on with people and encouraging them to get on with one another (what is now called public relations). He helped his newspaper and the opera house to run along as smoothly as possible despite all the difficult, spiky and quarrelsome individuals who inhabit Fleet Street and the world of music.

If his memoirs are less than lively it is probably precisely because of this smoothing and soothing quality of his. He says one of his friends described him as waspish, but there is small evidence of waspishness; except for a little dig now and again at some rather unpopular figure there are roses all the way.

When he writes about his mother the book lights up, but there is not nearly enough about her. After his parents were divorced she married a Mexican polo player, but the marriage did not last and she had a series of friends. During the war her friend was a handsome Albanian who was a marvellous cook. This in itself shows what a wonderfully clever woman she was, because marvellous cooks were rare and they were needed when spam and smog or whatever wartime foods were called were on the menu. Chatin Sarachi—we could have done with more about this delightful creature, and perhaps less about some of Lord Drogheda's colleagues in Bracken House. (There is a photograph of St Paul's seen from a window at Bracken House. But what about Bracken House from St Paul's? The post-war business community has a lot to answer for in the way the space made by bombs was used.)

This brings me to my chief complaint: the treatment accorded here to Brendan Bracken. It was through him that Lord Drogheda's career in Fleet Street was made: they were friends and colleagues for twenty five years. Bracken had bluffed and shoved his way to the top with the most amazing mixture of talent, effrontery and mendacity. In spite of being hideously ugly he was very attractive because of his intelligence, wit and oddity. Almost none of this comes through. Working so closely with Brendan for so long, there must be dozens of hilarious stories hidden in Lord Drogheda's memory. Loyalty is all very well, but there need have been nothing disloyal. Brendan destroyed his papers at his death, but this did not prevent his biography being written, more than once. To make him just another tycoon with his pockets full of directorships to shower on his favourites is not really doing him a service. At the end of his life he wrote Lord Drogheda a letter from South Africa with sound advice on how to make, and keep, money. On no account must it be held in sterling, said Brendan with commendable foresight.

One episode in connection with Covent Garden remains unexplained. Why, after the war, was one of the very few authentic musical geniuses these islands have produced carefully excluded. Sir Thomas Beecham would have been a giant among pygmies, is probably the answer. It would not have been comfortable for the pygmies. In 1956 Beecham wrote a sensible letter to *The Times*, suggesting 'a full and enlightened inquiry into every branch of its activities… undertaken by an independent body'. Lord Drogheda describes this letter as 'disgraceful'. He adds that an article in the *New Statesman* by Desmond Shawe-Taylor put Sir Thomas in his place. Desmond Shawe-Taylor is an excellent critic, but surely Sir Thomas's 'place' was at Covent Garden.

Another small complaint: Lord Drogheda's predecessor as chairman there was Sir John Anderson, with whom he worked for a long time, and who with his wife Ava was a source of endless amusement to friends. You would never guess it from this book; they are taken at their own, very high, valuation. (Imagine for one moment what Malcolm Muggeridge would have made of the Andersons, had he been harnessed to Sir John.)

The number of committees Lord Drogheda served on makes you dizzy; plenty of praise and bouquets all round are bestowed.

> As Don Carlos, Jon Vickers added greatly to his budding stature.
> He was proving a real feather in David's* cap.
>
> ** Sir David Webster, general administrator of the ROH.*

Well, it is perfectly easy to see what is meant.

Lord Drogheda has had an eminently useful life and he has enjoyed himself, which is admirable and disarming. His book could have been a bit shorter, and a bit cheaper, and jokes might not have been quite so strictly rationed; but it is not nearly as dull as the Edwardian lady's country diary* which heads the best-seller list.

* The Country Diary of an Edwardian Lady (1978)

Double Harness: Memoirs of Lord Drogheda, Earl of Drogheda, Books and Bookmen (1978)

Old Men Forget

To see ourselves as others see us—is it a gift? Or is it the very opposite, something we should on no account wish for anyone we care about? In his memoirs, Lord Norwich portrays himself, presumably, quite truthfully as he imagines himself to be—statesman, author, man of the world—and, as he writes well and almost succeeds in giving an impression of calm and balance, his book may be read in the future, and he taken at his own valuation, by those who seek to discover from contemporary sources why England finds herself in her present reduced circumstances.

This book is, of course, not only by, but also about, Mr Duff Cooper, who tells of his childhood, school, Oxford; of the years when he worked as a clerk in the Foreign Office, and the six months at the end of the First World War when he was in the army. He tells of his entry into politics, and the various ministerial offices he occupied; then his resignation after the Munich crisis, and how, on September 1st, 1939, when he heard that 'the second World War had begun my heart felt lighter than it had felt for a year'. He describes his indignation and worry next day—'we went to the Savoy Grill. I felt I could eat nothing, but dealt very successfully with a cold grouse'—lest, after all, the Allies should fail to declare war on Germany, and his relief when finally they did so.

His praise of his own talents he reinforces with numerous quotations from his fan-mail: 'I had a talent for public speaking', he tells us. The present reviewer never heard him in the House of Commons, so cannot judge his parliamentary performances which are said to have been on a high level; on the public platform he was very poor, delivering not a speech but a rather dull lecture, and losing his temper with interrupters. That is the key to much of his character. 'I am apt to become heated in argument' he says. At how many of the pleasant dinner parties and luncheons to which he refers did the veins on his forehead start out, as he seemed to approach apoplexy, as the result of some trivial difference of opinion? The interesting part about this performance was its effect on those present. Let no one imagine that the sight of a middle-aged Cabinet Minister raging in fury at a fellow-guest in a private house was alarming, for, unless an actual burst was feared, it was not. Any stranger present must have been rather amazed; but it was such an everyday occurrence that it aroused no more than a feeling of mildest irritation, embarrassment, or amusement, according to the temperament of the onlookers. 'Little Duff did a veiners last night' his companions would relate, and no one was in the least surprised to hear it. He tells much about his private, as a background to his public, life, so it is as well to get it in perspective; it is in the light of this rather excitable personality that the events described in his book should be read and judged.

It is worth while to take a careful look at the photographs he has chosen to illustrate it—the neat little boy, the vulgar youth with a cigarette hanging out of his mouth; the cocky MP standing beside his beautiful wife, wearing her famous 'Madonna' expression but minus the decorative bandages; the ambassador in his library, looking very weary, as if he had just calmed down after a particularly violent veiners.

Mr Duff Cooper first entered Parliament as Tory member for Oldham. He lost his seat in 1929, and was nursing the Winchester constituency when St George's Westminster fell vacant and the Press lords put up an anti-Baldwin Conservative candidate of their own in the resulting bye-election. He decided to fight as official candidate. This was an election which tested the power of the popular press: the *Daily Mail, Daily Express, Evening News* and *Evening Standard*—'every issue of each of them was devoted to damaging my cause'—had a good case. 'Discontent with Baldwin's leadership was not confined to those who doubted the wisdom of his Indian policy' writes the author. Lord Beaverbrook, who 'fought hard and spoke daily', sought to dissuade him from standing. 'He felt sure I should lose.' But 'I won by more than five thousand votes'—and as to Baldwin 'the Press lords by their attack had strengthened his position'.

The highlight of Mr Duff Cooper's political career was his resignation after Munich. He resigned, apparently, because he thought England should go to war then and there, though as First Lord of the Admiralty and a former Secretary of State for War he must have been fully aware of her unpreparedness. On 28 September, 1938, he notes in his diary: 'I lunched at Buck's with Diana and the Cranbornes. They are of course boiling with anti-government indignation'. Lord Cranborne must have been longing to resign, but could not do so for the excellent reason that he had resigned already a few months before, over Abyssinia. (He had boiled when the Prime Minister decided to discuss our differences with Mussolini, he boiled again when he went to discuss our differences with Hitler, and more recently he seems to have simmered at the thought of the present Prime Minister discussing with Malenkov ways and means of ending the cold war. Nobody minds such ministers resigning; unfortunately this time he did not do so; both his chiefs were ill and he was able to do his worst as Acting Foreign Secretary.)

Was Mr Duff Cooper's resignation the wise act of a selfless and high-principled statesman? Was it a futile gesture, a sort of veiners in public? Or was there a resemblance to Georges Mandel, who, like him, knew the state of his country's defences, but was quite happy at the prospect of war? He gives the following account of a visit to the latter in March 1940 when he was Minister for the Colonies: 'I saw Mandel, who was gay and brave. I asked him about the French air force, of which I had heard disquieting reports. He laughed and said that every time he asked about it he was told there were fewer machines than when he last enquired. He seemed so cheerful I thought I had mis-heard him, but he had meant what he said.' Very funny no doubt—for France; but considering everything, would not 'frivolous and irrespon-sible' meet the case better than 'gay and brave?' However all this may be, Mr Duff Cooper is proud of his resignation, pleased with the speech he made, and altogether very much satisfied. Perhaps he imag-ines he was being gay and brave too—brave, because 'political acquain-tances cut me' and because when he visited France 'I was distressed to find that my French friends were even more enthusiastic in their sup-port of the Munich policy than were the majority of my friends in England, and that there were fewer exceptions.' The Prime Minister was relieved to see him go, and Hitler saw that the war party in England had gained another recruit. Mr Duff Cooper frankly admits that many of his contemporaries regarded him as a war-monger, and quotes some of their letters abusing him. He seems to be proud of it.

So much for the statesman. Now for the writer. He has produced an excellent life of Talleyrand, a good life of Haig, and a novel with the embarrassing title *Operation Heartbreak*. He tells us that he has always loved poetry, and aspired to be a poet. He has composed verse on and off all his life, and is good enough to include a few examples of his work so that we may judge for ourselves the poetic talent of a man who, although he understands the German language, writes 'Heine is the only German writer in whom I really delighted.' Thus he dismisses Goethe, Schiller and Hölderlin—the very pinnacle of poetic genius. (He admits he is tone-deaf and does not like music.) Here are a couple of verses from a poem he wrote on the outbreak of war in 1939:

> Oh England, use us once again
> Mean tasks will match the old;
> Our twiddling thumbs can hold the skein
> From which the wool is roll'd.
> It may not be. Not ours to fight,
> Not unto us, O Lord,
> Shall twice in life be given the right
> To serve Thee with the sword.

He sent this effort to the Editor of *The Times*, but 'he neither published the verses nor answered the letter.' He probably felt it was the kindest thing to do.

The best part of *Old Men Forget*, and by far the most interesting, is about General de Gaulle and his relations with Sir Winston Churchill and President Roosevelt. It is an almost incredible story, from which Mr Duff Cooper, who served as Ambassador first in Algiers and later in Paris, emerges with great credit. He endured endless snubs, frustrations and rebuffs in his efforts to prevent England and France, or rather their capricious and huffy rulers, from quarrelling fatally at the end of the war. The fact that the two countries had every interest in common would not in itself have been enough to keep them united, given the characters of the men involved. Eight months after the end of the war, with Roosevelt dead and Churchill and de Gaulle out of office, this particular danger had passed. In 1947 Mr Duff Cooper was recalled, and an Ambassador whose views were more in accord with those of the English government of the day was installed in his place. He had, apparently, learnt nothing. Although in 1946 he wrote: 'Today the mighty arm of Russia is paramount in the countries that are nearest to her borders, and the muscular fingers of that arm are busy in the lands that lie beyond. In no European country is there a Communist majority, but almost everywhere the Communists are gaining ground because of the support from abroad on which they know they can rely,' yet in 1947 he says: 'He (Bevin) said there was only one point on which he agreed with me, namely that the danger still came from Germany rather than from Russia'.

Politician, author, man of the world—it is a far cry from the old song, referring to his famous wife, which went:

> Who is Mr Pankhurst? Who is Mr Humphrey Ward?
> Who is Duff Cooper—not Lady but Lord?

Unfortunately however, it remains true, as a witty person remarked, that a little Norwich is a dangerous thing. Such little influence as he was able to exert in the 30s was a dangerous influence, for England and for Europe, as we can now all too clearly see.

Lord Winterton's memories of the House of Commons cover the period 1904 to 1951. The book is not, in its terms of reference, an autobiography; there are no cold grouse, no *Miracle*, no poems to beguile us. Lord Winterton is obviously not such a practised writer, and possibly not such a clever man as Lord Norwich, yet his book is of lasting value as a record of English politics.

He has the rare gift, so valuable in a Parliamentarian, of being able to judge a speech, a debating point, or even a rude retort with himself as target, strictly on its merits, and distributes praise among the talented on both sides of the House. He also realises, which is very clever of him, and unusual in a real House of Commons'un, that House of Commons jokes generally seem much less funny when repeated outside than they did at the time they were made, so much do they depend on atmosphere and timing. He frequently compares the House with a school presided over by the Speaker-headmaster; (a Speaker like Colonel Clifton Brown was not nearly severe enough with the unruly boys, he tells us, and looked far too benign) and on 2 May, 1940, he notes in his diary: 'Very grave news. The Boches have now taken...

Amiens and Abbeville. Notwithstanding these events, the House of Commons at its very worst at question time—frivolity, foolish chaff and indulgence in ridiculous arguments...' and he adds: 'I have remarked before that the House of Commons sometimes shows its anxiety and nervousness on great and serious occasions during question time by behaviour reminiscent of an infants' school.'

The pages of Hansard for the last half century are sprinkled with Lord Winterton's interruptions and ejaculations; nobody was in more rows, and he was quick to anger. In moments of tension, he says, 'the centre vein of my forehead swells—a characteristic I share with Sir Alfred Duff Cooper.' Nevertheless he remained through it all a well-mannered, public spirited English gentleman, without a trace of spite in his character.

His fault, as an historian, is that he is often too generous. After writing a passage eulogising President Roosevelt he showed it to an American friend, who said: 'Yes, I know, it's the same story with everyone who meets him for the first time... that is his harlot's charm.' Lord Winterton was very much annoyed by this, and writes: 'It is easy to be cynical about Presidents and Prime Ministers.... But I prefer not to be cynical about Franklin D. Roosevelt.' There is virtue in this naïve approach, for it demonstrates a fact so often ignored by the historian who has never left his study—namely, the power of charm in a politician to dazzle even such an old hand at the game as the author of this book. It is a quality shared by all who rise to the very top in politics in every country in the world, and nothing is harder to explain or to define.

Lord Winterton visited another famous charmer, Lloyd George, in 1941. 'His main theme was that, whoever won the war, the end of it would see Western civilisation in ruins, with little chance of the re-emergence of Britain as a great Power within the lifetime of the youngest person alive. Though it was a dark and gloomy day, with deep snow on the ground, I left Mr Lloyd George's house without any great feeling of depression about what he had said to me, because I thought it represented the views of an old and tired man who would be naturally inclined to look at matters in a pessimistic way; but I have often pondered on his words since then. It was not a fashionable view at the time, as everyone forced themselves to believe that when Nazism and Fascism were destroyed a great new era of hope would begin for the world,' he writes.

Mr Lloyd George's plea in the House of Commons, early in the war, that we should negotiate peace while there was yet time to save England and Europe from disaster, had called forth a furious speech from Mr Duff Cooper, denouncing the old war leader for defeatism. It is easy enough now to see which of these two men was right; but the counsels of sanity, balance and foresight were disregarded, while silliness and hysteria triumphed.

Orders of the Day contains much that is interesting and much that is amusing; also the best defence of the Munich settlement and the most intelligent attack on Socialist policy in Africa yet written by any Tory. It is worth reading for these alone; let no one be put off this book by the rather unappetizing extracts which have been appearing in a Sunday paper.

Old Men Forget: The Autobiography of Duff Cooper, Cooper, D. (1953)

Orders of the Day, The Rt. Hon. Earl Winterton, P.C. (1953)

Kindly Con Man

Self-made men are two a penny, but whoever heard of a self-made boy? The answer is, everyone who knew Brendan Bracken. One was told: 'Brendan, an Australian orphan, sent himself to school in England and paid the fee out of money he had made.' The truth about his beginnings, which Andrew Boyle has so cleverly searched out, is much stranger than any of his friends can have imagined, and much stranger than the assorted fictions he himself indulged in. Who could have guessed that he was one of a large family who were alive and well and living only a few hundred miles away across the Irish Sea?

'Everything about the man is phoney. Why, even his hair, which looks like a wig, is real!' exclaimed an American who did not take to Brendan.

In the early 30s we dined with him sometimes at his pretty old house in North Street; we thought he was an Australian because he said so. He was very good company, held right-wing views, and was devoted to Winston Churchill. The Churchill children had a story that he was 'papa's' son, and we were inclined to think that perhaps he was and that his name, which suited him so well, was probably a brilliant invention of Mr Churchill's. Yet, like his fuzzy red hair, the name Brendan Bracken turns out to have been his very own.

He was born in 1901 at Templemore in Co Tipperary; his father, who sculpted gravestones and was an active Fenian, died when he was three and his mother married again. There were several brothers and sisters. Brendan was sent to a Jesuit boarding school where he was so unhappy that he ran away. His relations arranged for him to go to Australia, where he worked at various jobs including teaching and journalism. He also read enormously, and came to admire England so much that he decided to become an Englishman. For this purpose he considered it essential that he should go to an English public school, so having saved a few hundred pounds he sailed for England. Here he made his way to Sedbergh and called upon Mr William Nassau Weech, the headmaster. He told him several lies. He said he was an Australian orphan whose parents had perished in a bush fire, and that he was 15 years of age. Whether or not he was believed, Brendan talked Mr Weech into accepting him into the school.

Brendan, lapsed Catholic and lapsed Irishman, an enormous 'boy' aged 19, drew a cheque book out of his pocket and paid his fees there and then. He stayed at Sedbergh only one term, but the Weech family had grown so fond of him that they invited him to spend Christmas with them. When he left, he had an old school tie and a near-English accent; certainly it was neither Irish nor Australian, but what is now called mid-Atlantic. In his rather thick voice he talked incessantly, and if anyone else succeeded in saying a word or two Brendan kept up a sort of humming sound until he could break in and resume his monologue. Part of the reason why he and Randolph Churchill so often quarrelled was that they both wanted to talk and both became exasperated when neither would listen.

In order to keep body and soul together after leaving Sedbergh Bracken taught at a preparatory school near London, where he seems to have taken pleasure in beating the unfortunate boys. His vile behaviour there—and some of his pupils are still alive to tell the tale of the cruel 'red-haired master'—comes as a disagreeable surprise to those who only knew him as a kind friend, but it ties up with strange stories one had heard, and which Andrew Boyle mentions briefly, of Brendan many years later incongruously dressing up as a boy in shorts and wishing to be whacked himself. Except for one or two beautiful girls, who were miles beyond his reach but whom he pretended to court, one never heard Brendan's name linked with man or woman. His passion was directed elsewhere, to money and to power.

Andrew Boyle has mapped his rapid ascent in detail. When they first met, in J.L. Garvin's house, Brendan's hero Winston Churchill was not only out of office but out of Parliament. Bracken had no difficulty in attaching himself, but though the circumstances chanced to be rather favourable there is no doubt that he was exactly the sort of young man Churchill liked to have about him: brash, self-assured, amusing, talkative and efficient, with the news and gossip of the day bubbling out of him at top speed. Bracken's profession was now journalism; his ambition, politics.

In 1929 he was elected MP for North Paddington, and in Parliament he made Churchill's causes his own, sharing in his unpopularity and meanwhile making a good deal of money in business and in newspapers. After ten years on the back benches the war came; Churchill's star rose, and with it Bracken's.

There followed six glorious years when he was where he had always longed to be—at the very centre of things. As Minister of Information, 'God's greatest liar', as Randolph called him came into his own. He got on splendidly with journalists and was the most loyal of colleagues, and loyal as well to his subordinates, some of whose clever propaganda ideas misfired. For example, having heard from 'intelligence' that German officers guarding the Franco-Spanish frontier were homosexuals, 'a plan was devised for dropping suitable pornographic leaflets, beautifully illustrated and captioned, on these idle enemy units in the hope of undermining their morale.' The leaflets were to fly over in balloons, but unluckily a freak storm blew up and they landed on a golf-course in Surrey. A golfer who picked one of them up complained to J.B. Hynd, a new MP who 'held rigid views on the counter-productive nature of our sordid business'. Bracken, determined to shield his bright ideas man, received Mr Hynd and told him: 'You shouldn't be surprised at the lengths to which Goebbels will go.' He succeeded in convincing Mr Hynd that it was the Germans who had sent the beautifully illustrated pornographic leaflets. Since, presumably, they were 'captioned' in German this cannot have been too easy; but Brendan's deviousness amounted to genius and he was believed. In such care-free style did the Minister of Information run his 'lie-machine'. It cost a fortune, but it was only the tax-payers' money and it ran on oiled wheels.

It was Brendan's finest hour. When the war was over, all this fun came to an end. There was a Labour landslide, and Churchill and Bracken were plunged into the depths of gloom. Bracken lost his seat, and although he won a by-election soon afterwards the savour had gone out of politics for him. He accepted a peerage but never took his seat.

Bracken's letters to his great crony Lord Beaverbrook during the last years of his life are among the best things in this entertaining book. They are full of political gossip, some of it damaging. All he wished was for Churchill to become Prime Minister once more; that Churchill was unfit owing to repeated strokes did not weigh with the faithful Brendan. By the time the Tories got back he himself no longer wanted office, for Brendan was far from well. An injudicious doctor who treated a bruise with penicillin caused him untold misery and covered him with boils and blains. He died aged 58 of cancer of the throat. Sir Patrick Hennessy was with him at the end. 'Tell me one thing only, Pat' said Churchill, 'How did he die?','Very bravely,' said Hennessy. 'Poor, dear Brendan' said Churchill. And big tears welled up in his old eyes.'

Brendan Bracken made the best daily and the best weekly in English journalism—the *Financial Times* and the *Economist*. They are his memorial. He gave his 'old school' of a single term a magnificent library. His friends—a diminishing company—miss him still. We were completely divided from him by politics, yet I can never forget his kindness to us when our fortunes were at a low ebb.

Probably the present is the last moment in time when a biographer could have uncovered Brendan's carefully concealed origins. By his orders, all his papers were burnt at his death. Mr Boyle has written an enthralling book. I hope it is not curmudgeonly to say that there are too many misprints. Also, why cannot publishers employ, in addition to their inefficient proof-readers, some pedant to see that names are correct? There was no such person as Lady Sybil Colefax; Lord Stonehaven was not the father of Theodora Benson; and so forth. All quite trivial, but why not get it right?

Poor, Dear Brendan. The Quest for Brendan Bracken, Boyle, A., Books and Bookmen (1974)

On Love and Sex

The facts about what is called the Montagu case are well known. In the autumn of 1953 Lord Montagu of Beaulieu was charged with two offences, the jury acquitted him of the more serious one but disagreed about the other, and a re-trial was ordered. 'On December 16th' writes Mr Wildeblood, 'the day, significantly enough, of the ending of Edward Montagu's first trial, McNally had been interviewed by a member of the RAF Special Investigation Branch about letters which had been found in his kit. These had been written by a number of men, including myself. He was again "grilled" on December 23rd, and on the following day was arrested and charged by the RAF with indecency with male persons, no names being mentioned. He spent Christmas under close arrest, and was brought up before his C.O. on December 27th.

In spite of his plea of guilty, no evidence was offered and he was released "without prejudice". The Crown was after bigger fish than McNally. By this time he had confessed to offences with numerous men, but the police were interested in only one name—mine. This was because, in one of my letters, I had mentioned the magic word "Beaulieu"... None of the other men accused by McNally and Reynolds—of whom there were twenty four—was ever prosecuted.' On December 28th the police took over. Altogether McNally was interrogated for eighteen hours, and 'finally he was told that he would never be prosecuted for any of the offences which he had revealed, provided that he turned Queen's Evidence against Edward Montagu, Michael Pitt-Rivers, and myself'. McNally and another airman, Reynolds, were browbeaten into such a state of terror that they were prepared to say yes to any question that was put to them. The evidence of these airmen was accepted, and Montagu, Pitt-Rivers and Wildeblood were sentenced to varying terms of imprisonment. The airmen went free.

The offences were alleged to have been committed during a summer weekend almost two years before. The moral of Mr Wildeblood's book is simple; if he and his friends had not invited the airmen to their weekend party nothing would ever have been heard of it; they would have been left in peace; detectives would not have forced their way into their houses, read all their private letters, asked impertinent questions. The police would not have had an opportunity of altering a date on Lord Montagu's passport.

Now, less than two years since these disgraceful doings, one of the three victims of England's archaic sex laws has written an account of the case, against the background of his childhood and upbringing, and described his year in prison. To someone like myself, who knows prison from the inside, this part of Mr Wildeblood's book seems the truth, rather generously told. Those who have not been in prison can scarcely imagine how revolting are the lavatories, how uneatably disgusting the food, how freezing the cells in winter, what complete nonsense the idea that the prisoners are being trained for a trade, or fitted for life outside, or that anything at all is being done except to degrade their bodies and unutterably to bore and depress their minds. If people believe the comfortable tales that prison governors, prison doctors, prison visitors and prison commissioners tell them about prison, they will believe anything.

Has Mr Wildeblood performed a service in calling attention to the horror of our gaols? There is a theory that when educated people are imprisoned, and write about it afterwards, things are changed. In women's prisons sanitary towels are given to the prisoners supposedly as a result of agitation by the suffragettes who spent much time in and out of Holloway, and in such relatively small ways, no doubt, reforms are permitted to creep in. But to make (for example) the heating arrangements or the lavatories work in all the old prisons in the British Isles would cost millions of pounds, and many people might prefer to see the taxpayers' money spent on schools, or housing.

If the Home Office were honest enough to say: prison is dirty, smelly and insanitary, the food is filthy, the warders are rude, the beds are hard, the bedding inadequate, the work a heart-breaking muddle, but it is a punishment for breaking the law (except in wartime, when the Home Secretary can lock up anyone he dislikes) and therefore, if you wish to avoid its rigours, keep the law, that would be a point of view with a certain amount of commonsense in it. But spokesmen for the Home Office sing a very different tune; soon after his release Mr Wildeblood heard Lord Mancroft, speaking in the House of Lords, say: 'I want to draw attention to food, because, whenever food is bad, or someone complains, it becomes headlines in the newspapers at once. Food is now served in cafeteria trays, and is of a standard which might surprise noble Lords.' Mr Wildeblood comments: 'Yes, it probably might, particularly if they knew that the cafeteria trays had been washed in soapless water by prisoners who had not had an opportunity of cleaning their hands after going to the lavatory'. At least one of his fellow-prisoners, he says, was having treatment for syphilis. Lord Mancroft's fantasy was typical of Home Office pronouncements; the ponderous machinery of English hypocrisy is always set in motion when anything 'unpleasant' is under discussion, whether it be sex, or crime, or capital punishment, or just the diet of some poor wretch condemned to sit for a stretch in one of HM Prisons.

As to the 'psychological treatment' from which Mr Wildeblood was supposed to be going to benefit in Wormwood Scrubs, he says: 'the facilities for such treatment were not so much inadequate, as virtually absent' and 'once I was in prison… I was not only not encouraged to take psychological treatment but actively discouraged. Men in prison… do not merely remain as bad as they were when they came in; by a visible process of moral erosion… they become worse. This is particularly true of sex offenders.'

Although *Against the Law is* a history of spite and hypocrisy, Mr Wildeblood admits, as every prisoner must, that even in the misery of gaol the kindness of one's fellow prisoners, and of some of the warders, is a compensation; also he formed a sentimental attachment there, which no doubt helped to lighten the gloom.

Against the Law, Wildeblood, P. (1955)

❋

The Failures of Glandular Therapy

There was a notorious case a few years ago when three men were sent to prison for having, long before, had homosexual relations with other men—who were not only consenting partners but actually male prostitutes with pocketfuls of addresses of people to whom they had sold their favours but who, persuaded by the police to turn king's evidence, themselves went free. There was a good deal of criticism of police methods in this case, and, partly as a result, the Government appointed a Departmental Committee under the chairmanship of Sir John Wolfenden to enquire into the laws concerning homosexuality and prostitution.

In August, 1957, after sitting for three years, the Committee's report was published. With regard to homosexuality, while advocating very heavy penalties for offences against juveniles, it included the following statement:

> We strongly recommend that homosexual behaviour between consenting adults in private should no longer be a criminal offence.

One of the medical men who gave evidence before the Wolfenden Committee was a psychiatrist who has made the study of sexual abnormality his life work: Dr Clifford Allen. He has now published a book on homosexuality, its nature, causation and treatment. Briefly, he considers that it is a psychological disorder, often curable in the early stages by psychoanalytic treatment.

> … The basic cause for homosexuality is a psychological deviation. There is the possibility of subsidiary and ancillary factors such as endocrine dysphasias accentuating the psychological deviation, but these do not appear ever to be the prime cause.

The psychological basis is confirmed clinically by the response to psychotherapy, and the failure to respond to other measures such as glandular therapy.

He adds that psychiatric disorders such as schizophrenia, and in fact 'most of the psychoses which, with or without drugs, release abnormal behaviour are basically homosexual.'

He even cites the case of a homosexual mass murderer who, some forty years ago, killed a large number of boys, as though to demonstrate the lengths to which homosexuals may go—as if there were not plenty of heterosexual murderers such as Jack the Ripper.

The trouble with psychiatrists is that they spend so much time with their neurotic patients that they gradually come to imagine that most people are similarly ill-adjusted to life. Dr Allan, with complete intellectual honesty, admits that experiments show that male rats become homosexual if segregated from female rats, and that apes at a certain stage in their development are often homosexual. We do not need Dr Allen to tell us that dogs have homosexual urges, for a walk in Hyde Park will prove to us that they do. Leaving the lower animals and coming to mankind, he relates that many primitive tribes practice homosexuality as a matter of course (though some, like the ancient Hebrews, fiercely repress it), while Greek civilisation was to a large extent based upon it. Yet in spite of so much evidence of 'naturalness' he persists in his theory of psychological disorder. Nobody can deny, of course, that it is an abnormality, since only a fraction of men and women incline towards it.

Dr Allen's admirable reason for wishing to cure homosexuals (i.e., to direct their desires towards the opposite sex) is that he finds they are unhappy people. In England, where blackmail, prison and ruin threaten, they doubtless suffer from anxiety. Not everyone cares for 'living dangerously.' Most civilised countries have laws based on the Code Napoleon, which are infinitely less savage in this respect than our own which descend through the old ecclesiastical law, instead of from Greek and Roman law. In these countries, where, provided they are grown up, men and women can do as they please in private, homosexuals appear to be just as happy as anyone else. Of course they may suffer from jealousy, remorse, unrequited love and so forth, but no more, probably, than do heterosexuals. They are harmless members of the community, and the notion that they might suddenly change their habits and try to seduce young boys (a practise which the Code Napoleon punishes with severity) is almost as unlikely as that a normal heterosexual man should do so.

The neurotic anxieties and unhappiness of his homosexual patients disturb Dr Allen, who devotes his life to attempting to cure them of their homosexuality, sometimes with success. He might possibly find them less nervous, and thus less prone to alcoholism, 'violent psychotic fear-state,' suicide, and the rest of the tragic disorders from which he says they suffer, if the law were changed in the way the Wolfenden Committee recommends. He is concerned with their cure, and in his opinion prison is the very last place where such a cure can be effected. The threat of prison and the fear of blackmail, while seemingly not capable of deterring the compulsive urge to assault juveniles which a certain type of homosexual appears to be unable to control, and which is undoubtedly a dangerously anti-social form of mania, can render miserable the life of the harmless 'consenting adult' and make him, at the very least, drown his wretchedness in drink.

Most people, after reading Dr Clifford Allen's book, would be convinced that a change in the law such as that recommended by the Wolfenden Committee should be made without delay.

A few months after the report was published Lord Pakenham [Lord Longford] raised the matter in the House of Lords. Of course, according to the Christian religion homosexuals are living in sin. In theory all sexual intercourse is sinful unless it has the object of begetting a child; thus while heterosexuality is generally sinful, homosexuality is always so. The exception was only made because the emphasis on chastity in the Early Church was such that at one time there was a danger that the sect might die out for want of children to carry it on, while the lustful pagans multiplied themselves. Dr Allen is not concerned with sin; in the House of Lords debate, however, the concept of sin was given due weight. Lord Pakenham, a Catholic convert, said he spoke as a Christian. In addition, no less than four Anglican bishops took part in the debate, though true to their Protestant tradition, they did not all agree. Although Lord Pakenham and the Archbishop of Canterbury, while deploring the sin, bravely agreed with the Wolfenden Committee that homosexual behaviour between consenting adults in private should no longer be a criminal offence, they set the tone of sin-consciousness which gives this debate so unrealistic an air.

And, of course, in this context 'sin' is completely irrelevant. A decision to equate sin with crime would turn most people—who regularly commit several of the deadly sins; greed, sloth, anger, for example—into criminals. The House of Lords itself would dwindle away, nearly all the Peers would be locked up, until only the Bishops remained; and they would have little time for Parliament as they would probably be pressed into service as extra turnkeys by that other sinless group, the prison warders.

This was an occasion when the House of Lords might have been expected to show its alleged worth as an independent body not subject to the pressure of constituents, with, as we are so often told, experts in every field giving their services to the community. The only experts in evidence on December 4th last year were the sin experts. Where were the doctors and psychiatrists, the scientists, humanists, philosophers and historians? If they were present, they did not speak.

Three Peers made reasonable, commonsensical speeches—Lords Brabazon, Huntingdon and Lothian. For some of the other speeches—though the debate may have been 'as good as a play,' as was said at the time—it is difficult to find any excuse: ignorant, prejudiced, spiteful, stupid. An element of farce was introduced by the Bishop of Rochester with his account of Oxford and Cambridge sodomy clubs. Did he, or did he not, say that members of these clubs shamelessly wore a club tie? According to the newspapers the following day he did say so, but the tie does not figure in Hansard. A friend of mine who was listening to the debate in the public gallery surrounded by consenting adults, who were there in force to hear their doom pronounced, says that they looked self-consciously at their own and one another's ties during the Bishop's speech. (Another friend said: Oh, I know that tie; it's black with a narrow pale blue stripe.) But tie or no tie, the Bishop became quite eloquent at the thought of these 'plague spots,' where 'men were sucked in and held on to, [as] it were, by an octopus of corruption.'

Lord Huntingdon made the point, later in the debate, that 'extravagant denunciations in the most virulent terms of homosexuality.... (are)... invariably the result of suppressed homosexual tendencies. Many of these people, much to their credit, have suppressed these tendencies; but they boil over in abuse of homosexuality.' This remark of his nettled the next Bishop to speak, and in full flood of rhetoric— 'agony of soul and degradation of spirit,' etc.—he said crossly: 'If the noble Earl Lord Huntingdon thinks that that is an expression of suppressed homosexuality he may go on thinking.'

So much for the Lords and their debate. It seems strange that those Peers who are themselves consenting adults did not trouble to go down to Parliament and divide the House. They would have had plenty of support. Perhaps they feared the police. Whatever the reason, they stayed at home; the cowardly Government, who had set up the Wolfenden Committee, was panicked by the 'popular' press and decided to let things slide; the motion was withdrawn.

The controversy died down, but the problem remains. Can the doctors help? Undoubtedly they can, but reading Dr Allen's book it is impossible not to be struck by the complexity of the subject. For example, in dealing with the causes of homosexuality he gives four main attitudes which, in his opinion, may produce it. They are: 1— Hostility to the mother. 2—Excessive affection for the mother. 3— Hostility to the father. 4—Affection for the father, when the father does not show sufficient heterosexual traits. (Possibly that father was one of the 'cures'?) There is not much help there for parents who are anxious that their sons and daughters should grow up heterosexual.

There are so many exceptions to rules in this difficult matter. Most people know homosexuals who belong to the classic category of the rather nervous only child brought up by a doting widowed mother, but the writer can think straight away of four different cases of happy, large, united families in which one brother has grown up homosexual while the other brothers and sisters have not. Why should this be so? As Lord Brahazon said: 'One day, when we know more about sex, we may bring happiness to many. But do not think that that is going to be easy...'

Meanwhile it should he possible, in a civilised community, to live and let live. Four main points occur to the reader of Dr Clifford Allen's book:

1 Homosexuality is not 'catching,' like an infectious or contagious disease.

2 In the many countries where homosexual adults may behave as they wish in private there is no more homosexuality than in the few countries where such behaviour is a criminal offence.

3 Children and young people of both sexes must be protected by the law, and under the Wolfenden proposals the penalties for offences connected with juveniles are even more severe than at present.

4 Dr Allen considers that a traumatic experience in early childhood is usually the cause of homosexuality. If this is so. bearing in mind the behaviour of the segregated rats, it might be well to consider whether the English public school system is not designed to confirm and accentuate any such tendency at the adolescent stage.

As this article goes to press, a letter signed by (among others) Lord Attlee and Bertrand Russell has appeared in *The Times* (7 March 1958). They ask that the Government should introduce legislation at an early date to give effect to the reform recommended by the Wolfenden Committee, that homosexual acts between consenting adults in private should no longer be a criminal offence.

Perhaps the Government will now summon up its courage and do as they demand. Courage is required, and not only on account of the unpredictable reactions of constituents. A further letter to *The Times*, signed by Sir Charles Taylor, MP, consists of the verses from the Bible describing what happened to the Cities of the Plain.

If the law is changed, and (as Sir Charles Taylor seems to imply) English cities are consequently fired and brimstoned, it will seem to many people extremely unjust that they should be singled out for this treatment while the rest of the world, which never had the law, goes merrily turning round in the usual way. Sir Charles Taylor, as a Member of Parliament, has, of course, a duty to point to the risks involved, and in so doing he has earned the gratitude of those who had overlooked this dangerous aspect of the case. Nevertheless, it is to be hoped that the Government will, ultimately, consider it a risk worth taking.

Homosexuality: Its Nature, Causation and Treatment, Allen, C. (1958)

Louche Lounging in the Far East

This extravagant Feydeau-like farce is by an Englishman who has lived in Japan for many years, teaching English literature at a Tokyo university. It is not only that rarity, a really funny book, it also gives insights which must be valuable to hundreds of puzzled Europeans, losing their way in a vast city where they can neither speak nor understand the language, or read the writing. To be lost in Tokyo is to be truly lost.

Mrs Field, unattached and 50, has come to teach English poetry at the university. Her colleague in the faculty, Mathew, is a homosexual with a live-in Japanese boyfriend, but his adventures outside the harmony of his tiny flat are fraught with difficulty. His ideal, when seeking sex, would be to melt into the crowd, an impossibility where every Westerner sticks out like a sore thumb. He dreads being recognized by any Japanese from the university, and hides in the gloaming at the back of a cinema where others foregather for the same purpose.

Mrs Field's instinct is to confine what is louche in her life to her flat, so small that there is scarcely room for the actors in the dramas. When she is not explaining T.S. Eliot to her students, or being asked searching questions about the meaning behind *Lady Windermere's Fan* by one of the professors, she nevertheless manages to have a lot of quiet fun in her own way.

In Tokyo, the place of the red light district is taken by a skyscraper called Queen of Hearts. On each floor are two night clubs, catering for everything human lust or human oddity can desire. One of the clubs is Mr Lady. Tired businessmen, after a harrowing day on the telephone to America or Europe, turn in there to relax. They undress, don an elaborate kimono, and sit back while an expert in maquillage paints their faces and puts kohl round their eyes.

In the soft light surrounded by mirrors the client is transformed into a desirable houri; wherever he looks he sees this lovely creature. After a happy half hour of narcissism, the expert takes away every trace of make-up. Off comes the kimono, he puts on his Western-style business suit, and, totally contented, takes the train home to his wife. Mrs Field's charming lover is a bank clerk young enough to be her son. She is slightly jealous and disillusioned when she discovers that he supplements his salary by working one evening a week at Queen of Hearts. She cannot resist going to have a look.

Club New Love caters for lonely middle-aged women. They are entertained at small tables by young gigolos, who give them a bottle of wine and turn on the dance floor to old-fashioned music. Mrs Field leaves, after a very expensive half hour. She opens the door of Mr Lady, where there is also no sex; the idea of both clubs is to make their clients feel happy.

When Matthew hears what Sylvia Field has done, looking in on Mr Lady, he is incensed. 'It was wrong, because men, especially Japanese men, don't like to be seen in drag wearing make-up', he tells her. Perhaps he is right, and tweedy English ladies dressed for a point-to-point are better off at home. After the hilarious experience of the mysterious Orient, Mrs Field leaves.

One of the best comic writers, John Haylock excels also in the authenticity of his atmosphere and background.

Uneasy Relations, Haylock, J., *Evening Standard* (1993)

❋

Nothing Queer about Hitler

Dr Johnson defines the word bugger in his dictionary as 'a term of endearment among sailors.' Nevertheless, when the dictionary appeared in 1755, and for another two centuries, homosexuality was not only a sin, but also a crime, with terrible punishments attached to its commission. These ranged from the stake in the eighteenth century to hard labour a hundred years ago, as poor Oscar Wilde could testify.

Although Dr Johnson mentions sailors, who are cooped up together for months, they fact that sailors traditionally have a wife in every port contradicts the assumption that they are particularly at risk—is it a risk? Probably most people now would deny both crime and sin. We are luck enough to live in a permissive society, which, if it means anything, means each individual, man or woman, can choose a partner without having to fear either the law or the blame of contemporaries. In theory, at any rate.

But we also live in an age which seems to rate sex more highly, and of more general interest, than any other activity so that we have biographies of writers, artists, politicians, footballers, or royal personages, in which the whole emphasis is upon their sexual adventures or mis-adventure, to the near-exclusion of their talents or the interest attaching to their exalted rank.

The murder of a very popular and charismatic Dutch politician, which caused deep sorrow in his native city of Rotterdam and was followed by a spectacular funeral with thousands of mourners, hundreds of wreaths, and dozens of white limousines, in fact the funeral of a beloved star, such as we in England have also seen examples in recent years, has led the newspapers to wonder why this man, Pim Fortuyn should have evoked such enormous popular grief at his death. Scorning the obvious reason, that he was a politician who looked as if he might do something for them and for his country which other politicians were failing to do, and that therefore the people loved and trusted him and wanted to show their feelings in the only way they knew how, which was much too simple a truth, the media rushed to suggest it must be something to do with sex the all-important, the only reason for anything. Because he was on the right in politics there must be a link with homosexuality. Pim Fortuyn's own brother—said to have been his favourite brother—made a statement: 'I wish to make it absolutely clear, that my brother was never a right-wing extremist.'

However, to be to the right of centre connotes the dread word Fascist, in this case particularly inept. A book published recently tries to make Hitler into a homosexual' the link is soon forged. Hitler committed terrible crime. He was certainly not homosexual. What his sexual inclinations may have been remained a mystery. Perhaps they were not very important in his life. But such a simple explanation won't do. In a world where sex is king, we cannot allow anyone, let alone anyone famous, not to have been actuated in an important way by sex. It would be too dull, too lacking in the dubious joys experienced by the voyeur.

The whole of Europe, at the present time, is nervous about the number of immigrants coming to our continent. What Pim Fortuyn said is what most people think. France, England, Germany, Holland, Belgium, all the rich countries have a problem, which can and should be shared, and if possible a solution found, by Europe as a whole. Henry Kissinger said: 'If I want Europe, who do I call?' Who indeed. Perhaps, if he had lived, Pim Fortuyn might have been the man who could write Europe and make a reality of it.

What remains certain is that as long as the human race exists, so will sexual tastes differ. How could it be otherwise? What is important is to live and let live. Nobody should be tolerant about cruelty, but at least we can be tolerant about sex.

Spectator 2002

❋

The Marquis De Sade

Many people like porn, and nearly everyone has heard of Sade, whose novels banned for about 150 years, are now available in paperback.

Sade's taste, and the theme of his books, was flagellation and sodomy. Born in 1740, his was an extremely dangerous taste, because the penalty in eighteenth-century France for the crime of sodomy was death. Beating was another matter, and if he had confined himself to prostitutes, and paid them well, there might have been no trouble. But Paris brothels would not admit the little Marquis; he did too much damage.

Sade was an aristocrat with powerful relations; his aunts were abbesses, his uncle an abbé, his father a soldier and diplomat. He went to school at the Jesuit college Louis-le-Grand, married a girl of good family by whom he had three children, and he owned several châteaux in Provence. Yet because of his perverse tastes, he spent the best years of his life in prisons and fortresses all over France. Fatal to him was his love or orgies; one of the girls or boys who had taken part invariably gave him away, either to the police, or to his inexorable mother-in-law, who wanted him locked up to avoid further scandals for her daughter and grandchildren. It was she who got a *lettre de cachet** from the King; once incarcerated, and a trial refused, there was no chance of release. His wife did her best for him, and she wrote endless letters to the authorities, to no avail.

The worst of his dungeons was Vincennes, dark and cold, where his health deteriorated and his eyes failed in the gloom. Ten years passed, and he was transferred to the Bastille; his cell was in a tower, and it was there that he wrote his fantasies. He based his stories on a few facts, and used his fevered imagination for the rest.

In July 1789 he saw from his cell there was a demonstration outside the prison and improvising a megaphone he shouted to the crowd below to break in and deliver the prisoners. On the 14 July the mob did storm the Bastille, killing the Governor and freeing the seven prisoners; but Sade had been moved. He was soon released, and by a strange quirk of fate became a revolutionary judge, who had to try his hated parents-in-law for the new crime of being aristocrats. Showing that he was not, after all, a bad old fellow, he acquitted them.

His freedom did not last long. He was imprisoned again because of his obscene books. As Donald Thomas points out in his well-written and well-researched book, the monster Marquis goes to such extremes in his novels that sometimes his readers are more inclined to laugh than anything else. Even Swinburne, whose tastes were similar, was convulsed with mirth when reading *Justine* aloud to Rosetti. Laughter is the deadly enemy of eroticism.

Sade spent his last years in the relative comfort of Charenton lunatic asylum. Was he mad? Donald Thomas shows there was no evidence to convict him of crimes. He was wildly eccentric, and, as they say, his own worst enemy. Today, he would make a fortune. He was born too soon.

_* A royal order without appeal.

The Marquis de Sade, Thomas, D, *Evening Standard* (1992)

Elcho and Her Bunny Men

Balfour[*] was by way of being the cleverest and wittiest of the Souls; his public life was at the summit of affairs as Foreign Secretary, Prime Minister and elder statesman, until the Treaty of Versailles when he was over 70. These letters ought to show him at his best in private life—nobody could have been more adored than he was by the charming Mary Wyndham, Lady Elcho, who loved and flattered him for so many years.

Yet his best is not up to very much. There seems to be something flabby and bloodless about the man, and Lady Elcho was infinitely more than he deserved. He was like a cat which has 'been to the vet'.

The reader becomes so fond of Lady Elcho—rather stranded between a faithless husband and impossibly lukewarm lover—that it is a great relief when, in 1894 at the age of 32, accompanied by her three eldest children, she goes to stay with Wilfred Scawen Blunt and Lady Anne Blunt in the Egyptian desert.

Blunt did not care for the Souls, he said their coat of arms should be 'two flat fish osculant all proper'. Within a week he had seduced Lady Elcho; he called her his Bedouin wife. By the time the party went back to England, she was expecting his child. Lord Elcho accepted the situation, perhaps more easily than did Arthur Balfour. However, the *amitié amoureuse* went on as before, Wilfred Blunt fading right out of the picture. From then on, Lady Elcho seems self-assured; there is no doubt the adventure was exactly what she needed.

Balfour's letters are a mixture of social and political gossip, a good deal of emphasis on his philosophical writing, concerned with a synthesis between science and religion, and descriptions of endless games of golf.

His philosophy is as forgotten today as his golf, but it was considered rather wonderful for a politician to aspire to such heights, and it gave him additional cachet in the eyes of intelligent women friends like Lady Desborough and Lady Elcho.

He loved music, and a visit to Bayreuth was looked upon as amiable eccentricity. His letters are not witty, and they breathe the boredom he affected to suffer from. Everything except golf was a dreadful bore: country house parties, cabinet meetings, the chore of Balmoral or Windsor, all evoke yawns.

Lady Elcho was exactly the opposite, she enjoyed life. She loved her children and beautiful Stanway, simple and grand parties, her friends, art, nature, travel and home. As the years go by and her children grow up and marry, 1914 approaches.

Two of her sons were killed in the war, losses she never recovered from. There is an unforgettable description of these tragedies in the diary of her daughter, Lady Cynthia Asquith, most poignant being the death in action of Yvo, just finished school and dying before he had lived.

Whether Lady Elcho and Balfour were lovers is anybody's guess. Even if they were, it must have been less than satisfactory and not of the first importance to either of them.

Hints of his masochism cause no surprise. Why she loved him is a mystery unsolved by this amusing and cleverly edited book, which is illustrated by wonderfully funny photographs.

* Arthur Balfour, Prime Minister 1902-1905.

The Letters of Arthur Balfour and Mary Wyndham 1885-1917,

Balfour, A. and Lady Elcho, *Evening Standard* (1992)

❈

The Profumo Affair

A short time ago a friend who was for many years a conservative member of parliament told me that he had just been reading—or re-reading—the Denning Report on the Profumo case. He said it was almost impossible to believe that only fifteen years had passed since the whole country was seized with wild hysteria about something so essentially trivial and unimportant, and he added that such a fuss would be inconceivable now. Myself, I was in France at the time it was all going on, and found it extremely difficult to make the French understand why everyone had become so excited.

There is a saying in America: 'Nobody died at Watergate.' This is not true of the Profumo case. Dr Ward had been arrested and charged with living on the immoral earnings of prostitutes; he was out on bail. The judge's summing-up made him think (rightly) that he was going to be convicted, therefore he committed suicide. And when Lord Astor died less than three years later aged 58 his wife said his death had been hastened by evil gossip. His crime; he had lent a cottage near Cliveden to Dr Ward, who was his osteopath.

Maurice Collis was also a near neighbour at Cliveden. In his diary he describes Dr Ward as 'a most friendly and charming man.' He sheds light on the whole wretched business from the Astor point of view, and undoubtedly Lord Astor was very badly treated. The whole pack was in full cry. He should not have minded, but apparently he did.

The diaries have been edited by Collis's daughter; they were probably far too long for publication and she therefore picked out the days when Maurice Collis mentioned something to do with one or other of several themes: the Astors, or Cookham and Stanley Spencer, or Burma, where he had worked in the Civil Service as a young man, are among the themes. Perhaps this method of selection was inevitable, but it detracts from the essential diary quality when you skip weeks and even months between entries.

If a great deal is left out, things are left in which should not have been. Private conversations about intimate subjects recorded in a diary should not appear in print a very few years later, or at least if they do the person quoted is bound to be hurt and annoyed. The diarist some-times gets the wrong end of the stick, as for example when he says that Sir Osbert Sitwell, opening an exhibition, was so nervous during his speech that his hands trembled. In fact, they trembled because he had Parkinson's disease.

A rather curious man emerges from these diaries, not at all attrac-tive but with some of the talents which make a good diarist. He was observant, and clever. He was a prolific writer, and many of his books are excellent. *Cortes and Montezuma,** the fascinating life of Stanley Spencer, and above all Somerville and Ross, come to mind. In each case he probed to the heart of the matter, whether Mexico at the time of the conquest or the wild west of nineteenth-century Ireland among hunting Protestants.

A serious and odd omission in the volume under review is that no list of Maurice Collis's books is to be found there. But it is beautiful-ly produced, both paper and print beyond praise.

* Reviewed below.

Diaries: 1949-1969, Collis, M., ed. Collis, L., *Books and Bookmen* (1978)

Hypocrisy On High

Reading once again the sad and sordid story of Profumo, Secretary of State for War, and Dr Ward, the osteopath, it is impossible not to be struck by the foolishness of Profumo in constantly denying his brief, frivolous little affair with Christine Keeler. Perhaps he thought it didn't matter; it had all been over for more than a year, and everyone lies about sex. Maybe he preferred that his wife should not know.

It ended in disaster for all concerned; Christine Keeler was involved with a jealous West Indian who tried to shoot her, and she told her whole story to the police. They informed Military Intelligence.

At the same time as Profumo she had (only once, it appears) been to bed with Ward's friend, the Russian naval attaché, suspected of spying. He had left the country, but the mills of 'security' ground slowly until Profumo was crushed.

Wild rumours abounded. In a personal statement to the House of Commons he lied for the last time.

The House of Commons is well-accustomed to lies; a few years before Profumo's, about something unimportant, it had swallowed a capful by the Eden government about Suez, a vital matter. But the story of 'fun' in high places shocked thousands of people.

Dr Stephen Ward, fashionable osteopath and portraitist, liked to surround himself with pretty call-girls. His patients and sitters liked what they found in his mews flat. Lord Astor, a patient, lent him a cottage at Cliveden, where Dr Ward and the girls used the swimming pool. At the pool, Profumo, a guest of Lord Astor, met lovely Christine and dated her. A few weeks later the relationship ended.

According to David Thurlow, Dr Ward was the object of the intense hatred of John Lewis, a socialist ex-MP who suspected Ward had seduced Mrs Lewis, described as a 'Jewish princess', and had sworn vengeance.

Lewis fed the police with scandalous stories about Ward and, discovering the Russian connexion, also told George Wigg MP and other former Labour colleagues. Wigg raised the matter in the House. Profumo resigned, but Dr Ward was arrested.

The shocked establishment was determined on a scapegoat. Details of Dr Ward's activities made the trial a wonderful nine-day scandal and filled the newspapers with their favourite topic. None of his influential friends came forward to help him. The judge summed up in such a way that Dr Ward realising he faced a prison sentence, took an overdose and died.

Ken Tynan and John Osborne sent roses to the funeral with a card: To Stephen Ward, victim of English hypocrisy.

Thirty years on, David Thurlow tells the tale well. His theory is plausible. This is one of those affairs from which nobody emerges with much credit.

Profumo: The Hate Factor, Thurlow, D., *Evening Standard* (1992)

❋

Fate in the Shape of an Egyptian Rake

Marguerite Alibert, born in Paris of poor parents in 1890, had an illegitimate daughter when she was just 16. The child was adopted by her grandmother, and Marguerite became a prostitute. One client fell in love with her, donating a flat near the Bois de Boulogne. When she was 22, she attracted the attention of Mme Dénart, the madame of an expensive brothel. Mme Dénart taught her many accomplishments: she learnt to dress well, to ride, to play the piano, and she was provided with an assortment of rich lovers.

She was taken to smart restaurants and fashionable resorts like Deauville. She acquired a collection of valuable jewels. After a rather 'dubious' marriage she called herself Mme Laurent. Now having a surname, her daughter Raymonde was sent to school in England.

One of Marguerite's rich gentlemen friends took her and Raymonde for a trip to Cairo. Here she met her fate, an Egyptian playboy millionaire called Ali Fahmy. Ali pestered her to marry him. He was 22, she ten years older. From the beginning they quarrelled ferociously. He was jealous and possessive, she at times liked to go back to the old game.

They fought in Ali's palace, they fought on his yacht, they fought in restaurants and hotels; she often had a black eye and he had scratches on his face. It was a violent, unhappy marriage.

At the end of June 1923 they went to London and stayed at the Savoy. Marguerite slept with a loaded pistol under her pillow, as she always did, to defend her jewellery. The jewels meant a great deal to her. They were the visible sign of her success with men, which attracted other men. She was determined on divorce and busied herself collecting evidence of the physical cruelty she claimed to have endured at Ali's hands.

The hotel doctor was consulted about her painful haemorrhoids, which she told him had been caused by Ali Fahmy's unnatural vice. A specialist advised an operation. On July 9, a stifling hot night when there was an apocalyptic thunderstorm over London, the Fahmys went to the theatre and saw 'The Merry Widow'.

Back in their rooms they began to bicker and emerged fighting into the corridor. The night porter, who was taking luggage to another room, asked them to go back, but their little dog had escaped and Ali was seen crouching by the porter and whistling to catch it. The porter turned a corner with his load, and it was then that Marguerite ran out and shot her husband three times.

The porter contacted the manager and the police were called. Marguerite was taken to Bow Street police station. Ali Fahmy died on his way to the hospital. On July 11 there were headlines: 'A Prince Shot in London.' Fahmy was in fact a bey, not a prince. But for the newspapers the couple were a prince and princess; she a beautiful and elegant French woman, covered in jewels, he a fabulously rich Egyptian. Marguerite spent two months in the hospital at Holloway prison. Her solicitor secured the services of the most famous advocate to the Criminal Bar, Sir Edward Marshall Hall, and together they polished up her defence. As there was no question but that she had killed Ali Fahmy, Marshall Hall concentrated on extenuating circumstances. If found guilty, Mme Fahmy would be hanged.

The trial began on Sept 10 at the Old Bailey. It had a ghastly fascination for the public and the Press. The court was besieged. Long queues waited to get in.

Percival Clarke opened for the Crown. There was a rather perfunctory cross-examination of the prisoner. Then Marshall Hall, after cross-examining the prosecution witnesses, turned his attention to Mme Fahmy. He made his client seem an innocent white woman, seduced into marriage by a rich, wily, vicious Oriental, who was surrounded by black Sudanese servants eager and willing to do whatever he wished.

He alleged the operation she had to undergo was a result of Fahmy's perverted tastes, and that on the night he was killed he was crouched ready to spring on her when, maddened by fear and distrust, she shot him in self-defence. Nobody seems to have pointed out that Fahmy was shot from behind.

So emotional and so cleverly argued was Marshall Hall's defence that not only the jury but the judge, Mr Justice Rigby Swift, were won over. The judge summed up on the fourth day of the trial and the jury took only one hour to reach their verdict: not guilty. There was pandemonium in the crowded court.

Could a modern Marshall Hall similarly sway a jury (and to an important degree a judge)? Histrionics are no longer fashionable at the Bar, but juries, accustomed to the unlikeliest soap operas on television, have probably not changed very much.

It must be said that Marguerite was as effective an actress as could have been wished by counsel. Pale, tearful, half fainting as she was assisted to the dock each day, she also had plenty of time to think when asked tricky questions by the prosecution, as everything had to be translated for her. She never put a foot wrong.

Andrew Rose has written a vivid account of this drama of life and death. He has padded his book with a background of postwar decadence and extravagance, descriptions of Egypt in the 20s and the life of a Parisian *poule de luxe*.

After her acquittal Mme Fahmy tried in vain to get her hands on some of Ali's millions. Presumably she went back to high-class, well-paid prostitution. She died in 1971.

Scandal at the Savoy: the Infamous 1920s Murder Case, Rose, A., *Sunday Telegraph*, (1991)

❊

Prostitution

When is a whore not a whore? When she is the rich, lovely, clever, cultivated and powerful Mme de Pompadour, might be the answer, because strangely enough, the Marquise figures in this history of the world's oldest profession. From ancient Egypt to the present day, the author casts her net rather too wide, but she is on the side of the prostitutes, and does her best to present them as a persecuted class.

They have been persecuted at various times, and fulminated against by Old Testament prophets, Christian clergy and others, but above all annoyed by the police who harass them, arrest them and even (according to this book) beat them up. It is a hard-luck story

But is it? Some of the characters did amazingly well for themselves, living in a luxury to which they were far from accustomed. So much so that it is impossible to pretend they have anything in common with the pathetic street walker, tottering along on high heels, keeping her distance from bright lights for fear her age and ugliness would deny her a client. The kept woman, smothered in jewels by an adoring lover, lives in a different world.

It also seems odd to waste sympathy on happily married women without a care in the world, simply because they are living on their husbands' money. Why should they mind? In any case there are quite as many hen-pecked husbands in the world as there are battered wives, something feminists fail to notice.

It might be imagined that the permissive society would have made brothels redundant, but presumably there are enough people with unusual tastes to make them a paying proposition.

Rather unexpectedly, the Mothers' Union lately announced it was in favour of the inspection of prostitutes in brothels, presumably for fear of Aids as well as VD.

Why is kerb-crawling forbidden? It seems rather a sensible idea, both for crawler and crawled-after, but perhaps abduction is feared. It might be easier to push someone into a car than it was to hoist a Sabine woman onto a horse.

Marlene Dietrich, about sixty years ago, acted the part of a prostitute in a film. She sang, in English: 'I'm falling in love again.' The original, in German, had very different words: 'I am, from head to foot, adapted to love. That is my world, and absolutely nothing else at all.' Sung in her hoarse voice, it was the prostitute's hymn. No nonsense about falling in love.

Whores in History might qualify as soft porn, and thus caters to the English obsession with sex. It is too long and dauntingly heavy to hold. But you can't have too much of a good thing.

Dr Johnson once said: 'I always talk bawdy at the table, then everyone can understand.' His words have been taken to heart in a big way by publishers.

Whores in History: Prostitution in Western Society, Roberts, N., Evening Standard (1992)

Soft Porn and Scandals before the Terror

Not so long ago we had forbidden best sellers in England. *Lady Chatterley's Lover*, *Lolita*, *Ulysses* and others poured into the country and were burned if discovered. Now censorship is relaxed and books must take their chance without the boost of being forbidden.

Robert Darnton announces he spent twenty five years of research to discover exactly what the French read in the eighteenth century and whether their reading helped to cause the French Revolution. It is almost impossible to discover what people in fact read, as opposed to what adorned their libraries. Voltaire's works fill a large shelf but probably, apart from *Candide*, they were not much read.

There was strict censorship, not only of political books but of bawdy, and jokes and scandals about the royal family, or wicked cardinals and licentious abbés. Blasphemy was almost as popular as sex. When found, the books were burned, but they were easily hidden and became bestsellers. They came to France from Switzerland, England, the Netherlands, many of them printed by Huguenots.

King Louis XV was a gift to writers of scandals, his love life so public, his mistresses so powerful in making and unmaking governments, his ministers so unpopular and incompetent. It was very easy to hold him up to ridicule and contempt, as he grew older and corruption ruled. He was powerful and dangerous, distributing *lettres de cachet* to people who annoyed him, exiling them and imprisoning them for years without trial.

Taine, after deep research throughout France and writing one hundred years later, considered privilege, in all its unfairness and stupidity, had more to do with making revolution than any other factor. Doubtless the forbidden bestsellers amused their readers, with their unedifying tales of those in authority, King and Church, but people heartily disliked the police state and arbitrary injustice. As to the Terror, it grew year by year until it reached a climax four years after the taking of the Bastille. Unlike the Gordon Riots in London a few years earlier, the French Revolution was backed by the educated middle class, which had real grievances. But when every owner of property, however modest, became the target for pillage and murder by the mob the bourgeoisie took fright and has been frightened on and off ever since.

Robert Darnton's researches and his potted French history don't take us far in understanding what happened in 1789 and beyond, but they permit him to include lengthy translations of soft porn: *Thérèse Philosophe*, or stories of Mme Du Barry—always popular. Truth to tell, his book is disjointed, prolix and rather dull. The dust jacket, a reproduction of Jean Francois de Try's masterpiece *The Reading From Molière* is a colour-printing disgrace, the faces and hands of the elegant ladies and gentlemen bright scarlet. For a work of 'scholarship' the proofreading is shoddy and one of the French advisors mentioned might have told the author that Mme Du Barry's house near Marly was at Louveciennes, not 'Lucienne'.

The Forbidden Bestsellers of Pre-Revolutionary France, Darnton, R., *Evening Standard* (1996)

Golden Porn

Oscar Wilde said he took his diary with him when he travelled, to have something sensational to read in the train. Anaïs Nin would have loved to have her diary with her, but it was enormous. It grew and grew, to about a hundred volumes. It was her end all and be all. She stored it in vaults of which she kept the key.

She was part Spanish, part Danish, part French, of a mixed-up Cuban family abandoned by her musician father, who left his wife to bring up the children as best she could. Very beautiful, she considered herself a great artist, but her writing was refused by publishers over and over again, which made her furious. She lived near Paris with her rich banker husband, Hugo, and distributed the money he gave her for housekeeping among her penniless lovers, chief of whom was Henry Miller. Terrified of starvation he insisted upon his stipend, as he called her largesse. Everything went into her diary, her innumerable affairs, including one with her own father, every compliment she received, her rows with publishers and lovers.

Anaïs spent every day with Henry Miller, and when Hugo was away on business he moved in with her. There were many abortions, and she and Hugo spent fortunes on doctors and psychoanalysts. When the war came they all went to America, where she bigamously married a much younger man in California.

Then began a wild life of lies, two husbands, trying to believe in 'jobs' she pretended to have in Los Angeles and New York, commuting between Rupert and Hugo. As usual, Hugo paid. When no publisher would take her work she bought a printing press and published it herself.

Although the diary and her outsized ego filled her life, she was also a wonderful wife to her two husbands; they found her indispensable and swallowed the lies in order to keep at least half of her. Her avid self-promotion worked up to a point, and she often lectured at universities, charming dons and students. Hugo left the bank, and there were moments of financial disaster. Her old lover Henry Miller behaved well; as Anglo-Saxon Puritanism changed into permissiveness his *Tropics of Cancer* and *Capricorn* became best-sellers, he was rich, and considered a major writer. He allowed Anaïs to sell his love letters to her, a great help.

She herself had written a good deal of porn, which came in very handy. It was a little pot of gold for the old age of her husbands after she died. In her lifetime she was rewarded by becoming a cult figure, her old novels and edited diaries selling at last.

Deirdre Blair's book is immensely long, with copious scholarly notes. It is very funny in parts, which Anaïs would not have approved of. Nothing is left out, but far from boring the reader this biography fascinates from beginning to end. American dream or American nightmare? In any case, American.

Anaïs Nin A Biography, Blair, D., *Evening Standard* (1995)

On a Sea of Hope

The image is familiar. Robert Louis Stevenson was a delicate, sickly child, terrified by hellfire, full of dreams and nightmares, whose parents took him to the Riviera when the Edinburgh climate became too raw for him. The father, a prosperous engineer who hoped his only son would join the family firm, was bitterly disappointed when Louis decided to be a writer. It was even more bitter when Louis told him he had lost his Calvinist faith.

He made so little money with his writing and had such wretched health that his father, unwillingly, had to support him until he was 30.

At 30, he provided his parents with another dire disappointment by going to America to try to marry an American; she had a husband to divorce, several children and was ten years older than Louis. Yet, like all his decisions, it turned out to be the right one.

Fanny was tiresome, vain, possessive, jealous, but she looked after him devotedly. He suffered from frequent haemorrhages, was as thin as a rail with a concave chest, and his survival seems almost a miracle. Fanny did all he wished, living for months at a time on board a small yacht in the Pacific despite her seasickness because Louis felt relatively well at sea.

After his marriage, he wrote best sellers: *Treasure Island*, and *Dr Jekyll and Mr Hyde*, one of his nightmares put to good use. Finally, with Fanny and her children, he settled in Samoa, built a house and cleared the wild land round it. He wrote letters to his literary friends, including Henry James and Gosse, but had no wish to return to civilisation. He died, aged 44.

The South Sea islanders revered him, and he loved them. They carried him up the mountain to his grave, to which, Ian Bell tells us, there is now a chair-lift for tourists. The great charm of the man comes across in this biography, and Ian Bell, though unable to like her much, is perfectly fair in giving Fanny her due.

Robert Louis Stevenson: Dreams of Exile, ed. Bell, I., *Evening Standard* (1992)

Erotic Tales of Discovery

In the nineteenth century syphilis played the dread part Aids does now. Until a cure was discovered, mercury kept it at bay, but Gustave Flaubert changed in a few years from a beautiful young Viking to a fat, bald, middle-aged man with one tooth, his mouth blackened by mercury treatment.

Was Louise Colet the muse of this genius? They had a short, passionate love affair, but to her disgust Flaubert left her to devote himself to his art. Louise suffered from his neglect and consoled herself with other men, usually well-known writers, sometimes Immortals from the Académie Française. She was a poet, who won the poetry prize of the Académie several times. Whether it was awarded for her beauty or her verse is unclear.

Flaubert wrote her love letters from Normandy, where he lived with his mother. She was forbidden to visit him, but they sometimes met at Mantes for a day or two of lovemaking at a hotel. Louise had a little daughter at home, which made her small Paris flat less than ideal for her countless affairs.

She had several great qualities; she was beautiful and extremely courageous, and almost more than politically correct, really a red revolutionary, extravagantly anti-clerical, anti-Bourbon, anti-Bonapartist. After the disastrous Commune she went to Italy to help Risorgimento, and insult the Pope.

She wrote hundreds to letters to Flaubert, which he burned, but she kept all his. He began to write to her again when he was working, slowly as was his wont, on *Madame Bovary*. He was familiar with the Norman background to his story, but he wanted her to describe the feelings of a wildly romantic provincial housewife, bored by her life, which is what Louise had been until she managed to get to Paris. It was part of his eternal search for the mot juste. He loved her beauty, but her unending reproaches and tempers must have been tiresome.

Are muses tiresome?

He had seduced Louise in a cab driving about the Bois de Boulogne, called by the author a hansom cab. The idea of erotic gymnastics taking place in a hansom cab is hilarious. Flaubert is accused of indelicacy because of the scene where Madame Bovary and her lover drive round and round Rouen in a cab with the blinds drawn (also called a hansom). Yet it is something that must have happened hundreds of times in the history of men, women and four-wheelers. The muse is unlikely to have minded, but she disliked *Madame Bovary* intensely.

A much deeper and more rewarding friendship was Flaubert's with George Sand, but on the whole he preferred the company of his men friends, and from time to time undemanding prostitutes.

Mrs Gray's book is very well researched and she has discovered interesting details about her heroine. It is a lively picture of nineteenth-century literary Paris seen through American eyes.

Fire and Rage: A Life of Louise Colet: Pioneer, Feminist, Literary Star, Flaubert's Muse,

de Plessix Gray, F., *Evening Standard* (1994)

✸

La Belle et La Bête

Flaubert and George Sand began writing to each other in 1863 when he was 42 and she 59. Storm and stress were behind them: the 'scandal' of his masterpiece Madame Bovary, and Sand's well-publicised love affairs with Musset and Chopin.

They could hardly have been more unalike, he an inveterate pessimist, she a motherly old optimist who enjoyed her country life with her family while writing endless books. They had in common hatred of the emperor and strong anti-clericalism.

As to their writing methods, Flaubert could worry for a whole day about a single word—*le mot juste*—while George Sand churned out her books by the dozen. There are ninety six volumes of her collected works, and lately another twenty four volumes of letters.

Struggling slowly with *L'Education sentimentale*, Flaubert was fairly happy. They visited each other, she went to Normandy and he to Nohant in Berry, and sat up all night talking. They met in Paris often, and became devoted friends. The reception of his book by most of the critics was a devastating blow to Flaubert. The tone of his letters changes completely.

George Sand tells him to pay no attention, but though pretending not to care, his despair is obvious.

Pleased by the departure of Napoleon III, George Sand had great hopes of the Republic, which were not shared by the elitist Flaubert, and were soon disappointed. He was anti-Christian, advocating the promotion of the strong and clever, not the humble and weak. Universal suffrage he thought nonsense.

After the Franco-Prussian war he became permanently angry and miserable, and doubtless George Sand's loving and happy letters helped him to begin to write again, even if her optimism irritated him at times. Most of his literary friends died; only Turgenev and George Sand supported him at this sombre period.

She died in 1876. He went to Nohant for the funeral and was angry because her coffin was put in the church.

Beautifully translated with exemplary footnotes, to read this book is to understand Gustave Flaubert and George Sand. Henry James long ago summed them up: Flaubert was of 'a powerful, serious, melancholy, manly, deeply corrupted but not corrupting nature. He was head and shoulders above the others'; George Sand 'was a supreme case of the successful practice of life itself'.

Flaubert-Sand: The Correspondence, trans. Steegmuller, F. and Bray, B., *Evening Standard* (1993)

❉

From Hell to Paradise and Sexual Freedom

Mary Challans took the pen name Renault because her first novels were autobiographical and she did not wish to embarrass family and friends. She pronounced it Renolt.

Her adult life divides easily: England 1925-1948, a sort of hell on earth; and South Africa from 1948 until her death in 1983, a paradise.

Born in 1905, Mary Renault's quarrelsome parents could not divorce because the father was a doctor. The atmosphere at home was miserable, but Mary had a good education and went to Oxford, for women undergraduates in those days more like a school than a university.

She wanted to be a writer. Her father gave her £20 a year, hardly enough for shoes and stockings, let alone books, or theatre, or travel. There was no room in the house where she could write—Virginia Woolf's *A Room of One's Own*, so relevant to Mary's situation, came out in 1928.

To escape from her unhappy family and restricted life she took a job as a nurse; it was desperately hard and grossly underpaid, but at the Oxford Radcliffe Infirmary she met the love of her life, nurse Julie Mullard. During the war they had to go on nursing, seeing each other seldom.

Mary's first books were about hospitals, and sold quite well, but when *Return to Night* was published in America in 1948, it won a huge money prize from MGM.

Hardship, cold, poverty and austerity were cast aside, Mary Challans and Julie Mullard sailed to South Africa and Mary never set foot in England again, though she twice went to Greece.

Her wonderful novels *The Last of the Wine* and *The King Who Must Die*, and her many books set in ancient Greece, were based on extensive reading and research. She was intent upon getting all her facts right, her clever imagination did the rest. The superb scenery and perfect Greek climate at the Cape, where the two friends lived at Camps Bay between mountains and sea, probably helped.

Most of Mary Renault's men friends were homosexual, like herself. She loved the theatre and the company of actors. In England there had been a certain amount of backsliding by Julie, who had a couple of affairs with men, but Mary never wavered.

They had an ideally happy life together, Mary more and more successful and famous, Julie devotedly caring for her and keeping disturbers away when Mary was working.

Inevitably politics intervened, for these were the days of the most unfair and the most absurd aspects of apartheid. Mary was a fairly mild liberal; she did what she could, signed protests, wore a black sash, but living in the country she never saw the situation in quite the simple way its foreign critics did. She felt much more strongly about sexual freedom, and lived long enough to see it complete.

David Sweetman's book about this brilliant woman is a delightful success story. Like Marguerite Yourcenar, Mary Renault has shown that the historical novel can be a work of art.

Mary Renault: A Biography, Sweetman, D., *Evening Standard* (1993)

❊

At the Mercy of the Muse

Robert Graves was 19 when the First World War began; he was badly wounded physically, and also, like everyone else who had to endure the unendurable, psychologically. Brought up in a puritan family and sent to boarding schools he hated, he married a lovely girl, Nancy Nicholson, daughter of the painter William Nicholson.

From the Army he went to Oxford, and while he was a penniless undergraduate began a family. Still in his twenties he had four children, no money and a head full of poetry. He also had delayed shell shock and appalling nightmares.

Nancy Nicholson's life in an Oxfordshire cottage with four tiny children, the only money an occasional cheque from her father or Robert's mother, and presents from his friends Siegfried Sassoon and T.E. Lawrence, must have been hard. Finally Graves unwillingly accepted an offer to teach at Cairo University. They all sailed to Egypt, accompanied by Laura Riding, an American poet whose work Robert admired. They became so ill and miserable that he took everyone back to England before he had fulfilled his contract.

They soon left the cottage for London. Robert Graves and Laura Riding got a flat in Fulham, Nancy and the four children lived round the corner in a barge on the Thames. The ménage à trois worked rather well. The exhausted Nancy was only too pleased for Robert to have somebody to occupy his time: he was in thrall to Laura Riding, his goddess and his muse. Trouble came when they were joined by a fourth, Geoffrey Taylor, or Phibbs, a handsome Irish poet. Laura Riding fell in love with him, but he preferred Nancy. In a paroxysm of jealousy, Laura jumped out of a third-floor window. She broke all her bones including her spine and pelvis.

Amazingly, she recovered. Nancy and Geoffrey stayed on the barge with the children, Robert and Laura went to France and so on to Majorca, where they built a house near the sea. This had become possible because Robert had written a bestseller, his autobiography *Goodbye to All That*, a truthful account of the war.

He also wrote a short biography of T.E. Lawrence, at Lawrence's request. Apparently he was chosen because Lawrence felt he could trust him not to mention anything disagreeable, such as his Charlus-like predilection for paying a strong man to beat him to a jelly. The book sold well. Robert published his poems, but there was no money in that, and his two bestsellers set a pattern lasting all his writing life: the prose made fortunes and paid for the poetry.

In Majorca Graves wrote his Claudius books, still in print after sixty years. He wasted much time in the 30s and again in the 50s with cinema people who promised him enormous sums for making his books into films. Nothing ever came of these efforts. Although she liked the comfortable life, Laura Riding was jealous of Robert's financial successes, she herself failing to find a publisher for her writing. But she remained his perfect goddess and the inspiration of his verse.

In 1936 the Spanish Civil War sent them back to England. Robert was becoming slightly disillusioned with his muse, who for years denied him her bed while inviting her disciples and admirers to share it. 'Bodies have had their day,' she told him. She remained his muse and his goddess until they went to America and she fell in love with a man she subsequently married; Graves was free of her after thirteen years as her devoted slave. His new companion was Beryl Hodge, with whom he had four more children; they lived in England for the war, and in 1946 managed to leave high taxes and small rations behind and go back to Majorca. He earned money from books, lectures in America, poetry readings, translations. His career flourished. He gave the Clark Lectures at Cambridge, and in 1961 was elected visiting Professor of Poetry at Oxford. He delighted large audiences of undergraduates by telling them Yeats and Eliot and Pound, as well as Milton and Dryden and Pope, were rotten poets, which was just the opposite of what they had been taught by schoolmasters and dons. Nobody much minded all their swans being geese, but they were not so sure that his 'discoveries' were swans, the only poets except Laura

Riding and Graves himself.

He loved Celtic, Greek, Hebrew and Roman myths, he loved rewriting the Gospels, or Homer, or (rather disastrously) the Rubáiyát of Omar Khayyám. But as he grew older he fell in love more and more desperately with muses, who all betrayed him with younger lovers. Rather tiresome for Beryl was the fact that two of the muses were keen gold diggers; he never failed to provide whatever money they demanded.

Surrounded by family, friends, admirers and hangers-on, Graves was the emperor of his village, Deya. Even in the 30s it had been an artists' colony (dread thought) and needless to say in the 60s it became a haven for hippies with their joints and guitars. The police began looking for, and finding, drugs everywhere, and Beryl wisely threw away Robert's little store. He was far from averse to an artificial paradise, experimenting with magic mushrooms and the like.

Graves was awarded various gold medals, some of which turned out to be base metal. He was offered a CBE, but like Evelyn Waugh he declined. The end of his life was beyond words; frightful. For years he suffered from senile dementia and sat staring into space. He lived to be 90, if living it can be called. Beryl looked after the helpless carcass as Nancy had once looked after the neurotic, shell-shocked soldier.

The most balanced account of his life is Miranda Seymour's excellent biography. Martin Seymour-Smith takes the reader through Grave's poems, showing that in them can be found his whole emotional history. For someone who wants every single detail year by year, Richard Perceval Graves is the man; *The White Goddess* is the third volume of a vast trilogy. William Graves has described his father's wild superstitions and his love of Deya. Most importantly Carcanet has published poems, essays and lectures. These are what Robert Graves, with his inborn Puritanism and his goddesses, must be judged by.

Robert Graves: His Life and Work, Seymour-Smith, M.; Robert Graves: *The White Goddess*, Graves, R.P.; *Wild Olives*, Graves, W.: A Life on the Edge, Seymour, M., *Evening Standard* (1995)

Minimal Effort Required

There have been many biographies of Bernard Shaw, but none more quirky than this. Most people think of him as an old sage with a white beard who wrote splendid plays, as well as hundreds of letters and postcards, whose wise words made such excellent 'copy' that he was constantly besieged by newspaper men wherever he went. How he would have loved television! He would have been 'on' nightly, worldwide.

Shaw's sexual life was minimal, but his beard had not always been white. When it was red he behaved like most young men, flirting and sometimes going to bed with his flirts, but with a marked lack of enthusiasm. He was a hopelessly bad lover, didn't enjoy sex, and greatly enjoyed teasing. He liked beautiful people, both men and women, especially if they were connected with the theatre.

As this book is by way of discovering hitherto unexplored aspects of Shaw's sex life, it naturally begins with his unhappy childhood in Dublin. The drunken father, the uncaring mother, along with the mother's singing teacher, get close attention and plenty of psychoanalytical jargon. Shaw had the good fortune to be familiar with great music from birth. He loved music, it was the joy of his life. Otherwise his education was patchy, but when at 19 he followed his mother to London he educated himself in the British Museum Reading Room. The uncaring mother gave him a room in her flat, and never seems to have complained that for a decade he got no paid work.

He became a socialist, anti-vaccination, vegetarian, teetotal, and wore natural wool Jaeger clothes. He was, in fact, a crank of the first water, but such a charming, amusing, clever, courteous crank that he won everybody's heart, from Ellen Terry's to Sidney Webb's. He spoke at socialist meetings, wrote articles for the Fabians, all for nothing. His music and theatre criticism earned little, but he got free tickets for concerts and plays. When he wrote novels and plays his ideas and paradoxes and jokes made him famous. There were reams of love letters to actresses, but he wished neither to receive nor bestow caresses.

Shaw contracted a white marriage with a kind, rich lady; a great success. Sally Peters makes a valiant effort to weave some sex into his relations with men, in particular Harley Granville Barker, of whom he was very fond. To look for sex in Bernard Shaw is like looking for beauty at Shaw's Corner, his ugly little house which is now a place of pilgrimage. Neither is worth looking for, they are non-existent. His genius lay elsewhere, as is perfectly demonstrated by Michael Holroyd in his masterly life of the old magician.

Bernard Shaw: The Ascent of the Superman, Peters, S. (1996)

Diaries 1953-1959

The Vélodrome d'Hiver is an enormous circus situated in the factory-filled district west of the Eiffel Tower. As we went in, on a warm June evening, the smell of wild animals and damp straw hung in the air, although the place contained many thousand Christians and not a single lion.

All the best seats were already taken, and we climbed an iron stair to an upper balcony; a hymn was being sung by choirs massed behind the platform. We stood above the steep bank of seats in the balcony, and could see both performers and audience.

Either side of the platform were a piano and a harmonium, between them a dozen or so men, in front a smaller, raised platform, tastefully draped in red and gold. Among the group of men was Mr Billy Graham, fresh from his Scotch triumph and now for the first time trying his luck in Paris.

Two speakers in turn mounted the podium and addressed us in French. The first said that *le docteur Beelee Grum* had no financial backers. The loudspeakers blurred his voice and one could not hear much, though the name Beelee Grum recurred several times. The second introduced the boys in the ring to my left the pianist, to my right the harmonium player, a singer—all Mr Somebody or other from somewhere in America. Each rose from his seat when his naine was called, but we had been warned not to applaud. We were then told to get ready for Dr Beelee Grum's MESSAGE, and people wandering about the hall were ordered to sit still and keep quiet (the wandering, in fact, went on the entire evening; it appeared to have something to do with the loudspeaker arrangements).

Another hymn, and Mr Graham himself began to speak. I had never heard him before, and he was gravely handicapped by having to pause after each staccato sentence while the French pastor beside him translated his words. There was something unfairly comic about this proceeding. Mr Graham, a well-set-up youngish man with guinea-gold hair like his predecessor Miss Aimée Semple Macpherson's, held out his hand with a book in it:

'You all know this book; it's the bible.'

The French pastor held out his hand with an identical book:

'*Vous connaissez tous ce livre: c'est la bible.*'

'You all know the bible is a good book.'

'*Vous savez tous que la bible est un bon livre.*'

A finger is pointed at the audience:

'In the bible you will find an answer to every one of the problems in the world today.'

Another finger is pointed:

'*Dans la bible vous trouverez une solution pour tous les problèmes dans le monde d'aujourd'hui.*'

Mr Graham called for repentence, and told a story to illustrate the urgency of taking steps to be saved. An aeroplane at an airport is ready to take off for America. I have my ticket and my seat reservation. The passengers are being called, but I feel there is plenty of time. I go to the bar for a cup of coffee. While I am there the aeroplane leaves. I have missed the plane!

'*L' avion décolle! J'ai raté mon avion!*'

He told us to hurry along the path to heaven, warning us that God is not an old man with a white beard sitting on a cloud. One step along the path *au ciel* would be taken, if we came from our seats and stood humbly beneath the platform and dedicated our lives to God.

Surprisingly, hundreds of people did this, at first in twos and threes, then in a constant stream from all over the hall. While they left their seats and made their way to Mr Graham, the choir hummed celestial music. When all were assembled, the rest of the audience was told to go and wait for friends outside the hall; meanwhile the self-elected were shepherded into a curtained-off space behind the platform, where they were presently joined by Mr Graham.

From my high perch I could see everything. A prayer was said, and the speech began again, much as before. I had half hoped (since Mr Graham is a Baptist) that he would lead them all into the Seine.

***

In the *Irish Times* of 30 January 1956 there was a photograph of a portrait of the English Prime Minister made out of pieces of damp-looking fur, 'the work of M. J. Laroche.' It is a speaking likeness of the face that looked out recently from the television screen. This artist, of whom I had never heard before, has cleverly hit upon the perfect medium in which to portray Sir Anthony Eden. Marble for Roman emperors, bronze for eighteenth-century statesmen, oil paint for Victorian politicians, wet fur for Sir Anthony. How odd that such a man should be the son of the squire who, waking up on a shooting morning and seeing it was pouring with rain, was heard to exclaim furiously, 'Oh God! How like you!'

***

The *Figaro* is much annoyed by a report that Gaston Dominici* was recently given a dish of *filets de sole Normande* to eat in his prison cell. Far too delicious for him, says *Figaro,* which is also indignant because the yellow press calls the old man *le patriarche.*

When we were first in gaol in conditions of unspeakable filth and discomfort, during the summer of 1940, certain newspapers described the luxurious circumstances of our way of life in H. M. Prisons. We were said to call for alternate bottles of red and white wine; the dustbins of the gaols were supposed to be stuffed with empty champagne bottles, and so forth. For inventing and printing these lies the *Daily Mirror* and the *Sunday Pictorial* had to apologize in open court, and pay an agreed sum. I bought a fur coat with my share of the money, which kept me alive through bitter winters in unheated cells for the next three years.

Gluttony is one of the seven deadly sins; envy is another. The mere notion that somebody is indulging in the former sin causes many people to fall into the latter. The clever, if untruthful, journalists who wrote the fantasies about our champagne orgies reckoned, possibly correctly, that the thought of all the fun we were having in the middle of a war would infuriate many of those who were suffer-

145

ing privation and danger.

Unfortunately our opponents subsequently used less crude methods. They instituted a 'whispering campaign' and were careful to avoid libel. A friend, who hoped to hear an actionable slander uttered by one well-known 'whisperer,' asked, 'Why are they in prison? What have they *done?*' He received the answer: '*I know what I know.*'

About Dominici and his sole, perhaps the *Figaro* need not worry much. Prison is a grim place, even for a tough old peasant, and he has been there a long time now.

[*] Serving a life sentence for the murder of three tourists.

* Serving a life sentence for the murder of three tourists.

***

A buyer, described as a French bibliophile, paid 3,020,000 francs for the manuscript of M. André Malraux's *La Condition Humaine*. At another sale a few months ago the manuscript of *The Moon and Sixpence,* by Mr Somerset Maugham, fetched almost as much: £2,600. On the other hand, a lot consisting of a tooth and a lock of hair of Napoleon's, with the Legion of Honour he wore, only made £38 at a recent auction.

***

In the *Daily Telegraph* Late News column I read: 'A tourist boycott of Spain by German Protestants urged today by the annual congress of German Protestant pastors. Resolution adopted by five hundred pastors from West and East Germany said Protestants should make no holiday trips to Spain as long as a "hostile attitude" against Protestantism prevailed there.'

Poor things… But there is not much point, perhaps, in being a Protestant unless you occasionally protest against something or other; the pastors are merely fulfilling their function.

It is their loss, and I doubt if they will be much missed. German Protestant pastors in Andalusia, where song and dance and music and gaiety and sunshine are part of life, or in the Alhambra where every scented garden, every gushing fountain, is a symbol of love and pleasure, would, to say the least of it, be out of place.

***

It is only surprising that Conservative and Labour politicians should not have guessed long ago that nobody wants to listen to them. When they hire a hall to speak in, it always remains half empty. This has nothing to do with politics; simply they themselves are too dull.

A good speaker can attract huge audiences; crowds of people will go out on bitter, foggy evenings and sit on wooden seats to hear Sir Oswald Mosley, for example. But oratory is the rarest of gifts, and not one bestowed on the Edens, Macmillans, and Morrisons. It is not their fault, nor does it necessarily make them less good administrators; on the other hand they have the sorrow of knowing that they bore.

***

When the last war began, among a thousand horrors and inconveniences great and small there was one blessing the newspapers dwindled in size so that all the six dailies I took in weighed no more on the breakfast tray than *The Times* alone had done a few days before. Now they seem to be growing fatter every week, stuffed out with just the same nonsense one remembers from the 30s. The cheap papers fill up with photographs, gossip, and strips, while *The Times* gives full rein to the terrible whimsies of the fourth leader which have now spread over onto other pages, and has found in 'Oliver Edwards' the Mrs Miniver of literary criticism. It is all very well for people with dustbins, but what can country dwellers do about getting rid of kilograms of newsprint? A periodic bonfire is the only solution; a very unsatisfactory one, since burnt newspaper transforms itself into a fine light, black confetti and floats all over the garden.

***

The Eden government had a wretched press for their Egyptian outing. Except for one or two papers which rather overdid it. VAST ARMADAS NEARING CANAL was a headline in the *Daily Sketch they* were scolded by right and left in England just as they were by Mr Eisenhower and Mr Bulganin in the unfriendly outside world.

The weeklies were unanimous in their condemnation of Eden's police action. The most damaging attack on the Prime Minister was a cartoon in *Punch* which I saw reproduced in *Paris-Presse:* 'Eden, or the lamb in wolf's clothing.' A well-fed lamb with Sir Anthony's unfortunate physiognomy, badly disguised by a mangy wolf's skin, is taking a flying leap in a desert landscape. The expression of wild and meaningless excitement in the eye, the silliness of the teeth and chin, must be frightening enough to Eden's friends to contemplate, whatever emotions they may arouse in his opponents.

Presumably the picture of Port Said after the police action, flattened and burning, cannot do the government much good, although I notice that the Tories, between the storms of applause for one another with which they keep up their spirits in the House of Commons, pretend that nothing much happened when the 'police' landed. According to *The Times* unbroken windows still glint in the evening light, but French reporters see things otherwise. *J'ai vu le visage d'une ville frappée à mort'* [I saw a village trampled to death] was the headline in *France-Soir,* '*l'eau manque totalement a l'hôpital incombré de blessées'* [no water for hospital full of wounded]; and another reporter described the all-pervading smell of *cadavres.*

***

On the Hungarian revolution against Communism

English people are giving huge sums of money to the Lord Mayor's Fund for Hungarian refugees; in Paris the *Humanité** building was wrecked; these are two characteristically different ways of demonstrating European solidarity, but both of them are effective.

_{* French Communist daily.}

***

The English have so often told the world that foreign visitors think their policemen are 'wonderful' that they appear to have convinced themselves that the police force is one of the most alluring attractions the British Isles have to offer. Not long ago in the window of a Paris travel agency I noticed, incongruous among posters from many lands—snowy Alps, sunny islands, Spanish dancers, noble temples an English poster: it was a picture of a policeman. A coloured postcard on sale in London shows the outside of 10 Downing Street; the agreeable, unpretentious old house is almost hidden by the large policeman in the foreground.

A police force is a necessary evil, but it is a strange notion to imagine tourists planning a journey and saying to themselves, 'Shall we visit the Norwegian fjords? Or Sicily when the almonds are blossoming? Or Paris in the springtime? Or best of all shall we go to England and see the police? *Let's.*'

***

The note of complaint in the writings of television critics gets shriller every week. How they must envy Lord Beveridge, who said that he and Lady Beveridge looked at T.V. for a few days and did not enjoy it, and that they would not accept a television set as a gift. I suppose someone capable of writing a readable article about it is not likely to be capable of getting full enjoyment from viewing.

Nobody who had anything amusing or interesting to do, or to think about, would dream of abandoning it for the sake of tiresome T.V. Therefore the wretched critics, who view for a living, become more and more censorious and governessy as they describe the ghastly boredom of the programmes, and the way the BBC. is obliged to compete for silliness with I.T.V. Before we know where we are there will be an attempt to stop people wasting their time watching it. There is a lot of pleasure to be got out of interfering with the way other people waste their time.

How should leisure time, ideally, be spent? On winter evenings, at any rate, one cannot very well be out of doors taking healthy exercise. A good book? I have recently been engrossed, not for the first time in my life, in the memoirs of Saint Simon. My edition is in thirty-eight small volumes published in 1840 and printed in a neat 8-point type. It is very trying for the eyes, more so than even a speckly television. I can not pretend that it does me, or anyone else, the slightest good to read, for example, a long description of lunching with Louis XIV when he was with his armies, of how everyone kept his hat on at table unless addressed by or speaking to the King when he would doff it; of how dukes were invited to luncheon but cardinals were not, and so forth. But it happens to amuse me, it does no one else much harm, and in fact all the same arguments apply to it, as to television.

On the other hand, I can do without a critic's commentary, and so I daresay can viewers. The critics should beg to be excused and write their witty pieces about something they find more congenial.

***

The League Against Cruel Sports protested to the Bishop of Southwell because, in a churchyard in his diocese, a fox's brush was thrown into the grave of a M.F. H. It was 'more reminiscent of a beastly pagan rite of a bygone age than the modern conception of what is seemly behaviour in the consecrated area of a burial ground belonging to the Church of England.' The British Field Sports Society made a snappy rejoinder: 'Placing a fox's brush on a huntsman's coffin… is certainly no more pagan, as the League protests, than the firing of a volley at an Army burial.'

Very true; and what about an officer's sword, carried ceremoniously at his funeral? What are swords for, except to run people through? Do modern soldiers have tiny model bombs carried in their cortèges? 'Firing a volley' sounds more like the Crimean War, so very old-fashioned.

***

'You have probably never heard of George Howard, who farms outside York. But it won't be long before all America has heard his name and knows about his home. For that home, Castle Howard, has been chosen for a British Railways poster to be displayed in America in an attempt to encourage American tourists to come here. This castle was last in the news half a century ago, when that amazon of temperance and suffrage, Rosalind, Countess of Carlisle, had the complete stock of beer there poured into the lake.' This curiously-worded paragraph from the *Sunday Dispatch* gossip column was headed 'Beery fame.'

It is wonderful what the popular press can do in its ardour to reduce everything to the proportions of common mannishness which is deemed appropriate. It would not be easy for an ignorant but art-loving foreigner, keen on sight-seeing, to guess that the 'home' of Mr George Howard, who farms outside York, is the magnificent masterpiece built for his ancestor by one of our few architects of genius, Sir John Vanbrugh, and set in 'the noblest lawn in the world fenced by half the horizon' as Horace Walpole described it.

The 'complete stock of beer' which Rosalind Lady Carlisle poured into the lake was, unfortunately, the contents of a glorious cellar of vintage wines. As a child I remember hearing one of my uncles tell the story of this wanton act; he described it as sadly as though it had been the burning of the Alexandria library.

In London the battle of Albert Bridge is raging; in Paris the battle of the rue Barbet de Jouy. Well, perhaps not exactly *raging,* but at least Mr John Betjeman and M. Gérard Bauer are doing their best to rouse public opinion against senseless destruction of old buildings and their replacement by hideous new ones.

Albert Bridge is a delightful and unusual Victorian bridge, and it seems that the people who want to pull it down have got a plan to spoil Cheyne Walk as well while they are about it. The rue Barbet de Jouy is a pretty little street where several of the old houses have gardens; here it is proposed to build a nine-storey block. The old districts of Paris are supposed to be protected by law from desecration, but since it is a ministry which threatens to build, there is an interminable shadow boxing between departments; while this is going on it is feared the monstrous block may quickly be built and the damage irreparably done.

M. Bauer writes that this affair is symptomatic of an evil which all France is suffering from. Mr Betjeman has the same story to tell about England, each week in his *Spectator* column.[*]

[*] Albert Bridge and Cheyne Walk were saved. The rue Barbet de Jouy was irrevocably spoilt.

***

In Paisley the building of 255 new houses has been brought to a halt by teddy children, who pull down the houses as quickly as they can put them up. Although a fence costing £200 was erected round the building site it only lasted a week. 'Watchmen were stoned by bands of youngsters and forced to take refuge, with the result that the men left the job…. Half the glass in the windows of the houses had been broken, fresh brick-work had been knocked down repeatedly, and bricklayers had left their jobs as a result. It would often take bricklayers until midday to rebuild work knocked down during the night. Ceilings had been damaged by people walking through the roof space above and putting their feet through each plaster panel… piping and electrical fittings torn out… a child was seen to smash a panelled door with a pick, but could not be caught….'

I suppose it is too much to expect the dignified inhabitants of the 7th arrondissement or of Cheyne Walk to defend their districts in this spirited way, but might it not be possible for them to harness the local teddy-power? In Paisley it appears that the bricklayers became so discouraged that 'they left their jobs as a result.' If Chelsea and St

Germain des Prés cannot muster suitable children, might it not be possible to import some from Paisley? I expect the Paisleyites would love to see them go; they might even buy them single tickets. The child who smashed the panelled door would be perfect for special tasks the sculpture on the Ecole de Médicine, for instance.

***

According to the *New York Herald Tribune,* Lord Strathmore said that if he had a gun he would shoot Lord Altrincham.[*]

What are we coming to, when a Scotch landowner, in August, has not got a gun?

[*] As BBC Court reporter he had derided the Queen's style of public broadcasts.

***

A letter to the *New Statesman* from Professor Gilbert Murray's son shows that the great Hellenist died, as he had lived, outside any church. It appears to have been his gentle and courteous manner[*] towards a visiting priest which gave the latter an excuse to say that he was reconciled with the Roman Catholic Church into which he had been baptised ninety years ago. His ashes lie in Westminster Abbey; the Church of England is not particular about the outward and visible signs of inward and spiritual grace.

The successes claimed by priests sometimes remind one of the strange successes of modern doctors. One of the recent triumphs of medicine was the case of the man who died, had his heart re-started, and 'lived the "life of a vegetable"' for twenty three months, unconscious, in convulsions, being tube-fed by nurses once an hour day and night.

When Forain, the famous draughtsman, was dying, his doctor called a second opinion. After examining him from top to toe anti making every imaginable test this specialist declared that every part of the patient's body was functioning normally. Forain, as he drew his last breath, said: *Je meurt guéri* [I die a healthy man].

***

Just as the Russians, or rather the Soviet Government on their behalf, always claim to have invented everything from jet aeroplanes to washing-up machines, so Miss Elsa Maxwell[*] likes to say she has invented all kinds of rather well-known resorts. Her latest claim is that she 'invented the Lido in 1919.' When one surveys the beach today, where thousands of people are enjoying the sun and sea, one feels as grateful to her for her clever invention as I suppose the Russian public feels towards its government when climbing into a tram or writing with a fountain pen.

'There was nothing here,' Miss Maxwell is reported as saying, 'until I made it. You can say I *am* the Lido.'

Nothing here? Does she mean that she constructed the sandy shore, so conveniently adjacent to the loveliest city in the world? Hardly, for Lord Byron used to gallop his horse by the edge of the sea on the Lido when he lived in Venice. Or did she build the Moorish Excelsior, in 1906? Or make the place fashionable? She cannot quite mean that either, for it has always been used as a bathing beach by Venetians, and by anyone else sensible or fortunate enough to go to Venice in summer, since long before Miss Maxwell left her native America, even before she was born.

One hundred and thirty eight years ago Lord Byron, who had left Venice to be near Countess Guiccioli, wrote to a friend: 'A journey in an Italian June is a conscription, and if I was not the most constant of men I should now be swimming from the Lido, instead of smoking in the dust of Padua.'

[*] *Elsa Maxwell—the 'hostest with the mostest'—an American career gossip.*

***

When Chairman Mao referred the other day to certain intellectuals and

Oswald Mosley fishing for trout in the lake below Wootton Lodge.

Oswald Mosley defending Britain with the national fencing team,
after a match with a Swede 1932.

Unity and Diana during the Parteitag.

Tom and Diana at the Parteitag 1937.

Diana and Oswald Mosley before the beginning of the War.

Wootton Lodge in Staffordshire where Diana lived after her second marriage in 1936. Diana's son Desmond Guinness on the front lawn.

In the drawing room at Crowood, Wiltshire, Max, Diana, Alexander and Oswald Mosley after the War. The family left for France in 1951.

With the Duchess of Windsor in Paris in the 70s.

Evelyn Waugh in 1955.

Diana with Max Mosley, 1961.

Diana smiling in the 50s, flying to
Madrid airport (right).

others who maintain a critical attitude to the régime, he said with characteristically Chinese euphemism that these people have 'uneasy thoughts'.

It is difficult not to have uneasy thoughts about some of our rulers. When, like the present Minister of Education, they expose themselves to our uncomfortable gaze in a weekly poem our thoughts get uneasier and uneasier. Mr Graham Greene, in a letter to the *Spectator,* the paper which favours its readers with Hailshamia, wondered whether Lord Hailsham purposed to add Wilhelmina Stitch's poems to the curriculum in State schools. The implication seemed to be that Miss Stitch has served Lord Hailsham as a model for his own verse. Admirers of Miss Stitch's rhyming sermons may resent this. Her work was so polished, neat, and cleverly contrived, the moral so aptly pointed. A poem of Lord Hailsham's, recently published, called *Hopes and Fears,* beginning

> Is the fragile bark that's me
> Tossing on the stormy sea,
> At length to harbour drawn?

had, doubtless, something in common with Wilhelmina Stitch's verse as regards spiritual content, but technically the poetess was in another class. Stitch fans may care to know, if they are not satisfied with the hebdomadal offering of the Minister of Education, that the *Irish Independent* daily employs a delightful poet called James J. Metcalfe.
'Some would do anything they could… To live another day… While others wish to go to sleep… And quickly pass away… Both attitudes are wrong because… Our time upon this sod… Is only by the holy will… And by the grace of God.' This is an extract from one of Mr Metcalfe's recent poems; it bears an undeniable resemblance to some of Lord Hailsham's verse as to subject matter but Lord Hailsham is hardly Mr Metcalfe's peer as yet, when it comes to a really original rhyme.

***

An ex-Minister about whom some people may have had uneasy thoughts is Lord Salisbury. He was reported in the *Daily Telegraph* on the 16th March 1957 (when he was still in office) as having opened the 'Atoms and Health' Exhibition at the Royal Society of Health with a speech that 'could not have been more soothing'. 'He assured us' wrote the *Daily Telegraph* reporter 'that future generations had nothing to fear from atomic radiation.'

The very next day the *Observer* (which never stops treading on the toes of members of our Tory Government) published an article by its scientific correspondent, Mr John Davy. 'One thing is certain,' he wrote; 'every additional bomb test will do *some* damage. It will cause some people to die of bone cancer who would not otherwise have done so. It will also produce genetic changes, the majority of which are likely to be harmful. These will effect not us but our descendants.... The trend of recent expert reports—such as that produced for the World Health Organisation last week—indicates that the hazard is more immediate than earlier estimates suggested.'

Since Mr Davy is a scientist, while Lord Salisbury is not, his article unfortunately must be taken more seriously than 'No need to be nervous' (the heading in the *Daily Telegraph*). It might be better, in some ways, if Ministers left poetry writing to the poets, and scientific forecasting to the scientists. The English love of amateurishness and dislike of professionalism is sometimes carried almost too far.

***

Amateurs of the saga of America's golden age, those, for example, who enjoyed the biography of Harry Lehr ('King Lehr' as with apt literary allusion he was called), will love Mr Cornelius Vanderbilt the Fifth's book about his family: *The Vanderbilt Feud, The Fabulous Story of Grace Wilson Vanderbilt.*

The author's father, son of a multi-millionaire, was an extremely clever engineer who patented his many inventions and sold them all over the world. But his mother was America's top hostess for fifty years; a very arduous and expensive career.

The older generation of Vanderbilts loathed the beautiful Grace at first sight, and forbade Neily the Fourth to marry her. They more or less cut him off, so that Neily and Grace were obliged to rub along on fewer million dollars than they might have expected. Nevertheless, it was not long before Grace knew all Europe's crowned heads and the King of Siam, as well as everyone else who 'mattered,' and she never stopped inviting them to her brownstone 70-roomed mansion on Fifth Avenue or her seaside house at Newport. Her son says she was considered very exclusive; he also says that she entertained 37,000 guests in one year, which might appear almost conclusively inclusive, when the number of days she spent in ocean liners, cures and *nach*-cures *(sic)* is subtracted from the number of days in a year.

Reading this book one quickly forms the habit of adding and subtracting. Mr Cornelius Vanderbilt is very strong on figures and statistics; he knows exactly how much everything cost, from mansions and yachts to long-stemmed American Beauty roses for the dinner table. He also knows exactly how much everyone is 'worth' and what the dead ones left in their wills.

The secret of Mrs Vanderbilt's success as queen of society was a combination of money, snobbery, energy and attention to detail. Not only did she remember the individual tastes of her thousands of guests, but 'Mother was always careful to silence potentially envious tongues with small acts of thoughtfulness and gentility.'

Mrs Grace Vanderbilt had two lovely sisters, Belle and May. May's daughter, known as Baby May married the Duke of Roxburghe. 'Silly old May,' I remember Lady Cunard saying one day, referring to Baby May, 'no wonder she's tired, sitting up all night playing with her valves.' (The Duchess was a keen wireless fan.) An almost exact contemporary of Mrs Vanderbilt, Lady Cunard was also American and a hostess; but there the resemblance ends.

Neily did not take kindly to the role his wife assigned to him of man-about resorts as his son calls it, and dinner party host. Eventually this talented man took to the bottle: 'Poor darling Neily is *continually* drunk,' wrote Grace to her sister. He cleverly designed a lift which could be entered through a door concealed in the *boiseries* of their New York dining room. Sometimes in the middle of meals, when Mother became more than he could bear, Father disappeared into this lift and was not seen again for quite some time.

'My sister and I were given lessons in proper table settings. Followed by the butler bearing various dishes and condiments on a huge silver tray, Mother led us around and around the gleaming sixty-foot mahogany table. Before I was nine, I knew precisely which dishes remained and which disappeared during a complete seven-course dinner,' writes Mr Cornelius Vanderbilt.

English children, of course, were never allowed near the dining room. A congealed egg in the schoolroom was the best they could hope for.

***

The fuss about the new kind of advertising, where the name of a product is flashed on a cinema screen for a split second, so that though not consciously reading it the subconscious mind is supposed to register it and store it up for future use, seems rather exaggerated. If it persuades housewives to buy soap Y rather than soap Z (which is the most that is claimed for it), presumably Z could advertise in the same way; perhaps then the subconscious mind would get into such a muddle that housewives would give up buying soap altogether.

The idea that it could be politically dangerous and induce people to vote for A instead of B is far-fetched, and if A advertises himself in this way, B only has to look sharp and follow suit. Personally, I am very much in favour of advertisements which are invisible to the naked eye.

***

Ever since I happened to mention in this Diary how greatly I looked forward to the poems which Lord Hailsham used to contribute to the *Spectator,* there has been a stony silence—as far as poetry goes—from conservatism's bathing belle. He probably imagined that his photograph in his bikini on Brighton beach, which I saw in *France-Dimanche,* will carry more weight with the party than 'the fragile bark that's me' and that Conservatives will be more impressed by physical heroism (*France-Dimanche* says the sea was icy) than by the courage he showed in publishing his verse. This had unlucky results, for *The Times* reports that he introduced a hysterical note into the proceedings of the Tory Conference.

Small wonder; bathing in the English Channel in October would be enough to make anyone hysterical.

***

According to the *Star,* the Bishop of Chelmsford has appealed to people 'to queue up outside a church before service so that they would attract other people to see what was going on.' What a quaint idea of the Bishop's. Can it really be that people so love queuing that they have only to see a queue and they are impelled to join it? Has the Bishop considered what will happen when finally, with the ringing of the five minute bell, the queue moves out of the rain to lose itself among the deserted pews of an empty church? Might not even the most ardent queue-lovers then wonder whether the churchgoers had not taken leave of their senses?

If the Bishop of Chelmsford were to cross the Irish Sea he would find churches so full that queues are formed, not as a stunt but from necessity. Most Irish towns and villages have two churches, one old and charming, often eighteenth-century Gothic, the other ugly and modern. The pretty ones are empty and the ugly ones are full of worshippers. It always appears to me that it would be a generous, Christian and logical act on the part of the Church of Ireland if it were to give at least half of its empty churches to the Catholics It will take more than the attraction of imitation queues, or even the musical comedy ditties of clergymen popularising dogmas ('can anyone tell me an original sin?') to fill Anglican churches.

***

Last time I was in London two foreigners stopped me and asked, 'Where is Knightsbridge?' I replied that it was the very street we were in. They seemed rather doubtful, and said they had walked twice up and down looking for a shop called Harrods, but couldn't find it. When I told them that, though Harrods may call it Knightsbridge, the street it adorns is Brompton Road, they were puzzled. It is one thing to have your shop in a 'good address,' but very strange to muddle customers by giving a good address and then not being there.

***

This is the moment when the dozen or so best known literary folk of the Establishment are invited to state which book they consider has been the Best Book of the past year. As they are either authors who sometimes do reviews, or else reviewers who are occasionally authors, they naturally all choose each other's books in an orgy of love and harmony.

Personally, I see no harm in this. Many of the books chosen will have been well worth reading. The French system, whereby young writers have to spend months every year making love to old ladies and gentlemen in the hopes of winning one of the famous literary prizes, an activity which leaves them little time for writing, is much worse. In their case, of course, the afternoon calls, flattery and *petit soins* they bestow get them into training for the lobbying which, in middle age, will land them safely in the Académie Française.

Apart altogether from back-scratching (and after all, even writers must live), how much is one influenced in one's opinion of a book by friendship for the author? In my own case, I think it prejudices me a little in the book's favour. But on the other hand personal dislike, or dislike of a writer's politics, would never make me think, or say, that a good book was a bad one.

***

The winter collections, shown in August, and the new motors a few weeks later, are the terrible twin temptations for women and for men to indulge in dis-saving (as Mr Roy Harrod called it in an article in the *Financial Times*). Most men think it unnecessary to dis-save on a new winter coat when last year's is as warm as ever, and most women think it absurd to want a new motor when the old one still runs along. If women follow the fashion this time their spindly legs may be cold, but their heads will be beautifully warm. Anyone wishing to steal a hat will have quite a job to hide even one; to take five at a blow, as in the days of Nina hats, would be an impossible feat.

***

A French friend who visited London for the first time for a number of years said that he found English newspapers had become a great deal sillier during the interval; in fact, he said he could not make out from them what the news might be because they were filled with stories and photographs of actresses, dogs, runaway lovers, and other trivialities. Mr Randolph Churchill, in *What I Said About the Press,* scolds most of the cheap newspapers (though not, of course, Lord Beaverbrook's) for making money and degrading the public taste with pornography. Mr John Osborne, in his contribution to *Declaration,* complains that they contain too many articles about the private lives of members of the royal family.

The obvious answer to all these grievances is that if these three gentlemen had bought *The Times* or the *Guardian* they would have found plenty of news, no pornography and not a word about the private lives of members of the royal family.

While I have every sympathy with the Frenchman who did not know where to turn to find the news of the world (no capitals intended here), I have not so much for Mr Churchill and Mr Osborne, who were born and bred in London and should know by now how tiresome and stupid most English newspapers are, and avoid reading them. It may be, though, they are both fired with reforming zeal, like so many puritanical English people, and in that case they will naturally want to read more and more about their *bêtes noires* because it is no fun reforming if you have nothing to fulminate against.

In view of this possibility, perhaps the good idea I have had will not help them much, though it would be a boon to those genuinely seeking news. It is this. Newspapers should be obliged, like patent medicines, to print a formula on the front page giving a rough idea of the contents. If the formula reads as follows:

Police court reports:		
Sex crimes	27%	
Other crimes		18%
Sport		22%
Gossip and fashion		12%
Royalty		7%
Cheesecake		6%
Domestic news		5%
World news	3%	

those who bought the paper would know what they were buying. It should not be forgotten that some people love reading about crime and looking at photographs of girls in bathing gowns; there are even people, millions of them apparently, who greatly enjoy the *Daily Express*. Rather harmless tastes, one might think, even if one does not share them. It is easy not to read what annoys or bores. Personally, I dislike all ball games, but it does not worry me that large wads of newspaper space are devoted to describing them; I skip those pages.

A very good formula is that of the Paris edition of the *New York Herald Tribune*. It has eight pages, of which three are news, two leading articles and feature articles, leaving one each for Wall Street, comic strips and sport. The sport page is mostly about American games, with lovely headlines like Lakers Trampled by Knicks, and Wings Nip Hawks, or Buckeyes Edge Oregon, or Navy Mauls Rice. The words 'win' and 'lose' are seldom seen.

***

There is a new revue at the Lido in the Champs Elysées, where the famous Bluebell Girls are dreams of beauty. As they dale about sparkling with sequins and nodding plumes it is hard to imagine that in a few years they may be startling people by their inside knowledge of what is going to be done to the Bank Rate, Yet that is the way the world goes.

***

I once knew a man who was acutely sensitive to embarrassment. At the cinema, for example, if a child actor appeared on the screen, he had to cover up until it was no longer there. He kept a large white handkerchief for this purpose, which he threw over his head; he only removed it when one told him: It's all right, you can uncover now. A man of this sort would know better than to read the fourth leader in *The Times,* though I doubt whether he would go so far as to wish to forbid its appearance, even if he were a dictator instead of just a Tory minister. Similarly, Mr Churchill and Mr Osborne should cultivate the art of skipping, which is indispensible for newspaper readers.

A little further up the street there are queues outside *The Bridge on the River Kwai,* a war film in which all the English are incredibly brave and idealistic gentlemen and the Japanese rude, brutal, stupid (about the siting of the bridge) and not even as tough as one might suppose. Outwitted by the incredibly brave and idealistic English colonel, the Japanese colonel, who has been torturing him in vain for some days, feels so annoyed by what has happened that he has a good cry by himself in his steaming jungle study. The film was photographed in Ceylon, which seems to be the most beautiful country on earth.

Although there are moments when the friend mentioned just now would have had to 'cover up'—the whistling for example—excellent acting and the odd jokes make it worth seeing.

***

It is too late for the Society to save John Nash's Gothic castle, Shanbally, a pale grey house like a child's toy fort set in a park in County Tipperary with a view across to the Knockmealdown mountains. When I visited it lately on a cold afternoon the empty knocking of demolishers' hammers filled the air.

The castle was surrounded by an impenetrable barbed wire entanglement, as if they were ashamed of what was going on. At least I thought so at first, but perhaps they are really afraid that lumps of battlement will fall on the heads of the curious—not that there can be many visitors to this desolate and melancholy spectacle.

On arrival in Dublin I saw a poster: WHY NOT RE-BUILD TARA?

Well, why not? 'Tara's halls, where the harp that once...' No particular reason, I suppose, except that the reconstruction of a dark age monument might be frightfully ugly. It would be a puzzle to know what to do with it when it was finished (or what to do with *them,* if there were several halls). Harp recitals, of course, spring to mind.

Meanwhile it is not so much new building that should concern people in Ireland as the demolition of fine old houses. Just as in England, planners have only to see a well-proportioned, agreeable Georgian house, to hurry with their pickaxes; before you know where you are it has disappeared, leaving a gap which is quickly filled either by something hideous and 'contemporary' or else by a villa of the cosy cot variety.

The Irish Georgian Society has just been formed* with the object of preventing, where possible, this unnecessary vandalism, and preserving the eighteenth century character of Dublin and other towns.

In any case the Irish Georgian Society can hardly be expected to save country houses which have failed to find a buyer. Too many roofs to keep in repair... It occurred to me that television might he the answer to the problem. A homeless dog, shown on T.V., attracts thousands of people to clamour for it, people who had never thought of keeping a dog before. If country houses, in danger of demolition for want of an owner, could be shown for a few moments each week, who knows what might happen? Some rich Surrey-dweller, who follows his local hounds through the rhododendrons of suburbia, might suddenly feel an irresistible desire. Even if every house did not find an owner (and I believe many would) such a weekly programme would surely arouse widespread interest in the beauties that are being thrown away in England and Ireland.

[*] By Diana's son Desmond Guinness.

***

Mr Emrys Hughes says of his short life of Sir Winston Churchill: 'This is not the sort of admiring biography of which we have had so many in recent years.' He begins two hundred years before Sir Winston was born, pointing out that the great Duke of Marlborough was a great scoundrel, and going on to Lord Randolph, his American wife, and their son. 'Had young Winston been sent to an elementary school it is probable that his academic education would have ended there, for he did not show the abilities that would have won him a scholarship,' writes Mr Hughes. 'He had been nursed, waited upon, pandered to, mollycoddled, tutored, dragged through examinations, and had become accustomed to the world of wealth, rank, privilege and snobbery.' It is not at all clear whether MrHughes looks upon this upbringing as having conferred an unfair advantage on the young Churchill, or as an obstacle which he subsequently managed to surmount. But, in fact, nineteenth century public schoolboys were not waited upon, pandered to or mollycoddled; these early chapters should be omitted from an English edition of the book because they are rather misleading and wholly irrelevant. When it comes to Sir Winston's political career, however, it is well documented and fair. Mr Hughes quotes at length from Churchill's speeches, and shows how often in his life he changed not only his party but also his opinions.

***

Among the members of the Labour government in 1945, first as Minister for Fuel and Power and subsequently as Minister of Defence, was Mr Emanuel Shinwell, whose autobiography is called *Conflict without Malice*. Mr Shinwell is the son of a poor Jewish tailor who had come to England from Poland as a little child in 1868. His account of his own childhood and early life is the best part of the book; his father singing 'As I walk down the street each friend I do meet, says, there goes Muldoon, he's a solid man'; he himself buying a dish of hot peas for a farthing; collecting a library of books from junk barrows; marrying at 19 a girl with a wonderful feathered hat.

In 1919 he was sent to gaol for incitement to riot in Glasgow; he vividly describes prison conditions and food: the latter was unchanged twenty years later and is probably much the same to this day. Mr Shinwell could not and did not eat it; nor could he eat the food cooked in rancid oil given him by the Spanish reds when he visited their civil war. In the first case he lived on bread, in the second on oranges.

Perhaps the rest of the book suffers from too little malice; but it is interesting for its account of the early days of Labour, when those who came to break up their meetings were chucked out in a very rough way, and also for a chapter on Ramsay Macdonald.

Mr Shinwell refused to join the Churchill government in 1940; he was often critical of it in Parliament where he and Lord Winterton, another critic, were called Arsenic and Old Lace. Once Brigadier Harvie Watt, Churchill's P.P.S., reproached him for attacking his chief during a difficult moment of the war, and added: 'You mustn't forget the P.M. has great military gifts. His ancestor was the Duke of Marlborough', to which Mr Shinwell replied: 'My ancestor was Moses'.

***

Women this spring have achieved a really new look, especially about the head. Neat and tidy hair has had a long innings of just forty years, ever since the birds' nest bun coiffure was superseded by the shingle soon after the first war. Now the fashion seems to be for a large purple or orange chrysanthemum with a slender stalk, set on a tall thin body and spindly legs. These shaggy heads are not easily come by; it is no use thinking that to drag the hair through a hedge backwards will, get the proper effect—only a hairdresser can artfully arrange the artless disarray. A bell-shaped hat would add to the horticultural effect: a huge flower under a cloche.

***

The 42nd Salon de l'Automobile at the Grand Palais has drawn more than a million visitors. The most expensive motor was a very glamorous Rolls Royce, the prettiest, a Cadillac which looked like a brilliant, poisonous flying insect. The new Citroen is very cleverly made, you can go to bed in it, and put twelve suitcases in the boot—both very useful innovations, as anyone who has tried to get a room in a French hotel on one of the roads to the South in August.

***

On a newspaper placard in Dublin I saw the following:
BALENCIAGA
ARD RI FAISIUN
which made me wish I understood Irish. Has M. Balenciaga given an Irish periodical what he has, it seems, denied to *Vogue*—news of his spring collection?

***

English parents continue to be greatly harassed by the 11-plus exam, which, they feel, divides the children unfairly and prematurely into

167

sheep and goats. It is, no doubt, admirable that they should set such store by education. But the fact is, once a child has learnt to read he can learn two-thirds of the subjects taught in grammar schools by himself. Who wants to be 'taught' history, for example, by some prejudiced schoolmaster, when he can read all the great historians, and any number of memorialists and biographers as well, in a school library or a public library? Latin and Greek, mathematics and science—they must be taught if they are to be learnt; but not English literature, history, geography, and so on.

I have been reading the autobiography of an Eton master, M.D. Hill, published thirty years ago. His subject was biology.

'With a few exceptions,' he writes, 'only the duller boys are allowed to specialize in science... the truth is that many masters in the year AD 1927 believe that there is something a little "odd" or ungentlemanly in the pursuit of science, though it is better than nothing for a dull boy.... There is no shadow of doubt that valuable recruits have been lost thereby. I have known several cases of boys who would gladly have taken up science *con amore* if their tutors had allowed them. More than once boys have said to me: "My tutor hates science, he always laughs at it in Pupil Room."'

That was Eton in the 20s. It was just the same in the 40s. Of the 50s I cannot speak.

***

Mr Hill was before his time in many ways. He thought the birch and cane would soon be as out of date as the rack and thumb screw. I believe at Gordonstoun the boys are punished by having to run for a mile; something that many people do for pleasure. The latter objection, however, also applies to being beaten; so perhaps one punishment is as good as another who knows?

***

Eton may not shine when it comes to the teaching of hard subjects such as physics, but in what a scientist friend of mine calls the BBC subjects it excels, and the masters also excel in writing wonderful end of term reports which keep the parents quite amused and happy. Not for them the humdrum 'fails to concentrate sufficiently on his work,' or 'has made a real effort this term' type of report, which, they no doubt realize, is unreadably dull. One of my sons got this from an Eton master: 'He is an incorrigible oddity, and is fast becoming a museum piece here.'

Mr Hill relates some of the sallies of another master: 'His courage in tackling questions of which he does not know the meaning, much less the answer, is worthy of the highest praise.' And: 'His self-esteem is commendable, for while he believes that he has learnt something up to me this Half, I am quite sure he has not.'

***

The strangest event (it happened in December 1954, but has only just been published) was the Pope's second vision. This time, Christ visited the sick-bed of his Vicar on earth, which is perhaps less wonderful than that the sun should turn round in the sky, which the Pope saw after a three-day fast as he walked in the Vatican gardens four years ago.

Perhaps the reason why the newspapers give the Pope's visions so much less prominence than they give to a railway smash or a royal romance is that unbelievers do not believe in them and believers find them perfectly natural. Nevertheless, when a man of Pius XII's intellect and experience sees visions it is more interesting than when children guarding their flocks on the hillside, or nuns, or hermits, see them; from whatever point of view one considers it, it is news of the very first importance.

***

The case against the gamblers has failed. It turns out that what the policeman saw (when he climbed a fire escape and peeped into a London drawing-room) was not forbidden by law. Grown-up men and women who amuse themselves by transferring their own money from one to another in a private house, are not committing an offence. How farcical the English gambling laws must be if it could ever have been imagined that they were!

***

The prettiest town I have seen for ages is Alençon. Towns which have given their name to lace should be attractive, but a visit to Valenciennes soon demonstrates that they are not always so. Alençon had the good fortune to be rich in the eighteenth century and less rich subsequently; for this reason it has remained lovely, with hundreds of charming houses and many old streets and squares.

Climbing some stone steps in order the better to see the fine seventeenth century palais de Guise, I found myself at the door of a chapel dedicated to St Theresa, the Little Flower. Apparently she was born in the next-door house.

In the chapel there is a grille through which one can see St Theresa's parents' nuptial bed, a Second Empire mahogany bed hung with red curtains; and behind these curtains, a printed notice relates, the saint as a child used to hide when she wanted to think about God.

Round the top of the chapel walls are some delightful frescoes, depicting scenes from her life. In one of them she is shown, as a little girl, *'courant seule vers l'église malgré la pluie'* [rushing to church despite the rain]—an act of courage which could, I daresay, be paralleled in many an Irish village on almost any Sunday. It probably rains more in Ireland than it does at Alençon.

***

A museum of costumes is being arranged in Paris. French royal personages were surprisingly short; Louis XIV measured 5ft. 2½', but made himself several inches taller by wearing very high heels and a very high wig. And not only royalties were small; the robes Josephine wore when she was crowned are so tiny that in all Paris, it appears, there is not a mannequin who can fit into them. So these historic dresses will be displayed on dummies used nowadays for the clothes of boys and girls of fourteen

***

However wrong-headed the Aldermaston marchers may have been, however wickedly irresponsible their demand for unilateral disarmament, it was impossible not to feel sorry for them as they trudged along in the snow and slush and wind. Luckily, most of the men had very long hair and some of them beards, which must have been a great comfort; and I suppose the parsons could pile plenty of vests and jerseys on underneath their cassocks. But what about the poor women, in their thin tight trousers?

On Good Friday they kept the blood coursing through their veins by jam sessions of rock and roll; there was a spirited photograph of this in *The Times*. But by Holy Saturday they must have been too footsore for that kind of sport; and it snowed. Feeling worried about their fate I rushed to the French newspapers, but the march was not mentioned, and there were no English papers to be had. As so often happens, however, my sympathy turned out to be completely misplaced. For, according to the left-wing weeklies, it appears that the marchers loved their march and arrived at their goal after three days of it with heads (and presumably beards and cassocks as well) held high.

They were all a bit tired at the end, no doubt, which accounts for their behaviour to an Oxford geneticist, who, exercising the old English right of free speech, criticised the notion of unilateral banning of the H-bomb. It seems that on hearing his words some of the girls broke ranks, and tried to pull his motor car to bits. Only when the lady leader of the march, calling above the surrounding din, reminded them that they were supposed to be pacifists, did they resume their dignified progression.

**

The most amusing of all spectator sports in England now is television. Not the second-rate plays and films nor the actors and actresses, but the news, and the real people, heroes and heroines who voluntarily exhibit themselves under a merciless magnifying glass for the public to gaze at.

**

What is the vote? A right, a privilege, a duty. If to have the privilege of the vote is the right of every adult citizen, to exercise it is a duty. And since, of course, everyone has a duty to do his duty, voting should be made compulsory, This is an argument which is being put forward in the French press at the present time.

I imagine, if ever we have the compulsory vote in England, a new sort of suffragist or suffragette will appear; there are bound to be people who conscientiously object to voting; they will probably chain themselves to railings and have to be carried struggling into the polling booths. But though you can carry a man to the poll, you cannot make him vote—not, that is if the ballot is to remain secret. *How* can you make sure that he will not 'spoil' his paper? And if a policeman, or a WVS lady, or a boy scout, stands over him while he puts *a* cross in the right place—well then, no doubt, the fur would fly. Tiresome though it must be for people with a highly developed civic sense to see good votes going to waste, the alternative seems too difficult.

Perhaps it might he arranged otherwise; the electoral roll could be checked and a fine imposed on non-voters. In England now, when between a third and a half of those enfranchised abstain from voting, a rich harvest could be expected from a fine of, say, a guinea a head. Enough would be collected to pay for something popular, another 'fly-over' or two, for example, like the one being built at the beginning of the Little West Road, which is apparently costing nine millions.

***

I have never voted in a parliamentary election in my life, not that I am a conscientious objector to voting but simply because I have never been able to face the idea of sharing responsibility for sending either of the pair of troglodytes standing, in any constituency where I happened to be on the register, to the House of Commons. They were all the stuff of which back benchers are made; vote-fodder for the Tory or Labour whips; unwavering supporters of their disastrous leaders.

I once voted in a local council election in the depths of the country, but that was for a special reason. My vote, went to the Independent candidate, just in order to help keep out a particularly fatuous Tory do-gooder from the next village. Others must have had the same idea: my man won.

***

One of the great advantages of age is that you begin to know by experience the kind of thing you are likely to abominate. International exhibitions I long ago learned to avoid. The newspapers are so clever at making them sound wonderful that after a bit the most unlikely people suddenly announce that they are off to, for example, Brussels. A nightmare day-trip from Paris is highly recommended by the railways; it allows many weary hours for seeing all the sights.

Nothing would induce me to go; I have never forgotten how, as a child, I longed to see the Prince of Wales in butter at Wembley, where this original piece of sculpture was the high-light of the Empire exhibition. Having waded through dust and crowds to reach my objective in either the Australian or the Canadian pavilion, I forget which, I found the butter Prince slightly less lovely than I had pictured it in my imagination. From that moment of disillusion dates my aversion to these exhibitions: what you see is almost never worth the struggle involved.

173

At Wembley the amusement park quite made up for the disappointment, but now I should not care much for that either.

***

Attacks on Teddy boys continue to fill the newspapers, and an MP, Mr James Dance, is reported in the *Daily Mail* as having suggested in Parliament that if they have been found guilty of insulting behaviour, unless they pay their fines on the dot they should have their 'revolting curls' cut off. Some people might think that, however much insulting behaviour is to be deplored, this is scarcely the way to persuade a group of people to be more civil. Of course nobody would have dared to suggest that Louis XIV's curls, or even Charles II's or William III's, were revolting, or that a single ringlet from all those cascading locks could possibly be spared. If I were a rich Ted I would grow longer and longer curls, or even get myself a wig like theirs, just to tease Mr Dance.

For, according to the newspapers, the Teds are very rich indeed; much richer than public school boys, who, as a result, are inclined to give up their 'missions' to the East End of London. A good thing too, I should imagine. No self-respecting Ted wants 'missionaries' from public schools, foisting cricket, scouting and other distasteful games upon him. On the other hand (in order that contact, supposed by the do-gooders to be so valuable, should not be lost between the East End and the public schools) a few of the more affluent Teddy boys might well take a day off from work occasionally and send themselves on a mission to Harrow or Eton or some other suburban school. They could give the school boys a good feed (often much needed), and lend them their Elvis Presley records. As a special treat they might bring a pin-table, or even a few girls, along with them.

A mission of that sort would have an enormous success; the school boys would learn to look forward eagerly to a visit from the Stepney Mission, or whatever it might be called. Probably life-long friendships would be formed. And the Teds would enjoy the glow of self-righteousness, knowing how much they had done to brighten the drab term-time lives of their less fortunate contemporaries.

***

The art critic of a French newspaper complained (in connection with the Biennale exhibition at Venice, which is apparently even more ghastly than usual) that everyone now suffers more or less from what he called the Cézanne complex. Those with a Cézanne complex are terrified lest by laughing at or ignoring some ugly daub of abstract painting in 1958 they may be earning themselves the despised niche in the history of art which we now allot to the people who failed to recognise the greatness of the Impressionists.

Personally I do not care in the very least whether my grandchildren's generation despises and rejects my choice of pictures, or whether they themselves will blame me for not having bought a bunch of twisted iron arranged by a 'sculptor' whom they consider a genius. I suppose it is different for art critics, who are by way of 'knowing' something or other, but I cannot understand why anyone else should mind what future generations think about their taste. Yet it undoubtedly worries some people, even those who pride themselves on their indifference to contemporary judgment of their knowledge, opinions, good nature, or whatever it might be.

It is one of the strangest evidences of human vanity that a person should care about the opinion of posterity; the opinion, that is, of descendants of the crowds milling along Oxford Street, or the Boulevard des Italiens, or in and out of St Mark's on an August afternoon.

***

The following appeared in 'Comment' in the *Observer* recently: 'When General Serov was asked about the Press references to his forced deportation of thousands of citizens of the Baltic States by cattle trucks to Siberia, he replied that we had done as much to the Fascists. Some papers commented that we had, in fact, treated Sir Oswald Mosley and others well. That is perfectly true: and we can be proud of the restraint shown to them, in war-time, as political prisoners.'

Lady Redesdale* tells me she wrote to the *Observer*:

The writer of 'Comment' thinks that we can be proud of the restraint shown to Sir Oswald Mosley and his followers in war-time as political prisoners. This restraint consisted in imprisonment in the ordinary London prisons of Brixton and Holloway for 4 years, without charge or trial. During *this* time I often heard or read of politicians boasting of the great freedom enjoyed in this country, where according to Magna Carta, no Englishman may be kept in prison without trial. It was hard at the time to read without a bitter smile the effrontery of those words when compared with what was happening in actual fact... Sir Oswald and his followers were imprisoned because they opposed the war with Germany, on which our politicians were resolved, and for no other reason at all.'

The *Observer* did not print her letter. A few weeks ago the same newspaper published a 'profile' of Mr Arthur Koestler, and stated that he had been imprisoned by Vichy France. I wrote pointing out that in his autobiography *Scum of The Earth,* Mr Koestler describes how he was arrested and sent to a concentration camp by the French authorities during the winter 1939-40. He had managed to secure his release, and was living in England, by the time the Vichy government was formed. The *Observer* did not print my letter.

* Diana's mother.

***

I have been reading the Empress Alexandra Feodorovna's letters to her husband, the last Tsar, written during the war between 1914 and 1917.

They are love letters, but they are also full of advice about the conduct of the war, the appointment of ministers and so on, handed on from 'our Friend', the Holy man of God, Rasputin. She wrote in English, signing herself Wify, Sunny, and sometimes Girly. She continually urged the Tsar to assert himself, be more of an autocrat, make people tremble—the last thing poor 'Boysy' was capable of doing. He spent most of the time at General Headquarters, where 'Baby' (the Tsarevitch) often accompanied him. Do not allow Baby to put his elbows on the table, or throw bread pellets at meal-times, writes the Empress.

Knowing the end of the story, and that in a few months 'our Friend' is to be poisoned and shot, and not long afterwards the whole imperial family taken to Siberia and murdered, it is pathetic to read of the optimistic prophesies about her children's future happiness, the four Grand Duchesses married, Baby reigning over all the Russias—in which the Empress tried so hard to believe.

Her bitter hatred of the Grand Duke Nicholas, much the ablest member of the royal family, dated from his telegram to 'our Friend' when the latter proposed visiting the troops: *Viens, je te ferai pendre* [Come and I'll have you hung].

Deeply religious, she firmly believed in the power of prayer. When Goutchkov, a minister whom she particularly disliked, was going on a tour of factory inspection, she went to church and prayed that his train would he de-railed and he alone killed; but, as so often happened prayer remained unanswered.

***

Air travel can be exasperating. Years ago I was travelling to England from Spain and landed at Hurn because there was fog in London. With other passengers arriving from everywhere imaginable, we were herded into a hangar furnished with some straw chairs, locked in and told to wait. Every few minutes the door was unlocked and another twenty or so stranded travellers were pushed in. The hangar soon filled up: people began sitting on the floor. Outside the window several charabancs could be seen, their drivers chatting together and smoking. Luckily, my companion,[*] an impatient man, soon wearied of the dull situation. He threatened the officials with a writ for unlawful detention, and thus we made our escape. I expect the others are there still, their bones whitening....

[*] Oswald Mosley.

***

A study of English and German archives apparently shows that, on both sides, there was often a disparity between the number of aeroplanes claimed to have been shot down in the Battle of Britain and the true figure. A Mr Alan Brien has discovered the reason for this. Writing in the *Daily Mail* he says: 'Both the British and German Air Forces exaggerated the RAF through careless checking and wishful thinking; the Luftwaffe through arrogance and a lying propaganda service.' So now we know.

***

Mr Arthur Koestler, in his autobiography *The Invisible Writing,* describes the Budapest of the 20s, where he says there was a group of first-rate writers who would have been world famous had they been born in London, Berlin or Paris, but who were condemned to write for each other and a relatively small public because their language was Hungarian. Translation? Of course it is possible, in theory, though much gets lost in the process.

Certain words and idioms are untranslateable. In another category are translators' howlers, the Englishman who gave *lac du Japon* as Japanese lake (instead of lacquer), the Frenchman who turned Alexander Pope into *le pape Alexandre.*

General Spears, in his book *Prelude to Dunkirk,* says that Madame de Portes, a lady who had an influence on pre-war politics in France through her friendship with a member of the Government, was

known as *la porte à côté,* the side door. He does not add the other meaning of *à côté*—common, a person one does not receive—which is the
whole point of the joke. A German once told me that in a prisoner-
of-war camp in America he was classified as a rabid Nazi—*kaninchen
Nazi,* he said, laughing. Had he really confused rabid with rabbit?

***

Who has not. when learning a foreign language, read a book and labo-
riously noted down all the unknown words in order to look them up
afterwards in the dictionary? And who has not felt rather depressed,
when, having more or less mastered the language, he comes across
dozens of words in as many pages which he has never heard of?

Personally I never mark books. The only point of doing so is to
emphasize something for future reading, and as I dislike reading
books where words and sentences have been scored and underlined
this, for me, would defeat its own end. But I notice that lending library
books often have remarks written in their margins by people who cannot contain their furious irritation or disagreement with the authors'
opinions.

In small libraries the librarian sometimes makes a note, to refer to
when giving advice to borrowers. This had been done, for example, in
Holloway Prison library, where the librarian was a wardress and not
exactly what my father used to call 'a literary cove'. Yet I suppose she
had to know vaguely what the books were about; it would never do if
a new prisoner managed to borrow an exciting novel during the very
first week. The wardress goes from cell to cell accompanied by a prisoner carrying a tray of books; only boring or at any rate edifying
books are supposed to he offered to a prisoner during the early part
of a sentence.

In women's prisons hooks bound in red cloth used to he the
favourites, because the prisoners contrived to transfer some of the red
dye from the bindings onto their own lips. This is one of those brilliantly clever things, like splitting a match into ten parts each of which

will light a cigarette, that convicts learn in a trice. Probably they no longer have to trouble about the shabby old red hooks; I saw in a paper some time: ago that they are allowed to keep ordinary make-up in their cells now. I wonder whether peroxide is also available to them; one of the saddest sights in a woman's prison was the piebald heads, with a few inches of golden, crimped hair hanging down below the black, brown or sometimes grey.

I once borrowed a rather pretty leather-bound edition of Racine's plays, printed about 1840, from Holloway Prison library. The presiding wardress had written on the fly-leaf: *Wonderful language; dull.* If she considered Racine dull, whom would she find brilliant? It is anybody's guess

Prison has a very special effect on one's taste in reading. Where the surroundings are so desperately degraded, 'realism'—which generally means the description of disagreeable happenings against a sordid background—is not much cared for. The need is for either beauty, it and elegance, or else for what Germans call *'das Erhabene'* (which can he more or less translated 'the sublime').

This accounts for the fact that St John of the Cross was a best-seller to prisoners of war, or so at least I was told by somebody who worked in a bookshop. I wonder if they read him much now that they have returned to the world. There is no doubt that a very light diet, or in other words semi-starvation, combined with a completely sedentary life, tends to direct the thoughts of even a pleasure-loving and worldly person towards contemplation and mysticism. And the untempting temptations of St Antony as imagined by Bosch might he any light-headed prisoner's dream.

***

Lord Berners used to send me his books as they came out when I was in prison. They gave me great pleasure, but they were distressingly short; a prisoner wants to look up from a book and discover that several hours have gone by unnoticed—just the opposite of ordinary life when one never has time for all the myriad things one would like to do. We only had permission to write two letters a week, and mine were always mortgaged up to the hilt to go to children and other near relations. But for writing to a Member of Parliament it was possible to obtain special leave from the prison governor; many prisoners took advantage of this with the idea that an MP might summon up courage to raise the whole question of Regulation 18B in general, or of some constituent's case in particular, in Parliament. (One or two courageous M.P's actually did so). I used to get permission for an extra letter to thank Lord Berners for his gifts by saying that I must write to a member of the House of Lords. As a matter of fact he never took his seat or went near the place; his excuse was that the only time he had been there his umbrella was stolen by a bishop.

The day my arrest was reported in the newspapers he wrote to ask whether he could help me in any way; should he, for instance, send me a little file concealed in a peach? This letter was only given to me months later; it had meantime been the rounds in the Home Office and was riddled with pin holes.

***

On a raw November morning at Waterloo station a woman exclaimed in an indignant way to the world in general but also to me in particular because I happened to be near by:

'Look at that man! It's a shame! He's dressed in nothing but a blanket and his bedroom slippers!'

I looked. 'I think he's a friar,' I said. She calmed down a bit. 'Oh, is that what they call it, dear,' she murmured doubtfully.

***

The committee which formed itself in Mahatma Gandhi House has appealed for money to help it save liberty in France. I long to know 1. whether money is pouring in, and 2. how it will be spent. I suppose the committee will have to come to Paris on a fact-finding expedition. Rather a clever idea of theirs, really; but how surprised the French will be! English people enjoy giving money to 'save' some country or other. I remember at the end of the war ladies went from house to house in every village collecting 'for China.'

***

English pacifists certainly pick their weather for demonstrating with a noble disregard for their own comfort. The Aldermaston march took place in a snow storm; the attack on the concrete mixer at a rocket-launching site in Norfolk was made in bitter December fog. Climbing over barbed wire entanglements and rolling in icy mud, the demonstrators accurately reproduced for themselves conditions in the front line in the war before last.

I suppose the demonstrator called 'Arrowsmith' was compensating for an ancestor who, in medieval times, was an armaments manufacturer hammering out arrowheads on his anvil.

***

I see that the memorial designed by Mr Lynn Chadwick, to commemorate the crossing of the Atlantic forty years ago by the airship R.34, is not going to be erected at London Airport after all. Lord Brabazon complained that it looked like a diseased haddock.

Sculpture arouses much more furious controversy than painting because, I suppose, being set up in a public highway, it is seen by many more people. When I was a child, the target for angry denunciation was Epstein's *Rima,* a rather inferior work which we all felt obliged to defend because those who attacked it were art-haters.

The Sudanese have hit upon a rather original idea. Instead of *unveiling* statues in Khartoum they now *veil* them preparatory to removing them out of sight. A statue of General Gordon riding a camel and one of Lord Kitchener on horseback have recently been veiled, to the accompaniment of ceremonial music and military parades.

This is an idea Londoners might with advantage copy. My first choice for veiling would be Nurse Cavell. But I hope London will offer to purchase the Khartoum statues; I feel sure they would be popular, the camel in particular would give great pleasure.

What an excessively odd animal a camel is; the sight of General Chinese Gordon riding his across Hyde Park would beguile countless Londoners from now till doomsday, art-haters and art-lovers alike.

***

A doctor told a friend of mine that 700 different chemicals are used to preserve food. He said that nobody knows what effect they may be having on the human body. He added that of course food must be preserved if vast agglomerations of populations are not to starve. The same argument is used about chemical fertilizers. As the poor little suicide boy in Hardy's novel said in his farewell note : 'because we are too menny.'

Possibly we need a Bertrand Russell of chemistry to point out the dangers in our foods; in any case, patient research is required. Maybe the 700 chemicals do no harm at all to A but give B the permanent stomach-ache which makes his life such a bore. I suppose it is on the cards that if the brains and energy which are lavished on satellites were given to medical research, and if an equal international prestige attached to healing the sick as now accrues from the conquest of space, preventions and cures would in fact be discovered and mankind would suffer less.

Is the Devil at work in the world, or is it just the dark side of Nature which forces men to struggle on, trampling and discarding the weak as they go. Who knows?

***

A correspondent informs me that it is not the Sudanese who invented the veiling of statues, but Max Beerbohm; he thought of it in 1911.

Ah, but did it just stop at being a clever notion, or did Max Beerbohm actually succeed in veiling any? And if the answer is that he did, was there a military band and an ambassador at his veiling ceremony? The Sudanese veiled so stylishly.

The veil itself, on the Kitchener statue, looked like an immense ballet skirt, with the horse's legs playing the parts of Robert Helpmann and Margot Fonteyn in a *pas de deux*.

***

Sir Frank Medlicott, National Liberal and Conservative MP for Norfolk Central, is reported as saying: 'Imprisonment without trial is anathema to British people. We are getting slack about this.' Apparently they had nabbed a couple of foreign seamen and omitted to charge them. I agree with Sir Frank Medlicott about the slackness, but I do not feel too sure about the anathema. I don't believe the British people give a button for habeas corpus, though I suppose they might if they were nabbed themselves. I do, for example.

***

When I was at Holloway, concerts were occasionally given for the prisoners by well-meaning and philanthropic visiting musicians. They took place in the chapel. Although architecturally this chapel naturally could not compare with a Gothic country church, it was rather pleasant in its way. In the dirty, smelly, dark old prison it seemed clean, well polished and brightly lit. (I once asked per-mission to be allowed to buy a stronger bulb for my cell because—I could not see to read—the answer was NO).

One such chapel concert I went to I shall never forget. There was a man who sang folk songs and at the end of each line of verse he raised himself on tiptoe and poked his head out first to the right and then to the left. I began to laugh and couldn't stop—something that had never happened to me since childhood. I buried my face in my hands and tears of laughter ran through my fingers. Terrified that he might see and be deeply hurt, I did everything I could think of including biting my tongue; but still I shook with laughter which became more painful with every 'Hey nonny no' from the singer, who had so kindly come to Holloway to amuse the prisoners but had not meant to amuse them quite as much as that. It was agony; back in my own cell I was over-come with extreme exhaustion. I hope he did not notice; perhaps he thought that I was like Mme. Verdurin, who demonstrated her sensibility by listening to music with her face in her hands.

***

President Kennedy's Peace Corps is apparently considered such a good idea (*The Economist* calls it a 'noble experiment') that other countries may imitate it. But *The Economist* admits 'there is a good deal of scepticism in Washington about these "innocents abroad." Will they be mainly rich men's children hungry for adventure? Will pampered young Americans prove tough enough and humble enough? How many are likely to know or to learn quickly the obscure languages they will need later?'

I have been wondering just the same thing. Of course all foreign languages seem obscure until one has managed to learn them. But it might be better in some ways if the Peace Corps refrained from foreign languages altogether. It is so much easier to annoy people if they can understand what you say. And the under-developed will already be highly tried by the noble experimentalists sharing their homes and eating their food.

There is a brighter side for them (the under-developed peoples) however. They can get a bit of their own back. For 'President Kennedy does not rule out similar corps in the slums and depressed areas of the United States.' Well done him! It will be most instructive to observe the reactions of the American unemployed to a highly-powered team of, for example, Congolese, living with them, eating the same food, and speaking heaven knows what language. This will certainly deserve to be called an Experiment, though how Nobly it turns out remains to be seen.

***

'... *but not on us, the oysters cried...*'
The English love for dumb creatures is famous, and also their fondness for oysters. There was an outcry during the dock strike when it was feared that several hundred thousand oysters might die of thirst unless they were unloaded and given a refreshing drink of sea water. Like the Walrus and the Carpenter, people began shedding bitter tears over them. The dockers relented; the oysters were saved. For what? To be swallowed alive by fat business-men?

***

England ought to have a 'Day' like America's Fourth and France's Fourteenth of July. Like them, it should be in the summer, a whole holiday for everyone with fireworks and dancing in the streets.

It is true we have got Guy Fawkes Day, but it is a bit grim when you come to think of it gunpowder, treason and plot, ending in hanging, drawing and quartering. In fact it is a wonder Guy Fawkes Day has not been forbidden by the life-peeresses; I expect delinquents galore result from this concentration of minds on horrors, and the burning of the guy is anti-social.

In any case, November is a hopeless month for a Day. Last Guy Fawkes I drove round Trafalgar Square at midnight to see the fun. Through a fairly dense fog it looked as though a sporadic fight was going on between boys armed with firecrackers and police armed with batons, and although this is some people's idea of an amusing evening, the Day I envisage would have a more universal appeal.

What date to choose? It must commemorate something unchanging. 'Empire Day' would never do; it would upset people right and left, as well as laying us open to ridicule. Oak Apple Day would not commend itself to Cromwellians, nor the anniversary of Waterloo to enthusiasts for united Europe. The safest choice would probably be Midsummer Day, at present celebrated only by lunatics at Stonehenge.

***

What has become of Mr Kennedy's brother-in-law's Peace Corps? There was news six months or so ago of idealistic young Americans who were to be sent to countries all over the world where they planned to speak the same language, eat the same food, and live the same lives as the natives.

It is very strange that they have faded out of the news. Two explanations occur to me: either they are stuck at the language fence, or else they have arrived at their under-developed and under-privileged destinations and have all been eaten by their hungry hosts. One never knows. If the latter, they will have made their contribution to solving the world's problem of under-nourishment, particularly in respect of protein.

Unfortunately, in the present state of affairs people seem to be more concerned with Mr Kennedy's War Corps** In Vietnam, and this, as far as one knows, is not being run by any of his relations.

***

To smile or not to smile? American politicians treat us to miles and miles of smiles. On the whole, I am in favour of less smiling; we got very tired of poor Ike's gums, and we have had just about enough of Mr Kennedy's teeth. Public figures who do not smile are rare and precious; Queen Mary, for example, was delightfully glum.

When the world is in such deadly danger from its politicians as it is at the moment, they might at least pretend to be serious. At a cinema recently I saw a news reel of Mr Kennedy conferring with his advisers on the world crisis. It would be comforting if they could be persuaded to confer without being filmed at all, but this is too much to ask, I suppose. Did they settle down in a quiet room for their momentous conference? Of course not, because that would not seem a modern and young way to behave; the image is so important. The film showed them all climbing self-consciously into a little boat belonging to the President, while Mr Kennedy gave a fine tooth-display. I am not at all sure that this boat is a good exchange for last year's golf course.

***

All through the summer holidays, while the Berlin crisis has loomed, the politicians have indulged in their habitual fantasies. Mr Macmillan pretended to believe the whole thing has been invented by the newspapers. I was surprised at the intense irritation, not to say fury, caused by his Gleneagles utterance, for it is exactly in line with his usual fatuity, just the sort of thing he has taught us to expect. Life may or may not be better with the Tories, but when it comes to being fatuous they certainly beat all.

***

Hurricane Debbie interfered with the unilateralist anti-American demonstration at the Holy Loch. The anti-German demonstrators in Wales were pelted by the locals. And in London hordes of actors and actresses and clergymen sat in the streets and were carried away by the police.

Wouldn't it be a good idea to have sitting-streets, like the play-streets in populous areas of London which are reserved for the children to play in? If the sitters were shepherded into specially reserved streets, they could be left to sit quietly until their beards grew down to the ground, or until they got bored with sitting.

But perhaps their fines come in useful. One can never be sure of the motives of the Home Office.

***

I have been experiencing the joys of British Railways. I examined my train with interest, to see whether Dr Beeching is earning his keep. It was rather a horrid train. It went from Glasgow to Oban, stopping innumerable times. There was evidence that people had been smoking in the no-smoking carriage, and apart from that it was excessively grimy. The lavatory door not only had no lock: it would not even shut but swung about as the train lurched.

It is a good rule on British Railways to avoid luncheon and dinner and to eat breakfast and tea instead. They lavish a lot of thought and love on breakfast and tea, while the others are generally disgusting beyond belief. But even at tea a repressive spirit reigned in the dining car of my train. Two harmless ladies sat down at a table and were immediately ordered by the waiter to move. When they mildly asked why, he replied angrily: 'It's not laid up. You can see it's not laid up.' (Why 'up'?) He spoke as though a banquet was involved. The ladies moved. I should have felt inclined to stay and make enough fuss to get the table of my choice 'laid up'—i.e., a plate and cup put upon it.

I experienced another example of tyranny in Glasgow. I climbed into the airport bus, and the driver came hurrying along and said furiously that no one was allowed to get in his bus until the flight was called.' He was about to try and make me get out again when our argument was cut short by (to use BEA jargon) a flight being called. One of the most tiring things about travel in the British Isles is the strange and perverse delight the employees of the railways and airlines take in making everything as difficult as possible for the traveller.

Whether the Scotch are worse than the English in this respect I don't know. I met some people who were loving a coach tour through Scotland because their Scotch driver was so amusing. They thought him perfection.

To go back to poor Dr Beeching and his Augean stables: of the two trains I travelled in, one was 3 5 minutes late and the other 25 minutes late. As a result I could not visit the Burrell pictures in Glasgow Art Gallery because it was already shut. I was sorry not to catch a glimpse of the wonderful pink Matisse which so unexpectedly hangs there.

***

Once on my journey I was obliged by hunger to forget my breakfast-and-tea rule, and eat some dinner. I had Crème Solferino, which turned out to be a tin of warm tomato soup, and Poires Duchesse, which was a pear in a wine glass smothered in frightening green jelly and false cream. I draw a veil over what came between. Where this repast was perpetrated is a secret, but it was not on a train.

A friend of mine took some foreigners to a noted and reputed restaurant in Gloucestershire (yes, there is such a restaurant and apparently the food is good). Because they arrived at three minutes past two, they were not allowed to have any lunch. The sideboards were loaded with delicious cold food, hors d'oeuvre, lobsters, hams, saddles of mutton. But a rule is a rule in the catering world. My friend took the astonished guests, who were not accustomed to such cruelty on the part of restaurant keepers—an obliging race elsewhere in Europe—back home and fed them on bread and cheese.

***

I love the description in *Time* of the Kennedys' music party at the White House. Casals played Schumann and Mendelssohn. Those present included Aaron Copland, conductors Bernstein and Stokowski, Labor Secretary Arthur Goldberg, and 'the grandes dames... Rose Kennedy, Mrs Robert Woods Bliss.' Then there were Walter Lippmann, George Meany and 'a sprinkling of Puerto Ricans.'

Time comments lyrically: 'The evening was right out of the eighteenth century, it might have been a concert led by Haydn at the court of the Esterhazys or a command performance by C.P.E. Bach for Frederick the Great.'

Except that in the unenlightened days of the 'Aufklärung' Frederick the Great and the Esterhazys would never have had the opportunity to get to know those exotic guests, and except that Schumann and Mendelssohn do not happen to be eighteenth-century composers, and except a few other things…. I suppose *Time* was being sarky, but who can tell?

***

It was bad luck on Sir Martin Lindsay that the very day he tabled his motion deploring Lord Beaverbrook's and the *Express* group's alleged attacks on the royal family, the Duke of Edinburgh should have chosen to say to the press: 'The *Daily Express* is a bloody awful newspaper. It is full of lies, scandal, and imagination. It is a vicious newspaper.' Sir Martin Lindsay had just said that it was unfair to attack the royal family because royal persons are unable to answer back. The Duke's counterattack rather spoilt Sir Martin's knightly gesture.

I am an assiduous reader of many newspapers and periodicals. I nearly always disagree with the policies advocated by the *Daily Express,* which is notable for frivolous xenophobia, but I do not find it so scandalous, lying, or vicious as some others I could name, and furthermore I cannot recall a single word of criticism of the Queen in the *Daily Express.*

Sir Martin Lindsay says people can demonstrate their disapproval by cancelling the *Daily Express* and ordering a different newspaper, and so of course they can, all four million of them. Meanwhile, as the Duke of Edinburgh says, it is fun to be rude, and particularly so if nobody sues you for slander.

***

Next time Mr Harold Macmillan makes his countrymen feel embarrassed by wearing a white fur hat when he visits Moscow, or by saying, 'There ain't a'going to be no war,' so that they begin to wish they, or he, had never been born, they might reflect that things could be a good deal worse. Take Camelot. Mr Robert Kennedy, the Attorney General, and his wife gave a party at their home in Maclean, Virginia. Mrs Kennedy arranged a small table for three on planks across the swimming pool, and she invited a judge called Mr White and also Colonel Glenn, the astronaut, to sit with her there. She meant the judge and Colonel Glenn to fall into the pool, but according to a report of the party, 'Mr White, being an old friend knew what might happen so stayed away. Colonel Glenn managed to retain his balance and it was Mrs Kennedy who fell in. Later, Mr Arthur Schlesinger, the President's adviser, clad in a light blue dinner jacket, and Mrs Spencer Davis, a personal friend of Mrs Ethel Kennedy were pushed in.'

The Kennedys are so young that they and their personal friends have to push one another into pools at parties. Don't ask me what the difference is between a friend and a personal friend because I don't know, but in they all go.

Only a young country can contain so much youth. Stuffy old European judges and colonels might not want to be pushed fully dressed into swimming pools, but the fact that most of the personal friends are aged between 40 and 50 is the reason for ail the fun they have.

***

In the past, I have complained bitterly in this Diary of British Railways and their degraded and unpunctual trains, it is therefore only just to record that a recent journey to Newcastle and back was extremely comfortable.

The train was hot, in spite of snow outside, and the meals at least half as good as the meals on French trains, which, since they also cost half as much, seems about fair.

When the Channel tunnel is built the train journey between London and Paris will be roughly the same length as between London and Newcastle, and no doubt all comfort-lovers will choose to travel that

way. Quite apart from the chancy weather in northern Europe, which
has given rise to the adage:

Time to spare?

Go by air!

it is not everyone who cares, even in perfect weather, for the tedious
drive to London Airport and the numberless small irritations inflicted
upon the traveller when he finally gets there. Up and down moving
stairs which, as often as not, are stationary; herded into 'channels,' then
being made, after a long walk through the channels, to clamber into a
crowded charabanc in order to be driven a couple of hundred yards to
the aeroplane—none of this is much fun. Once inside the aeroplane, a
deafening roar heralds the distorted voice of the captain welcoming
you aboard the aircraft and hoping you will enjoy the flight, in two languages. Does anyone *enjoy* the flight? One does not fly for enjoyment,
but to get from A to B, it might be thought.

***

I often complain about the wrecking of the little that is left of beauty
in London, but there are one or two items on the credit side. Chief
among these is Apsley House, which, now that it stands alone, looks
enormously better than ever it did when it was the end of an undistin-
guished row.

On the blank part, where its neighbour was amputated, windows
and a cornice are being made. The usual mean grumbles at the cost of
this highly necessary and praise-worthy effort makes it doubly merito-
rious.

The Duke of Wellington, who generously gave the house and its
collection of glories to the nation, must be pleased at how splendid it
looks now.

Few people bother to go in to see the Goya portrait of the first
Duke, although thousands went to the National Gallery to look at the
empty space where the other Goya portrait, the one that was stolen,
had been.

***

Mrs Kennedy is so fond of art that she arranged for the Most Famous Picture In The World to be shown in Washington. This picture, which is also supposed to be the Most Valuable Picture In The World, but was not for sale, so that the Richest Country In The World couldn't buy it, is called by the French, who own it, '*La Joconde*,' and by the Anglo-Saxons, the 'Mona Lisa.'

When it arrived in Washington all the Best People were invited to see it unveiled. So were all the journalists, best and worst, and the television cameras. It was an occasion nobody was to be allowed to miss, because it was the outward and visible sign that the Kennedys were for art.

There were some complaints afterwards that everybody who was invited to see the picture had seen it before, without being half-crushed to death in the process.

***

Three Russian writers who sent their manuscripts to publishers abroad have been locked up in lunatic asylums by the Soviet authorities. The idea is that anyone in Russia who might come across some of their work would not be influenced by it because the authors are certified madmen.

The Russians have copied this straight from the Americans, who kept their poet, Ezra Pound, for many years in a madhouse in the most frightful conditions for the same bad reason: he disagreed with the government.

***

I see somebody wrote to the *Daily Express* urging people to spend their summer holidays at Waterloo. This was supposed to annoy the French, but I imagine it will annoy the Belgians more. It may end by annoying the holiday-makers most of all. There is nowhere to stay and nothing much to do at Waterloo but fight.

***

Probably most people were taken by surprise when they read that Sir Winston Churchill had been made an honorary citizen of the United States. They wrongly imagined that he was one already. He has always seemed very much a part of his mother's country, and has I suppose done more than any other single person to put it in the materially pre-eminent position it now occupies. From the American point of view he has earned citizenship many times over.

The message he sent across the Atlantic to be read at the ceremony is sad, in the context of today. It is over twenty years since Churchill proclaimed that he had not become first minister in order to preside over the break-up of the British Empire. Thus what happened was the opposite of his intentions, but many of us said at the time, if he lives long enough he will see it break up as a result of his policy: his 'great allies,' Soviet Russia and the United States, will make sure of it between them.

He has lived; he has observed the inevitable; and he emerges from his twilight to say: 'I reject the view that Britain and the Commonwealth should now be relegated to a tame and minor role in the world.'

But for him and for the politicians who succeeded him there would never have been the smallest doubt of a 'fertile and glorious' future for Britain and the Commonwealth. There is no doubt of it now. provided Britain will join with the rest of Europe to make the greatest nation the world has ever seen.

***

Mr Harold Wilson said in Parliament: 'there is something nauseating about a system of society which pays a harlot* 25 times as much as it pays its Prime Minister, 250 times as much as it pays its Members of

Parliament, and 500 times as much as it pays some of its ministers of religion.' Dame Rebecca West, commenting on this in the *Sunday Telegraph,* writes: 'Nobody sensible would go to a night club to see Members of Parliament coming down staircases dressed in sequins and tail feathers.'

Wouldn't they? I am not sure. As a confirmed loather of night clubs even I might be tempted from my hearth for such a Roman holiday.

* Miss Christine Keeler, who wrote her life story.

***

Mr Nehru has never been one of the most beloved foreign politicians in this country, in spite of his command of our language, his long terms of imprisonment under the British Raj, and all his other advantages and accomplishments. Now, however, there is sure to be a great swing in his favour. An opposition leader in the Indian parliament has angrily accused him of spending 3/6d a day on food for his dog. English people are bound to approve of this little extravagance; dogs to them are what cows are to the Indians, and they would rather vote for somebody who spent too much on his dog than too little. It is unlucky that Mr Nehru's dog has only just become a celebrity; there is no doubt that the massive aid to India would have been more kindly looked upon here had people known that some of it might find its way into some dear doggie's bowl.

***

The French wireless has a general knowledge programme. The other day I heard a boy who had chosen Napoleon as the greatest man of the nineteenth century asked his reasons for the choice. He replied after some hesitation: 'Well, he managed to annoy a good few people.'

Nearly every day one sees in the papers that some schoolmaster or other has forbidden boys to wear their hair with Beatle-like fringes. The masters' job is to impart learning and good manners, and it is not good manners to make personal remarks about other people's fringes. The way you cut your hair is a matter of fashion, and anyone who lives long enough will have the amusement of hearing schoolmasters of the future, who were boys when the Beatles were boys, forbid their pupils to brush their hair off their foreheads.

***

Headline of the month: LORDS IMPOTENT IN FACE OF FECUNDITY. The House of Lords debated the population explosion, and suggested several ways of damping it down, to which, doubtless, no attention will be paid. Since their last debate on the subject two years ago the population of the world has increased by a hundred million.

***

Although I sometimes love the amusing expressions they invent, I am not very partial to the way Americans use our language. 'He does not have' in place of 'He has not got' strikes oddly on English ears. Worse even than that, however, is the barbarous expression, 'as of now,' which is constantly cropping up in articles and speeches in the US. It means 'now,' and one would have thought 'now' would do.

***

Sir Isaiah Berlin, writing on the subject of Sir Winston Churchill's wartime speeches: 'This is the kind of means by which dictators and demagogues transform peaceful populations into marching armies: it was Mr Churchill's unique and unforgettable achievement that he created this necessary illusion within the framework of a free system without destroying or even twisting it.'

The trouble with newcomers who try to write about old England is that, no doubt through ignorance of our aged institutions, they perpetuate rubbish like the above. To imprison hundreds of patriotic people without charge or trial, and hold them in prisons and concentration camps for periods of up to five years as Churchill and his government did, can hardly be described as neither destroying nor even twisting the framework of a free system. Possibly Sir Isaiah Berlin has never heard of habeas corpus during his sojourn among us.

***

A friend writes from New York saying that whereas three years ago he was warned not to walk in Central Park after dark, this time he was told on no account to risk walking there at all, even in the daytime. He adds that nobody in his senses would 'ride the subway' (American for 'go by tube') at night, because even in a crowded carriage you may be knifed, and your fellow passengers would bury themselves in their favourite comics, pretending not to notice the corpse in their midst.

The day after I got this letter, I read in a paper that in future every underground train is to carry an armed policeman, in an attempt to check the number of murders.

The strange thing about these killings is that they are apparently not done for any special reason, like robbery for example. In this they resemble the murder described by André Gide in *Les Caves du Vatican*. As far as I remember, Lafcadio kills a man in the train between Rome and Naples, in order to find out what it feels like to be a murderer.

***

The Tory candidate who won the two Cities by-election last month is supposed to have wrecked the new image of the Tory Party. His crime or worse, his blunder was that he was educated at Eton. I don't imagine this was altogether his fault; most children have to go where they are told, and many of them would in fact much prefer to stay at home. An exception was the late Lord Bracken, who sent himself to school after interviewing various headmasters (or so he used to tell us).

In any case, the last three Conservative Prime Ministers all went to

Eton, and the one before that to Harrow, and it is only during the past few months that it has been ordained that nothing less than grammar schools will do. To have been to Eton is as bad, almost, as to have been caught shooting grouse.

It is somehow typical of the poor old Tories that they should be taken in by rubbish of this kind. Although there are many better schools than Eton, and many more profitable sports than grouse shooting—bingo, for example—it is not Eton and grouse that make one despise the Conservatives, it is what they have done to England. Their African policy, the subservience to America, the refusal to go into Europe: none of these evil things has much to do with education or pastimes.

A Talent to Annoy

GERMANY

Fly on the Wall

The author of *Eva and Adolf* tries to be a fly on the wall, for its subject is Hitler's private life. According to the publisher the book has been 'painstakingly researched'.

A clever man of my acquaintance uses a good formula when he is not certain of something: 'Don't know, so won't say'. To get at the truth about the sexual life of any individual is difficult; in the case of a politician or public man anxious to keep his private life to himself it is almost impossible. Although I met Eva Braun a few times and thought her pretty and charming, as to her affair with Hitler I don't know, so won't say. On the other hand, when it comes to Unity Mitford I know a great deal. The short chapter devoted to her is inaccurate. I counted twelve errors of fact. It would be tedious to list the inaccuracies; the most important of them is a scene supposedly enacted at Wahnfried, the Wagners' house in Bayreuth.

According to Mr Infield, Eva Braun and Unity both stayed there as guests of Hitler, in the house and in the annexe, for the festival. One evening Hitler and Unity were seen by a maid in a 'compromising position' on a veranda sofa. While the maid watched, Eva Braun, passing by, saw what was going on. She 'stared for a full minute then turned and disappeared into the darkness.' Everything about this tale is bogus. Anyone who knew Wahnfried would see its inherent implausibility, for during the Festspiele it is full of people, the family, musicians and other guests; a busy Bayreuth street would have been as good a choice for the scene described. But in fact neither Unity nor Eva Braun ever stayed at Wahnfried in their lives. Frau Winifred Wagner (the distinguished daughter-in law of the great composer) directed the festival and was hostess of Wahnfried in those days. She writes:

> Eva Braun was never in Wahnfried or in the Siegfried Wagner Haus (annexe) and, as far as I know, never in Bayreuth. Hitler never introduced her to me and never spoke about her. I never met her. Unity never stayed at Wahnfried or in the Siegfried

Wagner Haus, where Hitler lived when he visited the Festspiele. She visited me in Wahnfried, but I never met her in the Siegfried Wagner Haus when Hitler lived here.

Therefore whatever and whoever was seen by the 'maid' it was certainly not Unity Mitford or Eva Braun. When the *Sunday Express* announced its serialization of *Eva and Adolf,* I wrote to the editor telling him there were numerous mistakes in the chapter about Unity. On 9 September I expressed a letter to him with Frau Wagner's words, showing that the Bayreuth episode never in fact happened. He acknowledged this in a letter dated 11 September, but nevertheless published the story in the *Sunday Express* on 14 September.

In a second, subsequent letter Frau Wagner is categoric: she never had such a maid. Mr Infield's book has some rather interesting passages; all the more curious that he should include the silly story of 'what the maid saw'.

Eva and Adolf, Infield, G., *Books and Bookmen,* 1975

Truth, Lies and Opinions

Otto Dietrich, German *Reichspressechef,* was a pleasant, mild, well-mannered, modest little man, with (as was once said with less reason of an English politician) plenty to be modest about. After the war, finding himself in an English prison camp, he wrote this gossipy book about his twelve years at Hitler's court. It was meant, presumably, to explain away his past.

Apart from a few disobliging references to various colleagues he devotes himself to a lengthy attack on the Führer, whom he suddenly discovered, while he sat in prison, to have been the devil incarnate. His book would not be worth mentioning were it not that the gossipy facts it contains are true. Dr Dietrich's *opinions,* on the other hand, are of no interest, except to show how far sycophancy can go. Unfortunately they make up the bulk of his apology.

Many of them are incredibly naive. For example, he gives as his reasons for thinking democracy the best form of government the fact that Hitler did not consult the German electorate before he went to war. Perhaps he imagined that the English voters were consulted before Chamberlain declared war on Germany? If so, he was ignorant of the democratic way of life. The Americans, of course, had the benefit of a presidential election in November 1940, but Roosevelt, the successful candidate, pledged himself not to send American 'boys' overseas to fight in Europe's quarrels. He may have been determined to bring his country into the war, but he had to pretend that he was determined to keep it neutral.

Dr Dietrich says that Hitler's suicide was a shirking of his responsibility. 'His departure from life was in terms of: 'After me the deluge'. Europeans all through history have chosen what Germans call the *Freitod* in like circumstances, and this judgment in itself clearly shows that Dr Dietrich's conception of honour and of duty is faulty, even if his whole book did not demonstrate this.

The translators have done an excellent job, though they appear to be unaware that daemon and demon are not the same thing.

The Hitler I Knew, Dietrich, O. (1955)

Hitler's Court Jester

'Hanfstaengl was a gay and amusing companion,' writes Mr Brian Connell, the man who has set down these reminiscences in English. 'People have said I was Hitler's court jester,' adds Dr [Putzi] Hanfstaengl himself.

The Hanfstaengl family belong to Germany's intellectual middle class; they print art reproductions and sell them in a Munich shop. Putzi's mother was American: he was sent to Harvard and remained in America to manage the New York branch of the business. He was 27 when the first war began; he stayed on in the shop in Fifth Avenue. During and after the second war he spent seven years of considerable hardship in English, Canadian and American concentration camps, except for a short time when his offer to help the Allies in their 'psychological warfare 'against Germany was rather half-heartedly taken up by Roosevelt. (The Central European Jews who ran this side of the war never cared much for Putzi.)

His claim to fame is that he knew Hitler well, and saw a good deal of him between 1923 and the middle 30s. More than twelve years have passed since Hitler died, and it may seem astonishing that Dr Hanfstaengl should still feel obliged to write with such exaggerated spite about the man he was once so proud to call his friend. But in so far as he was a close associate of the Führer (and 'court jester' neatly sums up this association) or in so far as he was a National Socialist, he evidently feels bound to excuse himself to his Anglo-Saxon readers. It is as if he imagined they were lying in wait to see what he would say, ready to pop him back behind bars if he is not abusive enough. This attitude of his places him in a dilemma. He wishes to sell his memoirs, therefore he must write about the only interesting thing that ever happened to him—his connection with Hitler. He has to have been an intimate, yet the Führer must be a monster; he has to have been an influential counsellor, whose courageously sharp criticisms and sage foresight were nevertheless ignored; he has to have been prominent in the Nazi hierarchy, yet all the time devoted to the American way of life. Thus he calls upon memory for fact, upon imagination for fiction, and the unity of his book suffers in consequence.

It is a safe guess that most readers will skip the pages about the Hanfstaengl pedigree to get to the man in the shabby suit, spell-binding his Munich audiences and charming Putzi's dollars out of his pocket to pay for a printing press for the Party newspaper. It is the eye-witness account of the famous Bürgerbräukeller meeting, the Putsch, Hitler's trial and his imprisonment in Landsberg which, historically, is the valuable part of the book.

On the 9th of November 1923 the marching column of demon-strators, led by Ludendorff and Hitler, was fired on by the police in the narrow street near the Feldherrnhalle; sixteen men were killed, among them Scheubner-Richter whose arm was linked in Hitler's. His fall dis-located Hitler's shoulder, and it was in this condition that he made his way to the Hanfstaengls' country cottage at Uffing. Putzi, along with many others including the badly wounded Goering, had fled to Austria. Frau Hanfstaengl took Hitler in, and it was at the Uffing villa that the police arrested him two days later.

Dr Hanfstaengl's was far from being the only family of substance to support Hitler at that time. On the eve of his trial, for example, Frau Bechstein* visited him in prison. She gave him a bouquet of flowers and embraced him, saying: '*Wolf! Wir stehen immer zu Dir!*' ['We shall always stand by you.'] Back in his cell, Hitler discovered half a bottle of champagne concealed among the flowers, which he drank next morn-ing before going into court. The Führer told me this story himself.

Months later, when Putzi visited him in Landsberg, 'the place looked like a delicatessen store. You could have opened up a flower and fruit and a wine shop with all the stuff stacked there. People were sending presents from all over Germany.'

Apart from the loan of his invaluable dollars at a time of gallop-ing inflation Hitler liked Dr Hanfstaengl's company and his piano-playing and his drollery. Hitler himself, as Putzi relates, 'was a gifted mimic with a sharp sense of the ridiculous. His star turn was a sort of symposium of the type of patriotic orator then very common in Germany, and by no means extinct since—the politically conscious, semi-professorial figure with a Wotan-like beard. Hitler's nationalism was practical and direct, but they would boom away about Siegfried's sword being drawn out of its scabbard and lightning playing round the German eagle and so forth. He could invent this mock rhodomontade *ad infinitum* and be very funny about it.' He would also recite a poem written to him by one of his admirers 'with embellish-ments of his own, and have us in tears of laughter.' But Hanfstaengl, not content with being the boon companion of a leisure hour, hoped (so he says) to influence Hitler politically; an idea which anyone who knew both men would find grotesque.

When the National Socialists came to power he was given the job of foreign press relations officer. In a way he was well fitted for this; he spoke excellent English, knew many American newspaper men, and was popular and hail-fellow-well-met. What, then, went wrong with this enthusiastic Nazi, wearing a smart uniform he designed himself, enjoying his new status to the full (he says his telephone never stopped ringing, even the barest acquaintances were anxious to claim friendship with the man who was the Führer's friend), and playing the part—this I can vouch for myself—of *der treueste aller Treuen* [the most faithful of the faithful]—what went wrong?

This book provides the answer. Dr Hanfstaengl, while professing love and loyalty to Hitler himself, loathed with bitter hatred every single person in his entourage. Men like Goering and Himmler, who seldom saw the Führer, are let off lightly, but those who were frequently in his company, from the brilliant Dr Goebbels to the faithful Schaub, are heaped with scorn and abuse. He made no secret of his feelings, and it appears that he regaled foreign press correspondents with every kind of tittle tattle and stories of real or imagined strains and stresses within the Party. Naturally enough, this came to Hitler's ears, and the enemies Putzi so recklessly made saw to it that his attacks on members of the government were repeated to the victims. Annoyed by these reports, Hitler invited him less and less often, thereby increasing his bitterness. After a time his post virtually ceased to exist; foreign journalists were directed to other channels. For old time's sake this was done gradually and unobtrusively; the only wonder was that it had not happened sooner. A modern English equivalent would be the appointment of Mr Malcolm Muggeridge as Buckingham Palace press relations officer.

Not long afterwards he left Germany; the result of a practical joke. Court jesters seldom care about jokes against themselves.

Hearing one evening that Putzi was in the habit of saying that he wished he could have fought in the 1914 war, but that keeping a shop in New York of which the window was smashed by anti-German Americans had been more disagreeable than life in the trenches. Hitler said that if he really longed for battle he had his chance at last: he could volunteer to fight in Spain where civil war was raging. He then imagined how funny it would he to pretend to gratify this life-long wish, to pretend to he flying him to Spain to be parachuted behind the Red lines while in reality he was flown from one German airfield to another. Probably after elaborating this idea in his inimitable way and acting Putzi in the *Kampfzeit* when he thought there were Reds lurking round the next corner) the whole thing went out of Hitler's head. Among those who heard him, however, there were several with old scores to pay off. The practical joke was carried out. Starting from Berlin on a 'special mission 'to Salamanca, headquarters of the Franco press, Putzi was told in the aeroplane that he was to he dropped behind the Red lines. By the time he landed (at Leipzig) he was in a great stew. He took the first train to Switzerland, convinced that the Gestapo was after him. Goering, contrite that the joke had gone with such a bang, wrote begging him to come home and offering him a job in the Four-year-plan. He refused.

Dr Hanfstaengl announces with pride (or at any rate with satisfaction) to his Anglo-Saxon audience that after the war he found his name on a Gestapo blacklist. Probably it was there because during the war he was released from the Allied concentration camp for a time in connection with the Americans' psychological warfare, an activity which can take a very dangerous turn according to which side loses the war. But Putzi's hosts, of course, won the war.

Back in Munich since 1946, he has now broken his long silence. Some people might think he has got his values mixed up. He is ashamed of what he should be proud of, proud of what he should he ashamed of. However that may be, his book contains interesting material about events and scenes he lived through. Where he is forced, through lack of first hand evidence, to speculate about Hitler's private life, we cannot do better than quote Mr Brian Connell once again. when he praises Putzi for his 'inextinguishable capacity for embroidering an anecdote and total lack of inhibition in his remarks and comments.'

* 'Frau Bechstein belonged to the piano manufacturing family.

Hitler: The Missing Years, Hanfstaengl, E. (1957)

❋

The Lie Merchant?

Are these diaries genuine? The reasons for asking are twofold. First, where have they been all these years? Second, they would have been very easy to invent. They contain nothing that could remotely be called new. The bulk is made up of the OKW [*Oberkommando der Wehrmacht*] reports, which are frankly, in 1978, rather dull reading because everyone knows what was happening in Germany in March 1945. The Russians were nearing Berlin, having overrun Prussia, Pomerania and Silesia, raping and plundering and destroying everything they could lay hands on. The Allies were 'area bombing', with fire storms burning hundreds of thousands of men, women and children and demolishing the houses of those who survived. Roads were choked with refugees, everything had broken down. American and British armies were advancing in the West. There was nothing left of Germany, it was done for. The future was epidemics, starvation, humiliation, disaster.

This was the apocalyptic background of the diaries, which begin on the 27 February and end on 9 April, 1945. Anyone vaguely familiar with Goebbels could have written them; they are not in his hand but are supposed to have been dictated to a secretary, which makes them long-winded. Probably they are genuine. I expect they would have been spicier if they had been invented, and more in the style of *I Was Hitler's Maid.*

Why did Hitler, supported by Goebbels and others, not capitulate sooner? Probably because, knowing that confrontation between Russia and the West was inevitable, they thought the Allies might move to prevent the Soviets from occupying half of Europe. This was, of course, a delusion, but it was not so fanciful as it is sometimes made out to be.

In 1954 Winston Churchill made a speech in his constituency in which he said

> Even before the war had ended, and while the Germans were surrendering by hundreds of thousands... I telegraphed to Lord Montgomery directing him to be careful in collecting the German arms, to stack them so that they could easily be issued again to the German soldiers whom we should have to work with if the Soviet advance continued.

There was a fuss about this speech at the time, and the telegram to Montgomery could not be found. But it shows the trend of Churchill's thoughts after Yalta, and that his thoughts had been rightly guessed by Hitler and Goebbels. They did not reckon with the Americans, infinitely more powerful than the British, who in 1945 were so pro-Russian that on various sectors of the front they halted in order to give the Russians time to advance further into Europe.

In a way the most interesting part of this book is the introduction by Hugh Trevor-Roper. It is more than thirty years since he wrote *The Last Days of Hitler*. Although with the passage of time a fairly objective view might have been expected, the Professor sums up Goebbels's propaganda as 'crude and violent in form, utterly unscrupulous in substance, and quite indifferent to truth'. This is evidently still the accepted point of view; it has not been thought necessary to give examples of Goebbels's mendacity.

It is something of a mystery why Goebbels is always supposed to have been such a liar: a 'lie merchant'. I am very much opposed to a government-controlled press and to censorship, but there is no doubt that during the years 1933 to 1943 Dr Goebbels had such a success story on his hands that he had no need to lie. The economic revival of Germany under the National Socialists was speedy and impressive. Hitler's thesis, that a country's riches consist of the quality of its people (*Volk*), made him reject the idea that Germany was 'ruined' just because it had no foreign exchange, a stagnant economy and six million unemployed when he took over. It was their work that could enrich it. Industry, agriculture and the building of a modern infrastructure absorbed the unemployed, and Germany became prosperous in a remarkably short time. Although without doubt Goebbels as propaganda minister saw to it that 'the Whig dogs got the worst of it', he had no reason to lie.

During the first years of the war when German armies were winning battles the same thing applied. He only had to tell the truth. When the tide turned he had more reason to lie because of the importance of morale on the home front. But here again he was rather truthful; for example he did not seek to underrate the disaster to German arms at Stalingrad.

Describing Goebbels's character and personality, Mr Trevor Roper several times says he had an 'inner emptiness'. I am not quite sure what this means. Goebbels was an educated man, a doctor of philosophy, well-read. He was extremely busy and he obviously enjoyed his work. Was he suffering from 'inner emptiness'? Very hard to say.

I knew him fairly well. He was clever, good company, always ready with a sarcastic witticism. His wife and children loved him, his associates, several of whom I knew, admired and liked him. One of them, Prince zu Schaumburg-Lippe, wrote a book eulogizing him when this was an unpopular, even dangerous, thing to do, after the war.

I stayed with the Goebbels at their villa at Schwanenwerder on Wannsee—'luxuriously furnished', according to Trevor-Roper. It was comfortable, but by no effort of the imagination could it have been called luxurious. He also says that in Berlin Goebbels had 'his palatial residence near the Brandenburg Gate'. Palatial? I knew the house: it was his official residence as minister. It was not as palatial as number 11 Downing Street, where I also stayed long ago when Churchill was chancellor of the exchequer. To English readers a palatial residence means a big house, Londonderry House for example, or even a house in Belgrave Square or Grosvenor Square. The Goebbels's house in Hermann Goeringstrasse was not in the same league as any of these. Why get it so very wrong?

Maybe there is not much evidence to blast him with, and he must be blasted. Goebbels was against the war in 1939, as Speer has testified. His courage and his loyalty cannot be impugned. Hence the 'inner emptiness' and the 'palatial residence'. Goebbels's reading (Carlyle and Schopenhauer are mentioned) is disapproved of; it is not what we should wish an English propaganda minister to indulge in.

His opposite number in England during the war was Brendan Bracken. a man I also happened to know rather well. I was quite fond of Brendan, but even his best friend could not claim that he was truthful. His whole life was one long lie; he pretended to be an Australian orphan whereas in reality he was Irish and had a mother living in Templemore, Co Tipperary. While he was minister of propaganda a misfortune occurred. Illustrated pornographic leaflets, which had been concocted in his ministry by German-speaking émigrés, and which were supposed to be dropped on German soldiers stationed on the Spanish frontier in order to 'weaken their resistance' (sic), blew away in a freak storm, and one of them landed on a golf course in Surrey. J.B. Hynd, a prim Labour MP, went to complain to the minister.

Brendan was quite ready for him. He told Mr Hynd:

> As a man of the world who claims to understand the German mentality, you shouldn't be surprised at the lengths to which Goebbels will go. You're playing into Goebbels's hands at this moment. Goebbels knows of the divided counsels here about British propaganda activities, and that's no doubt why he and his henchmen have taken the trouble to despatch the balloons and those obnoxious leaflets just to exacerbate the divisions as you're now doing.

Mr Hynd was contrite. This tale is from Andrew Boyle's *Poor, Dear Brendan*, indispensable reading for anyone interested in lie merchants.

The Goebbels Diaries, ed. Trevor-Roper, H., *Books and Bookmen* (1978)

❄

A Liturgical Bob and Go

One chapter in Father Brocard Sewell's delightful autobiography is 'At odds with the Red Hat'. There's none called 'At odds with the Triple Tiara',* but there very well might have been. Father Brocard regrets, as all lovers of beauty and tradition must, the abandonment of the ancient liturgy. Because it was in Latin, it made the Catholic Church truly universal, with the same services in the same words the whole world over. He bitterly regrets the impoverishment of religious life in its outward manifestations. The distress caused by the Vatican Council was widespread. It killed Evelyn Waugh.

Father Brocard is a Carmelite priest, an expert on type and printing, and the author of several books on fairly obscure writers of the end of the nineteenth century. He was born to Protestant parents, and says he became a Catholic because, as a very religious boy, he suffered from acute boredom in the chapel of his low-church school.

After his conversion, as a young man, he worked for G.K. Chesterton's magazine *GK's Weekly*. Deciding that his vocation was for monastic life, he became a novice of the Dominican Order.

In 1941 he joined the RAF, and is wonderfully funny about his wartime adventures. He ended up in Germany, in 1945. There were strict rules about no fraternisation, of which he took not the slightest notice. He still sees his friends from Wulfrath, which is now 'twinned' with Ware.

After the war he decided not to go back to the Dominicans, and joined the Order of the Canons Regular of the Lateran; though finally he transferred to the Carmelites, and was ordained a priest at Aylesford Priory in 1954.

For many years he edited the *Aylesford Review*, in which he often supported unpopular and unfashionable causes if he thought them right. It was his courage and independence which got him into trouble with the hierarchy and the Cardinal. When the spirit moved him he did not hesitate to write to *The Times*.

Perhaps we should be thankful that at least Cardinals still have red hats, even if their trains have been docked. Father Brocard is glad that during his time in Rome, at the Carmelite college, there was still the old Roman splendour, before, as he says, Popes were given paupers' funerals.

* The Pope.

The Habit of a Lifetime, Sewell, B., *Evening Standard* (1992)

A Matter of Class

When General Fuller was appointed military assistant to the CIGS the *Sunday Express* described him as 'probably by far the cleverest man in the Army'. This was in 1926, when Fuller was 47; he was already well known as a writer on military matters. A professional soldier, he had fought in the Boer War as a very young man; during the First World War he served on the stall in France. He did not invent the tank, but when this new weapon appeared on the scene in 1916 he was the soldier who immediately understood its potential. Since he had no power to direct the method of deploying the tanks they were largely wasted, but then and after the war he devoted his brilliant intelligence and far-seeing imagination to tanks and mechanized warfare.

It goes without saying that although a younger generation of army officers agreed with them, the old generals paid little attention to Fuller's theories. Field Marshal Montgomery Massingberd, for example, was still talking about the necessity of using tanks to support cavalry at the end of 1928. But if Fuller's books were largely ignored in England they were read, admired and understood, and his precepts acted upon, in Germany. Shortly before World War II General Fuller was invited to a military parade in Berlin. Thousands of tanks thundered down Unter den Linden. Hitler greeted him afterwards with the words: 'I hope you were pleased with your children?'

Some of our generals were stuck in 1914, but it was the politicians who ruled Britain in the 20s and early 30s who were criminally negligent of our country's defence. Completely frustrated, Fuller left the army in 1933 to devote himself to writing. The only politician who insisted that Britain must be armed in an armed world, and that it must be equipped with a modern mechanized force, was Oswald Mosley. For this reason General Fuller joined the British Union of Fascists in 1934.

Brilliance is not always considered an asset in England, but how did it come about that General Fuller, who was not only the cleverest man in the army but a military thinker of genius and a first rate writer, was completely unheeded in official circles? The author of *'Boney' Fuller: The Intellectual General* gives a wonderfully frank answer:

> His relative lack of success as a soldier was in part due to the cause of mechanization, which he espoused too strongly and too early from the point of view of his career interests; but it was also due to central factors of his personality, his extreme intellectual competence, his superlative rationality, his barbed and irrepressible wit, his somewhat clinical human relations, his rejection of compromise even when his future was at stake.

He was regarded by many senior officers as 'too clever by half', and he had an 'impossible wife'. 'He was an uncomfortable and all too aggressively cerebral member of the military organization' writes Brigadier Trythall. 'Uncomfortable' is strangely enough the very word used about him by Fuller's noted disciple, Adolf Hitler. A great admirer, he once asked me whether the General might not be an *'Unbequemer'* in an organization. Mosley never found him so, he was a loyal and splendid colleague. On the other hand for stupid people he was uncomfortable, with his rapid and sarcastic manner of pointing out their inadequate processes of thought. Liddell Hart, the other English military genius of the century, maintained close friendship with Fuller for many decades: he sought his company and obviously did not find him uncomfortable. As to the 'impossible wife', Mrs Fuller's admiration for Boney was boundless and her loyalty to him absolute. True, she had a strong foreign accent, either Polish or German, but as a convinced European with an ineradicable English accent I cannot accept that this made her 'impossible'.

It was Fuller's patriotism and concern for our defences that took him into the British Union of Fascists, and it was his patriotism which made him oppose the second World War. He saw at once that, win or lose, this war would be the end of Britian's greatness. If, however, once the fatal war had been declared, his advice had been asked, there would most likely have been no lightning defeat of France in 1940. The Allied armies had more tanks than the Germans, but it was the Germans who used their armour in accordance with Fuller's text books on mechanized warfare. As he used to say: 'The greater the mass of the opposing infantry the greater the victory of the armoured divisions.' Even if some of the soldiers had found him uncomfortable his expertise, his professionalism, his intelligence, would have been of incalculable value to Britain, fighting for its life. 'Extreme intellectual competence' is not considered a grave disadvantage by everyone. General de Gaulle is quoted as having asked in 1943, 'What about your best soldier, General Fuller?... I have often wondered why he is never used.' Admittedly General Fuller had no great opinion of Mr Churchill, whom he once described as the greatest mountebank since Nero, 'but Nero had the better of him in that he committed suicide when comparatively young; that, at least, was a decent act', he added characteristically. He had an 'intellectual disapproval of Churchill's political aims and military strategies, and emotional distaste for Churchill's style.'

A letter in *The Times* recently pointed out what strangely childish nicknames our generals in World War II were known by: Squeaker, Boy, Jumbo, Pip, Bubbles. Fuller's nickname was Boney, the name the English gave Napoleon during the Napoleonic wars. With his small stature and sharp intellect it suited him admirably; a name any soldier would be proud to bear.

Brigadier Trythall's biography is excellent in many ways, an enthralling book. He often allows Fuller to speak for himself, and when he does so the brilliance and charm of the man come across.

Perhaps I should declare an interest: I was devoted to General Fuller and delighted in his clever conversation and sarcastic, unkind jokes; I was also very fond of Mrs Fuller.

'Boney' Fuller: The Intellectual General, Trythall, A.J., *Books and Bookmen* (1977)

More Violence than Politics

A book called *Political Violence and Public Order*, by an American, might well be about the tragic situation in Northern Ireland, but a glance at the photograph on the jacket shows mounted police, not armoured. cars and tanks. In fact, Mr Benewick's book (a product of the flourishing PhD industry) deals with not very violent violence. He has no bombs to record, no gunmen, no arms and legs blown off, not a single death. It is a history of fascism in England in the 30s, but only of a fractional part of fascism: the part connected with violence.

The hundreds of public meetings, where attentive audiences listened to Sir Oswald Mosley's economic and social policy for what was then a very sick country with over two million unemployed, are hardly mentioned. It is not politics but violence that interests Mr Benewick. Meetings and marches where there were clashes between fascists and communists are described at length. They were fascist meetings and fascist marches, and they were attacked by communists. This is known as fascist violence; had a communist meeting been attacked by fascists, presumably it would have been communist violence. If a notable orator, putting forward a quite difficult argument., has assembled a crowd of people many of whom have paid for their seats to listen to a speech, he and his stewards are unlikely to attack their audience.

After the Olympia meeting, which a large number of communists, drummed up for days before by the *Daily Worker*, tried to smash, Lloyd George wrote (*Sunday Pictorial*, 24 June 1934) 'The Blackshirts secured an audience of 15,000 people to pack the huge exhibition hall.... I feel that men who enter meetings with the deliberate intention of suppressing free speech have no right to complain if an exasperated audience handles them rudely.' Strangely enough, this defence of Mosley by an ex-Prime Minister is not mentioned in the long account Mr Benewick gives of the Olympia meeting. It is omissions such as this which show a certain bias.

The other charge made is that Mosley and his fascists provocatively marched through East London, said to have been hostile to them. It is worth remembering that a large proportion of the men who marched were in fact citizens of East London, and that it was there the fascist candidates polled 19 of the votes at municipal elections in 1937, elections where only householders, that is by and large older people, had the vote. Among young people in that part of London Mosley had mass support.

Far from it being the fascists who 'invaded' East London, they considered it was they who had been invaded from foreign parts by people who could not even speak English, but who were handy with foreign notions of how to fight a man they disagreed with, such as throwing potatoes with razor blades stuck in them.

In Mr Benewick's book there are slovenly mistakes and misspelt names, and he is at times grossly inaccurate. There is a bad example of this on page 162: 'Mosley could say without any hesitation... from the bottom of my heart, "Heil Hitler".' These words were in fact written by Captain Gordon-Canning MC, an ex-10th Hussar, in a contribution to *The Blackshirt*. In both style and content they are so unlike anything Mosley ever wrote (*le style c'est l'homme*) that no intelligent person who had made a detailed study of him could conceivably make this particular mistake, and Mr Benewick is not unintelligent. An historian would check the origins of so controversial a statement.

'The combination of slow promotion, unsettled beliefs, personality conflicts...' these according to Mr Benewick are the reasons why Mosley left the old parties. Slow promotion? At the age of 32, Mosley was the Minister charged with the hardest task facing the government of the day: how to solve the unemployment problem. It would not be easy to find an example this century of quicker promotion. It was because not only the policy he devised but any action at all was refused that he decided to build a grass roots movement. He had no support-ing press and had to speak, and be heard, or give up. Mr Benewick describes him as 'an outstanding leader whose appeal reached charis-matic dimensions', which sounds like an American compliment. Attacked, he and his men defended themselves, and that is the begin-ning and end of fascist violence.

Would an Englishman's thesis on the burning and looting of American cities by rioters in 1967, or on the Democratic Convention in Chicago in 1968, be any better than Mr Benewick's? In order to rank as history, it would certainly need to be more carefully researched.

Political Violence and Public Order, Benewick, R., *Books and Bookmen* (1969)

❋

Blood on the Walls

The dust jacket of *To Build a New Jerusalem* is as old-fashioned as the title. Watched by the founding fathers, from Marx to Attlee, a grim looking 'worker' emerges, brilliant sun behind him, from the ruins of Westminster, St Paul's, and some factories. Below is a photograph of a vast crowd, wearing caps, hats, or even boaters, which must be very ancient. Superimposed, giving the V sign, is Neil Kinnock, strayed into the revolutionary past.

A.J. Davies has written a fair, useful history of the Labour move-ment, its idealism and its internal quarrels, so bitter at one time as to make it unfit to govern. During the long years in opposition it has shed its most unpopular beliefs, Clause 4, and unilateralism. The word socialism seems to be taboo, presumably because of socialism's eco-nomic failure wherever it has been seriously tried. 'Labourism' is what A.J. Davies calls it, just when the name Labour is under threat, as being outworn.

What he calls 'the battle of Cable Street' in 1936, never in fact took place. The British Union obeyed a police order to about turn before contact with its enemies, to the great disappointment of all. There was no fight, let alone a battle; just a few scuffles of left-wing supporters with the police dispersing them. It is a myth, believed as myths so often are.

Can Labour win this time? We shall very soon know. It is anybody's guess.

Willie Hamilton is a Durham miner's son, famous for disliking the royal family and for trumpeting his republican views in and out of Parliament. *Blood on the Walls* is a fearsome title, which puts us in mind of a cellar at Ekaterinburg, or torture in some vile prison. But Hamilton's rather engaging book is not about red revolution, and contains no diatribes against the Queen. All his hatred is concentrated upon Mrs Thatcher. As she has retired, like Willie Hamilton himself, it is already out of date.

He thinks our monarchy is unnecessary, he would like to see it abolished, along with the House of Lords, but he is realist enough to know the huge majority would never allow any such thing to happen. He only wishes the Queen would pay taxes, which is rather tame after so much sound and fury for so many years.

He describes the frightful life of a miner in the 20s, and of the miner's wife, his parents. There were no pit-head baths. She washed the coal dust off him in her kitchen. She cleaned and cooked and baked, there was one cold tap, she struggled to feed her family on a miserable wage, and to buy them clothes and boots. Baldwin's wicked deflation in 1926, the starving of the miners into submission after the General Strike collapsed, all this is well told and grim enough, even if the blood on the wall comes from the bugs which infested their wretched slum.

Anyone with enthusiasm for the good old days should read about Willie Hamilton's childhood. It explains his dislike of Mrs T. Nobody could pretend the grinding poverty, the bitterness of unemployment the frightful conditions of those days were the fault of the royal family. The Tories were in power and they did nothing.

To Build A New Jerusalem: The Labour Movement from the 1880s to the 1990s,
Davies, A.J. (1992); *Blood On The Walls*, Hamilton, W. (1992), *Evening Standard* (1992)

Spies Good and Bad

The Germans have a proverb: 'He who betrays once, will always betray.' Or in other words, a traitor is a traitor. The game of foxes proves the truth of this again and again. Spies, double spies, triple spies, they probably hardly cared whom they doublecrossed in the murky world at war wherein they flourished.

The game of the foxes is a dirty game, without rules. The stakes are high because you play with death, the rewards are meagre because nobody can acknowledge the cat's paw. Only half trusted by his superiors, the spy ends by being completely untrustworthy, a flawed man. From the humble agent right up to the very top there is a vileness met with in no other profession. Admiral Canaris, for example, sometimes served his country and at other times sought to betray it.

According to the author, who has had a good look at the secret files of the *Abwehr*, Canaris tried to recruit agents in England among members of British Union. He failed, as anyone familiar with English politics could have told him he was bound to do. There is a whole world of difference between the political opposition of patriotic men to a war which, win or lose, they considered was certain to be disastrous for their own country, and helping its enemy to secure its defeat. There has been an English tradition of political opposition to war; Charles James Fox's attitude during the Napoleonic wars is one example. Mosley and his party followed this tradition, during the first months of the second world war, sometimes called the phoney war period.

Quite different from ordinary spying is the skilled work of decoding and unscrambling. When Churchill, ensconced in his bomb-proof shelter, spoke on the telephone to Roosevelt in Washington, both men imagined that their conversations were private because their hot line was scrambled to the last degree. Sometimes, apparently, they talked frivolously, but often what they said was of great value to the Germans, and in particular to the U-boats. One guesses, given the nature of the two men, that they talked far more than was strictly necessary. Every word was heard and recorded in Germany; not by the *Abwehr*, but by the Post Office. It was the triumph of the German equivalent of our Postmaster General, Reichsminister Ohnesorge, and a brilliant team of engineers. They invented an unscrambler, so that within a couple of hours the Allied leaders' conversations were received in the appropriate quarters.

The British government also had its successes. One of these was Operation Doublecross, the object of which was to mislead the Luftwaffe into dropping its bombs on non-strategic targets that would in no way impede the war effort. This it brilliantly did. The choice of the actual targets lay with the politicians, and Mr Churchill was considered 'rather callous'. This 'led to a violent clash between the Prime Minister and Herbert Morrison.' Morrison objected to the selection of working class residential districts as targets for the bombs.

Now that we are all friends again in what we hope is to become united Europe, it may be of interest to the Germans to learn that long before he had the opportunity to order the blanket fire-bombing of German civilians in non-strategic open cities, Mr Churchill had chosen English working class residential districts as targets for the Luftwaffe. *C'est la guerre*. Mr Farago calls Mr Churchill's Operation Doublecross 'somewhat fiendish'. But a very great many of the doings recorded in this exciting book are fiendish to a degree, and it shows there is no limit to the devilish ingenuity of the civilised countries once they are bent upon destroying one another.

For the politicians, and even for the soldiers, all that matters is to win. If you win you are given a statue; a doubtful benefit, perhaps, for we lack a Verrocchio. But if you lose, everything from run of the mill contingency planning to the deliberate bombing of civilians may land you in some Nuremberg of the victors' devising.

The Game of the Foxes, Farago, L., *Books and Bookmen* (1972)

✳

Hitler and British Politics

The impact of Hitler on English politics was heavy. During the 30s, policy practically came to mean foreign policy. Recently published figures show that from 1933 to 1937 the Cabinet discussed foreign and imperial affairs 1,480 times, compared with 11 for education, 20 for housing and 47 for unemployment. The old familiar quarrels about protection versus free trade, or whether the prayerbook should be revised, faded into insignificance. As the author points out, in the 20s few could be found to defend the manifest anomalies of the Versailles treaty; the Labour party in particular was loud in demanding revision. But when Hitler came upon the scene and wanted the talk translated into action there was a lukewarm response both from England and from the League of Nations.

Collective security had been the keystone of League policy. It was an excellent idea, but when it came under pressure at the time of sanctions against Italy over Abyssinia it melted away until England remained as its sole protagonist. Since the English had no wish to fight for Abyssinia, sanctions were a half-hearted fiasco, and collective security collapsed and was shown to be an illusion.

The 1935 plebiscite in the Saar was another turning point. English newspapers had argued as to whether the Saarlanders would vote for the status quo (League of Nations rule) or for France. English soldiers kept guard to ensure the secrecy of the ballot. A little over ninety per cent voted for incorporation in Hitler's Reich. This was about the usual proportion in plebiscites within Germany, but the English press always pointed out that these votes were faked, therefore it came as a surprise. After this disappointing result in the Saar nobody wanted plebiscites in disputed territories: self-determination, once a popular League idea, had lost its savour in the democracies.

With the failure of collective security and the certainty that self-determination would mean that the brand-new country Czechoslovakia and the artificially swollen Romania and Poland would lose extensive territories which should never have been allotted to them in the first place, Britain's foreign policy was in disarray.

The author, by means of innumerable quotations from his victims, has no difficulty in showing the politicians of the 30s in an unfavourable light. Never enamoured of them myself, it is ever so disheartening to see the whole lot, from Lloyd George and Churchill down to the very small fry, so avid of place and power, so jealous, disloyal and hypocritical, and so notably lacking in the essential talent of a statesman: that of being able to see a little further than the next man.

The vitally important question is, should England have intervened in a frontier dispute between Germany and Czechoslovakia? Was it a British interest? Was Britain's frontier on the Rhine, the Oder or the Vistula? It is merely an academic question; we cannot 'learn from history' because England was so weakened by the war that such a role is now unthinkable.

Chamberlain's whole policy may have been misconceived, but according to his lights he did his best for peace. He had to take into account not only 'Herr Hitler and his methods', deprecated by everybody, but also France, the alliance between France and Russia, Italy, the Balkans, Japan and its aggression in the Far East, and above all the strains and stresses within the Tory party and its unfortunate accretions (a legacy of 1931) of National Labour and National Liberals. The rump of the Labour party in parliament and in journals like the *New Statesman* demanded intervention in every war from Spain to Manchuria, while at the same time ardently advocating the disarmament of Britain. Chamberlain was sniped at from all sides, although he was encouraged by a mild popularity among non-politicians; it is doubtful whether any available leader of the Conservative party could have done much more than he did.

English politicians were wonderfully ignorant of European history and Chamberlain spoke but the bare truth when he said Czechoslovakia was a far-away country of which they knew little. The same applied to Poland, guaranteed in 1939, that the prophecy of Lloyd George in 1919 might be fulfilled when he pointed on the map to the Polish corridor and said: 'Here is where the next war will start.'

For members of parliament, to declare war on Germany was the answer to many things. All the great neglected domestic problems of the day, unemployment, housing, poverty, were solved at a stroke. 'There's a war on' was sufficient answer to any complaint, however pressing. None of them had to bother his head about a general election, a major worry which had been looming near.

Thus the great disaster hit mankind. More than fifty million are estimated to have died, some in battle, some murdered, some starved, some burnt alive with fire bombs or annihilated by atom bombs. After what the author calls the Russo-American victory half of Europe was occupied by Soviet Russia, and thirty years on there are Russian tanks in Prague. England, under Churchill who loved the British Empire and detested socialism, had been reduced to poverty-stricken impotence. As this book demonstrates, Churchill's coalition ensured socialism's electoral success; and Churchill himself recognised that the war had gone awry when he called his own book *Triumph and Tragedy*. He lived to witness the end of the Empire.

Oswald Mosley is denounced for predicting 'collapse', but he has unfortunately been proved right in the event. (As to the insulting suggestion that Mosley would in some way have benefited from a German occupation of England, it is enough to say that from 1932 he never ceased to press for rearmament, and that given his character and record it is impossible to imagine him as the lackey of a foreign power.) He foresaw that whatever the outcome war would be disastrous for Britain.

The author makes extensive and subtle use of inverted commas, often with hilarious effect. An example: 'Halifax's "soul" had "risen in indignation" against Mussolini's "crimes" in Abyssinia'. Written thus, the soul and the crimes appear equally dubious.

It may be a mistake to refer to people by their surnames alone. While there was only one Hitler, there were in those days two

Macmillans, two Morrisons, two Chamberlains, two MacDonalds; as to the Wilsons, not only were there Horace and Arnold but there is a reference to 'Wilsonism' which relates to Woodrow of blessed memory. Another oddity is the disregard of double names. Few, without a glance at the index, will guess that Monsell and Croft are Eyres-Monsell and Page-Croft. Unimportant? Yes; but if they are to be mentioned, the names they were known by might as well be used. The same applies to Hart, generally known as Liddell Hart. it would be too bad if some callow undergraduate were to imagine that Hart refers to Judith, or that one of the Wilsons was Harold, or that 'Wilsonism' meant galloping inflation.

The author's brilliantly interesting book costs £15; this is a steep price but it is worth every penny.

The Impact of Hitler: British Politics and British Policy 1933-1940, Cowling, M.,

Books and Bookmen (1975)

❋

Of Pigs and Boars

'*Après deux grandes guerres inutiles et ruineuses, réjouissons-nous de savoir qu'une personne au moins, pendant ces sinistres années, s'est amusée.*'
[After two pointless and ruinous World Wars, let's at least cheer the one person who during those disastrous years enjoyed himself.]

'Two farmyard pigs and a wild boar' was the comment of De Gaulle on the photograph of Churchill, Roosevelt and Stalin at the Yalta conference—a photograph which has lately been seen again, illustrating an article about this book entitled *The Day We Lost the Peace.* They are sitting together in the sunshine; Sir Winston in a 'funny' fur hat, smoking a cigar, is beaming at the other two who look in his direction—Roosevelt, hatless, wearing a theatrical cloak and vacant expression, and Stalin, dressed in his plain uniform. The proximity of the two politicians in fancy dress does not, as might be supposed, make him too look ridiculous, but rather the reverse. Because he is the wild boar.

Sir Winston has called this last volume of his account of the Second World War *Triumph and Tragedy*; unfortunately his triumph was transitory, but the tragedy persists. He begins, however, on the triumphant note to which we became so accustomed during the war. It is D Day; the Allies are advancing; he is having the time of his life. 'I had a jolly day on Monday on the beaches and inland' he wrote to Roosevelt on 14 June, 1944. 'We are working up to a battle which may well be a million a side... How I wish you were here!' He sang Rule Britannia in a wardroom, visited the ruins of Caen, stayed at Arromanches: 'They wanted to call the harbour "Port Churchill." But this for various reasons I forbade.'

In one of Sir Winston's favourite expressions, the Hun was being made to bleed and burn on all fronts. The Red Army was advancing from the East. 'Every victory that you gain is watched with eager attention here' he wrote to Stalin. 'This is the moment for me to tell you how immensely we are all here impressed with the magnificent advances of the Russian armies.'

Best of all, he was able to 'go into action' on one of His Majesty's ships, the destroyer Kelvin. 'Admiral Vian... proposed that we should go and watch the bombardment of the German position... Accordingly we passed between the two battleships, which were firing at twenty thousand yards... and soon we were within seven or eight thousand yards of the shore, which was thickly wooded. The bombardment was leisurely and continuous, but there was no reply from the enemy. As we were about to turn I said to Vian, "Since we are so near, why shouldn't we have a plug at them ourselves before we go home?" He said 'Certainly,' and in a minute or two all our guns fired on the silent coast. We were, of course, well within the range of their artillery, and the moment we had fired Vian made the destroyer turn about and depart at the highest speed. We were soon out of danger and passed through the cruiser and battleship lines.' No doubt as they sped away from the silent wooded shore he made a whole series of V signs—a gesture of defiance to the continent of Europe upon which he was soon to inflict such fatal wounds.

His finest hour was sweet, but very short. Already, with unconditional surrender almost a year away, a black cloud loomed, a worrying, nagging thought that almost succeeded in spoiling the sport of that exhilarating, victory-laden summer. What would the wild boar do, once he had been let into the garden?

'Evidently we are approaching a show-down with the Russians about their intrigues in Italy, Yugoslavia, and Greece. I think their attitude becomes more difficult every day.' This was a minute addressed to the Foreign Secretary. Strange words to use about our ally, who was fighting the Hun with all his might, and was now approaching the Polish frontier. It was almost five years since we had declared war on Germany in order to free Poland from the invader, but apart from setting up an *emigré* Polish government in London and allowing Polish soldiers and airmen to fight with our armies, England, for geographical reasons, had not been able to implement the guarantee given in 1939. But now our Russian ally was advancing into Poland, which was about to be liberated and take its place once more among the free and democratic nations.

Reviewing this book, the *Times Literary Supplement* commented on the single, unpolitical, war-aim of the author—to win the war. Clausewitz said that war is the pursuance of political ends by other means. To Sir Winston the means and the end were so confused that he apparently had no other thought in his head than the defeat of Hitler. He seems to have imagined that once this was accomplished there would be a Peace Conference, and Europe would assume its pre-1933 aspect, with Germany enjoying the blessings of democracy and mass unemployment, while the League of Nations was hard at work once more in Geneva. It was not until the summer of 1944 that the fatality of his policy began to dawn upon him, and even then his enjoyment of the triumph often obscured his vision of the approaching tragedy. Those who had warned were silenced; foresight in this matter had been strictly forbidden.

In order to defeat Hitler he was prepared to cast away the wealth and strength of England and see her reduced to a second rate power. That was not all: English honour was held to be involved in the liberation of Poland; yet after the efforts and sacrifices of a six years war Poland is not free. 'The Germans are a cold in the head but Russia is the pox' is an old Polish saying; the massacres of Katyn and what happened in Warsaw were not likely to change this opinion. Readers of *Triumph and Tragedy* know the end of the story, and so did Sir Winston when he wrote the book. It is a piece of special pleading; he wishes to show the world how great was the effort he made during the last year of the war to avoid the results of his colossal errors of judgment. But however hard he tries to shift responsibility, it falls back upon him.

As long as his war-aim was to 'kill Germans' it was all straightforward. Not only did England and America pour arms into Russia; they also provided arms and money to 'Communist banditti' as Sir Winston calls them, wherever they might be, if they would promise to kill Germans too. (The fact that these 'Partisans' put the arms to other uses as well was one of the reasons for the great unpopularity of their English and American benefactors in Europe after the war.) It did not matter whether those killed were soldiers, or even men, so long as they were German. A few weeks before the end of the war, Dresden, an open city full to overflowing with refugees, provided an opportunity for making them bleed and burn in their tens of thousands. The farmyard creatures were determined to show that they were in no way behind the wild boar when it came to being 'tough'; the bombing of Dresden had no other object, since it did not affect the course of the war.

In the summer of 1944 grave doubts as to the intentions of Russia began to loom, doubts which became certainties after the Warsaw rising. Sir Winston tells the story in full; the Russian wireless appeal to the Poles in Warsaw to rise against the Germans, now that their liberators were at the gates, how they bravely did so, encouraged by the sound of Russian guns on the outskirts of the city, how the Russians then halted their advance, and gave the Germans several weeks in which to put down the rising, refusing all help to the desperate Poles and even forbidding English and American aeroplanes to land with supplies on the airfields within reach.

Thus (again for geographical reasons) were the Poles for the second time buoyed up with promises which could not be kept. Stalin achieved his object—Poland minus its fighting men was easier to occupy and has since been no trouble to rule.

One of the last broadcasts from the heroic city was picked up in London. This is the stark truth. We were treated worse than Hitler's satellites, worse than Italy, Romania, Finland. May God, who is just, pass judgment on the terrible injustice suffered by the Polish nation, and may he punish accordingly all those who are guilty.

This chapter, The Martyrdom of Warsaw, might well have been called instead The Result of England's Guarantee of Poland. On the 30 August General Smuts wrote to Sir Winston as follows:

Please do not let strategy absorb all your attention to the damage of the greater issue now looming up. From now on it would be wise to keep a very close eye on all matters bearing on the future settlement of Europe. This is the crucial issue on which the future of the world for generations will depend. In its solution your vision, experience, and great influence may prove a main factor.

It is hard to say whether Smuts meant the last sentence sarcastically; it was already plain that, whatever might be said of his experience, the Prime Minister's influence was pure illusion. He had summoned up the barbarian from the East and the simpleton from the West—Europe meant nothing to the latter; it meant riches, plunder and power to the former. He could write and telegraph to Stalin every day, he could sometimes persuade Roosevelt to join in his appeals, but it made no difference whatever. He did his best. He told Field-Marshal Alexander, still fighting in Northern Italy, 'if the war came to an end at an early date… to be ready for a dash with armoured cars'—a dash for Vienna, to forestall the Russians. 'Difficult as the world is now' he wrote to the Foreign Secretary, 'we shall not make our course easier by abandoning people whom we have encouraged by promises of support'; while to Tito he said 'we had no desire to intervene in internal Yugoslav affairs, but…we ought not to let the King down.' Seemingly bewildered by the difficult world, minutes, memoranda and telegrams flowed from his pen while the people whom he had encouraged by promises of support were, in fact, abandoned one after another.

In October he went to see Stalin in Moscow, and made another half-hearted attempt to back up the 'London' Poles. He reported optimistically to Roosevelt, who replied: 'I am delighted to learn of your success at Moscow in making progress toward a compromise solution of the Polish problem.' Stalin, as always, was adept in keeping the ball rolling, with memoranda, exchanges of views, and the rest of the meaningless manoeuvres which make democratic politicians feel at home. He knew he had Poland in the bag.

It was in February 1945 that the Three met in Yalta, when the photograph referred to above was taken. Between banquets they discussed everything, and settled nothing. They even discussed 'the all-important question of voting rights in the Security Council' of the World Instrument for Peace, which was to be set up after the war—a question which had been shelved at Dumbarton Oaks. After much talk they arrived at a world-shaking conclusion: 'unless the Big Four were unanimous the Security Council was virtually powerless. If the United States, the USSR, Great Britain, or China disagreed, then it could refuse its assent and stop the Council doing anything. Here was the Veto.' In other words, the whole idea made nonsense from the start, just as did the Atlantic Charter and its four freedoms. They might promise freedom from fear of the policeman's knock (the present reviewer well remembers reading about this excellent notion in a cell at Holloway Prison) but what did the wild boar care? It was all moonshine. Even with his restricted vision and trustful nineteenth-century outlook Sir Winston must have realised this.

At Yalta, six months after the Warsaw rising, when Russian intentions in Europe were already plain for all to see, he quotes himself as saying: 'It is no exaggeration or compliment of a florid kind when I say that we regard Marshal Stalin's life as most precious to the hopes and hearts of all of us,' and again: 'We feel we have a friend whom we can trust.' Is it unfair to quote the idiocies, the indecent nonsense of an after-dinner (or should it be after-banquet) speech? No, since he gives the words in his own book.

Poland, as usual, was on the agenda; the Prime Minister made his contribution: 'Honour was the sole reason why we had drawn the sword to help Poland against Hitler's brutal onslaught, and we could never accept any settlement which did not leave her free, independent, and sovereign.'

The last part of the book is an account of submitting first to Russian force and then to American ignorance and obtuseness. Sir Winston could neither control nor influence events in the least degree. It is astonishing that the Americans should have paid such slight attention to his views; he cared far more than they did what happened to Europe, for after all he is half English. He did his utmost to persuade Eisenhower not to withdraw his armies from thousands of square miles of the European heart-land in order to allow the Russians to 'wend' their way into it. But nobody listened to him any more.

President Roosevelt died on 12 April. Sir Winston spoke of him in the House of Commons: 'What an enviable death was his! He had brought his country through the worst of its perils and the heaviest of its toils. Victory had cast its sure and steady beam upon him.' The German wireless said: 'Roosevelt will go down in history as the man at whose instigation the present war was spread into a Second World War, and as the President who finally succeeded in bringing his greatest opponent, the Bolshevik Soviet Union, to power' and Stalin: 'The friendly attitude of President Franklin Roosevelt to the USSR will always be most highly valued and remembered by the Soviet people.'

He had done irreparable harm to Europe; had he died five years sooner our continent might have been spared the worst. As it was, he did not live to see the consequences of his actions, as his friend Sir Winston has done.

Throughout the victory celebrations he had, he tells us, a heavy heart. He concealed it most cleverly, and a spectacle Europeans found unnecessarily incongruous at the time when their continent was the scene of tragedies of a magnitude hitherto unknown was that of the politician who bore so great a responsibility for these events, electioneering with his cigar and his grin and his V sign, seemingly well satisfied with the turn of events. Perhaps the fact that, although they laughed and cheered, they did not vote for him, shows the electors felt it should be possible to rejoice (if rejoicing at such a time is the order of the day) in a more dignified manner.

'While the rejoicings in our victory over Hitler and the Nazi tyranny transported the peoples of the Grand Alliance my mind was oppressed with the new and even greater peril which was swiftly unfolding itself to my gaze,' he writes, and, in a message to President Truman, 'we hope that the V.E. celebration will... occupy the public mind at home.' What is this distinction between his mind and the public mind? Does he imagine that no one but he was concerned with the danger? He had got his heart's desire—he had fought and conquered Germany. Had he never paused till now, to wonder what might happen next?

However, almost at once he thought of a way to solve all out-standing problems and dangers. 'It seemed above all vital that Stalin, Truman, and I should meet together at the earliest moment, and that nothing should delay us.' Incredible though it may appear, in spite of his experiences at Teheran, Moscow and Yalta, he was once again longing to repeat the futile discussions, to eat and drink at the banquets, and to listen to and bestow the ridiculous compliments in the after dinner speeches. 'Nothing can save us from the great catastrophe but a meeting and a show-down as early as possible at some point in Germany...' he wrote, yet a few pages later he admits: 'The agreements and understandings of Yalta, such as they were, had already been broken or brushed aside by the triumphant Kremlin. New perils, perhaps as terrible as those we had surmounted, loomed and glared upon the torn and harassed world.'

Again and again Sir Winston refers to this or that problem being settled 'at the Peace Treaty.' He never understood that he was fighting a new kind of war with a new kind of ally—who but he could refer to the conquerors of 1945 as the Grand Alliance? A Peace Treaty would have been just as meaningless as all the other commitments and undertakings of his Soviet friends. He looked forward, no doubt, to a Peace Parade and plenty of banquets and endless opportunities for making his V sign, but it was not to be.

However, one last meeting of the three Great Powers was vouchsafed him, this time with the cheerful, energetic Mr Truman representing America in place of the empty opera cloak. It took place at Potsdam in July. Sir Winston writes of the proposed Oder-Neisse frontier for Germany: 'For the future peace of Europe here was a wrong beside which Alsace-Lorraine and the Danzig corridor were trifles. One day the Germans would want their territory back, and the Poles would not be able to stop them,' but he was again unable to influence events in any way.

There were several more banquets. He thought it time Stalin learned to drink brandy out of a bigger glass. 'So I filled a small-sized claret glass with brandy for him and another for myself. I looked at him significantly. We both drained our glasses at a stroke and gazed approvingly at one another.'

After the Conference Sir Winston heard the result of the General Election. He says:

I intended, if I were returned by the electorate, as was generally expected, to come to grips with the Soviet Government... For instance, neither I nor Mr Eden would ever have agreed to the Western Neisse being the frontier line... The over-running by the Russian armies of the territory up to and even beyond the Western Neisse was never and would never have been agreed to by any government of which I was the head. Here was no point of principle only, but rather an enormous matter of fact affecting about three additional millions of displaced people.

These are brave words. If they mean anything at all, they mean that if Mr Churchill had won the election he would have sent English armies to turn the Russians out of Germany. But of course they are empty, bragging words, meant to discredit his successor as Prime Minister. Certainly, by his own account, not Mr Attlee, not even Mr Eden himself could have carried less weight in the counsels of the Three than he did. The Polish question, the German frontiers, the fate of Austria—his impotence in these matters was plain long before the British electorate turned him out of office. He had won his war, but he lost everything else—much of the British Empire, English honour (so he tells us in connection with Poland) and the General Election.

The number of people living under Communist domination was increased, as a result of the war, from 170 million to 770 million. In Sir Winston's own words:

> The territories under Russian control... include the Baltic provinces, all of Germany to the occupational line, all Czechoslovakia, a large part of Austria, the whole of Yugoslavia, Hungary, Romania, Bulgaria.... This constitutes an event in the history of Europe to which there has been no parallel, and which has not been faced by the Allies in their long and hazardous struggle.

An auto-criticism which can compare, in its frankness and scope, with the confession at a Soviet state trial.

The Second World War, Vol. VI: Triumph and Tragedy, Churchill, W. (1654).

Hollow France

Hollow Years? Yes, perhaps. Anyone who has suffered a major haemorrhage knows well the empty feeling and the extreme weakness, such weakness that looking over the side of the bed is enough to make him faint. When Alistair Horne was writing about the fall of France in 1940 he decided it could only be explained by what happened at Verdun in 1916, and that again by 1870 in the Franco Prussian war. The result was three brilliant books, which put the hollow years and what they led to in perspective. France in the 30s was too tired, to weak to do much except recover gradually. It had summoned the whole world to help it defeat Germany, and fresh soldiers from America and Canada and Australia had helped exhausted France and England to victory. A peace, which even those who helped draft it had grave doubts as to its durability, followed.

Huge bits of Germany were lopped off and given to Poland, or made into brand new countries with outlandish names, in order to weaken it further, with French guarantees. Then the French lay down to recover. Mr Weber, with hundreds of interesting statistics, demonstrates that their lethargy was fatal to national revival. They thought they had fought and suffered enough; it was a long convalescence. Of course there were extreme nationalists and patriots among them; France would not be France without that. But as far as governments went, ambitious men who went into politics played musical chairs, taking turns in various ministries, the interest and fun of intrigue making the practically oblivious to what was happening elsewhere. East of the Rhine there were revolutions, and at one time it looked hopeful for Marxism. France hardly cared, it had its own Marxists and the people were not enamoured of their bourgeoisie.

The turning point was the vote in the Saar. National Socialism had routed Communism in Germany as democracies looked at it antagonistically, and thought, or wished to think, that the Saarland, rich in coal and administered by the League of Nations, would vote either for status quo or to join France. The English press predicted that although the inhabitants were German, if they were allowed a properly conducted secret ballot they would not vote to join Germany where Hitler ruled. The votes that had brought him to power had been rigged, they said. English soldiers guarded the voting stations; there should be no jiggery pokery. The result was over 90% for Germany. A year later the Germans marched in to the demilitarized zone of the Rhineland, and ever since there have been voices in France and England saying that it they had been thrown out then there would have been no war three years later. But France had no wish to begin fighting long before its wounds were healed, and England said after all the Germans were only walking into their own back yard. In the climate of that time nobody could have induced the Allies to move. Weber's account of France's backwardness and the misery in which the majority of people in big towns lived is horrifying though not more so than Orwell's *Road to Wigan Pier* about conditions in the North of England It is a pity this book is confined to France. It should be interesting to compare what was happening in Germany. At the beginning of the 30s unemployment was a scourge in al three countries. The Germans put their men to work on the infrastructure. How did they and the French compare in essentials such as higher education, consumption of food, percentage of dwellings with running water an indoor sanitation, purchasing power of the workers, holidays, and so forth? Germany's huge losses in the war make the comparison meaningful. Both, of course, were re-arming.

The great men of our century are those who saw, after the disaster of the Second World War, that Europe must unite or go under. France and Germany must be found together and never fight again. The vagaries of Brussels are bewildering but unimportant. Weber's interesting book is less depressing, in the light of the huge rise in the standard of living compared with those days. You cannot make people happy, but they can have some leisure and comfort.

It showed what would have happened if plebiscites had been allowed elsewhere.

The Hollow Years: France in the 1930s, Weber, E. (1994)

❄

A City of Ruins

'We are confident that Hitler's mechanised hordes will never get to
Paris. But should they come so far... we shall defend every stone, every
clod of earth, every lamp-post, every building, for we would rather
have our city razed to the ground than fall into the hands of the
Germans.'

These words, from a French Government spokesman on 9th June
1940, may be set beside Sir Winston Churchill's well-known speech to
the House of Commons a few days earlier: 'We shall fight on the
beaches, we shall fight in the fields' and so on. Both were typically
politicians' utterances; the difference between them, looked at historically, is that the Frenchman's words were put to the test of reality within a week, whereas the Englishman's boast was destined to remain an
empty one, since the Germans never crossed the Channel.

It is idle to speculate on what would have happened if the Channel
had not existed. One thing is certain: the speeches of politicians, however brave and stirring, would not have affected the issue, which would
largely have depended, as it did in France, upon the relative strength of
German and English armour and aircraft, and also, to some extent,
upon the behaviour of the civilian population. The only evidence we
have to go on is what happened to the English army in France in May
1940.

Throughout his book, General Spears pretends that the realities of
war do not exist. All that matters is that politicians, and generals too if
they can be so persuaded, should continue to shout defiantly that they
are winning the war, however obvious it may be to everyone that, in
fact, they are not. No wonder the French generals were irritated
beyond endurance by this attitude, and by the censorious admonitions
to France to go on fighting while English troops were embarking for
home in French ports, and the bulk of the exiguous English air force

was (quite rightly) being saved for the defence of the homeland. The French begged for more fighter cover for their armies; the English turned them down. Half the book is taken up by these reiterated demands and refusals.

Sir Winston Churchill's promise to France, on 11th June, of a couple of divisions within a fortnight and twenty five more by March 1941, made when the French armies were at their last gasp facing one hundred and twenty four German divisions, was described by General Weygand as *dérisoire*. He might well have used a stronger term. At the same conference, which took place at Briare after the Government had left Paris, General Weygand 'was launched on his favourite theme, the folly of having embarked on war at all. "I wish to place on record that I consider that those responsible embarked upon the war very lightly",' he said. Churchill and Eden quickly changed the subject, as well they might. The cap fitted.

After further argument about whether the RAF could be used in the battle, Marshal Pétain spoke. 'He was calm, detached…. He wished, he said, to support General Weygand in his contention that the present war in no way resembled the last one…. He then paused and said gravely, alluding to Churchill's advocacy of fighting in Paris: "To make Paris into a city of ruins will not affect the issue". There was a rather painful pause, brought to an end by Eden 'who told one of those cheering stories which were being spread by neutrals about the very heavy losses the Germans had suffered. For Churchill, with his usual disregard for the consequences, 'urged the French to fight in Paris, describing how a great city, if stubbornly defended, absorbed immense armies,' writes General Spears. He adds: 'The French perceptibly froze at this'. Not only Frenchmen, but the whole civilised world owes a debt of gratitude to General Weygand and Marshal Pétain for saving Paris from this senseless destruction. General Weygand declared the incomparably beautiful capital an open city that same evening.

But Sir Winston was determined not to let France fall without making one supreme effort to bolster her strength and morale. On 16th June he made his great offer on the telephone; France and England were to be united as one country, 'the Franco-British Union'. Since no soldiers or airmen could be spared to help France on the eve of defeat, the Prime Minister offered himself and a bunch of politicians instead—as if France had not enough politicians already. Reynaud at first received the idea enthusiastically, but presumably the soldiers pointed out that it would not make a pin of difference. No more was heard of it; the battle of France was lost.

General Spears' book should be read by everybody interested in the Second World War, for his work placed him at the very centre of affairs, where he was an observant onlooker. He can describe men and events vividly. Even those who agree with the French lady who said to him: 'I hate the war. It is the fault of your country. You bear a heavy responsibility, *you* were a *belliciste*, like your Churchill'—even they must be glad that General Spears was there to describe Reynaud, Pétain, de Gaulle, Weygand and the rest, their words and their actions, in those fateful June days.

The Fall of France, Spears, E. (1954)

❋

Jungle Knights

The third and last volume of M. Benoist-Méchin's* history of the summer of 1940 is in some ways the most interesting of the three. It describes the early days of Vichy, the formation of the new government, and how full power was conferred on Marshal Pétain by the National Assembly voting 569 for to 80 against with 17 abstentions. This overwhelming parliamentary majority accurately reflected feeling in the country as a whole.

The extent to which this was so is illustrated by the fact that even André Gide, most liberal of men, who was subsequently attacked by Vichy as a writer who led youth astray, had noted in his *Journal* a few days earlier: *L'allocution de Pétain est tout simplement admirable* [Pétain's address is brilliant], after listening to a broadcast speech.

The second half of the book consists of a series of portraits of the principal French actors in the drama of the sixty days, and of two foreigners, King Leopold and Sir Winston Churchill. Although, like everything he writes, these essays are full of illuminating anecdote and intelligent observation, they nevertheless have the defect (probably inevitable, yet so admirably avoided in the remainder of this detailed history) of being partisan. Thus, while admitting his brilliant cleverness and power of managing men, the author does much less than justice to Laval, and perhaps more than justice to the Marshal and the King of the Belgians. These two honourable men have been meanly treated, and M. Benoist-Méchin's view of them as perfect gentle knights is very well as a corrective to vilest denigration, yet his readers are bound to ask themselves whether these qualities alone, in the jungle world, are adequate. M. Benoist-Méchin, in redressing the balance, insists perhaps rather too much. However this may be, there is no corresponding failure of objectivity in his account of General de Gaulle.

The great value of this enormously long book is precisely that it recaptures the day-by-day atmosphere, through the use of contemporary memoranda, diaries and the like. The portraits, on the other hand, may be slightly coloured by subsequent events, by successes and failures, developments and changes which subtly altered the size and shape of the personages themselves. Yet, at a time when almost all France was agreed in giving the Marshal *pleins pouvoirs* [full powers] to get the best terms possible from the conqueror and to negotiate the difficult details of inevitable collaboration, M. Benoist-Méchin does not deny a certain nobility to the lonely figure of de Gaulle. Snubbed and used by the English government, kept in the dark about military projects, his correspondence censored; spurned by many of the French soldiers and sailors who happened to find themselves in the island, unable to induce a single governor or prominent personality from the French overseas empire to join his revolt, suffering the humiliation of appearing to have condoned the bombardment of the French fleet by the English at Mers el Kebir, he yet persisted, and huffed, and believed in final Allied victory. (True, he had passed the point of no return.) In the summer of 1940 the liberation and the terrible events accompanying it were infinitely remote and unpredictable; and M. Benoist-Méchin does not allow their shadow to cross his sad little sketch of the General as he was then.

It would be impossible to over-praise this book as a whole. With M. Fabre Luce's *Journal de la France* it presents a detailed, accurate, vivid and absorbing picture of a vitally important episode. In English we have nothing comparable; translators should be found for the *Soixante Jours*.

* A Minister in Pétain's government.

Soixante Jours qui Ebranlérent l'Occident: III La fin du régime, Benoist-Méchin, J. (1956)

Hanging Offence

If a militarily unprepared country declares war on a militarily stronger neighbour it must envisage the possibility of defeat. If this unprepared country is alone in the fight it will then have to accept the best peace settlement it can get. If, on the other hand, it has unbeaten allies it must await the final outcome of the war, enduring meanwhile, as best it may, occupation by its conquerors. All this seems self-evident, and would not be worth stating except that ever since 1940 an unrealistic argument about what should or should not have been the attitude of the French during the four year armistice has raged with inconceivable bitterness.

This was not a case where a stronger aggressor country pounced on a weaker country in order to conquer it. France declared war on Germany, not the other way about. And the consequence of this declaration of war might have been foreseen.

There were then, roughly speaking, four courses open to Frenchmen. They could completely withdraw from public life; or they could choose co-operation with Germany, working for the so-called New Order in Europe; or they could harry and sabotage the occupying power by every possible means; or they could hold a balance between these two extremes while waiting to see which side would win the war. The vast majority preferred to take this last course, and meanwhile were content for France to have a number of extremists on either side, to be ready for any contingency.

At the same time, it was also obvious that 'resistance' was not analogous to, for example, the resistance of the Irish forty years ago to the English. In that case every act of violence might he thought to be hastening the end of a hated foreign domination. But there was never any question of Germany occupying and ruling France except for the duration of war, and therefore acts of violence were gestures of defiance which led only to immediate reprisals suffered by the whole population, and for that reason were disapproved of by many patriotic Frenchmen.

To hold the balance, to keep the life of the country going, defending its interests in every sphere and ensuring that a maximum of sovereignty remained in French hands was the difficult and ungrateful task performed with admirable skill by the brilliant Pierre Laval. That his efforts on behalf of France should have cost him his life was due to the fact that he was a great opponent of communism, and at the end of the war it was the communists who ran France (and indeed all Europe) for a time. The surprising thing is that communist politicians and leaders of the resistance should have found non-communist Frenchmen willing to work with them. General de Gaulle's first act was to bring Thorez back from Moscow to a seat in the government.

These three large volumes of documents, collected and published by the Hoover Institute, contain the testimony of hundreds of men who worked for the Vichy Government, and in particular for Laval, between the armistice and the German retreat in 1944. Soldiers, politicians, diplomats, police, businessmen, all agree that Laval's tireless efforts spared his country the worst rigours of an oppressive occupation. His policy was to endeavour to save France from the harsh treatment meted out to Poland. One of his hardest struggles, of which there is massive evidence in these volumes, was to limit as far as possible the number of French workers sent to Germany. His method here, as elsewhere, was to prevaricate, argue and delay, and the difference between the numbers asked for and the numbers sent represents the success of his design.

Almost all the witnesses speak of Laval's love of country, and many end their testimony by saying that, had he had a trial, this is the evidence they would have given. Because he had no trial, the Hoover Institute, in the interest of history, has published this lengthy hook. One of the witnesses thus sums up Laval's attitude: '*Chez lui, le patriotisme c'était l'amour de son pays et non pas, comme chez la plupart des Français, la haine de celui des autres. Il voulait le bonheur des Français et comprenais que celui-ci ne pouvait être réalisé que dans la paix par une large compréhension européenne.*' [For him patriotism meant the love of his own country and not, as with most of the French, the hatred of others. He wanted the best for France and he understood that this couldn't be realised except through peace and a greater European understanding.]

Laval, one of the first Europeans, had always worked for peace: he thought it a grave error for France to declare war in 1939. But in the hour of defeat he set himself to do whatever was possible, in the difficult circumstances, for his country. Forty million Frenchmen could not all find rooms in London's Connaught Hotel, somebody had to help them through dangerous, hard, disagreeable years.

Although *La Vie de la France sous l'occupation is* immensely long it is far from dull—a great deal of it is of extreme fascination: small wonder it has been a best seller in France this winter.

The Hoover Institute should follow it up with an account of the collaborators—the Déats, Doriots and Darnands. Then the picture of these years would be complete.

La Vie de la France sous l'occupation, Hoover Institute (1957)

Uneasy Alliance

Allies of a kind indeed. After Britain and France declared war on

Germany, Roosevelt gave us as much help as he dared, but he had to keep an eye on the presidential election in 1940. In order to be re-elected he was obliged to make various pledges; American boys (a politicians' expression meaning soldiers) should not be sent overseas to fight in an European quarrel. Once elected, his hands were free.

Harold Ickes, Secretary of the Interior, wrote in his diary: 'For a long time I have believed that our best entrance into the war would be by way of Japan... which will inevitably lead us into war with Germany.'

Roosevelt increased the 'pressure on Japan by denying her vital raw materials, notably scrap metal in the autumn of 1940 and above all oil at the end of July 1941.' To this threat of strangulation the Japanese riposted violently; in December they attacked Pearl Harbor, precipitating war in the Pacific.

Christopher Thorne's interesting book deals with the resulting British/United States alliance, and shows what an uneasy alliance it was. The common policy of war with the Axis powers was sometimes almost lost sight of in the general acrimony which resulted from the totally different war aims of the Allies. Churchill was concerned to defeat Germany and Japan and yet to preserve the British Empire intact, while Roosevelt was pushing towards the dismemberment and destruction of the Empire. Mr Thorne continually feels bound to remind his readers (and perhaps himself) that in spite of the recrim-inations the Allies did work together and they did defeat Japan. Soon after the death of Roosevelt the British Empire disappeared, but by then the war had been won.

The episode which best illumined the whole enterprise was the devising and signing of the Atlantic Charter. Under its terms there was to be 'freedom' for peoples everywhere in the world. Mr Churchill, who had light-heartedly signed, seems to have been sur-prised and chagrined when the Indians and Burmese asked if their turn for freedom would soon come. To him, they were lesser breeds without the Charter; he had not had them in mind when he signed it. He was thinking, so he said, of countries under the Nazi yoke. Mr

Roosevelt on the other hand meant every word of it; there were to be no more colonies, and no more military bases like Singapore. Panama, Hawaii, and the various bases the Americans acquired (for 'the President still had a keen eye for the possible acquisition by the US of bases that would enhance her strength at sea or in the development of new air routes' says Mr Thorne) were a different matter. It is wonderful to see the workings of Anglo-Saxon hypocrisy under the strong light shed here.

To begin with, the Japanese were ridiculously underrated. President Roosevelt was full of strange theories: 'the evil-doing of the Japanese might be due to the less-developed skulls of their basic stock' he thought. (He told Stalin at Yalta that the Vietnamese were 'people of small stature... and not warlike.') Mr Churchill also had wishful thoughts. He sent two warships to the Far East in order to stabilize the situation and impress the enemy, rather in the same way as a gunboat in an African river might impress the local tribe. The Prince of Wales and the Repulse, with no air cover, were sunk by the Japanese. Singapore fell and many thousands of prisoners were taken. For Churchill, this was the blackest day of the war.

If the Japanese were underrated, China 'was built up in Roosevelt's imagination into a great power whose mighty inexhaustible armies were to help defeat Japan.' General Chiang Kai-shek accepted money, arms and flattery but he did not move. He well knew that his own particular enemy was Mao Tse-tung.

Determined that India should be freed from British rule, Roosevelt suggested to Stalin, when Churchill was not present, that he felt the best solution would be reform on the Soviet line. 'To this ingratiating observation Stalin merely replied that the matter was a complex one, and that reform from the bottom would mean revolution.' Roosevelt and Churchill vied with one another in their courting of Stalin and there was a certain jealousy between them. 'Poor Neville Chamberlain believed he could trust Hitler', announced Churchill. 'He was wrong. But I don't think I'm wrong about Stalin.'

Just as the war in the Far East was coming to a successful conclusion the atom bomb was ready for use and the Allies dropped one on Hiroshima. They then dropped another on Nagasaki. To its credit, the Far Eastern Department of the Foreign Office, which had not been informed that the bombs were to be used, wrote a strong protest:

> A more intelligent way would surely have been to have given publicity to the discovery and its possible effects, to have given an ultimatum with a time limit to the Japanese before using it, and to have declared the intention of the Allies to drop a bomb on a given city after a given date by way of demonstration, the date being fixed so as to give time for the evacuation of the city.

Something on these lines is what most people who thought about it considered should have been done, but Mr Churchill agreed with the American plan to drop the bomb on a crowded city 'without a moment's hesitation' as he himself put it. Soon afterwards there were war crimes trials in Tokyo, but only Japanese were in the dock. General MacArthur was sent to Japan with full powers and thousands of bibles. We know the outcome. The clever, hard-working Japanese turned their attention from the arts of war to the arts of peace, and the yen, like the mark, soars into the empyrean.

Allies of a Kind is scholarly and thorough, but it is not a page too long. It is a book that even the most ignorant layman will read with deep interest.

Allies of a Kind: The United States, Britain and the War against Japan, Thorne, C.,
Books and Bookmen (1978)

Hard Lessons: Regulation 18B

'No charge, no trial, no term set.' Yes, regulation 18B was certainly odious in the highest degree. Cast into prison with no charge, hence no trial, by the Home Secretary, for as long as he pleased, for years, was exactly like being kidnapped. Useless to count the days, as there had been no sentence. Actions by 18B prisoners for habeas corpus all failed, the judges showing themselves in a poor light as the creatures of the executive.

The 18Bs appeared before an Advisory Committee chaired by Norman Birkett KC. In Mosley's case his house, flat, safes and even bank account were carefully searched; as there was nothing sinister to find, nothing was found. He was interrogated for hours by Birkett, and convinced he would be released. Instead, I was arrested as well. I left four children, the youngest eleven weeks old.

Having a naive belief in British justice, I considered Birkett dishonest. He should have advised Mosley's release, and if his advice was rejected by the Home Office, he should have resigned. By the time he interrogated me, my opinion of him was very low.

The excuse for all this? Summer 1940 was a time of panic; German armies swept west, the Low Countries and France fell. Stories of fifth columns in defeated countries were believed, though subsequently found to be fantasies. The British Union was hardly a candidate for suspicion; it was super-patriotic.

But it had campaigned during the phoney war for negotiated peace, and hundreds of loyal men and women were arrested. This was quite a popular move; the Government was seen to be 'doing' something. Hitherto, there had been only defeats.

A new criminal offence was invented: the spreading of alarm and despondency. The great disseminator of alarm and despondency was the BBC, which had only bad news to give. Anyone but a traitor who might be pleased at the turn of events in 1940 was bound to feel a certain alarm when Churchill, with his record of failure, recently added to by the tragic farce in Norway, became Prime Minister.

Busybodies had the time of their lives, seeing strange lights in neighbours' houses, or marks on telegraph poles, or a man in a pub doubting a swift and final victory. All was reported to the police, and led to prison. It was one way of aiding the war effort.

MI5 is the villain, and the clown, of the book. Professor Simpson's story is a good one, but its results were sad and horrible. MI5 invented a huge fifth column, but when required to produce evidence of its existence was unable to do so; it was a figment of its imagination. Yet I and women were imprisoned, families broken, businesses ruined, dependants left with no means of support, health undermined.

Since the riots and publicity of recent times people are probably fairly familiar with the degraded vileness of prison life, but in those days the public knew nothing. The grimy filth was incredible, since prisons dispose of plentiful slave labour. The lavatories, the kitchen and eating utensils coated with grease, were indescribably disgusting. The cold, even in summer, was piercing; no ray of sun could penetrate the small heavily barred windows encrusted with London soot. The lights, turned out in air raids, were too dim to read by.

Churchill at first was all for 18B and pretended to think in the event of defeat Mosley might head a puppet government, a grotesque notion. Quite apart from Mosley's patriotism, no ambitious politician aged 43 would accept a position which at a stroke would earn him the hatred and contempt of all his countrymen.

However, as time went on Churchill began to wonder if 18B were not incompatible with his role of democrat fighting totalitarianism, and when, after three and a half years, we were released, he called the regulation 'in the highest degree odious' and asked for it to be abolished. By then, the Home Secretary had become addicted to the power he enjoyed and he paid no attention. For some time previously Churchill had ensured better conditions, and we now went on to house arrest.

Professor Simpson has done a thorough job, though impeded by the death of most of the prisoners and the shredding of papers he wished to see, also finding some still 'closed'. The secret service, with its lies and fantasies, keeps its secrets to itself

He is witty and sarcastic about jailers and jailed alike, and his conclusion, no doubt the right one, is that the war was entirely unaffected by 18B. All the misery, the suffering, the vast expense, not to speak of the permanent dent in any British justice, was for nothing. Fifty years on, his scholarly book is in the highest degree welcome.

18B, in the Highest Degree Odious; Detention Without Trial in Wartime Britain,

Simpson, A.W.B., *Evening Standard* (1992)

❋

Reforming Prison

Only the most devoted fans of books about prisons will wish to fork out £3.50 for Mr Caird's little effort. It tells a great deal about Mr Caird himself, and everything he can remember about Wormwood Scrubs, where he spent seven weeks, and Coldingley, where he was incarcerated for the remaining forty five weeks of his sentence. A twenty-page pamphlet would have provided ample space for the information he imparts, and, allowing another twenty for himself and his feelings about being sentenced and going to prison, it still only adds up to forty pages. Whoever heard of a book of forty pages? The padding is shameless, the repetitions inexorable.

Strangely enough, the thrilling chapter he might have written about his crowded hour of glorious life at the Garden House Hotel in Cambridge is nowhere to be found. It would have relieved the monotony, but for some reason he decided barely to mention it.

Coldingley, a relatively pleasant prison where he worked as a clerk, and where there are facilities for reading and other pleasures, was only less hateful to him than Wormwood Scrubs, and the reason is that the worst thing about prison, in England at any rate, is the loss of liberty. Conditions in the cage come second. Nevertheless they do count, and he had a clean cell to himself, was allowed several books at a time, got fairly decent food, fresh air, cinema, wireless and television, and could listen to the Beatles on a record player. The work he had to do, even if less amusing than writing for the *Sunday Times* and the *Morning Star* (as the blurb says he has done since) was at least better paid and less boring than sewing mail bags. Mr Callaghan, when he opened Coldingley, said it was a leap into the future of penal reform.

Wormwood Scrubs is one of those disgusting old prisons where three prisoners are crowded into a cell built for one, and where the lavatories are revolting in themselves and completely inadequate for the hugely swollen number of men using them. The dirt and degradation are a disgrace, but when there are so many institutions competing for money—hospitals, homes for the aged—and because the rate of criminality is high, the idea of razing the foul old prisons to the ground is hardly practical. What could be done at once is to redesign the 'recesses' as they are called, and have at least eight modern lavatories with WCs and basins to each landing.

Mr Caird is interested in the Soviet Union; he repeatedly mentions having read six volumes on the subject. He even heads a chapter 'One Step Forward, Two Steps Back', although it does not fit the context, which is the gradual relaxing of rules that irked him. If he has also read Solzhenitsyn's novels he will have found a first-hand description of prison life in Russia. Since he considered himself a political prisoner, this will have given him a yardstick against which to measure his own experience.

Not that there is any but the most tenuous resemblance, because Mr Caird was locked up not for his opinions but for a violent demonstration against a group of people who were dining at the Garden House Hotel in Cambridge. The purpose of the dinner was to promote tourism in Greece, Mr Caird did not think anyone should be a tourist in Greece; he disapproved of the Greek régime. Nobody suggested forcing him to visit the most beautiful country on earth, but in England people can travel as they please. It is breaking the law to demonstrate violently, even against someone planning a Greek holiday.

A mob of between three and four hundred assembled at the front and the back of the Garden House Hotel 'intent on wrecking a non-political dinner.' They banged on the doors, the windows and the roof, rushed in and 'once in the dining room they used typical hooligan methods, overturning tables and smashing crockery.... Before long a really threatening situation developed. It needed eighty police to restore order…. The shambles had been achieved.' Mr Caird was convicted of 'causing a riot, unlawful assembly, assaulting a policeman, and carrying an offensive weapon' and Mr Justice Melford Stevenson sentenced him and several of his friends to prison; he was given eighteen months. On appeal, Lord Justice Sachs said: 'When there is wanton and vicious violence of a gross degree the Court is not concerned whether it comes from gang rivalry or from political motivations. It is the degree of mob violence that matters and the extent to which public peace was broken.' Most of the sentences were confirmed, including Mr Caird's.

These stirring events are not described in this book. Mr Caird, in a couple of pages, contents himself with saying that he did not mean to be violent, and that a dinner guest 'wielded a chair with great effect'. Probably the dinner guest had arrived unarmed and defended himself with what came to hand. The description of the riot given above comes from the judges as reported in *The Times* (7 April 1970) and the *Daily Express* (20 August 1970).

The author appears to think all the security, the counting of heads, the searching of prisoners for offensive weapons and so forth was completely unnecessary. He should put himself in the warders' shoes. Although in his photograph he looks harmless enough they were probably terrified of him. Supposing it had got about on the prison grapevine that one of them planned a holiday on, say, the Soviet shore of the Black Sea? Mr Caird might have felt irresistibly impelled to beat him up. He has doubtless heard tell of thousands held in Russian prison camps and obviously feels indignant about their harsh treatment. One can picture the scene in the fevered imagination of the warden: Mr Caird (THINKS): Here is this disgraceful warden taking himself and his family to a country where the prison régime is unacceptable to ME! to MR CAIRD! It won't do. Perhaps if I give him a good thump he will go to the Isle of Man instead. No! What am I thinking? Not the Isle of Man, where I've heard there's birching. Certainly not a holiday at home, where the prisons are so nasty; where CAN I send the warder for his holiday? The Scillies?

The warder might look readier to deal with such an attack than men and women dining at a Cambridge hotel, but Mr Caird's feelings could have got the better of him. It was not long, however, before the Wormwood Scrubbers realised he was a sheep in wolf's clothing, and he was sent off to graze at Coldingley.

Mr Caird is interested in penal reform. Do prisons 'reform' the prisoner? Hardly ever, is probably the right answer. All the same, the odds are that Mr Caird will now think twice before he behaves as he did at the Garden House Hotel. This, only time will show. Is prison a deterrent? There again, not as a rule; but Cambridge undergraduates have not smashed up any hotels since Mr Caird and his friends went to gaol. It may be a coincidence, but on the other hand it may not.

The 'good and useful life' of the book's title is what prison is ostensibly designed to encourage ex-prisoners to lead. Very possibly Mr Caird will be a model the Aldermaston variety and writing about better way of reforming people might be prison commissioners can point to, busying them afterwards for the *Morning Star*. Yet found than the expense of spirit and waste himself with demonstrations of the old it is difficult not to agree with him that a of time and money which is prison.

A Good and Useful Life: Imprisonment in Britain Today, Caird, R., *Books and Bookmen* (1974)

Each in His Prison

English prisons are in the news. Cells in Hull prison were allegedly found to be spattered with blood after the warders beat up the prisoners. Warders elsewhere have been 'going slow'. They protest that their work has become impossible, there are too many prisoners. The gaols are overflowing, they have become even more disgusting than formerly because of desperate over-crowding. They are disgusting for the warders as well as for the convicts; hence the protests of prison officers. Yet crime, violent crime, increases year by year; there is unlikely to be a reduction in the numbers of unfortunate wretches packed three to a cell built for one. When warders 'go slow' the prisoners are locked in for twenty three hours of the twenty four. They are seldom beaten up, but it is not necessary to look exclusively abroad for the horrors of captivity. They are here, now, in our own country.

England is hardly mentioned in Elizabeth Basset's anthology. She concentrates on three great villains: Russia, Germany and Japan. Englishmen are seen as victims, never as aggressors. Yet most of the Commonwealth heads of state, notabilities and prime ministers of the past fifty years have been gaoled by the English: Mahatma Gandhi in India, Kenyatta in the infamous Hola camp, the list is long. De Valera staged a brilliant escape from Lincoln prison, but most of them languished for years. These events are passed over in deafening silence. Perhaps none of the prisoners wrote inspiring words in their cages. Pandit Nehru is the only one quoted: 'Must the State always be based on force and violence?' He knew the answer, but it is the sort of rhetorical question that sounds well. The unfortunate Nehru spent, in all, sixteen years in British prisons in India. Sixteen years. It does not bear thinking of.

This anthology is highly selective, it produces no uncomfortable surprises or controversial contributors. Solzhenitsyn puts everyone else in the shade; many strive too hard for effect, others are mawkish. There are tortures for the sadistic or masochistic reader, but they can be skipped. The last war and the unspeakable miseries it engendered take up most of the book, but since there are also quotations from many centuries ago, for example from the Bible (spoiled by the banality of a modern translation), space could have been found for Socrates' prison dialogue with his disciples. If, as a non-Christian, he is ineligible, other inspired prisoners come to mind, Sir Thomas More, John Bunyan, and many a victim (in a purely Christian context) of the Reformation and Counter-reformation. Perhaps it was just as well to stick mainly to the three villains listed above. Even if they are over-familiar, custom does not appear to stale them. If Arthur Koestler's account (*Scum of the Earth*) of his experiences in a French concentration camp at the very beginning of the war had shown that brutal and bullying camp guards are not exclusively Russian, German and Japanese, it might have confused the reader.

The choice of what to put in and what to leave out in a melancholy book of this kind is so vast that a central idea must govern it. There are moving passages, and beautiful ones, but what does the whole add up to? 'Stone walls do not a prison make, nor iron bars a cage?' Although it is true that man's indomitable spirit, his courage, his nobility, his love of beauty, can rise triumphantly above sordid and terrifying circumstances, it should be pointed out that Lovelace's comfortable little poem does not correspond with the facts. It was bound to be quoted here, and it is a great favourite with people unfamiliar with the insides of gaols. In truth, however, stone walls and iron bars do make a prison, and prison is a very terrible place. As Oscar Wilde wrote

> All that we know who lie in gaol
> Is that the wall is strong;
> And that each day is like a year,
> A year whose days are long.

Each in His Prison, Bassett, E., *Books and Bookmen* (1979)

Inhumanity

This is a perfectly ghastly book, not commended for holiday reading. The depressing thing about it is that appalling cruelty and torture are practiced just about everywhere on earth, man's inhumanity to man is universal.

The palm for the refinement of disgusting cruelty must go to the Chinese, keeping their victim alive while cutting bits off him here and there, to prolong his suffering. Yet though widespread, everyone who thinks about torture identifies with the sufferer. Few people would imagine they could possibly find themselves in the role of torturer, but, in fact, there are legions of them.

Why resort to torture? Algeria is a typical example; there was guerrilla war and Arabs were tortured to get information without which the French army would be in danger. There was an outcry in France, and General Massu had himself tortured (electric shocks) to see how much it hurt. But, of course, half the agony is the prisoner's utter helplessness surrounded by cruel enemies, while the General only had to say 'Hold! Enough!' to get up and go home.

Terrorists are very cruel. When the oppressed revolt they become oppressors, and are not noticeably more merciful. How can people, 'of all races' as they say, be so wonderfully brave under torture? Apparently, it is because their rage against the tormentor makes the adrenaline flow. Nobody feels anger against his dentist, or because he has a painful corn. These ills must be borne, but when somebody deliberately hurts, it infuriates.

Kate Millett has bravely read through the records of unspeakable horrors. Her book, though well written, is repetitive and much too long. She is preaching to the converted, it is highly unlikely that she will be read by police anywhere on the globe.

Can nothing be done? Possibly an energetic government might catch and punish those who have tortured in its name. But what am I saying? 'Punish'? What a frightful idea. The only hope is to change human nature; a vast programme.

The Politics of Cruelty: An Essay on the Literature of Political Imprisonment,

Millett, K., *Evening Standard* (1994)

Charlotte Despard

Because Charlotte Despard lived to be 95 she is always thought of as old, an old rebel, an old saint. As Charlotte French, one of a large family of fairly rich orphans, she married Max Despard, and her real life began when he died and left her a widow of fifty with a good deal of money. She had energy, imagination and courage.

One of a group of ladies who took country flowers to the London slums to brighten the lives of the poor, she found her vocation. She realised that charity could hardly alleviate the misery she found, it was not only not enough, it did not even dent the surface of the appalling poverty and injustice she saw. Her aim was to change society radically and permanently.

In order to help them she decided she must live among the poor, and she bought a house in Nine Elms, a noisy, dirty neighbourhood with an all-pervading smell of coal-dust. Her house became a club, a clinic, a soup kitchen, and headquarters of her fight against the conditions in which her neighbours lived, with rotten houses, starvation wages and the threat of the workhouse always hanging over them. Mrs Despard became a socialist, a Marxist. She believed that if Liberals and Conservatives could be defeated the world would completely change; misery, and with it crime, would disappear. Life in the workhouse, particularly for old women with no hope of getting work, was cruel. They were harried, insulted, 'bullied and half starved'. Their diet was 'stringy, half-cooked meat, thin gruel and black rotten potatoes'. One towel was provided for twenty four women; they were made to wear coarse, ill-fitting clothes and hard boots; the wards were not ventilated and smelt. When Mrs Despard asked the women why they did not complain to the Guardians she was told that if they did the Master put them on a bread-and-water diet as a punishment. She became a Guardian herself and worked from inside the system to change it.

Mrs Despard joined the suffragettes; she was convinced that once women were enfranchised there would be no more wars, justice for all, and slums would vanish.

Like many another saint, Charlotte Despard was hard upon those near her. She worked a willing helper, Rosalie Mansell, almost to death, and the unfortunate woman took to injecting herself with laudanum to obtain relief and had to go away and be cured of her addiction. In an account of her own childhood Charlotte boasts of her rebelliousness, but when in an impulse of generosity she adopted a little girl, who grew to be 'mischievous and emotionally insecure', she found herself lecturing the child on proper behaviour in exactly the same way as her governesses had lectured her.

During the Boer War Charlotte was a pacifist; it was the war in which her only brother, John French, made his reputation as a cavalry general. Her fondness for him was such that she managed to overlook their differences of opinion.

As a suffragette in and out of prison Mrs Despard was as courageous and uncompromising as she had been in her fight against the Poor Law. When the Great War came she was shocked by Christabel Pankhurst's pro-government and conformist attitude. She herself was the target for many a rotten egg when she spoke in favour of a negotiated peace. After the war, women were given the vote, and although she once stood for parliament, the idea of being a back-bench MP would have seemed like a death sentence of boredom to her fiery nature.

Mrs Despard looked around for another 'cause'. She found it in Ireland. Her family had Irish roots and Charlotte had become a Catholic (rather a strange one, since she dabbled in theosophy and also spiritualism, and when in doubt was in the habit of consulting Mazzini* in the great beyond) and she was also an ardent Sinn Féiner. Like many rebels she loved to annoy, and her adherence to Sinn Féin was made more fun for her by the fact that her brother, now Earl of Ypres, was Viceroy in Dublin. She was a great embarrassment to the unfortunate man, whose name she never hesitated to invoke whenever, during the troubles and the civil war, she and her Republican friend Maud Gonne were held up by troops here and there as they went about their revolutionary business.

The troubles over, she settled in Belfast where she took up the cause of the Catholics who were discriminated against in every way. At the time of the riots in 1935 as an old lady of 91 she was threatened and abused 'by Protestant hooligans'. This would once have delighted her, but now she was ill and old, and becoming rather poor. She had spent nearly all her money on her 'causes', now she was in pain and lonely but for two companions in favour of whom she made a new will in 1939. A few weeks later she fell downstairs during the night, and died in hospital. People said she had been pushed. There was a case about her will, and legal expenses accounted for what remained of her fortune.

Her causes never turned out to change the world quite as she would have hoped, nevertheless she was one of those pioneers who make things a little less vile. It was not her fault that her enthusiasm for Soviet Russia was misplaced, or that the Nine Elms workhouse had so many features in common with the Gulag archipelago.

If she were alive now, Mrs Despard might turn her attention to English prisons, where three men are cooped up in a cell designed for one. Or to another scandal of our time, the way in which old and suffering people are artificially kept alive by doctors. As long as the heart beats, each unhappy day that passes is counted a triumph for modern medicine. There are still causes worth the attention of a Mrs Despard.

Andro Linklater has written a most interesting book about her. On its cover is a wonderful photograph of her addressing an anti-fascist meeting, frail, indomitable, age-old.

_* Giuseppe Mazzini, Marxist philosopher and Italian statesman.

An Unhusbanded Life: Charlotte Despard, Linklater, A., *Books and Bookmen* (1980)

Singing in the Dark

— Why produce another biograpy of Wagner?
— To write a book on Wagner—trying to turn a deaf ear to the muttered incredulity of 'Another book on Wagner?'

A quote from each of these biographies. The answer is that Wagner, as man and as artist, is an inexhaustible subject, and also that after being hidden in a bank for almost a century we at last have Cosima Wagner's diary. It is indispensable reading for understanding the years between 1869 and 1883, the years of *The Ring*, of Bayreuth and of *Parsifal*. It is a human document of intense fascination, and a considerable work of art in its own right. Through it we get to know Wagner as never before; a companionable, high-spirited man, not robust, often depressed, but full of loving kindness and real goodness; and at the same time an artist who knew the importance of his art and who strove for it ceaselessley. The words from heaven in *Faust*:

> *Wer immer strebend sich bemüht,*
> *Den können wir erlösen*

(He who strives, we can redeem) could have been written with Wagner in mind.

A poet with pencil and paper can produce his poetry. Wagner's poems and music, his music-dramas, in order to be born, needed enormous energy and large sums of money. Even when the money was forthcoming there were vast problems to be solved; singers had to be found and trained, a huge orchestra mobilized, difficult stage effects achieved. Small wonder that, to begin with, it was not easy to persuade opera houses in various parts of Germany to devote such a large proportion of their resources to a new work by an unknown composer. Suppose Wagner had been born an Englishman (an impossibility, since he is the most German of German artists) and instead of Leipzig, Dresden, Hamburg, Berlin, Würzburg, Nuremberg, Munich, Vienna, Königsberg, he had had to try Cardiff, Newcastle, Norwich, Leeds? Would his operas have seen the light? Covent Garden would have been his only hope. Despite a festival with visitors from far and wide, Edinburgh has not troubled to build itself an adequate opera house. Wagner complained bitterly of his countrymen, their blindness and meanness, when he was bestowing upon them works of incomparable grandeur and beauty. Yet in any other country he would have fared worse.

He abandoned all thought of finishing *The Ring*, four evenings, until the accession of Ludwig II to the throne of Bavaria, at the age of 20, solved the seemingly insuperable problem. Wagner was deeply in debt and very near despair when the 'mad' king, one of the rare examples of a ruler who spent his leisure and money on art rather than sport, gave him an allowance and subsidies which made *The Ring* and finally the Festspielhaus at Bayreuth possible.

Naturally this generosity caused intense jealousy. Wagner's love of 'luxury' was violently attacked. (He needed quiet, a garden, silk clothes for an exceptionally delicate skin—not impossible demands in return for what he was giving the world.) His other need was for a loving and intelligent woman; his wife Minna had been neither. When he ran off with Hans von Büllow's wife Cosima his enemies in Munich were given a wonderful excuse for their furious condemnation. Büllow himself, an ardent Wagnerian, wrote to Cosima:

> You have preferred to devote your life and your incomparable mind and affection to one who is my superior, and far from blaming you I approve your action from every point of view and admit you are perfectly right.

But Cosima suffered from a bad conscience about Hans for years, hardly a day goes by when she does not moan in her diary. At Tribschen on a Swiss lake she and Wagner led an idyllic family life. He loved the five children (two were Büllow's and three his) so much that he even enjoyed hearing them romping on the stairs; a high test. He and Cosima read together in the evenings, Shakespeare, Goethe, Carlyle, Aeschylus, Schiller, Cervantes, all the classics. By day he went for long walks, and composed.

Before Ludwig appeared on the scene the man who had helped Wagner most with understanding and support had been Cosima's father, Liszt. The great spirits of the age supported Wagner, it was the mean and petty who attacked him. As he said, Goethe had fared no better. After the famous riot at the Paris Opéra performance of

Tannhäuser, when members of the Jockey Club shouted and whistled because they wanted a ballet, Baudelaire defended him. 'What will people in Germany say about Paris?' he wrote: 'This handful of scoundrels has brought down infamy on the heads of all of us'.

When debts became pressing, as they did despite Ludwig's help, Wagner gave concerts. He was evidently a conductor of genius; Cosima's description of his way with an orchestra is deeply interesting. His fame brought full houses, but he was a perfectionist who insisted on many rehearsals, and he rarely made much money in the end, though sometimes laurel wreaths were showered upon him in such profusion that players in the orchestra feared for their instruments. These concerts tired and exasperated him, he felt all his energies should be concentrated on his real work. Yet money had to be found, the builders of the Festspielhaus and of Wahnfried had to be paid. The King often gave only at the last moment; he was spending fortunes on building his palaces, now an asset for Bavaria but at the time the despair of his treasury officials.

Wagner's gods were Beethoven, Mozart and Bach; and Goethe and Shakespeare, and Schopenhauer. He transformed the way Beethoven's symphonies were played, in particular the choral symphony.

These two biographies inevitably cover much of the same ground, but they are aimed at different readers. Ronald Taylor modestly says his book might interest someone who had heard the prelude to *Tristan*, or Wotan's farewell, and who wished to find out about the composer. It is very well done, although the slightly apologetic note, as though to excuse himself for admiring Wagner so much, is strange. He covers the whole life: family circle, disastrous marriage with Minna, all the operas, love affairs, the trouble in Dresden in 1848, exile; and then Ludwig, Cosima, and Bayreuth. The print is rather small, but it is a book that can be recommended.

Curt von Westernhagen is altogether more ambitious. He has written a splendid book to set beside Newman, and it includes all the latest discoveries in letters and diaries. He is excellent on the friendship with Nietzsche and its tragic end, and astute at exposing Elizabeth Förster-Nietzsche's lies. Above all he devotes many enlightening pages to the music.

Wagner often went to Italy to escape from Bayreuth's harsh climate. He and his family were living in a villa at Posillipo when three young musicians, with the daughters of the house and Wagner himself playing and singing, performed the Grail scene from *Parsifal* in the drawing room. As the young men left the villa they heard a voice singing the aria from *Zauberflöte*: '*Drei Knäblein, jung, schön, hold und weise...*' [Three boys, young, beautiful, wise.] They looked back; it was Wagner, on the balcony. They immediately answered with Papageno and Tamino's '*So lebet wohl! Auf Wiedersehen!*' [Be well until we meet again.] Curt von Westernhagen, in such a typically German story, presupposes some knowledge of German culture because he is writing for Germans. (The translation is excellent.) His book will take its place in the library of every music lover.

When Wagner went to London to give concerts at the Albert Hall he met the Pre-Raphaelites, and Burne-Jones painted Cosima. Neither book tells what Wagner thought of the famous echo, of which Beecham said it ensured compositions by English composers would be heard at least twice.

Curt von Westernhagen relates how at the end of his life Wagner was persuaded by Renoir to give him a sitting. Renoir: 'He was very cheerful, I very nervous and sorry that I was not Ingres... At least it's some sort of souvenir of that wonderful head'. The portrait was said to have looked like a poached egg; nevertheless it is moving to think of these two great artists meeting for a brief moment.

Wagner died, in Venice, in 1883. Bruckner was working on his Seventh Symphony when the news reached him. 'I wept! Oh how I wept!' King Ludwig cried out: 'Horrible! Dreadful! Now leave me alone.' And he said proudly: 'I was the first to recognize the artist whom the whole world now mourns. I saved him for the world.' When Hans von Büllow's second wife told him, he said he felt: 'as if his own spirit had died with the spirit of fire', and hearing that Cosima could neither sleep nor eat, he sent her the famous telegram: '*Soeur, il faut vivre*' [Sister, live]. And live she did, for another forty seven years. She, and her son Siegfried, and then his widow Winifred Wagner followed the Meister's detailed instructions, and Bayreuth flourished, as it still does with the composer's grandson in command.

Wagner once said, referring to the orchestra pit at the Festspielhaus, 'I have hidden the orchestra, now I should like to hide the singers'. After the advent of electricity, with clever use of light and dark, mostly dark, Bayreuth partly succeeded in doing this, particularly in the 30s. Wagner also said he did not want only an audience rich enough to pay for the very expensive seats. This wish of his also came true for a time, during the last war when Winifred Wagner was in control. The State paid for the Festivals, the Festspielhaus was filled with soldiers and nurses and factory workers on leave; all the seats were free.

In the frenzy of destruction at the end of the war Wahnfried and the eighteenth-century Eremitage at Bayreuth were bombed. Fortunately, with the best will in the world, you cannot bomb music.

Wagner: A Biography, von Westernhagen, C., trans. Whittall, M.;

Richard Wagner, His Life, Art and Thought, Tayler, R., *Books and Bookmen* (1979)

Pointing at the Ring

Wagner deprecated Jewish influence in theatre and music; he wrote *Judaism and Music* to make his opinion clear. In private life he had many Jewish friends, as well as admirers and disciples. Hermann Levi, one of his conductors, wrote: 'That he is not just narrowly anti-Semitic is shown by his attitude to me... The most wonderful thing I have experience in my life is the privilege of being close to such a man, and I thank God for it every day.'

Wagner was extremely kind and patient with Joseph Rubinstein, a Russian Jew who idolized him and caused him and Cosima acute anxiety, because of the unbalanced character and suicidal tendencies of this talented young man.

Yet the author of *Wagner: Race and Revolution* says he believes that had Wagner been alive in the 30s instead of dying two generations earlier, he would have admired Hitler as much as Hitler admired his music, and that he is therefore in some way guilty of crimes committed by Hitler. It seems a far-fetched hypothesis, for even supposing Wagner had joined the Nazi party, which is unlikely, he would quite obviously have been horrified by genocide; his life is well-documented enough for this guess at least to be valid.

Mr Rose quotes Berthold Auerbach, who wrote in 1881: 'Is it compatible with the last remnant of honourable feeling for the Jews to throng to performances of Wagner's works?' this, because of Wagner's outspoken views in *Judaism and Music*. And here we have the point of Mr Rose's book. It is a plea to Israel to keep its ban on Wagner's music, and thus hardly affects Europeans either way. It is a matter on which Israelis have to make up their own minds.

Auerbach wrote in Wagner's lifetime; his words were not published. Since then, as everybody knows, terrible things have been done, and Mr Rose angrily disapproves of modern Jews who go to Berlin 'for the music'. According to him, all Wagner's operas are shot through with an anti-Semitic message, even *Tristan*, even *Parsifal*. There are also caricatures of Jews: Alberich, Mime, Beckmesser in particular. They were not given Jewish names, because the composer relied on the 'subliminal' level to convey his hateful message. Another hypothesis.

In Cosima Wagner's diary, 26 November 1878, she and Wagner are reading Disraeli's novel *Tancred*, and Wagner remarks: 'The whole thing is so unsettled because of its message. Conveying messages always fails in art, however good the intention.' Clear enough?

Rose's message is explicit, there is nothing subliminal about it. It is even as Wagner called his works 'the music of the future', he wished to dispense with the music of the past. Given his well-known and frequently expressed love of Bach, Mozart, Weber and Beethoven, this is another theory not to be taken seriously.

Does this book succeed in making its point? It reads like a rather clumsy translation from German. Will it be read, taken to heart, and shorten queues for *The Ring*? Perhaps so; but it would take a very credulous person to swallow the wild guesses.

Wagner: Race And Revolution, Lawrence, P., *Evening Standard* (1992)

An Enterprising Sister

To write a biography of Elisabeth Forster-Nietzsche it was not necessary for the author to visit the failed colony she and her husband founded in the 1880s. She only stayed a few years; it was a harebrained undertaking. After the inevitable financial disaster, Forster committed suicide, leaving the unfortunate colonists to exist in appalling conditions. He had issued a false prospectus, of a land flowing with milk and honey, and during an agricultural slump a few dozen Saxon peasants, rather like the Irish in similar circumstances, decided to leave Germany for what Forster promised would be a prosperous and easy life. That he was an anti-semite had little to do with it. Peasants in Saxony in the eighties were of German stock. Where anti-Semitism was rife, and Jews numerous, as in Berlin, the Germans laughed at Forster's colony.

In any case, Ben Macintyre went to Paraguay. For days he journeyed up a river on a filthy boat, eaten alive by mosquitoes. Then, with a guide, he rode many miles through a forest on a jogging nag—'the inside of my knees were raw'—and he finally found a few Germans, scratching a living from intractable soil, plagued by insects, snakes, unbearable heat, and tropical rain. He lived in a chicken coop for the weeks he was there. All it tells us about Elisabeth Nietzsche is that she was rather brave about all the miseries, and very dense not to have seen at once that the venture was doomed. The few remaining Germans had been too poor to leave, apparently.

All this pads out the book, but we might have been spared pages of potted history of Paraguay from the sixteenth century to a few decades ago when war criminals and train robbers hid round about. It is totally irrelevant.

Soon after her husband's death Frau Forster, hearing that her brilliant brother was gravely ill, went back to Germany to look after him. Friedrich Nietzsche cannot have been overjoyed to see his sister, who was 'the embodiment of precisely what her brother fought against.' She was a Christian, an anti-semite and a nationalist. He was none of these. But he was desperately ill, and was certified insane until his death in 1900.

The bossy sister took charge of the many books he had published, some at his own expense, and of the archive of notes, jottings and fragments he left. With the help of his disciples she pushed his books, and they sold. He became world famous, translated into many languages, and she was sought after as guardian of the archive. She was detested by most Nietzscheans, and accused of tampering with texts. But at least she did not burn. She reveled in his fame.

Frau Forster-Nietzsche looked back upon days with her brother and the Wagners, before the famous quarrel, as the happiest of her life. Reading Cosima Wagner's diary, it is easy to see why. At Tribschen there was a lovely house in beautiful country, music, books, and the company of two geniuses.

Forgotten Fatherland: The Search For Elisabeth Nietzsche, Macintyre, B., *Evening Standard* (1992)

The Karajan Dossier

When Goethe was told there was a dispute as to whether he or Schiller was Germany's greatest poet, he said why not be pleased there are two poets, and left it at that. The same applies to Furtwangler and Karajan; both were supreme musicians, albeit with very different characters. Frau Furtwangler is quoted as saying: 'It's a blessing having a husband who isn't vain.' Karajan was absurdly vain. Not about his music, where any amount of pride and vanity were in order, but about his appearance, or his driving of fast cars or speedboats, and other irrelevances.

The Karajan Dossier is a collection of interviews, reminiscences and reviews of great fascination. Round about the time when the maestro reached the preeminent position as Furtwangler's successor with the Berlin Philharmonic Orchestra, what he called the 'music explosion' occurred. Great conductors have always been idolized in Germany, but now they became world idols, and their recordings brought immense riches.

It is the orchestra which chooses its artistic director and conductor, and when Furtwangler died in 1954 the Berlin Philharmonic voted unanimously for Herbert von Karajan. He was 46, and very experienced. For seven years he had been Aachen's music director, he had conducted at the Bayreuth and Salzburg festivals, and at the Vienna State Opera, and had been guest conductor at the BPO a few times. Together they made wonderful records and videos with Deutsche Gramophon and Sony between concerts and world tours. He is said to have left 500 million marks to his family when he died.

He and the Berlin Philharmonic were a splendid team, but there were frequent disputes behind the scenes. When Karajan wished to annoy his great orchestra he cancelled their concerts and went down to Vienna, where he was also artistic director of the State Opera, or to Salzburg, and stayed there.

Intelligent and articulate, everything he has to say about conducting and music is deeply interesting. Thanks to modern recording everyone can hear the perfection of sound he and the Berlin Philharmonic achieved. As a young man Karajan joined the Nazi party, not once but twice. He was not interested in politics, but it was necessary for his career. This earned him a few little hostile demonstrations when he took the orchestra to America.

He was an extremely brave man, often conducting when in acute pain from operations for intervertebral discs. He carried on right up to his death aged 81, when once again the orchestra had to choose its conductor. It voted unanimously for Claudio Abbado, who when he heard the news 'for two minutes I couldn't breathe,' so overwhelmed was he by the honour of being chosen by the greatest orchestra on earth.

There is not a dull page in *The Karajan Dossier*, and Klaus Lang has found a superlative translator. Steward Spencer reads like a first class English journalist, with never an awkward sentence.

The Karajan Dossier, Lang, K., trans. Spencer, S., *Evening Standard* (1992)

Rebuilding Germany

It is arguable that the Allies, in a back-handed way, were largely responsible for the 'German miracle'. When, after nearly six years of war, they had defeated and over-run their great enemy, they tried to ensure that Germany should never rise again, or at any rate not within the lifetime of the allied politicians then in power. Roosevelt died just as the war was ending, and he died happy in the thought that Germany was a heap of rubble. His 'experts' told him it would take thirty years to rebuild the cities, for a start, and he doubtless relied on his Russian friends to see that it should take longer still. Roosevelt said that if he had his way he would 'keep the Germans on the breadline for twenty five years'. The idea, heard with monotonous frequency during the war, that it was not the German people but their leaders we were fighting, turned out to be just Allied propaganda. Probably the Germans had no more believed it than had the men who broadcast it.

The Morgenthau plan, which an enthusiastic Roosevelt induced Churchill to initial, was to deprive Germany of all its heavy industry. It would have entailed the death of millions. Part of the plan, the dismantling of factories and the stealing and using of patents, was in fact carried out. The armies of occupation behaved to the civil population in a way nobody has reason to be proud of; Aidan Crawley describes torture and starvation in the prison camps, and brutally undisciplined behaviour in general. De-Nazification, he says, 'lost all semblance of purification and became an act of indiscriminate vengeance'. He adds that 'more Germans died in the first two years of the occupation than had been killed in nearly six years of war'.

In the millions who survived, however, this bitter challenge evoked a brilliant response. They re-built their towns, their infra-structure and their factories in a very short space of time, being not only hardworking but skilled and inventive. The dismantling, which had seemed to the Allies at the time to be a clever way of punishing them, turned to the advantage of the Germans, who were not burdened with out-of date machinery. Before Roosevelt's twenty five years were up, Germany had become the richest country in Europe and the deutschmark was giving a helping hand to an ailing dollar.

The Allies had helped in another way too. Konrad Adenauer, mayor of Cologne under Weimar, was elected mayor once more after the defeat. An English brigadier earned himself a footnote in history by dismissing him from this office for being obstructive. Thus a small-scale dictator bestowed upon Adenauer the status he needed among his fellow-countrymen, which shot him into politics. As Chancellor he served his country well. He was a good European. and he chose in Erhardt, a professor of economics from Munich, the very man to preside over Germany's vertical take-off from rags to riches.

Fate helped the West Germans in other ways besides dismantling and the general behaviour of the occupying powers, though these gave a great impetus to the effort. Refugees from Prussia, Silesia, Pomerania, Saxony and other provinces, fleeing from communism, arrived in their millions. To begin with they were an additional burden, but they speedily became a precious asset.

When, as was inevitable, the Allies fell out amongst themselves and the cold war began, there was an inexorable tug-of-war for Germany. By far the most interesting part of this very intelligent book is the chapter dealing with communist subversion in West Germany.

The Russians never abandoned the hope of creating a united communist Germany with satellite status. They shrink from atomic war and attempt to attain their objective by other means. Blackmail is a powerful weapon, and a deadly threat to their relations in the DDR has induced many West Germans to work for the Soviets.

Besides blackmail there have been kidnappings and murders. Unlike the kidnappings in South America, they seldom make the headlines. In a very real way, the Germans have lived with fear. Now that the DDR has been able to install consulates in West German cities, and the West German Communist Party has been revived, things have been made a good deal easier for the Russians. 'The object of this underground warfare, which was carried on by thousands of Russian and East German spies, agents, and even assassins, was to undermine morale so completely that West Germans would come to prefer a reunited country under communist 'protection' rather than live in a perpetual state of fear and suspense', writes Aidan Crawley.

In his summing up, Mr Crawley tries to sum up the Germans. He says they eat a good deal; so do the French, and so does anyone in his senses if the food is worth eating. Their houses, unless built before 1850, are not very beautiful. Unfortunately the secret of building beautiful houses was lost everywhere at about that date. At least the Germans have repaired their cathedrals and not let loose any local Sir Basil Spences.* They are very polite, but do their good manners come from the heart? They call the rectors of their universities Magnifizenz, and Mr Crawley is not too sure whether this might not be a sign of 'supine' respect for authority. (Yet it is only a relic of medieval times, the equivalent of calling a king who may be anything but majestic, 'Your Majesty'.) He doubts that the Germans have acquired a 'passionate belief' in democracy. But what is this democracy? He approves of the fact that although an estimated eighty per cent of the population want the death penalty restored, the Bonn parliament refuses to pay any attention. Passionate believers in democracy might attempt to define it, since it by no means coincides with the will of the benighted majority.

Whatever the Germans turn to generally turns out to be wrong in the eyes of Anglo-Saxon commentators. One can easily imagine the strictures if the opposite of the behaviour here criticised chanced to be the norm. Mean and ascetic, hoarding their riches, rude to foreigners, insulting to the dons at their universities (incidentally 'don' is quite out of tune with modern egalitarianism. The Oxford Dictionary gives 'a Spanish lord... a distinguished man, a leader. Hence, in the English Universities...'). No wonder the Germans are inclined to laugh at foreigners who are so ready and anxious to teach them the ABC.

They have performed one 'liberal' act which is little short of sublime: they allow their Turkish guest-workers to use Cologne cathedral as a mosque. However surprising for the crusaders buried there, this must be gratifying to anyone inclined to wonder how broad-minded they really have become.

Germany is not just a chunk of materialist America planted in Europe. The Germans would probably rather be rich than poor, it is one worry the less, but there are plenty of tragic things to worry about in Germany, even in the Federal Republic, now and in the foreseeable future. Awareness of this fact is the great merit of Aidan Crawley's book.

* In charge of the modernist rebuilding of bombed Coventry Cathedral.

The Rise of Western Germany 1945-1972, Crawley, A., *Books and Bookmen* (1973)

Goodies and Baddies

A well-known writer of historical biographies once told me: 'People love reading about what they already know.' This is probably true, as witnessed by the popularity of the item 'yesterday's weather' in the newspapers. Professor Joll has written a painstaking account of a period most of his readers know very well, and some of them almost too well, and his book will be enjoyed by them accordingly. There is nothing much in it that could be called original, or that might shake their preconceptions and set them thinking. All the *idées* are comfortably *reçues*.

The book is well-written and objective, but suppose it were to be judged from the point of view of a completely ignorant newcomer, a

273

man from Mars who knew nothing of the last hundred years, how would it rank? Rather high, I should say.

Nevertheless, for somebody who has lived through half the period, as Mr Joll says he himself has, absolute objectivity is an almost impossible goal. A small example of the difficulty is to be found in the words he uses to describe the killing of a political opponent; they vary according to his view of the government which kills. Thus the pre-Franco Spanish Republicans 'execute', the Russians 'purge', the Germans 'murder'. This will be acceptable to most of his readers; it is important to differentiate between goodies and baddies. It is axiomatic that freedom fighters are heroes while rebels are thugs; heroic resistants execute but cowardly terrorists assassinate or strike in the dark. Violent death has been the fate of countless millions of Europeans, in wars, in camps, as refugees fleeing from their homes, by fire bombs raining down and turning their cities into raging infernos. Were they heroes or villains, were they murdered or executed, were they martyrs or brutes? It depends upon who writes their history.

To come down to details, there is a muddle in connection with the Balkan troubles of the 1870s. First, Disraeli 'threatened to intervene in support of the Turks', then a few lines further on we read of 'Disraeli's desire for unilateral action against the Turks.' This is obviously a case of careless proofreading, but although nearly every schoolboy knows that Disraeli and Queen Victoria were pro-Turk, and Gladstone pro-Bulgarian, there might be the odd one who wished to learn; an erratum slip would not come amiss.

After the First World War and the break-up of the Austro-Hungarian Empire the Balkans and other small countries came into their own. The fashionable parrot cry was 'self determination'. This was an idea and an ideal which, like Christianity itself, had never yet been tried. At Versailles the small countries had powerful lobbies and the defeated central powers were not heard. The predictable result was that great chunks of Germany and millions of Germans and German Austrians were included within the territories of the now swollen 'small' countries.

In the long run, their excessive greed did not benefit the small countries. Poland and Czechoslovakia, to maintain whose arbitrarily drawn frontiers Britain and France declared war on Germany in 1939, are to this day firmly in the grip of Russia.

Sometimes Professor Joll indulges in fantasy, as when he writes: '… democrats not only weakened the Weimar Republic, but also contributed to the establishment after the second world war of two rival German states, based on rival conceptions of society, one liberal and democratic and the other communist and authoritarian.' Does he really believe that German attitudes, opinions or preferences were taken into account when the 'zones' were carved out by the Allies in 1945? The truth is, in 1945 Britain and France were only slightly more influential than Germany itself, and the map of our continent was drawn by a ruthless expansionist Russia, aided by a complacent America ignorant of European history.

Leaving wars, treaties, politics aside now and again, an attempt is made to assess the vast European contribution to science, engineering, art and literature. The author disarms criticism in his introduction by saying that 'some of the greatest imaginative writers, painters and musicians have not been mentioned'. In a book of this length there has to be choice. Among the elect is André Gide, but not Céline; Debussy, but not Alban Berg. In the realm of musical comedy, Kurt Weill but not Franz Lehár; Weill is sanctified by his collaboration with Brecht. Not that it matters, since nobody is going to read a short history book in order to glean knowledge of the arts, particularly one which must deal with such an unusual number of wars, revolutions, executions, purges, murders and other miseries.

It ends, as end it must, on a note of interrogation. Nobody can be dogmatic about the future of Europe. Is Spengler's pessimism justified? Will Toynbee's new Christianity transform the violent continent? According to Professor Joll: 'To some people the Europe of the Treaty of Rome seems rather a provincial affair'. What a province! United Europe can be not only a world power the equal in strength of any other, but is already infinitely richer in everything that makes life worth

275

living.

Europe Since 1870: an International History, Joll, J., *Books and Bookmen* (1983)

Old Russia and New China

A German, an American, and an Englishman, have written these books within the last few months; they can conveniently be reviewed together, different though they are, because they all contain eye witness accounts of Soviet Russia. Dr Starlinger describes nine years spent in Russian prisons and concentration camps; his book is the most serious of the three, though Mr Salisbury, with the trained eye of the journalist who misses nothing (or, at any rate, nothing superficial) is well worth reading, and even frivolous, splenetic Mr Gale has a contribution to make.

Dr Starlinger is a Königsberg doctor who was arrested in 1945 and released in 1954. At the end of the war he was at first permitted by the Russians to organise a hospital at Königsberg, full to overflowing with typhus patients, but after a few months they arrested him and sent him to Russia.

The first part of his book describes life in a big town (Königsberg) where everything has been bombed to pieces—where the drains are smashed, and the water mains out of action; where food and medical supplies are almost non-existent; where there is neither electricity, gas nor fuel. (Perhaps the moral, for those who wish to survive the next war, is to live in the country, with an earth closet, near a spring of clean water and a well stocked vegetable garden.) Dr Starlinger writes with admirable calm and objectivity of his captors and of the incredible hardships he has endured at their hands, such as a journey lasting seven days and nights shut up in a railway prison cage truck of eight cubic metres, designed to hold six men but in which he was confined with *twenty six* others.

After one or two prisons he was sent to a camp where there were many educated Russians: intellectuals, politicians and generals, the survivors of various purges. Here he learned to know them in an intimate way such as no foreigner, outside a concentration camp, could hope to do. Mr Salisbury, after five years in Moscow, says that he had not a single Russian friend; he hardly even had an acquaintance, for so much as to pass the time of day with a foreigner was an unhealthy proceeding for a Russian, inviting the immediate intervention of the ubiquitous MVD. Dr Starlinger, on the other hand, spent many years in closest proximity with the most articulate of Russians, the political prisoners.

Life in the prison camp was hard, grey, hopeless. Between two barricades of barbed wire was a no-mans-land, covered day and night by machine guns mounted in towers. To attempt to escape meant instant death by shooting. Curiously enough, Dr Starlinger relates, although the prisoners often spoke of ways to commit suicide when their existence seemed intolerably hard to bear, he never saw a man take this obvious way out of life.

Everything was discussed in the camp, including politics and religion, and happenings outside were quickly known to the inmates. Dr Starlinger inside his concentration camp, and Mr Salisbury living in Moscow and making lengthy journeys all over Russia dogged by MVD. men, both come to the same conclusion: the death of Stalin, and to a lesser degree the fall of Beria, have altered everything in Russia. No one can calculate the extent of the change, and it is even now too soon to draw optimistic conclusions, but there is no doubt the terror has lifted a little, the man in the street feels less afraid, life has become a shade more normal.

The most important result so far has been the release of many German prisoners, among them the author of *Grenzen der Sowjetmacht*. Usually when a man is released from a Russian prison or camp he is made to sign a paper promising not to speak or write of what he has seen inside. Dr Starlinger was let out with no formalities of this kind, and so were many others with him.

Other results of the lightening of the atmosphere are small but numerous; it is now permitted to take photographs of the Kremlin, tourists are once more allowed into Russia, a vast shop selling every description of consumer goods, from toys to televisions, has opened in Red Square—the biggest store in the world, say the Russians, who, like the Americans, admire hugeness for its own sake; and, they could truthfully add, the most expensive.

Mr Harrison Salisbury was Moscow correspondent of *The New York Times* for several years until September 1954. He travelled all over the country, including Siberia. Both he and Dr Starlinger point out that life there is just about as disagreeable whether you are a prisoner or not. The slave workers very often have more to eat and warmer bedding than their 'free' counterparts.

In the vast areas of permafrost everybody is miserable, the only consolation is the evening drunkenness, which brings brief oblivion. The cold light of June ushers in a thaw which is quickly followed by another long winter. Drains and water mains are an impossibility at those latitudes, where the soil is permanently frozen six inches beneath the surface. Mr Salisbury gives a nightmarish description of Siberian towns; again, so much worse than the country, as readers of Mme. Krupskaya's life of Lenin will agree. When she and Lenin were living in a Siberian penal settlement, before the first war, they had a hut to themselves and Lenin went out duck-shooting.

Dr Starlinger, looking into the future, sees China occupying the position that Russia at present occupies *vis à vis* the West. He tells the following ancedote. When, in 1949, Mao won his war against Chiang Kai Shek, the most intelligent and well-informed prisoners were discussing the matter, and they agreed that it was the greatest victory for Russia and Communism to date. In the circle was an old Russian General whose views carried great weight among them. He sat silent. They urged him repeatedly to give his opinion about the triumph in China, and finally he got up saying: 'Yes, yes; six hundred million men, and soon there'll be more still—and then what?' and went out of the room. This was followed by a long silence: nobody had anything more to say. The General had served for many years in the Far East.

This is where Mr Gale's amusing little book comes in. He accompanied the Labour Party delegation to Russia and China last August as correspondent to the *Guardian.* They stayed a few days in Moscow, where (not having known it under the Stalin terror) Mr Gale duly noted the drab drear, and M. Malenkov's bunch of flowers for Dr Edith, and then they all flew on to China.

The delegation, Mr Attlee, Mr Bevan, Mr Morgan Phillips and *genossen,* may have been the knock-about turn he describes, but it remains in the background, for the press representatives seem to have been kept at arms length by everyone. Although he was only in China a month, Mr Gale looked about him, and what he saw was a well-organised, unimaginably large country, most of whose six hundred million inhabitants are better off than they have ever been before, with more to eat, more to wear, and less disease. If one per cent or so happen to be worse off, there are plenty of prisons and firing squads to take care of them, even though one per cent in this case means six million souls. The remaining five hundred and ninety four million men and women are working hard for their country and Chairman Mao, and rapidly developing their industries, and having millions of healthy babies; and it is not surprising that thoughtful Russians look at them with a certain apprehension.

Dr Starlinger says: Russia is a *Raum ohne Volk* [Room without people]. China is rapidly becoming, despite its vastness, a *Volk ohne Raum* [People without room]. He foresees the day when the West will have to protect Russia's western frontier while she defends her eastern frontier against expanding China. This may be in the distant future, but he believes that it accounts in part for the *détente* in Russian relations with the rest of Europe in recent months.

Of the three authors, he sees furthest and his book is the most important. Mr Salisbury's book is excellent journalism. If English readers feel inclined to put it down in disgust because of its tiresome style, I suggest they should read it (as an English poet once told me one should read Longfellow) with an American accent. This enables one to imagine that an American is telling a number of interesting things, and the infelicities of language cease to irritate.

Diana Mosley

Grenzen der Sowjetmacht, Starlinger, W (1955); *American in Russia,* Salisbury, H.E. (1955); *No Flies in China* G. S. Gale (1955)

※

The Chairman Trap

Dr Li was an enthusiastic young communist when he left Australia for his homeland, hoping to help build the new China and study in hospital to be a neuro-surgeon. But his destiny was to become Mao's personal doctor, a position of considerable danger. He started off with tremendous admiration for the Chairman, and only gradually the atmosphere around him of intense suspicion, jealousy and ambition brought disillusion.

Dr Li often tried to get away from the Chairman's court, but with no success. Mao liked him, partly because he had done his studies with Americans and Australians in the magic capitalist West, supposedly the great enemy, but deeply admired by Mao. The Chairman was a strong, healthy 61, his only problem insomnia. He was often awake for as much as thirty hours on end, and never hesitated to ring for Dr Li in the middle of the night, to come and teach him English, or just to chat.

Twenty two years passed, and Dr Li was at Mao's deathbed; although suffering from several serious diseases his doctors had every reason to fear they would be blamed and punished for killing him, even though he was eight-three, when his tired old heart stopped beating. Instead, Dr Li was told to arrange that the body should be preserved 'for ever'.

Mao loved, and half believed, the fulsome flattery of his courtiers. He liked pretty young women, gave dances for them and took any he fancied to his room. Not much harm in that; the girls were overjoyed, he was their god. The enigma is the Great Leap Forward.

Mao was absolute master of China. He realized the huge country was very backward and he feared the Soviet Union. Convinced that what made countries strong and powerful was linked to steel production, he set hundreds of millions of people to the task of melting iron and forging steel. Every village had its little furnace, using fuel in the most wasteful way imaginable, melting down old nails, pots and pans, even agricultural implements, all destroyed in the hope of reaching some impossible target. Failure meant imprisonment in a cruel labour camp. At the end of the process there were innumerable lumps of useless iron all over the countryside, and the peasants had no ploughs or even spades to work with. A bumper harvest was left to rot in the fields while able bodied men fed the back-yard furnaces. Mao in his luxurious train journeyed around China and pointed out to Dr Li the glow of little furnaces everywhere, fondly imagining his steel production would soon pass that of the powerful West. What happened was famine; millions of people starved to death. It was a disaster of the first magnitude.

Was the cultural Revolution, with its nationwide destruction of everything from irreplaceable works of art to the contents of any bourgeois house by Red Guards and students, allowed by Mao as a distraction to 'save face' after the fiasco of the Great Leap Forward? Why did Mao behave as he did? Can he have been as stupid as he seems?

This book is far better than most translations, probably because Dr Li knows English. It is a relief to learn that he got away at last, and lives in America with his sons. He closely observed the relation between success and health. When things went badly, Mao became ill, when they picked up health returned. His wife, the witch-like leader of the Gang of Four was a hypochondriac, but when Mao allowed her to wield political power her ills vanished overnight. It was what Churchill called 'the royal jelly of success'—if naked power to produce disasters can be reckoned 'success.'

The Private Life of Chairman Mao, Li, Z., *Evening Standard* (1994)

Faustian Knowledge

C.G. Jung's father was a Swiss clergyman of German origins, a rather sad person who lost his faith, and died when Jung was still a student. The vicarage where Jung lived as a little child was perched above the Rheinfall, an amazing, dramatic waterfall. At the age of three he had a dream which haunted him for the rest of his life. He dreamt he descended into a dimly lit chamber underground; a red carpet led to a platform upon which there was a golden throne. A sort of tree-trunk made of skin and naked flesh was standing on the throne; it had an aura of brightness. On the very top of it there was a single eye, gazing upward. He heard his mother's voice: 'Yes, just look at him. That is the man-eater'. The little boy was terrified. He knew even then that he had dreamed of a subterranean God; later he considered that this dream anticipated his life and work, impregnated as it was by the creative principle striving toward the light of consciousness.

At a very early age, too, he realised that God has a dark side. The vicarage was near the churchyard and, when village people died and were buried there, he was told that 'Jesus had taken them unto himself.' This laid the foundation of his life-long preoccupation with the 'dark side' of God. When at 16 he first read *Faust* it 'poured into his soul like miraculous balm'. Goethe's vision of God not only allowing but positively encouraging 'evil', because without it man slumbers in inactivity, exactly corresponded to the boy Jung's own conception of God. 'The figure of Mephistopheles made the deepest impression on me. I vaguely sensed [he] had a relationship to the mystery of the Mothers'. When Eckermann tried to induce Goethe to elucidate 'the Mothers' he only got the reply: *'Die Mütter! Mütter! Es klingt so wunderlich!'* (so strangely wonderful) but Jung was determined to try to shed light in the dark and hidden world where the Mothers dwell.

He became a doctor and psychiatrist and worked for nine years at a mental hospital in Zürich. While he was there he read Freud's books. The two men became friends, but there was a rupture when Jung found himself unable to agree with Freud's exclusively sexual explanation for every neurosis. He did not accept that the unconscious was as simple as Freud made out, and he determined to search deeper down. Hence the quarrel which divided these two eminent men.

Jung set himself to explore his own unconscious. He devised a diagram which showed the conscious mind as a peak and beneath it ever deeper layers of the unconscious—individual, family, nation, continent, race, the primeval ancestors in an area common to the whole of the animal kingdom; and beneath, the 'central fire' from which a spark or current ascends 'through all the layers to every living creature.' His discovery of the collective unconscious was Jung's contribution to understanding mankind. In his diagram it is easy to see, for example, that the deeper you get the harder it is to achieve unity between different groups. The nations find it difficult to understand each other, the continents and races well-nigh impossible.

Jung's attempt 'to probe the depths of my own psyche' led him along perilous paths. He said the only parallel journey that he knew of was in *Faust II*, where the poet had 'an alchemical encounter with the unconscious'. It would probably not be too much to say that having Goethe as forerunner and Faust as companion kept Jung sane. He writes: 'I was afraid of losing command of myself and becoming a prey to the fantasies—and as a psychiatrist I realised only too well what that meant'. Elsewhere he refers to men who did in fact go mad in pursuit of fantasies, who were 'shattered by them—Nietszche, and Hölderlin and many others'.

In the depths Jung met with archetypal figures, and, says Miss Hannah, 'He told me that at this time he made it a rule never to let a figure or figures that he encountered leave until they had told him why they had appeared to him'. In an attempt to throw light on this seeming impossibility she tells the story from the *Odyssey* of Menelaus and Proteus. Because 'he knows the sea in all its depths' Proteus could tell Menelaus all he wanted to know about what had happened since he left Troy. But how to seize him? Proteus turned himself into a snake, a lion, a giant boar, even into running water. Finally he grew tired of his magic repertory and told Menelaus all he knew. 'This story shows us... how to deal with the figures we meet on our confrontation with the unconscious', writes Miss Hannah. Does it? Doubtless what she says Jung told her is what he did tell her, but he himself constantly refers to the archetypes with whom he talked in the unconscious as 'my fantasies'. What he does stress is that his fantasies produced ideas which he could not recognise as 'his'.

Jung's archetypal figures included an old man and a girl, who told him they were Elijah and Salome. They were accompanied by a large black snake, but Elijah seemed to Jung the most reasonable and intelligent of the three. The figure of Elijah gradually developed into that of Philemon, who was to be the most important figure in Jung's exploration. Philemon is familiar to readers of *Faust* as the last victim of Mephistopheles' guile and cruelty. This pair—Philemon and Salome had a far-reaching effect on Jung, because at the very time of his encounter with them in the unconscious he was consciously falling in love with a young girl who turned out to be the only person 'able to follow his extraordinary experiences and to accompany him intrepidly into the underworld.' This was Toni Wolff, whose mother had taken her to Jung to be analysed on account of deep depression. Miss Hannah says 'it seems hard, just at the time he was tried to the uttermost by his confrontation with the unconscious' that Jung had to deal with the most difficult problem that can face a married man: that of convincing his wife that his love affair was necessary. He hit upon a splendid idea: 'he had seen all too often (in analysis) the untold damage that fathers can do to their daughters by not living the whole of their erotic life... the father's unlived life is then unconsciously displaced onto the daughters'. Fear that this might happen (for he had several daughters) kept Jung awake a whole night. He realised that if he refused to 'live the outside attraction' he would ruin his daughters' *eros*. Therefore it was his plain duty to go ahead with his love affair. I commend this thought to other husbands requiring an excuse for their infidelities.

Jung felt a need to 'see the white man from outside'; he went to New Mexico where he made friends with a chief of the Taos Pueblo Indians called Mountain Lake. They had long talks. One day Mountain Lake told Jung: 'The Americans want to stamp out our religion. But what we do, we do not only for ourselves but for the

Americans also. Yes, we do it for the whole world. Everyone benefits from it.' This observation produced great emotional excitement in Jung; he felt he was approaching the central mysteries of Mountain Lake's religion. He asked in what way the whole world benefited, and was told that the Pueblo Indians live on the roof of the world. nearest to God. 'We are the sons of Father Sun, and with our religion we daily help our father to cross the sky. If we were to cease practising our religion, in ten years the sun would no longer rise. Then it would be night for ever'. Mountain Lake had a poor opinion of white men. He said they look so cruel, and their eyes have a staring expression; 'the whites always want something. We do not know what they want. We do not understand them', an observation which confirmed Jung in his opinion that different races have the utmost difficulty in understanding each other. It is interesting that the Indians and the Americans each accuse the other of cruelty. The Indian with his scalping knife is an image familiar to every Anglo-Saxon child, an image sedulously fostered by the Americans while they wiped out whole tribes of redskins.

Jung found another noble savage in Africa, where he made a journey from Uganda to Egypt. He loved Africa. He said that the same conditions prevail in very primitive countries as in the collective unconscious. He was disappointed to discover that the tribes were no longer guided by the dreams of their medicine men. This was because the medicine men themselves laboured under the delusion that their dreams were no longer necessary, since the English district commissioner knew everything.

Jung lived for most of his life near the Zürich lake, where he built himself a house. Some distance along the shore he built a tower where he could escape from his family and the demands of his patients, and contemplate the water in peace. He was a very strong personality, loved and revered by his disciples. In this somewhat claustrophobic atmosphere, surrounded by adoring women, grateful patients and rich American benefactors, he strove to achieve *Ganzheit*. The English word 'wholeness' does not quite convey the meaning of this typically

German conception. The disciples accepted not only the idea of the collective unconscious (an idea which has thrown light on many things previously not understood) but also his claim to have explored it, and to have forced the archetypes he met there to disclose to him their secrets. Miss Hannah knew him well for thirty years, but she has perforce relied to a great extent on the only autobiographical writing he left: *Memories, Dreams, Reflections.* There he says he had to try to understand his own fantasies in order to help his patients with theirs, but in her book the whole question hovers on the frontier between medicine and religion, or magic.

One thing is certain: Jung never achieved *Ganzheit* in the Goethean sense. Art completely passed him by. His own carvings, hands stretching out to the udder of a mare, for example had little to do with art, whatever his anima may have told him. He kept his lively interest in odd phenomena into old age; he was delighted by the flying saucers and similar UFOs. He was pleased that people wanted them to be real, and that all over the world they were seeing round objects in the sky. 'Roundness is the symbol for the self, the totality, and this fact in our sceptical, rational modern world is of overwhelming interest in and for itself' says Miss Hannah. She often seems to be thinking in German.

I wish she could have told a few facts, such as the percentage of cures among the patients Jung analysed. Perhaps this is not possible, for what is a 'cure'? Her book is gossipy but interesting, and she herself emerges as a clever and agreeably quirky old lady. If Jung is slightly diminished, that is not her fault. Hagiography always diminishes its victim, and Jung was Miss Hannah's infallible idol.

Jung: His Life and Work: a Biographical Memoir, Hannah, B., *Books and Bookmen* (1977)

Thomas Mann

Thomas Mann was the best German novelist since Goethe, a very popular writer whose books sold in millions. He must also have been a talented actor: his readings from his works attracted enthusiastic audiences.

Thomas and his brother Heinrich decided not to carry on the old family corn business in Lübeck, and when their father died at 51 the family moved to Munich. Thomas wrote *Buddenbrooks* when he was twenty five, a best seller about himself, his family and Lübeck, thinly disguised. All his life he must have offended people he knew, who found themselves caricatured in his novels.

Heinrich loved Italy, but it meant little to Thomas, child of the Protestant gothic north. He married a Jewess, Kata Pringeheim, his perfect and sympathetic wife for more than fifty years. They had six children. Nothing could have been more bourgeois than this large family living in the hideous house he built in Munich.

Thomas was39 when the First World War began. He wrote enthusiastically for the Fatherland, saying it was a conflict between the German spirit and the material West, and defending the attack on neutral Belgium by comparing it with Frederick the Great's on Saxony. He dreaded being called up, but never was. He denounced democracy, which he was afterwards to extol. There are political quotes for all seasons to be found in Thomas Mann. After the war he felt very German and nationalist until the early 20s, when National Socialism erupted. His hatred of the Nazis governed his life henceforward. In 1933 he left Germany to live in Switzerland and managed to get most of his manuscripts out. But a box was inadvertently left behind, which caused him sleepless nights, because it was full of diaries to which he confessed his secret.

This respectable family man, and much-admired writer, was homoerotic. Although he remained buttoned up, never indulging in more than a hand clasp or a furtive hug, he dreaded the Nazis finding his confessions and blackening his character. They never did.

Nobody now, reading his story *Death in Venice*, could doubt where the writer's sympathies lay, but when it was published in 1913 the permissive society was undreamt of. Thomas Mann minded deeply what people thought of him.

Was he tortured by impossible, unassuasive desire? Probably not. His wife, his children, his enormous success, his fame and fortune and his Nobel Prize were extremely important to him. His diaries are full of complaints about health, teeth, ears, nausea and various ill that flesh is heir to. Sex seems to have been a mild and harmless pleasure, though possibly he regretted never having known passion. Even before the first war he was in and out of clinics. There was nothing he liked better than a rich sanatorium—health was a major preoccupation, and the mise-en-scène of *The Magic Mountain* perfectly familiar.

From Switzerland he lectured all over Europe; on Goethe, Schiller, Wagner, Freud and Nietzsche. But as war approached he and Katia began to feel uncomfortably near Germany so they went to America, where they had a powerful benefactress in Agnes Meyer, whose husband owned the *Washington Post*. She smoothed the way for Thomas even finding him a sinecure to ensure an adequate income. However, in return she wanted to be his muse, his mentor, his possessor. The unfortunate Thomas wrote her flattering letters, stayed with her, pretended to welcome her, while all the time confiding in his diary what a pest she was. Ronald Hayman, in his dry way, relates this richly comic episode to perfection.

The Manns lived in California and became American citizens. After the Second World War Thomas Mann who knew nothing of the gulags, used to say he could happily live under communism. Accustomed to adulation as an anti-Nazi and Nobel Prize winner, he suddenly found the climate changed. Denounced by McCarthyites as soft on communism, his situation was like the 30s all over again. He longed to leave America, which he called 'an air-conditioned nightmare'.

Eventually the Manns got back to Europe, and settled near Zurich. Thomas was showered with prizes and honorary doctorates.

A sort of jealousy shines out of the pages of Mann's Goethe novel, *Lotte in Weimar*. Probably what he envied in his great predecessor was Goethe's classic and uninhibited attitude to love, and that he went on falling in love when he was old and didn't care who knew it, whereas Thomas had to make do with a glance at an attractive waiter, or a glimpse of a boy playing tennis. Whether he truly wished for more is something we shall never know; probably his inhibitions had become an integral part of him.

Ronald Hayman has written an excellent biography of the great storyteller.

Thomas Mann, Hayman, R., *Evening Standard* (1996)

The Pulse of Ideology

For a very large part of the world, there is now no ideology with pretensions to universality that is in a position to challenge liberal democracy—this is the theme, constantly repeated, of this optimistic book [*The End of History and the Last Man* by Francis Fukuyama]. There are tables showing that more and more countries have succumbed to the charms and opportunities of liberal democracy, all of them rather rich and upwardly mobile. Their citizens enjoy freedom, and are no longer subject to the vague terrors of war.

Soviet Russia has fallen to bits, and revealed its appalling poverty and inefficiency to the delighted gaze of the more fortunate denizens of the west. Spengler should evidently have called his book *The Downfall of the East*.

China? Still by way of being communist, it has been obliged to allow a measure of market economy here and there, to keep things going. Perhaps we should not be too anxious for it to change. A glance further East than Russia can be rather alarming.

The brilliantly clever Japanese have pointed the way to Taiwan, South Korea and the rest of them. What Chairman Mao called 'uneasy thoughts' assail us in the comfortable, smug West. Can we compete? Are they too clever by half? What about their terrifying work ethic, just when we prefer the ethic of idleness? Might it interfere?

When the author speaks of 'extremely powerful passions—religion and nationalism', he is too politically correct to mention the dread word 'race'. Yet race is as powerful as either of the others. Disraeli said 'all is race', and certainly this book bears him out.

Riches and prosperity and ease are the goal. The only worry left to those of us with no more history is that some demented little country might blow us up with its nuclear bomb, thus putting an end to history in a manner almost welcomed by Shaw at the end of his life, when he despaired of irrational man.

Democracy is nowhere defined, and it takes many forms. Universal suffrage is only a beginning, and solves none of our problems. Somebody has to make decisions, choice is of the essence. What Asquith called 'the pervading influence of a commanding mind' is extremely important in the enterprise of government. But commanding minds are rare. In the teeth of bitter opposition from a large proportion of his countrymen, General de Gaulle, for example, once in power, was a dictator for ten years. Yet France is 'a democracy'.

Fukuyama dismisses local difficulties such as the Northern Ireland impasse, the hatred between Arab and Jew, the famine in Somalia, wars in the Balkans, and the hideous poverty in the very heart of America and the EC, as not particularly important. Some are soluble, others perhaps not. But he totally ignores the greatest and most intractable problem of our time: over-population.

He seems to be a clever don in a rich American university, becoming more and more optimistic as the old enemies and the cold war dissolve, while democracy advances with the calm firm tread Spengler once associated with Caesarism. Does he underrate the envy, hatred and malice in the world?

This enjoyable book is not unduly marred by the sort of jargon associated with American academics, though we could do without words like directionality, marketisation and explicated. It is pleasant to think that owing to the powerful scientific civilization created by the Europeans, the Americans and the Japanese, we can continue to be liberal democrats, and shall not be deprived of our harmless amusements, such as

Prime Minister's Question Time 'live' on the wireless. The cries of yes I did, no you didn't, you're another, and so forth, are the essence of the democratic process. So, for the matter, are American presidential elections. Small wonder we are the model and the envy of the entire world.

The End of History and the Last Man, Fukuyama, F., *Evening Standard* (1992)

❉

A Gleam of Hope

Mr Wyndham Lewis' first novel for fourteen years is, on the human level, as bitter and disillusioned as its title suggests. There can be no doubt that the author dislikes and despises people in general and English people in particular. Almost every character is a savage caricature, a grotesque. The central figure, Professor René Harding, is half French, and (as war-time England is, in a sense, the villain of the novel) this half-foreignness is evidently meant to mark his superiority. When war approaches, in 1939, he throws up his history professorship, because he disapproves so deeply of the war and the trend of events in Europe that he decides to start a new life in Canada. Why does he not continue to teach, and try to convert others to his point of view? Because he is nervous, vain, touchy, and—in the last resort—conventional. Feeling an atmosphere so hostile to him he retires before the fight begins.

In Canada, he and his wife are virtually prisoners for three years. They inhabit a room in a cheap hotel which they are too poor to leave, with no friends, no work, and no comfort, where they suffer deeply from the Canadian climate, which according to Mr Wyndham Lewis consists of ten months of bitter freezing winds and two months of glaring, panting heat accompanied by swarms of dangerous, stinging flies. Extremely unpleasant for both of them, these years are harder to bear for the wife than for the husband, as imprisonment must always be harder for those with empty heads than for those whose intellectual life is an unending adventure. Finally the dreadful squalid hotel is burned down; and when, soon after, René Harding is offered a chair of history at the local university, his wife, realising that Canada is to be their permanent lot and neurotically homesick for Kensington, chooses freedom by throwing herself under a lorry.

There are scenes which are so well described that they are unforgettable—the Hampstead dinner party, the hotel fire, the police morgue—but it is not these alone which are the point of the book. The loving care most writers lavish on their characters is reserved by Mr Wyndham Lewis for the ideas of his hero. Professor Harding, 'outraged by the events of the past thirty years beyond endurance', writes a book. In it he points out that: 'History is the record of the quantitive... Unless the notion of significance can be detached from this misleading "quantity" association, no proper History can be written... If a new attitude were to be introduced, banishing the record of the silly, the criminal, or the commonplace (which, as it is, relegates History to the plane of a crime-yarn, a Western Story, or a body of statistics) then it would be necessary to attempt to expunge from our daily life, as far as possible, the things we condemn in History... He hoped that the discredit of a certain kind of event in the past would reflect forward (to some extent) to how we all acted today.'

He goes on: 'We obviously would perish ignominiously if we continued as we were at present. We must train and compress our-selves in every way, and breed an animal superior to our present disorderly and untidy selves. He added that there was very little chance of our doing this, but that it was just worth stating that this is the only possible solution.'

The discussion of these neo-Nietzschean ideas makes this book unusual. For those who do not like didactic novels, perhaps it should be pointed out that they (the ideas) take up very little space; the remainder is full of dramas and melodramas; and of cads, mad charwomen, toughs, bearded Canadian pansies, thieves and murderers, revolving round the solitary figure of *homo sapiens* personified by Professor Harding. The result is an intelligent, funny, rather savage novel, deeply pessimistic about man as he is but with a gleam of hope for man as he might be.

Self Condemned, Lewis, W. (1954)

Les Champs Elysées

FRANCE

Yes, Wallis Was a Woman After All

The news that Michael Bloch, well known for his Windsor books and with access to the Windosr archives, had written a book to prove that the Duchess had been a man was startling. What had he discovered, and how? It conjured up the strangest vision among anyone who knew the Duchess (he did not know her) of a tiny man, a very thin midget, beautifully dressed in drag by Balenciaga, wearing a cleverly made wig, because few men could summon up enough hair for the bouffant style she favoured—but here the vision fades, and the real-life Duchess is remembered as she was, feminine and elegant.

The truth is, Michael Bloch does not say she was a man. He says she never had what other women have, but he doesn't say she had what men have. He says that her three marriages were unconsummated. Of course, he is only guessing. Perhaps he advanced his theory as an excuse for dishing up once again the whole Windsor story, from Mrs Simpson's meeting with the Prince of Wales, his passion for her, the abdication, their life together for thrity five years, her seemingly endless illness and her death ten years ago at the age of 90.

Wallis Warfield's first marriage was to a very manly and rather brutal looking officer in the US airforce, Winfield Spencer. She was 20. If he had discovered on their wedding night that sexual intercourse was impossible because of some physical deformity, there can be little doubt they would have departed next day. He drank too much and was often violent; he would not have been violent to her had they been living as brother and sister. This is just a fact of life. The marriage failed because of his drinking quite simply.

Mr Simpson was the sort of man who might well have married her in order to acquire an entertaining companion who was also a housekeeper of genius, but her marriage to Spencer was a love-match ruined by drink, hardly an unusual event.

The Duke's love for her was so deep, and so obvious to anyone who saw them together, that it is no good pretending it had some abnormal physical reason. It lasted until he died and she looked after him superbly.

There are happy married couples in the world, and the Windsors are an outstanding example of this. It seems just as perverse to pretend she was a freak to have pretended that she was not a royal highness, when legally she was.

Bloch writes well and there are plenty of photographs for the fans. It is the non-fans who may be slightly disappointed by the flimsy evidence he advances for his fantasy.

The Duchess Of Windsor, Bloch, M., *Evening Standard* (1996)

'Something Must Be Done'

Frances Donaldson's biography of Edward VIII was published a few years ago, and now she has abridged the text, added many excellent illustrations, and given it the coffee table format. More than half the book is devoted to the abdication, the tone throughout being censorious. It is a book by a governess doing her best to be fair to her charge, and sometimes succeeding.

She describes the rather sad childhood, the aloof mother, the sergeant-major-like father, and the poor education bestowed upon the children of George V at York Cottage, the house Harold Nicolson called 'a glum little villa'. She admits that the Prince of Wales had 'a very real talent for natural feeling and natural behaviour in an impossibly artificial sitution', for the 'narrow, nice line that, pursued with increasing confidence, would soon carry him to amazing heights of popularity almost all round the world.' It is no exaggeration to say that he was idolised; in England, in the Dominions where he undertook exhausting tours and in fact everywhere he went. Many quotations here emphasise this. Lord Mountbatten said of him: 'He had an absolutely magnetic charm.' Being an idol is probably not as easy as it sounds.

The abysmal failure of successive British governments in the 20s and early 30s to deal with the problem of poverty in the midst of plenty and of unemployment is notorious. The Prince of Wales, like other ex-servicemen of the First World War, saw the suffering of his fellow-countrymen and doubtless felt (and it was the truth) that it was due to the inadequacy of government. When, as King, he spoke the famous words 'Something must be done', millions of people agreed and approved; but the politicians, disliking the implied rebuke, murmured about bringing the Crown into politics.

When he came to the throne as Edward VIII he was already deeply in love with Mrs Simpson; it was a love which lasted every day of his life for nearly forty years. A great deal has been written about the abdication, and about his selfishness, and dereliction of duty, and putting his private happiness before his duty to his country, and all this is stressed here. It is a theory which does not stand up.

The point is continually made, that in a constitutional monarchy the monarch cannot play any political role. He must be 'above politics', in other words simply a figurehead and a living symbol. Suppose, for one moment, Edward VIII thought a war with Germany would be the disaster for us that it has proved to have been, he could have done nothing to prevent it had he remained on the throne. Even in purely domestic affairs he could not have interfered. 'Something must be done' was a cry wrung from him at the sight of ghastly despair in the distressed areas caused by political failure, but even that was disapproved of (perhaps rather naturally so) by a government which was convinced that nothing either would or could be 'done'.

If this point is agreed, that the sovereign must on no account intervene in any way at all, and that the word 'reign' is nothing but a word left over from olden times, then it follows that it does not matter so much who the sovereign is, what matters is continuity. The proof is that six kings and queens in the last one hundred and forty years have all been popular and successful, yet all unlike one another.

Edward VIII had a strong sense of duty; he would undoubtedly have sacrificed his private happiness had he been an only son, for he was a firm believer in monarchy. Since he had three brothers, all of them married and each with a wife eminently suitable to be queen consort, there was no reason for his doing so. It was perfectly true that he could not fulfil the role of King without the help and support of the woman he loved (as he put it). A royal family is needed. He knew that the brother who was to succeed him, the future George VI, with Queen Elizabeth and the Princesses, would be ideal for England and for what was then the Empire; and so it proved.

King George V is quoted as having 'exclaimed passionately' a few weeks before he died:

> I pray to God that my eldest son will never marry and have children, and that nothing will come between Bertie and Lilibet and the throne.

We are not told to whom he is supposed to have made this observation. It could, presumably, only have been to Queen Mary, and in strict privacy, and she is unlikely to have repeated it. However, there is no reason to doubt that such were indeed the thoughts of the old King. Edward VIII made sure that his father's prayer was answered.

Nevertheless, many people, Churchill and Lloyd George, among them, were very sorry to see him go. At the time of the abdication Lloyd George was in the West Indies; in those days the journey took weeks and he could not get home to take part in the House of Commons debate. He cabled to his MP son and his MP daughter: '... Had King not as prince and sovereign exposed continued neglect by government of chronic distress, poverty and bad housing conditions amongst his people in realm, convinced they would not have shown such alacrity to dethrone him. You may make any use you like of this telegram.'

With such high-powered statesmen on his side there must have been a temptation for the King to sit tight, but he was resolved not to divide the nation. In the interest of continuity, he abdicated. Sir Colin Coote, in his obituary of the Duke wrote: 'It was very largely due to him that his going was not cataclysmic. His determination that what he did should not be politically upsetting was as strong as his resolve to do it.'

The Duke himself shall have the last word: 'I played fair in 1936,' he said, 'but I was bloody shabbily treated.' The late James Pope-Hennessy quoted this. He had planned a biography of the Duke of Windsor, and it is a thousand pities that he did not live to write it. The Duke is apt to bring out the governess in people, but there was no trace of the governess in James Pope-Hennessy's make-up; only vivid intelligence and humour.

Edward VIII. The Road to Abdication, Donaldson, F., *Books and Bookmen* (1978)

❋

Goody-Goodies

In the last war Lady Donaldson had a farm; the description of her experiences is the best part of this memoir. Apparently she has already published two farming books, so there may be readers aware of her courage and skill in the enterprise. Her last venture, battery hens, seems less admirable.

She and her husband were lifelong members of the Labour Party, but left for the more seductive 'Alliance'. Far from breaking the mould of British politics it was so fragile that it came to pieces in their hands, losing handle and spout like an eggshell china teapot. She writes as if we were still living in 1988, before the world completely changed after the fall of communism, praising Crosland's book *The Future of Socialism*. Would there not now be more point in reading Taine?

It is sad to be told how nearly the biography of the Duke of Windsor was written by James Pope-Hennessy, so witty and perceptive. Frances Donaldson's book was a bestseller and she goes through the story again here. It is a pedestrian affair compared with what it might have been. Both Donaldsons were what Churchill used to call goody-goodies, which though very nice is somewhat inhibiting for writing on Edward VIII. Where Pope-Hennessey in the fragments that remain, makes the reader laugh aloud, but always with a scenes of pathos and waste, she is unconsciously comic, as when she says the Duke cruelly left his assistant Major Metcalfe behind in Paris when France was falling. It would have been much more unkind to drag him south, Metcalfe's goal being England where his wife lived. From Paris to London was easy compared with sailing from Bordeaux or Nice.

As to Freda Dudley-Ward, a very charming person, if she felt about the then Prince of Wales in the way described, what was she doing as his greatest friend for sixteen years? Could there have been a touch of snobbishness? Followed by a hint of the woman scorned? The account somehow fails to add up. It is an abiding mystery why people who find the Duke of Windsor unsympathetic and feel he would have made a 'bad king' (whatever that may be) should nevertheless be so critical of his abdication. They ought to be delighted that he gave them the slip.

Frances Donaldson is more successful with the Waughs, whom, unlike the Windsors, she met and knew quite well. Her friendly description might do something to counter hostile biographies of recent years about this excellent writer and wonderfully clever and amusing companion to his cronies. He was not at his best when drunk, but who is?

A Twentieth-Century Life: A Memoir, Donaldson, F. (1992); *Evening Standard*

Surrounded by Love

I knew the Duchess of Windsor fairly well for a good many years; she and the Duke were our neighbours in the Vallée de Chevreuse, and we often dined with them in the Mill house at Gif, where the Duke had made a lovely English garden round a millstream. They often came for luncheon or dinner with my husband and me, about five miles away at Orsay.

I was fond of the Duchess, and very much admired her wonderful efficiency, her great talent for making comfort and happiness for the Duke, her delicious food, and her unfailing high spirits. Nobody more appreciated wit and humour than she did. In conversation, as Cole Porter once said, she always threw back the ball. She was one of the most outstanding hostesses I ever knew. She made everything fun, and nobody in her house was ever allowed to feel out of things. The French loved her and appreciated her elegant appearance; she wore her clothes so well and chose them so cleverly.

Of course, as everybody knows, or at least everyone who knew them, the Duke adored her until his dying days. He thought her completely perfect in every single respect.

When he died she must have missed his love and admiration more than words can say. He was happy when she was there, sad when she was not, for nearly 40 years. There is no doubt about this deep and unchanging love. She felt he had given up so much for her sake that she simply had to devote her life to him, and this she did.

The last years were terrible. She was alive, and yet not alive. Doctors have become very clever at keeping the heart beating. Who knows what she suffered? I do not mean so much physical pain, or even discomfort, but who can tell whether someone in her condition feels sorrow, has illusions, or nightmares? Nobody knows. What we do know is that her nurses loved her.

So did her devoted couple Georges and Ofélia; their loving care of her was marvellous in its unselfish devotion.

The Duke, as he often said, felt very bitter that she was refused the title of Royal Highness. The Duchess, except for his sake, did not mind this curious piece of illnatured bad manners in the very slightest. It seemed to her, though it did not to him, something completely trivial and unimportant. His wish that she should be buried by his side in Frogmore is granted.

When he lay in state at Windsor fourteen years ago, sixty thousand made the journey to pay their last respects. He was greatly loved, and for his sake she was loved by many. I have been shown some of the hundreds of letters she used to get on birthdays and other anniversaries, full of touching affection for a lady the British people can never have seen. She has been much maligned, but they had paid no attention whatever to spiteful books or newspaper stories.

The Times (1986)

❊

Debunking a Dark Fairy Tale

A few years after the death of the Duke of Windsor in 1972, the Duchess, aged 80, had a brain haemorrhage and nearly died herself. Unfortunately she was saved by clever doctors and lived on for a decade: a living death. Her heart beat strong, but she had to be fed artificially through the nose. Her mind and memory had gone. She had three nurses and the best medical care as a rule, in her house in the Bois de Boulogne, with sojourns at the American Hospital in Paris. She became paralysed, but no details of the course of her long illness have ever been revealed. Her affairs were looked after by Maître Blum, her lawyer.

Apparently in 1980 Lord Snowdon wanted to photograph the Duchess for the *Sunday Times*, but this was of course impossible. However, he got in touch with Maître Blume, and Caroline Blackwood, who was to have written the text, became fascinated to the point of obsession with the old lawyer, who guarded the Duchess so secretively and with the aid of press cuttings sued anyone who libelled her. Nevertheless in her account, which she herself calls a 'dark fairy tale', she has made a cardinal error which persists from beginning to end.

It was not Maître Blum who stopped people seeing the Duchess, it was the doctor. The notice in the hall which the butler could show to callers who persisted in demanding to go up to her room was signed by him. Visitors made her blood pressure rise, and he forbade them. In any case she was in no fit state to wish for them so far as we know, though sometimes Maître Blum said she was sitting up listening to Cole Porter.

At my last visit she never spoke, but lay staring like the Greek mask of tragedy. I was appalled and haunted by the thought of her total loneliness and helplessness. Friends were all very well, but in a medical context only relations count. Only they can question and badger and insist, and examine and cross-examine. The Duchess had no relations of her own, nobody at all.

My view, as time went on, and it has not changed, was that the in-laws should have done what they could. They probably paid for her very expensive treatment, but a member or trusted friend of her late husband's family, accompanied by a famous neuro-surgeon and a lawyer, should have gone over to Paris from time to time to see for themselves. The doctor would most likely have agreed with the French doctors, but a second opinion is in order. They had not only a right but a duty to do something of this kind; a duty to a very old woman who had been married for thirty five years to their close relation. Perhaps they did! There was so much secrecy surrounding the Duchess and her illness that I for one have no idea.

Who can ever know what a human vegetable feels? Did she feel pain? Did she have nightmares? Nobody knows, but the heart beats, therefore she is 'alive'. Among the secrecy and uncertainty there was one comfort: the presence in the house of Georges the butler. Like all those who worked for her he was fond of the Duchess, and above all he was there. Daily visits by lawyer and doctor were no insurance as to what went on most of the time. Georges promised me that he would telephone at once if any of the nurses was less than kind and gentle. I went to see him in the morgue-like house, just to have a talk now and again. He was absolutely trustworthy.

Of course a photograph was out of the question, but Snowdon and Caroline Blackwood decided to switch to Maître Blum. She consented to pose, and gave an interview which sounds to have been a furious quarrel. According to the author Maître Blum had a crazy view of the Duchess's character and way of life. She screamed at the idea of her heroine at a night club, or downing a drink or two, and insisted she had spent her evenings reading or listening to classical music. She obvious-ly had no idea that the 75-year-old Duchess went gaily off to learn the Twist, and drank vodka out of a silver mug. She said all the books about her were lies, but the Duchess was much more fun and more gal-lant and unusual than Maître Blum, who scarcely knew her, seems to have imagined.

Maître Blum had a power of attorney, the Duchess had great possessions. Her jewels were amazing. None of them had anything to do with the Crown Jewels, as asserted here, but they became more valuable year by year. Queen Alexandra had left some personal jewellery to the Duke, but it must have been swapped or recut, as the Duchess only wore modern jewellery, most of it bought by the Duke for his beloved. He did not spend millions. The millions were realized by Sotheby's after the death of the Duchess; her things fetched huge prices, partly because they had been hers.

Caroline Blackwood writes of 'royal swords' so craved by Lord Mountbatten that they were always hidden when he was expected. They otherwise lived on the piano for all to see. They were made of dark jade, sharpened to a razor edge, and had been used for executions in Burma. The victim stood erect, and with one tremendous swipe by the executioner the head was severed from the body. These ancient swords had been given by the Burmese to the Prince of Wales on one of his Empire tours. Probably Mountbatten longed for them because he called himself 'of Burma'. Where are they now?

This book is full of mistakes, as becomes a fairy tale. Unity Mitford shot herself not in 1945, but in 1939 on the outbreak of a war she did not wish to live through. She was never 'incapable of speech'. The man who got pictures of the Duchess looking half dead took them from the road, he never got near a window. The Duchess was being carried into the garden. I never called the Duchess Wallis, or Hitler Hittles, nor did I say General Spillmann was Prussian; I met him and knew he was from Alsace.

All these inaccuracies cast doubt on the wild things Maître Blum is quoted as saying, and the little jokes and ironies fall flat. They are too repetitive. As to the description of Michael Bloch, Maître Blum's assistant, it is a silly caricature. He is a clever writer who made use of the Windsors' papers for some informative books.

When she died at last, in 1986, the Duchess left her money to the Institut Pasteur, a fact not mentioned here. Her funeral at St George's Chapel at Windsor was attended by all her household, they went with the Royal Family to the burial at Frogmore. The Queen decorated

Georges Sanègre for his devoted service.

Friends had places in the choir, I was put next to Laura Marlborough, who whispered: 'I went to see Diana Cooper last night. When she heard I'd hired a car to come here she said 'Oh! Do take me!' but I said sorry chum, no way, I'm not going to lug you up the steps.' Laura and Diana Cooper were two of the old ladies interviewed by the author for her gruesome little book. She has padded it out with chunks of extracts from the Windsors' memoirs. Its theme is suffering and death, and the ethics of modern medicine, more and more in question as the century ends. At present the Hippocratic oath to save life reigns supreme.

All this interspersed with many a giggle. Yet had it come out when she wrote it in 1980 (1970 she says, but that must be another mistake as both Windsors were alive in 1970), I should have welcomed it, spite and all.

Unfortunately, the author was too afraid of Maître Blum, who inconveniently lived to be 95. Any light shone upon that secret misery would have been better than nothing. Now, though every anti-Windsor story is raked up and raked through, none of them new and all so far away, it seems pointless.

The Last of the Duchess, Blackwood, C., *Evening Standard* (1995)

A Gay Life

James Pope-Hennessy was a charming and gifted homosexual. Affectionate, talented, beautiful to look at, he was addicted to very rough men. Generous, improvident and always hard up, at the age of 57 he was commissioned to write a book about Noël Coward for which he was to get a large advance. Chance acquaintances who heard this piece of news were ignorant enough to imagine that the money would be in his cupboard; they were dishonest enough to wish to steal it, and brutal enough to threaten James with a knife unless he showed them where to find it. When he cried out they gagged him in such a way that he choked to death. Len Adams, described by Peter Quennell as James' 'best, staunchest and most resolutely patient' friend, arrived too late to save his life. He had been out shopping, for this frightful tragedy happened in the daytime. This, at least, is the story of James Pope-Hennessy's death as I heard it at the time. It is more than seven years ago, but Peter Quennell evidently thinks everyone knows it, while in fact young people do not.

This book consists of letters, a scrappy diary, and short sketches of the royal personages James interviewed when he was researching for his biography of Queen Mary. According to his diary my husband and I met him in 1950, dining with the painter Derek Hill; I think it was Len Adams who arranged it. We remained friends and sometimes went to his house in Ladbroke Grove; he often sent his books to Mosley, whom he describes in his diary as 'so remarkably intelligent'. Peter Quennell speaks very highly of *Verandah*, a travel book about the grandfather, Sir John Pope-Hennessy, who governed various colonies. My own favourite is his incomparable biography of Queen Mary. It is incomparable because it succeeds in giving a real, accurate portrait of its subject, and in being perfectly polite, and yet there is a laugh on every page. The only royal portraits to compare with it are those which were kept hidden for several generations, like St Simon's. Yet there was nothing to offend, none of the impertinent, boring insults of the authors now busy publishing libels on the Duke of Windsor.

Pope-Hennessy's hilarious account of life at the Windsors' Mill in France is the best thing in the book, and of the Duke he has this to say: 'I was startled to find that... he is not only the one member of our royal family for whom one needs to make no allowances whatever, but that he is exceedingly intelligent, original, liberal-minded and quite capable of either leading a conversation or taking a constructive part in one. He is also one of the most considerate men I have ever met of his generation.' This makes one regret that Lady Donaldson, who, though not as clever as James Pope-Hennessy, is no fool, so resolutely refused to meet the Duke when she wrote her life of him. She was probably afraid that her preconceived idea of him might be upset.

James wrote the above in 1959 when he had become something of an expert on royal personages all over Europe, as he gathered impressions from them about Queen Mary. He was a good letter writer, but with his books he took endless trouble, re-casting, re-writing, working really hard to achieve excellence.

He had a number of devoted women friends to whom most of the letters are addressed. In his expressions of love, admiration and esteem for them one clearly sees the fatal exaggeration of his delightful nature, its fickleness, the way he found the irresistible star of one moment the near-bore of the next. He was not a faithless friend, but his wild enthusiasms cooled rather quickly, and collapsed like an overdone soufflé.

Publishers are in a poor way at the moment, but it is unforgiveable that there should be no photograph of James Pope-Hennessy inside this book. There are two on the dust jacket, a horribly uncharacteristic one on the front which has been widely reproduced and in which he looks like a querulous old woman. Ideally, there should have been a frontispiece of the portrait Lucian Freud painted of him, one of those rare, jewel-like Freuds, when affection for his subject is not marred by a desire to preach; where the avenging puritan so evident in much of his work is momentarily absent.

Peter Quennell has edited the book with a preface and notes which are all that could be needed or desired.

A Lonely Business: A Self-portrait of James Pope-Hennessy, ed. Quennell, P. *Book Choice* (1981)

Wonder Years

Here they all are, from Josephine Baker to Brancusi, from Cocteau to Chanel, from Gamelin to Gide, the old familiar Parisians, some French, many from abroad. Vincent Cronin gives each one at least a paragraph, because for the under-seventies the names are not always enough. His thesis is that hundreds of talented writers, painters, sculptors and musicians, and a sprinkling of geniuses, made Paris a brilliant city of self-centred individualists, hardly conscious that they were rushing towards world war, to be followed by decades of colonial wars and a potentially dangerous cold war.

One good and valid political idea came out of the First World War: self-determination. It was never tried. Even Clemenceau, who insisted that Germany must be encircled, described the new countries with their outlandish names as 'an absurd hotchpotch'. Lloyd George pointed on the map to the Polish Corridor and said: 'Here is where the next war will start.' The Versailles and Trianon treaties could have been designed to ensure disaster. Disarmament was a farce; Germany offered not to re-arm if France would disarm. France declined. An attempt was made to outlaw bombers. England declined. (It 'needed' them for the North-West Frontier of India.)

The truth is European countries were not wholehearted in advocating self-determination, even in Europe. They did not want it to spread to North Africa, the Middle East, India, Indo-China and elsewhere. All these anxieties are over and done with, but they seemed real at the time. Other anxieties have taken their place.

The twenty years described in this book were just about perfect in Paris, if you could put the international situation out of your mind. It did not unduly worry painters, or nightclub proprietors, or the givers of fancy dress parties; there was gaiety, beauty, amusement and the joys of the intellect. This loveliest of cities was shabby, but not yet choked with traffic.

The miracle of the last war is that Paris was not bombed. If you shut your eye to the outskirts it is very little changed and as beautiful as ever. It may not be a centre of great art now, but there is still a *douceur de vivre* hardly to be found elsewhere.

War is no longer an option, there will be no more fighting on the beaches; the choice is between Europe and a radioactive desert. The Balkans must do as they please.

Paris on the Eve: 1900-1914, Cronin, V., *Evening Standard* (1995)

❊

Dark Side of the Boom

This is a clever scissors-and-paste book with a theme: Paris in the 30s had a flare-up of the best of everything—the best painters, sculptors, composers, writers, as well as the best dressmakers, cooks, restaurants and parties, the wittiest talkers and the most elegant ladies. All this gathered in the loveliest of cities.

But there was a dark side. Dim and old-fashioned soldiers were controlled by vile politicians, some short-sighted, some wicked, while war threatened. Bernier hardly has words strong enough to condemn them.

He finds one shining exception: Léon Blum. This mild, cultivated and charming individual became Prime Minister, waved his Popular Front wand, and everything changed over night. The miserably paid workers had their wages raised, their hours cut, and holidays with pay became statutory.

A few months later, unsurprisingly, 'the budget deficit was growing alarmingly, a pause in the reforms had to be proclaimed. It was, Blum explained, not a retreat but a phase of prudent consolidation.' The government fell.

So much for politics, but most of the time Picasso, Brancusi, Stravinsky, Schiaparelli and Josephine Baker take the centre of the stage. They were none of them French, but they were all part of Paris. Daisy Fellowes was the best-dressed woman in the world, Princess Edmond de Polignac gave splendid musical evenings, Comte Etienne de Beaumont the most amusing parties. People loved fancy dress and they loved dancing, young, middle-aged and old. Elsie Mendl, a great party goer and party giver, was 80.

At the end of this wonderful decade of great art, luxury and silliness, the politicians blundered into war, so that after the fireworks came the dusk. That is the thesis.

Well, yes and no. Paris was never bombed, except by the Allies who had a go at factories on the outskirts. It was short of food and fuel but there was no English austerity after the war. There was a short, sharp, bitter civil war, after which it recovered speedily. The late 40s and 50s were the 30s over again. Picasso was painting, Cocteau being witty, Schiaparelli making lovely clothes—though Balenciaga was king of fashion—M de Beaumont giving grand parties, and Elsie Mendl, now 90, standing on her head every morning.

There were new plays by Sartre, Marcel Aymé, Montherlant and Thierry Maulnier. Céline, Aragon and Paul Morand were writing their best books. Paris was fortunate, it survived. It is now ringed with ugliness, but the centre is relatively untouched. There will always be people willing to give madly luxurious parties and others delighted to go. Rather harmless, perhaps.

In the 50s, just as in the 30s, some were terrified of war, and thought Soviet Russia about to invade. Maybe if Spain had been communist it might have tipped the scale—there was a massive communist vote in France at that time. Bernier's high praise for the French Left reads oddly in 1993 after its striking electoral defeat, the French would not agree with him there.

His source for high life is Janet Flanner, on the whole reliable; for politics the newspapers. He illuminates the Stavisky affair, which has close parallels with Robert Maxwell's, except that Stavisky swindled rich corporations.

Whizzing from the Chamber of Deputies to the Folies Bergère, from Picasso's studio stacked with unsigned pictures to descriptions of pink ruffles edged with gold, it is recognizably Paris, even if dawn followed dusk. The style and the spelling are American. What on earth is a car 'with a huge custom body'? Oh yes, of course, quite easy really.

Fireworks at Duks: Paris in the Thirties, Bernier, O., Evening Standard (1993)

Paris after the Liberation

The authors of this account of the Liberation describe the Paris of half a century ago. They give a balanced summing-up of political Paris, intellectual Paris, commercial Paris and silly Paris, with a slight bias towards the latter. They are probably right to do so, because there are several histories where the muddled story can be found. It is such a dismal tale that a little light relief in café society is in order. Essentially, it is the story of a civil war.

François Mauriac is far from being the only writer to emphasis that civil war has been part of French life for hundreds of years; in his recently reprinted political diary he says it again and again. Perhaps it is tribal, Frank versus Gaul, as he seems to think. With the trauma of defeat and four years of enemy occupation, this Franco-Gallic war assumed a violent aspect of the Liberation. Even now, half a century later, it still surfaces from time to time. There will always be argument about the extent the Resistance movement during the war was Communist-led. So many lies were told at the time that even now it is anybody's guess.

De Gaulle was said by Bidault, his Foreign Minister, to love France and hate the French. De Gaulle himself was the object of intense love and bitter hatred. He loved myths, and one that was highly important in his eyes was that Paris was liberated by his small army and by the Parisians themselves. The Americans obligingly stepped aside, and the Germans were pulling out as quickly as they could in the summer of 1944. Parisians were so happy to be rid of them and so intoxicated with joy at the arrival of French troops that there was an orgy of love-making, flag-waving and bell-ringing, a *Te Deum* at Notre Dame and General De Gaulle marching down the Champs Elyseés. A few shots were fired from roofs and windows, which made it seem more thrilling and realistic. The French then turned from the vanishing Germans and began killing and tormenting each other. De Gaulle stuck it for a few months and then retired to Colombey, where, as it turned out, he had to wait twelve years before returning to power.

Who had collaborated with the enemy? There were plenty of obvious targets, but they shaded down from people who had denounced their compatriots to the Germans, to petrol-pump men who had not refused enemy custom, or *artistes* who had sung in nightclubs patronized by German soldiers. It was a prime time for settling private feuds in an atmosphere of terror and hatred. People went to bed at night far from sure they would not be dragged out at dawn and thrown into a filthy, overcrowded prison. It was easy to get away with murder if the motive was patriotism, and sometimes it seemed as if only the few who had been in London with General De Gaulle were quite safe, leaving fifty million or so at risk. Every Frenchman alive at that time has his Liberation story, if he can be induced to tell it.

On a bigger stage, there was the developing American-Russian quarrel. What was to be done with Germany, defeated and in ruins? De Gaulle hated the Americans even more than he did the English, lumping them together as Anglo-Saxons, which, considering the ethnic composition of the US, seems bizarre. Americans had been rude to him during the war and he was in vengeful mood. But they were so powerful that his visit to Moscow hardly caused a stir. He hated every aspect of American civilization, but he was also deeply anti-Communist. What he craved was a great and powerful France; what he found was a bankrupt, half-starved country overrun by Anglo-Saxon armies on their way to crush Germany. Americans were bombing towns and villages in Normandy to smithereens.

A few years later when I came to live in France, I asked friends how they fared during the occupation and its aftermath. One told me he had been sent a miniature coffin by the Free French, but nothing untoward happened. His mother dispatched a hamper of food from the country every week for four years. He went to the Gare d'Austerlitz and trundled it home. I asked whether, when shortages became acute, the hamper was ever stolen on the railway? Never, he said. Of course he could have lived where the goods came from, but Frenchmen would rather be hungry in Paris than bored elsewhere.

Another friend, a member of the Académie Française, told me that even now, in the Nineties, the 'Immortals' are split down the middle, twenty a side. There is something reassuring about such a balance. However much they loath each other's opinions they manage to pre-

Lady Redesdale, Diana, Nancy, Unity, Jessica, Tom, Deborah, Pamela, Lord Redesdale.

Mrs Hammersley protected against illnesses.

Mrs Hammersley writing from her house in the Isle of Wight.

Lord and Lady Redesdale with Nancy before the arrival of Pamela, 'a screaming orange.'
The last photograph of Tom who was killed at the end of World War II.

Carrington in her thirties, wearing one of her cotton dresses and ankle socks.

At the Villa d'Este in 1933 with
Desmond Parsons.

Near Rome with Peter Watson.

Lord Berner

tend to be making a dictionary which will purge the language of Anglo-Saxon words.

The English love travel and hate foreigners. Do they dislike each other as much as the French do? We have never had occasion to discover the answer to that question.

When a Great Nation Turns Against Itself: Paris after the Liberation

Beevor, A. and Cooper, A., *Literary Review* (1994)

❈

Paradise on Earth

If my sister Nancy thought Paris an earthly paradise, it must be remembered that ten of the years she lived there were the 50s, an extraordinary decade the like which we have never seen since. From the War years and Occupation, Paris splendidly recovered; disliking austerity and shabbiness it quickly resumed its addiction to fashion, luxury and delicious food, helped by a flourishing black market.

In London the slogan was 'Fair Shares', which is nothing but a cruel illusion when poverty and riches live side by side. London seemed almost to revel in 'shortages', even paper was rationed (and murmurs that it was all being hoarded to accommodate the many volumes of Churchill's war memoirs) and Lord Berners was heard to complain that for the very entrance to a bookshop one was greeted by the cry: No Tolstoy! No Dostoyevsky!)

Paris rejected austerity. Far from rationing clothes, for example, dressmakers, led by Christian Dior, changed the fashion overnight, and decreed that each garment should consume many metres of silk, wool or cotton, thus giving a boost to the producers of these materials, as well as enchanting their clients, who had got so tired of their old clothes, and of clattering about in shoes with wooden soles.

Marshal Aid seems to have been well spent on modernising public transport and putting an efficient welfare system in place. But the exciting aspect of the 50s that the Arts flourished as never before. Picasso

315

produced surprises as he did throughout the War, but now painters flocked to Paris. The theatre led the genial atmosphere of renewal which prevailed. There was an explosion of talent, led by Louis Jouvet, Montherlant's thrilling play Le Cardian L'Espagne was in the repertory of the Comédie Française and his Port Royal at the Odeon, a play which gave the illusion that the audience was actually witnessing the drama of Jansenism, the nuns actionas of the pitiless autocracy of Louis XIV. Sartre wrote his powerful *Diable et le Bon Dieu,* Julien Green a twentieth-century homosexual drama, *Sud,* in the romantic setting of the Deep South. Cocteau's star actor was Jean Marais, Madeleine Renaud and Jean-Louis Barrault had their own troupe, and there were great beauties, Edwige Feuillère and Danielle Devrieux, as well as the irrepressible Arletty and the child-like quality of Zizi Jean Maire. This constellation of talent performed on both stage and screen, in films like *Les Enfants du Paradis.*

At the same time there were constant balls and parties given in sumptuous houses decorated by Georges Geoffreoy. Much, though not all, of the money spent on these extravagances came from South and North America. Daisy Fellowes, Mona Bismarck, Marie-Laure de Noailles, Etienne de Beaumont, Patino, Beistegui were generous hosts.

Novels and journals were written by Paul Morand, Montherlant, Sartre, Mauriac, an endless array of talent. Towards the end of this unusual decade, it was realised it was too good to last. As so often in human affairs, politics and war replaced gaiety and happiness. The terrible War Algeria affected every French family. No more balls were given, a sombre cloud descended. General de Gaulle came back from his twelve years at Colombey. He 'settled' Algeria, but it never knew peace.

Paris became hard working and serious, the Paris we know now. It is as beautiful as ever, but its elegant inhabitants wear blue jeans and fashionable black rags and tatters. The dress makers floated away, leaving only their names behind. Could that decade of half a century ago ever again materialise? The décor is still in place.

Unpublished (2003)

✳

Paris Intellectuals

Paris is a haven for intellectuals in a way that London has never been. To make a comparison, you would have to imagine not only Parliament, the British Museum and the palace of the head of state, but also Oxford, Cambridge, and the major public schools, all gathered in London. Of course there are clever boys in the French provinces, but they make a bee-line for Paris as soon as they possibly can.

Not many English writers live in London. They prefer the country, and go to London to see their publishers or agents, more than to see each other. The physical proximity of French writers and academics generates an abnormal amount of envy, hatred and malice, fuelled by the literary prizes which ensure the sale of novels which might otherwise languish. Television also plays a part in sales promotion, and Bernard-Henri Lévy is a popular performer, interviewing writers and intellectuals dressed in black and white to match his black hair and white face.

He starts his adventure on the freedom road with a backward glance at the Dreyfus case, but it would be difficult for anyone not familiar with the Affaire to make out what happened. In his version, Conservatives, the Army and the Catholics sent an unfortunate and totally innocent man to prison on Devil's Island. They undoubtedly did, but except for the few who were guilty of this injustice most people imagined Dreyfus had sold military secrets to Germany, a crime which appalled the patriotic French, terrified as they were of another war. By the time, owing to the efforts of Dreyfus's brother and his powerful allies Clemenceau and Zola, his innocence was as good as proved and the real culprit, Esterhazy, unmasked, France was in such a fever of fear and hatred between those who supported Dreyfus and those who condemned his supposed guilt that it was like a civil war. There was a famous caricature at the time of a dining room filled with a party of men in white ties and ladies in long gowns and jewels, all gesticulating, chairs broken, china and glass smashed. The caption was: 'They had spoken of Dreyfus.'

Proust's description of the Prince de Guermantes, who had gradually become convinced that a terrible crime had been committed by the Army, backed up by the Church, and who seeks out his old friend Swann, a Dreyfusard from the beginning, to tell him of his change of mind, is one of the most moving scenes in his novel. Needless to say, Proust does not let the Guermantes off the hook. The Duchess makes her bad-taste joke when people say how unattractive Dreyfus is: 'They'll have to change victims.' Words that echo through the Faubourg St Germain, finding itself on the wrong side in the bitter dispute. Since most of M. Lévy's 'causes' are to do with nationalism, still so powerful after the demise of ideologies, he is right to start with the most famous of them all. He is more indulgent to nationalists of other climes.

After the first war the surrealists were paramount among Paris intellectuals; some were communists and others were not. The Communist Party was never happy with its intellectual adherents, they were too unreliable. They went to Russia to see the workers' paradise and admire the revolution, and often saw too much and came back disillusioned and wrote, like Gide in *Retour de l'URSS*, books denouncing the regime.

After the second war there was another civil war between resisters and collaborators, still raging quietly when France embarked upon its colonial wars in Indo-China and Algeria. Inevitably they failed, and the generations of intellectuals described by Lévy played a part in trying to assure some sort of 'Freedom' for the wretched people caught up in these interminable struggles.

After 1989 and the collapse of communism old values such as the Rights of Man asserted themselves once more, and the intellectuals, disillusioned by the failure of the students' revolt in 1968 to effect radical change, seem to have settled down to arguing on television and writing.

Naturally the old bitter divisions of the last war remain. Lévy's hero is Malraux, his villains Drieu la Rochelle and Céline. Yet when the dust has finally settled, what remains is the writing. Sartre's and Montherlant's plays, Céline's *Voyage au bout de la Nuit*, Aragon's *Semain-*

Sainte, along with the Journals of Gide, Mauriac and Julien Green will be read when their politics have faded.

Lévy's book, well translated, may prove rather puzzling to English readers. They will be like the people in the rue du Quatre Septembre who, when asked what event that had given the street its name, hadn't the slightest idea. The word Billancourt means nothing to most of the English, and the footnote is not much help. The 'sixth February' is apt to pass them by. But they will enjoy some of the interviews, even if they seem rather anti-French, and perhaps congratulate themselves that our native writers are mostly fuddy duddy liberals, and not quite so furiously 'engaged.'

Adventures on the Freedom Road: The French Intellectuals In the Twentieth Century,

Lévy, B.-H., trans. Ceasey, R. (1995)

❋

Grief on a Front

The pitiless, everlasting rain of Loire Atlantique is the rather gloomy setting for the *petit bourgeois* characters to live their lives, where nothing much happens except births, marriages and deaths.

Jean Rouaud wrote his book in a newspaper kiosk in Paris during the slack periods, or at least so it was said when he won the Prix Goncourt in 1890. The Paris rain, and covering his wares with mackintosh aprons, must have reminded him of his home in Brittany.

Like most first novels, this seems to be autobiographical. His grandparents and his great-aunt Marie had been born in the 1890s. Their seemingly dull world and their quiet, harmless lives had been catastrophically broken into by the Great War.

Two brothers were killed—one of them, Joseph, suffered the torture of burned lungs in a gas attack upon the trenches, where he and his comrades lived like rats, with rats, in mud and slime. His sister Marie, who adored him, had been young at the time. Her love and her memories of him became more vivid, as in old age she lost her wits after 'a long, secret repression of grief… her life forever thrown off course'.

The grandfather, who also survived, and, in fact, a whole generation, were traumatized by the unbelievable horror of that war. Verdun is only the most spectacular example of the agony and senseless sacrifice they experienced. They endured and did not mutiny.

On to the 60s, when young people knew little of either war. The grandparents, leaving the rain for a while, went to stay with a daughter in a hot, sunny vineyard. The grandfather, contentedly chain-smoking, sat day after day in a chair, watching the men at work.

One day he disappeared and the whole neighbourhood turned out to search for him. He came back with a story of having seen exotic plants at Hyères, but in reality, mildly lecherous, he had been to see the nudist colony on the Ile de Levant.

His old wife found the boat ticket in his pocket. She said nothing, and, when he died a year later, he thought he had taken his secret to the grave.

In a frightful eternal recurrence, *Fields of Glory* ends with a young man in a cemetery on All Saints' Day, when French graves are smothered in chrysanthemum. The date is 1940. They are at it again. France is occupied. There are no trenches, but it is terrible in another way.

In the first war there was no choice; in the second, decisions had to be taken by individuals, the memory of which is at the back of every Frenchman's mind. An undeclared civil war, a near anarchy.

Perhaps Jean Rouaud will write a sequel to *Fields of Glory*. He could probably do it better than anyone, perceptive and subtle as he is. Not an easy book to translate, but Ralph Manheim has done it excellently.

Fields of Glory, Rouaud, J., trans. Manheim, R., *Evening Standard* (1992)

African Hell

Drastic cutting would greatly have improved this enormous book, at half the length and half the price it would have been worthwhile. Unwieldy and repetitive, it yet contains much new information, such as Ambassador Jebb's excellent dispatches from Paris to the Foreign Office in London. From these an authentic portrait emerges of that very curious and devious individual General de Gaulle, the loved and admired, the hated and despised dictator of France for ten years.

His enemies thought he had thrown Algeria away unnecessarily and hypocritically, while his adherents were certain he had saved France from civil war, from communism, and totalitarian Russia, immensely powerful in the late 50s.

The Algerian war coming immediately after France's defeat in Indo-China was appallingly savage. The tribes of Arabs, Berbers and Kabyles had always fought each other, and their losses in the war are reckoned to have been eight times those of the Europeans. Kettle's account of the massacres, murders, mutilations and tortures of the years when the war raged show that for all its inhabitants Algeria was a dangerous and fractured society, and possibly in their secret hearts most of the French, Spanish, Greek and Corsican *pieds noirs* were fairly thankful to leave when the time came, loudly though they cried for Algérie Française. The big *colons* had investments outside the country, but the small farmers and shopkeepers had to leave all their possessions behind. On the whole they did brilliantly in France, where they settled, saying bitterly they had to choose 'a valise or a coffin'. They thrived on deep hatred of de Gaulle, were sorry when bullets missed him and rejoiced when he was finally toppled. But the French army felt betrayed. Kettle ends his book after the abortive barricades, we are not given the revolt of the generals.

It is impossible to be dull about General de Gaulle with his sybilline pronouncements, faith in himself and dismissively contemptuous attitude to everyone else; when he is on stage the book comes alive.

Algeria remains a problem. Arabs, Berbers and Kabyles still fight each other. The economy has never flourished since independence; the land, so productive for its European owners, is nationalized, and what belongs to everybody profits nobody. Misery and poverty are the rule;

as to democracy, when the Fundamentalists were winning an election there was a military coup and the army took over. Algerian immigrants pour into France and swamp the social services. They are no more liked by the French than Europeans were by the Muslims in colonial days. The whirligig of time has brought its revenge, the outlook is bleak.

If the war killed upwards of a million people, and nobody knows the exact number, the population, owing to French medicine and dwindling infant mortality, has exploded. General de Gaulle got the Europeans out and they hate him for it. Do they regret it still?

De Gaulle and Algeria 1940-1960, Kettle, M., *Evening Standard* (1993)

A La Recherche du temps perdu

Scott Moncrieff's translation of *A la recherche du Temps Perdu* was a flawed attempt at a fiendishly difficult task, but with these revisions it seems to be as right as is ever likely to be. Three times Proust was inspired to write his masterpiece by sensations which evoked scenes from the past with startling clarity. The taste of a madeleine dipped in tisane brought back his childhood at Combray and in Paris. His adoration of his mother, family walks by the pink hawthorn bordering Swann's park; Swann dining with his parents without his wife, who had a 'past', visions of Gilberte Swann, a lovely child he was not allowed to play with; the church with stained glass windows commemorating the noble Guermantes of centuries ago; a glimpse of the Duchesse de Guermantes at a village wedding, her gold hair, brilliant blue eyes and high-bridged nose; Françoise the cook killing a chicken, the taste evoked lost years he was searching for. He had fallen in love with Gilberte, and his heroine was Oriane de Guermantes. Neither could he approach, so that feelings intensified in his imagination.

Later on, hearing the little shriek emitted by a porcelain coffee cup touched by a silver spoon, he was transported to the Balbec train, where a workman, banging the line with an iron hammer, had made the same sound. He was on his way to the coast, adolescent, delicate, with his grandmother. It came vividly back; the hotel flooded with light from the sea, his grandmother's friendship with the Marquise de Villeparisis (his first Guermantes), their drives around Normandy in her barouche, his friendship with her nephew St Loup, who seemed to him the acme of manly beauty and elegance, and the troupe of young girls he longed to get to know, who ran along the beach, arms entwined, and whose loud behaviour horrified his grandmother. One of them was Albertine, who was to make him suffer appalling jealousy because of her supposed lesbianism.

As a little boy in Paris he had dragged the unwilling Françoise all the way to the Bois de Boulogne to see the lady in pink driving in her smart equipage. She was Odette, a courtesan, with whom Swann, most fastidious of men, had fallen so deeply in love that he married her in the vain hope of possessing her completely, despite the fact that he knew his Faubourg St Germain friends, with whom he passed his time, would never receive her. Swann's painful jealousy, watching Odette's vulgar little house to see who was with her among the orchids and chrysanthemums, was the very same as the narrator is tortured by a generation later, when he imprisons Albertine in his flat. Love, for Proust, is agonizing jealousy; there is no room for fondness or companionship. Finally, there is disillusion and indifference, and the sorrow felt by Swann when he realises he has wasted his life pining for a woman he doesn't even like.

The narrator sees a poetic vision of beauty and elegance, the Guermantes and the friends framed in a box at the theatre, glistening with jewels and unattainable glamour, but already ironic laughter is not far away. When he meets them, and is invited to dinner, he soon discovers the distressing banality of the world of the rich and nobly born. It is one more disillusion. Even the celebrated wit of the Duchess herself is simply paradox spiced with malice. (For the reader, on the other hand, Oriane is one of the greatest heroines of fiction, bright and beautiful and elegant, with an unfailingly wicked tongue.) M de Charlus is a monster of another kind, another

Guermantes. When the narrator blunders into a male brothel he finds M de Charlus being flogged by a sailor hired for the purpose. Many of the characters are homosexual, (even in the end St Loup, which stretches credulity), and all are caricatures. Tenderness is reserved for his mother and grandmother.

The third occasion the narrator is projected into lost time is when he treads on a loose cobblestone in a Paris courtyard. He finds himself in St Mark's, walking on the uneven marble floor. Venice, for him, is art. Unlike love, or Paris society, art never disappoints, or disillusions. He knows he has within him a work of art waiting to be written. After one last party with his friends grown old and wrinkled, where he finds the grandees, formerly so exclusive, married to the very people they refused to receive, he shuts himself up and works until his dying day.

Proust had moved into a cold house where the fire smoked. His brother, who like their father was an eminent doctor, implored him to move to a warm clinic, but he refused. He died aged 51.

Proust's is one of the greatest novels ever written. Well-translated and well printed, these volumes are a publishing achievement to be proud of.

A La Recherche du Temps Perdu, Proust, M., trans. by Moncrieff, S.,
rev. Kilmartin, T., again rev. Enright, D.J., *Evening Standard* (1997)

Simple Pleasures

Like *Hamlet,* and like *Faust, A La Recherche du temps perdu* continues to occupy the minute attention of critics in all countries; there is even a risk that, while recognising it as the greatest achievement of imaginative literature of the first half of the twentieth century, they may spin around it such a cocoon of legend, myth and prestige that they will obscure the delights and glories of the book itself.

Some of these critics, seeking to illumine the psychological complexities of its author, fall over themselves in their eagerness to, discover a new 'truth,' like the American who recently announced that the name Robert de Saint-Loup derived from Proust's brother Robert and 'mon petit loup,' a term of endearment used by his mother. If this critic had crossed the Atlantic he might have hit upon a simpler explanation. Among the villages and castles in Seine et Marne whose names Proust borrowed for his noble personages—Guermantes, Villeparisis, for example—is the château of Saint Loup, well known to a number of people since it has been occupied for years by a hospitable English lady. Thus, although the novel and its author are inexhaustibly interesting subjects, readers are becoming wary of some of the far-fetched and inexpert criticism to which they constantly give rise.

Retour à Marcel Proust falls into an altogether different category; here the critic himself is one of France's foremost writers. biographer, historian, internationally famous authority on military matters, M. Benoist-Méchin was a minister in Pétain's government and is a great European.

His book is divided into two parts: the first, a long essay on 'La Musique du temps retrouvé,' he wrote as a young officer in the French army of occupation in the Rhineland immediately after the first war; in the second, thirty five years later, he looks back at his youthful self across the gulf of strange and tragic happenings which this troubled period represents, and at Marcel Proust. He re-read A *la recherche du temps perdu* almost reluctantly, he says. He feared to break the Proustian spell, and that the enthusiasm he had formerly felt for a magnificent work of art might prove to be illusory. But the novel appeared to him once again as fresh, as intelligent and as brilliant as it had done when he read it first, and more comic than ever before. '*Quel plaisir intense, vivace, inespéré m'a procuré cette nouvelle lecture de* La Recherche du temps perdu!' he exclaims, adding: '*et j'ai compris alors que son oeuvre était impérissable*' [the work is indestructable].

The theme of M. Benoist-Méchin's first essay is the role of music throughout the whole work; Proust's love and understanding of music were profound, and *la petite phrase* from Vinteuil's sonata is the *leit motiv* not only of Swann's love for Odette but also of love itself, in all its aspects—down to the sordid antics of Vinteuil's daughter and which, for Proust, was synonymous with tormenting jealousy. Those whose down-to-earth realism persists in discovering real men and women in all Proust's characters have also attempted to guess the original of *la petite phrase*. A complete answer to such pretensions is quoted here, from a letter in which Proust himself says it may have been suggested by Saint Saëns, or the Good Friday music in *Parsifal*, or César Franck, or *Lohengrin*, or Schubert, or possibly Fauré. In other words, by all and by none.

If Proust were living now, a prisoner to asthma in a darkened, blanketed room, he would most likely listen to faithful recordings of his favourite music. He would probably hear so much music, repeated so often, that the intensity of the pleasure he felt in it might be dissipated, and the power of evocation lost. Instead of thinking about Beethoven's string quartets, and writing down his thoughts, he might have played them on a gramophone. There may be too much music in the modern world. Madame de Cambremer, whose mouth watered when she heard Chopin so that she dribbled, might have learnt to listen unmoved, while Madame Verdurin could hardly have demonstrated her extreme musical sensibility by burying her head in her hands if she were obliged to do it several times a day.

'*La musique*,' said Proust, a few months before his death, to M. Benoist-Méchin, '*a été une des plus grandes passions de ma vie, je dis a été, car à présent je n'ai plus guère l'occasion d'en entendre, autrement que dans mon souvenir.*' [Music was one of my greatest passions, I say 'was' because I am no longer able to listen to it other than through what I remember.] Through memory, he communicates his passion for music to the reader; M. Benoist-Méchin also possesses the power to recapture and to set down in words the deep though transitory impression that music can make on the individual and on the crowd. His description of a performance of *Meistersinger* at the time of the Ruhr crisis is unforgettable.

Retour à Marcel Proust, Méchin, B. (1957)

❋

Proust on the Shelf

Proust died in 1922, but his name and his novel were so famous that Scott Moncrieff's translation was already a classic in the 30s. Aged 51, he died of cold. He had moved to a flat in rue Hamelin where the fire smoked and gave him asthma. With no fire, he lay swathed in rugs, shawls and hot water bottles, his bed, the floor, every table and chair covered in paper: galley proofs smothered in almost illegible corrections, carnets full of writing, even scraps and envelopes. He knew he had not long to live, and was trying to finish and correct *A la Recherche du Temps Perdu*. His brother (like their father, a doctor) implored him to move to a warm clinic. He refused. Only he knew how his life's work could be deciphered; the precious proofs and papers must not be touched. He worked until he died, and then artist friends made drawings of his thin white face, half covered in black beard. Might he have cut, or altered his work?

The first volume, *Swann's Way*, had been published at the author's expense in 1913. The next volumes, highly praised, some published after his death, completed his enormous novel.

Stepping on a broken cobblestone in Paris, Proust had been transported to St Mark's, with its uneven mosaic pavement. For him, Venice was art, and in that moment he realised that only art brings no disillusion. *Le Temps Perdu* is the novel of disillusion. Love is but jealousy, beauty fades, fashions change, friendships grow cool, art remains. Resolving to devote his life to the work of art he knew his novel could be, he turned night into day, working in the silent hours, seeing only a few old friends for an occasional midnight feast at the Ritz.

His last party is in the final volume, *Le Temps Retrouvé*. Everyone is changed by white hair, baldness, wrinkles, but even more from a worldly point of view. The aristocrats whom Proust had longed to know in his youth, and who had become his friends, were now mixed up with the middle-class people they had formerly so rigidly excluded. The Great War had been the catalyst, rich bourgeois gifts to war charities had broken the taboo, and the snobbish Proust becomes disillusioned.

All Proust's characters are caricatures, from the Duc de Guermantes and his brother Charlus to Mme Verdurin, all three so grossly rude and absurd that Charles Dickens's grotesques pale beside them. Oriane de Guermantes, however, is a real heroine, like Trollope's Lady Glencora. The narrator has loved and admired her ever since, as a boy, he glimpsed her at a country wedding; her brilliant blue eyes, gold hair and beaky nose have been his ideal of what an aristocrat should be. Yet even she lets him down. Her witticisms are only paradoxes spiced with malice.

The only tender and loving portraits in the novel are of the mother and grandmother, and, up to a point, Swann. The most fashionable man of his day, a recognised expert who advised his grand friends about pictures and music, he is perhaps what Proust himself would have liked to be; but he makes him spoil his life by marrying a woman not received in society. He marries in an attempt to assuage his jealousy of her many lovers, a jealousy that foreshadows the narrator's own suffering with Albertine.

I once asked an old French duke to what extent Proust had known 'Guermantes' during his party-going years before the First World War. '*Mais pas du tout!*' was the reply. Not quite true, but much imagination supplemented small acquaintance.

I read Scott Moncrieff's translation in 1934, having been put off for years by Clive Bell, who wrote that the novel was difficult. In 1935, I read it in French. The translation is a delightful book, but it is not Proust. The jokes that make one choke with laughter are not so funny, the descriptions of flowers and rivers and churches lose their poetry.

Mine is the old NRF (*Nouvelle Revue Française*) edition of 1929 in 15 volumes. One of them, *Sodome et Gomorrhe II*, succumbed to damp in an Irish house. They have moved with me from place to place, books to re-read. Newer editions, over-burdened by the scribbles found in Proust's room when he died, have become holy writ, but I prefer the beautifully printed NRF of Gallimard.

Sunday Times (1998)

❋

A Fight for Justice

Every few years somebody writes a book about the Dreyfus case, and this is likely to continue until kingdom come, because it is a story containing every ingredient of the most thrilling thriller and it never fails to enthrall. David L Lewis's is the latest version, written in American.

Alfred Dreyfus was a Jew from Alsace. He was eleven when the Prussians took his native province from the French. His brothers remained in Mulhouse looking after the family business, but Alfred was educated in Paris and joined the French army. He became a captain in the artillery in 1889, passed through the staff college and received an appointment on the staff. He was fairly rich, and married with two small children at the time the drama begins in 1894.

A charwoman who worked at the German embassy was paid by the French secret service to collect the contents of the embassy waste paper baskets. The German military attaché threw most interesting things into his, including love letters. He employed various French spies, among them a raffish officer who was always short of money, Major Esterhazy. One day Major Henry, who worked in the Statistical Section of the War Office—a parallel section to the Second Bureau, the formal Intelligence branch—found among the waste paper a letter offering a list of five items of military information, none of them top secret, but nevertheless clearly emanating from a spy. This was the famous '*bordereau*'. Major Henry passed it on to his superiors, and it was circulated to the chiefs of all the War Office departments. Somebody thought the handwriting on the *bordereau* resembled Dreyfus's hand. Graphologists were called in, who disagreed with one another. In spite of this, it was upon the slender evidence of his authorship of the *bordereau* that Dreyfus was arrested, court martialled, publicly degraded, sentenced to life imprisonment, and sent to Devil's Island.

He continually protested his innocence. No motive for his treachery could be found. He was passionately devoted to the French army, and he had plenty of money. He was unpopular among his fellow officers. They said he was inquisitive, forever asking questions about things which were no concern of his. There were a few who resented a Jew being on the staff at all, but it would not be true to put down his unpopularity to anti-semitism; he simply was not liked. The idea that a rigidly Catholic, Jesuit-educated aristocratic army caste manufactured evidence of treason because Dreyfus was a Jew is not borne out by the facts. On the other hand, the shrill cries of the anti-semitic press influenced the outcome. Once the journalists had got hold of Dreyfus's name, to acquit him was to be accused of being in the pay of the Jews, and through them in the pay of the Germans. No law of libel curbed these rabid men, and they succeeded in frightening both politicians and generals. Also, since even a court martial held in camera might not have convicted on the *bordereau* alone, Major Henry recklessly added forged evidence in order to obtain a conviction.

David Lewis describes the dreadful ceremony of the degradation, when Dreyfus had the buttons and braid torn off his uniform and his sword was broken across the knee of an officer. As he was marched back he cried out in his harsh voice: '*Soldats! Je suis innocent! Vive la France!*' The angry crowd shouted: '*Salaud! Silence! Mort au juif!*' [Bastard. Shut up. Death to the Jew.]

How could such a terrible thing happen? A few people suspected almost from the beginning that there might have been a miscarriage of justice, but they had nothing to go on and they kept their thoughts to themselves. There were several reasons for this. The most respectable was that some of the items on the *bordereau* concerned the artillery, and the French were then developing their famous 75 mm gun. It would have been a disaster if details of this had reached the Germans. Then, whenever during the weeks leading up to the court martial awkward questions were asked, Major Henry produced new 'evidence', some of it highly dramatic. He even said he had intercepted a letter from Emperor William II to Dreyfus, though nobody actually set eyes upon it. The German ambassador, an old-fashioned aristocrat, Count von

Münster, gave his word that neither he nor the military attaché had ever heard of Dreyfus. This shook the Foreign Minister, but the gutter press said it was another German lie.

As time went on many of the 'intellectuals' became violently pro-Dreyfus; some of them convinced of his innocence, others for party political reasons, but they often did more harm than good. 'The intellectuals have all more or less lost their national mentality,' wrote Maurice Paléologue, who called them 'these presumptuous pedants who believe they are the aristocrats of intelligence'. To the ordinary patriotic Frenchman they simply represented a group of nondescript writers and publicists who put every other country before their own, ready and willing to knock the government, the army, and France itself. There is no doubt that most of Dreyfus's supporters managed in their tactless way to stiffen the opinion that '*raison d'état*', or the life of the country, mattered infinitely more than the fate of one man.

A very terrible fate it was. They sent him across the ocean to be the only prisoner on Devil's Island. His wife and brother were unremitting in their efforts to get the case re-opened. Mathieu Dreyfus, afraid that the whole thing was being forgotten, almost managed to finish him off: he arranged for an English paper to print a story that Dreyfus had escaped from Devil's Island. The result was that he was no longer allowed to walk on the island, or to look at the sea; a high palisade was put up to contain him. Worst of all, he was riveted to his bed at night, by the ankles and the wrists. The misery of this in a tropical climate in a cell buzzing with insects can easily be imagined.

The hero of the 'affaire' is Colonel Picquart, who had become head of the Statistical Section. Picquart had been present at the court martial; at the time he never doubted that Dreyfus was guilty. Some time later, following the traces of the amateurish spy Esterhazy, he saw Esterhazy's handwriting and immediately recognised it as the writing on the '*bordereau*'. He told his superiors. They said there could be no question of a re-trial; it might set off a diplomatic 'incident' with Germany; it might even lead to war. Picquart, now convinced that Dreyfus was innocent, continued his inquiries. Nothing would induce him to throw up the case, he could not bear the heavy load on his conscience. As a result, in order to shut his mouth, Picquart was ordered to the Tunisian frontier where a colonial war was in progress. There were those who fervently hoped he might leave his bones in North Africa; but eventually he returned, more determined than ever to get the Dreyfus case re-opened. Major Henry's forgeries and lies gradually came to light, and he was arrested. Alone in his cell, he took his razor and cut his throat.

Major Henry's suicide excited the press of the entire world. Even French newspapers, hitherto neutral, now demanded revision. One of the court martial judges announced publicly that his eyes had been opened. When Mercier, Minister of War, heard the news he uttered the one word: '*Foutu!*' [Screwed].

This was in 1899, four years since Dreyfus had been languishing on Devil's Island. The new trial was staged in the lycée at Rennes in August. The town was stuffed with generals and lawyers and Dreyfusists and anti-Dreyfusists and journalists from every country on earth. The best account of this trial and of the atmosphere at Rennes is to be found in the diary kept by Maurice Paléologue, a diplomat in the Intelligence Department of the Quai d'Orsay. It was published in 1955, twenty years after the death of Dreyfus; the same year as the excellent English book on the Dreyfus case by Guy Chapman. Paléologue believed Dreyfus to be innocent, yet he felt sure he would be found guilty all over again. Passions ran high. One of the 'facts' which damned Dreyfus in the eyes of most Frenchmen was the alleged letter to him from their arch-enemy the Kaiser. Paléologue ridiculed the mere idea of the Emperor of Germany, King of Prussia, Margrave of Baden, Landgrave of Hessen, and so on and on, taking up his pen and writing to a spy. But neither the generals nor the lawyers were men of the world, and they swallowed such fantasies.

International interest in the trial was such that the Lord Chief Justice of England, Lord Russell of Killowen, went over to Rennes for a few days busman's holiday. He was given an armchair near the judges and Paléologue sat beside him. They had breakfast at 5.30 am, for the court sittings began at 6.30. When the accused was brought in, Lord Russell half stood up the better to gaze at this man who had so bitterly divided France and indeed set the whole world arguing his guilt or his innocence, this martyr with his legendary sufferings, this victim of lies, forgeries, and a monster miscarriage of justice. After a long look, the Lord Chief Justice turned to Paléologue and whispered in his ear: '*Comme il est antipathique!*' And that seems to have been half the trouble. Nobody liked him, he was quite exceptionally uncharming. Nobody, that is, but his own family. His wife and his brother were devoted to him.

All the same, he aroused deep pity in some observers. An English journalist at Rennes described him thus: 'There came in a little old man—an old, old man of 39, a small-statured, thick-set old man in the black uniform of the artillery—his hair was gone white as silver, and on the temples and back of the head he was bald.'

Lord Russell was loud in his criticism of the conduct of the trial. Hearsay, even at second or third hand, was admitted as evidence and readily listened to. The trial dragged on for a month. Amazingly enough, with two of the judges dissenting, Dreyfus was again found guilty at Rennes. Partly the reason was the poor impression made on the military judges by the melodramatic demagogy of the defence lawyers, but principally, and disgracefully, it was the old question: Mercier, Minister of War, or Dreyfus? Mercier carried the day.

However, there was no more Devil's Island. Dreyfus was speedily amnestied, and a few years later the whole trumped-up case was reviewed and the verdicts quashed by the High Court. Dreyfus was reinstated in the army and given the Legion of Honour. It was twelve years after his degradation. Picquart, who had been abominably treated, was also reinstated. He could not abide the Dreyfus brothers and refused to meet them. His motive for interfering in the case had been singularly pure; there was nothing personal about it; it was love of justice and of truth: no more, and no less.

Mr Lewis's book is never boring. There are one or two tiresome little mistakes (for example, he says the German Embassy in the rue de

Lille is in the eighth arrondissement which is the other side of the Seine) and it is written in American. For English readers it should perhaps have a glossary, some of the words are so curious. What do finagle and feisty mean, and how about sworling? One can make a wild guess, and on the whole the fascinating and dreadful tale is well told. Madame Straus, hostess of Marcel Proust, would have been as amazed as delighted to find herself and her guests described as the crème de la crème of Paris Society, even in a book from across the Atlantic. But such small details are unimportant. *Prisoners of Honour* is interesting and well illustrated. The only one of the protagonists who looks at all attractive in his photograph is Colonel Picquart: and that is as it should be.

Prisoners of Honour: The Dreyfus Affair, Lewis, D.L., *Books and Bookmen* (1975)

Sabre-Toothed Politician

'There are some people who think themselves progressives who say quite seriously: We accept the principles of 1792, but we reject the violence of the Revolution. Those who say this are either stupid or hypocrites. Can they not see that the violence was the inevitable result of the appearance of such principles?' These words were written by Clemenceau when he was 20. Ten years later he was himself to witness the violent horrors of the Commune.

This long and scholarly book is apparently the first biography of Clemenceau in English. Born in 1841, he was, like his father, a devoted worshipper of the Revolution and a convinced atheist. At home in Vendée, he was brought up to venerate St Just and Robespierre, whose portraits hung on the walls. He insisted that the Revolution was a bloc and must be accepted whole.

A left-wing opponent of Napoleon III, after the Franco-Prussian war he was elected member of the National Assembly and also mayor of Montmartre. To this day it is sometimes alleged that Clemenceau was in some way to blame for the murder of General Thomas and

General Lecomte, who had been ordered to remove the cannons that the National Guard had dragged up to the Butte. The cannons were no danger to the Prussians, who sat outside Paris preparing the German Empire, while civil war was brewing in the city. In truth, as soon as he was told that the Generals had been seized, Clemenceau ran up the hill from his town hall to try to save them. They had already fallen victims to mob violence, and a ghastly sight met his eyes: 'Soldiers, National Guardsmen, women and children, all were shouting like savage beasts, without realising what they were doing. I saw there the pathological phenomenon of bloodlust, children perched on top of a wall were waving indescribable trophies, dishevelled women... uttering harsh, inarticulate shouts.' Thus Clemenceau described a scene reminiscent of Paris during the Terror, seventy eight years before.

Politics were his passion. Clemenceau was a violent tornado of a man, brave, clever, quick, ready with wounding sarcasms and insults in debate, prepared to fight as well as to quarrel. His duels were almost as numerous as his love affairs. 'His personality was combative through and through' writes Mr Watson, and 'he had an extraordinary facility in debate... he was able time and time again to make his opponents look foolish. Naturally they did not like it.' Déroulède, attacking him in the Chamber for the part he was alleged to have played in the Panama scandal, said he inspired fear 'fear of his sword, fear of his pistol, fear of his tongue.' Considered 'too arrogant, too assured of his own ability, of his intellectual superiority, and of his political judgement', he was kept out of office until he was 65.

During the first three years of the war he constituted himself a sharp critic of the government and its conduct of the war. He had a paper, *L'Homme libre*, which was in constant trouble with the censor; he changed its name to *L'Homme enchaîné*. In 1917, when the war was going badly for the Allies, Clemenceau at the age of 76 became Prime Minister.

There is no doubt that his courage and fierce tenacity, the way in which he backed up the generals when they were being blamed for every reverse, his frequent visits to the Front, and the fear of him which silenced opposition, all contributed greatly to the final success of Allied arms. He incarnated an intractable will to victory; the Tiger, transformed, became Père-laVictoire. He despised and disliked—hated is hardly too strong a word—almost all his colleagues in the government, most of the generals including those of his allies, and all the allied politicians. But he hated the Germans even more. He subordinated, as it were, his little local hatreds until after the victory, when they blossomed anew.

For France and for Europe it might have been well had this furiously determined old man chanced to die at the end of the war. Clemenceau's warlike gifts and virtues were singularly inappropriate to the infinitely delicate task of peacemaking, yet as France's Prime Minister he was to be the principal architect of the Peace Treaties. His sole preoccupation, the German danger—dictated his every move. At the very moment when a far-seeing Talleyrand was needed, France was represented by a vengeful politician. Of course public opinion insisted upon revenge; it is no good pretending that Clemenceau did not represent the feelings of the average Frenchman at that time, but it is for statesmen to show more common-sense, not to speak of wisdom. He wanted to hang the Kaiser, and to exact crippling reparations from Germany, as well as to change the map of Europe. Until his dying day he never understood that reparations caused stagnation in France and hurt the receiver more than the donor.

Harold Nicolson's story, quoted here, of Clemenceau being 'rather high-handed with the smaller powers: Any objections? No? Adopted! Like a machine gun' is frightful in its implications, and reminds one of Stalin and Roosevelt at a Yalta banquet, when they moved pepper pots and forks representing millions of Europeans around on the table cloth, deciding who was to be merely bullied and who to be enslaved.

The 'smaller powers' got everything they wanted, provided it injured Germany or Austria-Hungary. They emerged from the Treaties swollen with immense tracts of central Europe to which they had no possible claim, whether historical or ethnic. The author skates over all this with a strange indifference. There is no mention, for example, of Masaryk or Benès, and the Treaties of Trianon and St Germain are ignored. Yet, for the future, what timebombs they contained! Europe is still suffering from the cruelty and stupidity of Versailles, St Germain and Trianon, and no-one more so than the foolish 'smaller powers'.

Clemenceau went banging on, paying scant attention to his ignorant though well-meaning allies. He had a distinct weakness for Anglo-Saxons and particularly admired the United States, but his theoretical friendliness did not extend to their representatives at Versailles. He hated Lloyd George, House and Woodrow Wilson hardly less than he hated Poincaré, Foch, Briand, Painlevé, Millerand, Léon Blum—the list could be tediously prolonged. When, after the war, Clemenceau allowed Mandel to put his name forward as candidate for the Presidency, he was convinced that he was bound to be elected. He was genuinely amazed by the victory of Deschanel, and his bitterness increased. The fact that Deschanel went mad soon afterwards was a slight comfort. He was beaten by his many enemies, and by the Catholic vote; his old passionate hatred of the Church of Rome had not been modified by the years. At the end of his life he proclaimed that the bolshevist peril was an illusion, the real danger was the Church.

He hated nearly everyone, but whom did he like? He liked his family, except for his American wife. He liked Monet, and admired his painting. He liked writers and painters and actors and especially actresses, and he liked a few cronies and toadies. He could not tolerate an equal, who might turn into a rival. One of his secretaries, Jean Martet, an unconditional worshipper, became his Eckermann or Boswell, producing several little books full of amusing details which find no place in the author's more serious and specifically political biography. Martet describes his hero's life in Paris after the war, and the speedy dashes by motor car to his house near the sea in his native Vendée. The simplicity of his flat and his cottage did not include plain fare. He sent his cook to have lessons from the chef at Claridges, and when Martet complimented his host upon the *omelette soufflée, mouton à la tomate* and *crème au chocolat*, the Tiger, gulping down a boiling *pêche pochée* which burnt his mouth, said: 'That's nothing. You should try my *poulet Soubise*.'

He could never resist a tease, and when Martet asked him whether he did not consider that Mme Curie, for example, was more qualified to vote than some drunken sot, Clemenceau replied that he was all for taking the vote away from the drunkard, but that he didn't feel too sure about giving it to Mme Curie, who kept very bizarre company.

Always ready with a sarcasm or an irreverent joke, Clemenceau's company was greatly enjoyed by young people. Hearing that an equestrian statue was being made of Marshal Foch (perhaps the one in Grosvenor Gardens) he remarked that Foch had never ridden a horse in his life. 'It's as if I had a statue made of myself riding a camel', he said scornfully. His statue, in the Champs Elysées near the métro station bearing his name, has neither horse nor camel. He looks as he must have looked in life, striding along into the east wind, bursting with energy; bold, malevolent, rough, ugly and ferocious.

Georges Clemenceau: A Political Biography, Watson, D.R., *Books and Bookmen*, (1974)

Paris and the Nineteenth Century

Counting from 1789, Paris had four revolutions in less than a century. Small wonder if the bourgeois inhabitants were frightened by rivers of blood. Napoleon built the Rue de Rivoli to make it harder to reach the palaces; in theory a few soldiers could prevent a mob crossing from East to West. Yet in 1871 the Tuileries palace was burnt down, and the Louvre only just escaped burning.

Christopher Prendergast is too much concerned with what happens to the mountains of filth and waste, the hundreds of dead bodies, which had to be disposed of in a city of millions. There is nothing special to Paris about the problem, and in fact it used the enormous underground space whence the stone that built it had been quarried.

He also dwells on human waste, the rag and bone man, the vagabond, encountered by the typical middle class flâneur as he strolls through the streets.

Haussmann during the second empire destroyed much that was beautiful in order to build wide, straight boulevards, and make it easier for police and military to contain trouble. He also made parks and green spaces to calm spirits. Yet the mob and the students threw up barricades in no time, when revolution was in the air.

Prendergast lightens his rather turgid prose with excellent quotes from Balzac, Baudelaire, Hugo and Flaubert to make his points. Some important contributions to Paris as 'capital of capitals' are entirely missing from his book: the beauty of the architecture; elegance and fashion. The uniquely delicious food gets a passing mention, but the exquisite minor arts of couture and decoration, the brilliant intelligence of conversation, the gaiety and fun, all are ousted by squalour, dirt and evil smells. Proust is mentioned, but there is no hint of a Guermantes to be found.

The Continual Pilgrimage opens with the liberation of Paris in 1944, American soldiers smothered in flowers and champagne. The honeymoon was short, the drunken boorishness of Hemingway and his like changed the scene, and on every empty space 'US go home' was the ungrateful message to the liberators. A few GIs made a bee-line for Gertrude Stein, who had spent the war in France and welcomed her compatriots in her grandmotherly way. Paris was a beacon for young writers, and over the Atlantic they came, both black and white. The blacks were entranced by the apparent absence of racialism in the French. They were accepted as they had never been by white people at home. They quarrelled among themselves, James Baldwin nourishing deep hatred for Richard Wright.

None of the young writers made French friends, they herded together and got their work into print at English language publishers and bookshops which catered for them. Most were very poor, and lived in seedy, bug-ridden hotels, or damp basements with no running water. They liked Paris, apparently because of the cafés.

When the Algerian war began they were disappointed to discover the French were racialists after all, and anti-Arab attitudes fashionable. They drifted away, and probably lived happily ever after in Greenwich Village. Even if some of Sawyer-Lauçanno's swans are geese, it is nevertheless a touching story in its pretentious way.

John Betjeman said that to read American books in an American accent is a great help. Presumably the pilgrimage continues; there is no end to the attraction Paris can exercise for artists, even now. Its tower blocks made the great ex-American writer, Julien Green, looking over the city from the heights of St Cloud, exclaim: 'It could be Detroit!' But, fortunately, it still could not.

Paris and The Nineteenth Century, Prendergast, C. (1992); *The Continual Pilgrimage by American Writers in Paris 1944-1960*, Sawyer-Lauçanno, C. (1992)

Napoleon's Children

Besides his legitimate son, the King of Rome, Napoleon had three other children. His son by Countess Walewska became a diplomat, the other two were of scant interest, therefore the title of this book is rather misleading since far the biggest role is that of Napoleon's nephew, the son of Napoleon's brother Louis, King of Holland. Louis-Napoleon's mother was Hortense de Beauharnais, daughter of Josephine. La Reine Hortense, as she was always called, had a younger son by her lover the Comte de Flahaut whose father was Talleyrand. This Auguste, afterwards Duc de Morny, engineered the coup d'état which brought his half brother to the throne as Napoleon III.

The caste is enormous, Napoleon had many brothers and sisters as well as his step-children Eugène and Hortense. Even someone familiar with the period might get muddled not only by the sheer numbers but by the determination to leave nothing out, resulting in what Lytton Strachey once described as 'an unwieldy accumulation of facts'.

The Bonaparte clan, and above all the great man himself, are so much disliked and so keenly denigrated throughout that it's a wonder the subject was chosen. Physically, mentally and morally they are attacked: fat, ugly, stupid, mean, cruel and dishonest. Even beautiful Pauline (disguised here in one of the many misprints as Paulette) is not given her deserved praise for refined elegance.

After Napoleon's defeat his son lived in Vienna where he bore the title Duke of Reichstadt until his early death from tuberculosis. He is the hero of a tear-jerker play by Edmond Rostand, *L'Aiglon*, which had Sarah Bernhardt in the name part.

Napoleon III was certainly a disastrous ruler. Queen Victoria, who stayed at St Cloud with him and Eugénie after the Crimean War, was enchanted by Paris, and she found the Emperor strangely seductive. But over the years he became unpopular for many good reasons, and when he provoked war with Prussia his armies were beaten in a matter of weeks. Eugène fled to England, where Napoleon joined her. The bloody Commune and the white terror which followed in 1871 were his legacy, matching the bloody coup d'état which had brought him to power twenty years before.

That was the end of the Bonapartes as rulers, though Napoleon's cousin Princesse Mathilde lived in Paris and is familiar to us through her literary friends, the Goncourt brothers, Flaubert, George Sand, and as a character in Proust. She died in 1904.

Napoleon's Children, Susan Normington (1993), *Evening Standard* (1993)

The Upper Hand

The Prince de Talleyrand was one of the wittiest, cleverest, most charming men who ever lived. He had inherited the celebrated *esprit* Mortemart from a grandmother, and there are Frenchmen today who give, as a reason for believing that the Duchesse de Dino's daughter Pauline was fathered by Talleyrand, the fact that the *esprit* Mortemart cropped up once again in Pauline's grandsons, Boniface de Castellane and his brothers.

There is probably no such spur to ambition in a brilliantly clever child as being utterly neglected by his parents. Lady Randolph Churchill's letter to her son refusing to go down to Harrow for some school festivity, as he had implored her to do, (she was going to the races), must have filled him with a feverish desire to succeed in life.

In the nineteenth century the children of the rich were hidden in their nurseries, but at least the nursery was only at the end of a corridor which led to their parents' part of the house. Charles-Maurice de Talleyrand-Périgord was sent miles away from home to be brought up by a poor woman in a cottage. He never saw his parents. As a baby, he fell off a chest of drawers and injured his foot; nothing was done about it, and he was lame for life. His uncle, who had the curiosity to seek him out, found him limping and dressed in rags and carried him off to his mother. He was four years old. She sent him away to his great-grandmother, an old lady who taught him the graces and manners of an eighteenth-century aristocrat, until at the age of eight he was sent to a boarding school in Paris.

Because of his infirmity, his parents (who never received him in their house) bestowed the family titles on his younger brother and forced Charles-Maurice to go into the Church, a career for which, to say the least of it, he had no vocation. In his memoirs he expresses deep bitterness about his upbringing.

Born in 1754, and destined to live in times of violent change, he grew up with three passions: politics, money, and women. He became a deacon at the age of 21, and, staying with his uncle the Archbishop of Rheims, he was present at the coronation of Louis XVI. Here he met for the first time the beautiful and high-born young ladies who were to become his bosom friends for life. He had a genius for friendship, and he was seductive and charming with his blue eyes, turned up nose and witty jokes. Ordained priest in 1779, he never allowed his vows of chastity to interfere with his gallantries, nor yet with his pursuit of riches.

He sensed that he was gifted for politics, and he was bent upon making enough money to be able to live not in comfort, but in luxury. '*Il ne faut jamais être pauvre diable*' [never be a poor sod], he said. He loathed his priest's soutane, and the measure of restraint it might put upon his vaulting ambition, for he realised that the days of the great political Cardinals, the Richelieus and Mazarins, were past. When Talleyrand was 34, he was made Bishop of Autun. Before taking up his duties he went into retreat at Issy, to prepare himself for the sacred order. The Abbé Ducloux, his spiritual director, complained that in the midst of his exhortations to the Bishop-elect the door would fly open and frivolous *gens du monde* would rush in for a gossip. The whole point of the bishopric, for Talleyrand, was the large income that went with it.

He visited his See once and once only, and impressed the local clergy with his brilliance. When he had to celebrate Mass in the cathedral it was a slight disaster because he was so obviously unfamiliar with the service. Nevertheless he was elected by his clergy as deputy for the Etats Généraux at Versailles, for this was the fateful year 1789, and the King had been prevailed upon to call the Estates together.

The fall of the Bastille was the prelude to riots and troubles, and what was known as *la grande peur* [great terror] swept through the upper classes and even the royal family. Talleyrand asked to see the King; he had a plan for reforms which might have saved the throne. Instead, he was granted an interview with the Comte d'Artois, who put the plan before Louis. When the King refused to budge, the Comte d'Artois and the Comte de Provence decided to flee. This precipitate emigration of his two brothers did great harm to Louis XVI, whose own disastrously bungled attempt to get away two years later was the beginning of the end.

On the first anniversary of the fall of the Bastille it was decided to celebrate with a Fête and a Mass in the Champ-de-Mars. The Bishop of Autun was called upon for this bizarre ceremony. Louis XVI and Marie-Antoinette, sporting the tricolour, and a huge crowd assembled. Talleyrand, as he climbed the steps to the altar, set up in view of all, was heard to say: '*Pourvu qu'on ne me fasse pas rire!*' [hopefully they won't make me laugh] Lafayette, who was rather a prig, was deeply shocked.

All his life, Talleyrand was a man of the centre. He now resigned his bishopric and took the oath of the Civil Constitution of the Clergy; for this, the Pope excommunicated him. He worked with Mirabeau and other moderates, and had Mirabeau lived it is possible that the monarchy might have been saved and the worst excesses of the Revolution avoided. Possible, but not probable. Armies of the central powers were massing on the frontiers of France, the King's brothers were with them, and they were in constant communication with Marie-Antoinette. War was imminent.

In 1792 Talleyrand was sent to London to attempt to secure English neutrality in the war. He was not well received by the Tory government, which looked upon the ex-bishop as a dangerous revolutionary, nor by his émigré countrymen who called him traitor, renegade, unfrocked priest, nor by the King and Queen. On the other hand, he was made much of by the Whigs, and welcomed by Charles James Fox and Lord Lansdowne. From this time onward he and Lord Lansdowne were close friends; they would doubtless have been pleased, could they have known that their descendants were to marry, and that the daughter of Talleyrand's natural son, the Comte de Flahaut, was destined to be a future Lady Lansdowne.

After his return to Paris the horrible massacre of the Swiss Guards at the Tuileries was followed by the imprisonment of the royal family in the Temple, and in September there were mass killings of aristocrats, priests and nuns in an orgy of bloodshed. Moderates like Talleyrand were in grave danger, and he decided to go back to London, though he waited for a passport signed by Danton, for he did not wish to be classed with the émigrés.

When Louis XVI was guillotined there was a great revulsion in England against anyone connected with the Revolution, and the ex-Bishop of Autun was ordered to leave the country. He sailed for America, where he attempted to improve his depleted fortunes by dealing in real estate. It was not a success, and when he heard the great news of the fall of Robespierre and the end of the Terror he made his way home as soon as he could: 'If I must spend another year here I shall die,' he wrote to Madame de Staël. Die of boredom…

The false step taken by Robespierre which led him to the guillotine was one of those outdoor fêtes so beloved of revolutionaries. He proclaimed that it was in honour of an '*Etre Suprême*', and this was more than his colleagues, or the cynical Parisians, could stomach.

Germaine de Staël worked diligently among her political friends to ensure that Talleyrand could return safely, which, via Germany, he did in 1796. Then he waited and watched, for a chance to get into politics. He joined a political group, the Constitutional Club, made up of like-minded moderates, and quickly gained an ascendancy over the other members. He read learned papers to the Academies. He made friends with all the influential women in Paris: Mme de Staël, Mme Tallien, Joséphine de Beauharnais. Mme de Staël arranged for him to meet Barras, the most powerful man of the moment. Barras was greatly impressed, and before long named him Minister of Foreign Affairs. He was 43.

According to Benjamin Constant, who rode with him in the carriage when he went to take up his appointment, Talleyrand murmured: '*Immense fortune! Une fortune immense!*' [Good fortune, a large one.] Mr Bernard dismisses the story as 'spurious'. But whether he said it or not, he undoubtedly thought that he could make vast sums of money as Minister, and make them he did. In two years he acquired twelve to fifteen million francs, taking presents and bribes, '*douceurs*' as he called them from foreign powers. He made no secret of it, and perhaps the French felt they had suffered enough from a 'sea-green incorruptible'.

All was flux. Looking at the Directors, Talleyrand knew that their government could not last. He decided to join forces with the brilliant young soldier who had conquered Italy, and regularly corresponded with him. After the coup d'état of the 18th Brumaire, he worked closely with Napoleon. These two extraordinary and dissimilar men, despite an antipathy, needed one another. Each admired the other's qualities, but they never became friends. When Napoleon flew into one of his rages it irritated him beyond endurance that Talleyrand was neither angry nor cowed, but stared into the middle distance maintaining a contemptuous silence. Even when Napoleon shouted that he was 'shit in a silk stocking', Talleyrand's only comment was *'dommage qu'un si grand homme soit si mal élevé'* [so great, so badly raised]. Napoleon thought it essential that a *grand seigneur* should deal with foreign courts and give *ton* to his own court. It was one of his fatal mistakes.

During the Consulate Talleyrand was living openly, in his official residence, with a Mme Grand, a beautiful woman with an empty head and a disreputable past. Napoleon insisted that he either get rid of her or marry her. Although he had been excommunicated, Talleyrand had not been granted lay status by the Church. He now asked to be freed from his vows and allowed to marry, but this was more than the Pope was prepared to do. Talleyrand raked up such precedents as he could find, among them the case of Cesare Borgia, who although a Cardinal had been permitted to marry a French princess. It was pointed out that Cesare Borgia had never been ordained a priest, moreover the Pope, Alexander VI, was his father, which made all the difference. However, Napoleon twisted the Papal decree; he announced that Talleyrand had been secularised and granted the right to contract a marriage. Paris was stupefied. That the proud and disdainful aristocrat should marry Mme Grand seemed unbelievable. Mr Bernard thinks he probably did it from indolence, and in order 'not to disturb a pattern of life which he found agreeable'.

Meanwhile Napoleon pursued his conquests all over Europe. There seemed to be no end to the wars. At St Helena, Napoleon admitted he had made two mistakes: the campaigns against Spain and Russia. Talleyrand, moderate as always, was the advocate of peace, and of the natural or ethnic frontiers between nations. He knew that the defeat of one country by another was never final, but engendered first resistance and then another war. Napoleon was unconvinced; after crowning himself Emperor of the French he crowned himself King of Italy, and bestowed kingdoms upon his brothers and his marshals. Although heavily engaged in Spain he invaded Russia, in the disastrous campaign which led to his downfall. Long before this, Talleyrand had perceived that while Napoleon ruled there could be no peace, and he intrigued with the Russians, the Prussians and the Austrians to encompass his defeat. In his memoirs, Talleyrand seeks to justify this odious and reprehensible treachery by saying that Napoleon was bleeding France and Europe to death.

After the departure of the Emperor and the return of Louis XVIII from his long exile, Talleyrand was sent to Vienna to represent the people of France at the Congress. He took with him his last love, Dorothea de Courland, wife of his nephew Edmond de Périgord. Talleyrand's brilliance, and the persistence which ensured that he sat as an equal with Metternich, Wellington and the other delegates, were admirable; often he imposed his will on his country's victorious enemies. France was indeed fortunate to possess such a man at such a moment.

However, as the Prince de Ligne said, '*Le Congrès danse, mais il ne marche pas*' [The Congress dances but doesn't budge], and when Napoleon escaped from Elba a great deal remained to be done. The events of the hundred days, and Waterloo, made Talleyrand's task harder than ever. That he succeeded in keeping France's natural frontiers was a measure of his success. Not for the first time, nor for the last, representatives of the European powers were astonished at the ignorance displayed by the English in the elements of history and geography, an ignorance which has continued to our own day and which has accounted, in part, for the mistakes made by the anglo-saxons when they have taken a hand in re-drawing the map of our continent.

After the second restoration, Talleyrand was out of office for several years, though he had a position at Court. He and Dorothea (now Duchesse de Dino) lived at his hotel on the corner of the rue St Florentin, and spent their summers at his grand castle of Valençay and at Rochecotte, her delightful house near the Loire. In 1820 a daughter, Pauline, was born. Talleyrand loved her tenderly, and was generally thought to have been her father.

Louis XVIII loaded him and his family with titles and honours, but it was only after the abdication of Charles X that Talleyrand was brought once more into public life, when Louis Philippe appointed him ambassador to London. He and Dorothea spent four years in London. They made the embassy a sparkling centre of fashionable society, with the best food and the best talk at their table.

At the age of 80, Prince de Talleyrand retired, and he and the Duchesse de Dino resumed their life between Paris and Valençay. London friends paid them visits at the Château; Lady Granville enjoyed herself and said it was like an English country house. Mme de Lieven, on the other hand, a difficult guest, was bored to tears.

When his old wife, from whom he had been separated for so many years, died at last, Talleyrand began to consider a reconciliation with the Church. Mme de Dino and Pauline, now a pious young lady of eighteen, never stopped urging him to sign a letter to the Pope making his submission to Rome. He finally did so, on his death bed, to their extreme satisfaction. Jean Orieux, author of a recent biography of Talleyrand, describes the scene when, after making his confession, he was to receive the last sacraments. The abbé was about to anoint his palms, but the prince clenched his fists and held them out, saying: 'Do not forget, Monsieur l'abbé, that I am a Bishop.' More than forty people were present at his death, and all Paris knew what had happened between the abbé and the prince '*Après avoir roulé tout le monde, il a fini par rouler le bon Dieu*' [After taking advantage of the entire world, he ended it by taking advantage of god], people said.

Mr Bernard's book is the best and most complete biography of Talleyrand in English. There is little to complain about. When he makes James II a contemporary of George III it is obviously a slip of the pen: he means the Stuart pretender, the Cardinal of York. The organiser of the ill-fated flight to Varennes was Axel Fersen, not Fernsen, and the Prince de Ligne has become, rather absurdly, the Prince de Linge [Linen]. (Both these mistakes appear in the index as well as in the text.) To an English eye the American spelling is unpleasing, and Lady Elizabeth Holland and Lord Charles Grey will hardly do for Lady Holland and Lord Grey. Apart from these relatively trivial errors, the publisher is to be congratulated on an excellent production at a very modest price.

What made Talleyrand so greatly loved and appreciated by his many friends of both sexes and of all ages? Above all, it was his brilliant conversation. Mme de Rémusat speaks of his 'method of approaching serious subjects in the most frivolous possible manner', and she says: 'Although more artificial than anyone I had ever known, he was able, out of a thousand affectations, to construct a perfectly natural manner.' There was not a trace of pomposity or hypocrisy in him, and Mme de La Tour du Pin, who disapproved of him, says: 'in spite of everything, he had more charm than any other man I have ever known', while an observer at the Congress of Vienna declares: 'He seemed to dominate that illustrious assembly by the charm of his mind and the ascendancy of his genius.'

Talleyrand: a Biography, Bernard, J.F., *Books and Bookmen* (1973)

Madame Du Deffand

Mme du Deffand had the good fortune to live in eighteenth-century Paris, where her surroundings were of perfect beauty. She was pretty, and rich enough to be comfortable, as were her many friends. Versailles, with its jealousies and stifling etiquette, was no longer the magnet it had been the century before; and Mme du Deffand, after a fling in her youth with the dissolute Regent, settled down to what must seem an ideal life. Wit and beauty assembled in her yellow silk drawing room and amused themselves with chat and cards, only interrupted by delicious food.

If an interesting foreigner came to Paris he soon found his way to Mme du Deffand. There was even a spice of danger; free-thinking men and the encyclopaedia they were writing were sometimes confined in the Bastille. Mme du Deffand was a comfortable reactionary, but Voltaire, a great friend of hers, lived on the borders of Switzerland. He had been in the Bastille once, and had no desire to go back.

Mme du Deffand partook of the *douceur de vivre*, which Talleyrand said only those who had lived before the French Revolution had known. Yet long before she went blind she was discontented. She said over and over again she wished she had never been born. Cross and sharp with her servants and companions, when her sight faded she took her niece Julie de Lespinasse to live with her. After a while Julie escaped from her tyranny and set up on her own. She had no money, but all Mme du Deffand's friends combined to give her what she needed, and annoyed the marquise by making Julie's salon as brilliant as her own. They were perhaps tired of the eternal grumbling and pessimism, although Mme du Deffand could be excellent company.

When Horace Walpole appeared on the scene Mme du Deffand fell madly in love with him. She was old enough to be his mother, and Walpole fled, terrified of becoming an object of ridicule. He wrote her very cruel and repressive letters, while she tried her best not to allow her love expression in her replies. The whole episode is painful; she lived only for his occasional visits to Paris.

Her letters to Walpole, Voltaire and others, are not to be compared with those of the other marquise, Mme de Sévigné, a century earlier. They are full of complaints, and one feels both Walpole and Voltaire were terrified she might descend upon them, at Strawberry Hill or at Ferney.

Benedetta Craveri's enjoyable book tells the story well. The footnotes are at the end instead of at the bottom of the page, where they belong, and the translation is riddled with Gallicisms. But Mme du Deffand and the appalling ennui she suffered from demonstrate that perfect surroundings, peace, plenty and wit, do not necessarily make happiness, something twentieth-century grumblers may find it hard to admit.

Madame du Deffand and Her World, Craveri, B., *Evening Standard* (1994)

Doting Mothers

In theory, everybody is familiar with the letters of Mme de Sévigné. And in practice? Probably a few of those considered suitable were read in the schoolroom and have scarcely been glanced at since. Mrs Hammersley has changed all this; beautifully translated, beautifully produced, her book deserves to be a bestseller, for it is guaranteed to delight, amuse and instruct, with its excellent introduction and scholarly footnotes.

About one sixth of the letters are here; most of them addressed to Mme de Grignan. 'It is ordained there should be a Mme de Sévigné whose love for her daughter passes the love of mothers, from whom she has constantly to be parted' wrote the Marquise. Mme de Grignan (who was also a faithful correspondent, but whose letters have not survived) has often been blamed for her coldness-this 'dry stick of a daughter' as Irvine calls her-but there is nothing harder to put up with than the sort of possessive, enveloping, passionate love which the mother heaped upon her. And with all this exaggerated adoration, Mme de Sévigné did not scruple to marry *la plus jolie fille de France* [the most beautiful girl in France] to a forty-year-old man, twice a widower, who had the pox (though this she could not know).

'All his wives are dead,' wrote the bride's mother, cheerfully, 'and by extraordinary good fortune his father and son as well, so that he is richer than ever before'.

Was seventeenth-century France a different world from our world? Mme de Sévigné's letters from Les Rochers could almost have been written yesterday. She walked in the woods, received her grand neighbours, chatted with the abbé, read a great many books, and never stopped assuring her correspondents that she was not in the least bored, but on the contrary occupied country sympathise; and amused. Those who love the country will sympathise; they are amused and happy, but Paris could believe it that they feel obliged to mention it each time they write.

Illness, the weather and money troubles were other stock subjects, whether she wrote from country or town. The doctors were very rough;

yet to this day any French doctor will put his liverish patient on the diet of rice which M de Grignan found so *adoucissant* [soothing].

Politics, and church politics, were an unending source of gossip, and in those days everyone, however intelligent, was an amateur Crawfie. Certainly the doings of the royal family were spicy enough; births, deaths and the marriage nights of princes and princesses and of the King's large family of bastards were attended by the curious courtiers and every detail passed on to friends.

Mme de Sévigné, staying at Grignan for grandson's left wedding, notes with surprise that the young couple all night and that nobody made a bawdy joke when they came down to breakfast.

It was to celebrate this wedding that local ladies, we read, 'though they knew we wish to dispense with their presence, break the windows or crawl under the doors to come and pay their compliments at the peril of their lives.' ['*qu'on avait priées de ne point venir, ont rompu des glaces, ont pensé tomber dessous, ont été en péril de leur vie, pour venir faire un compliment...*'] It was bitterly cold weather that February in Provence just as it has been this year; even the rushing Rhone was frozen, she writes. Surely it was ice, not windows, they broke in their polite efforts to reach the château?

Not the least of the book's great virtues is the elegance of Mrs Hammersley's English, which never jars by being too and yet never irritates by being self-consciously antique.

The illustrations show what we want to see, the prettiness charm of Les Rochers, the grandeur of Grignan, and the exuberance of the letter writer.

Can one imagine a Mme de Sévigné of today going to watch a woman burned at the stake? I do not feel as certain, in saying no, as I should once have done.

Letters from Madame de Sévigné, ed. and trans. Hammersley, V. (1956)

U and Non-U

BRITAIN

If I were a novelist I should think twice before allowing pre-publication extracts of my books to appear in newspapers. In some shiny journal a chapter from *Anglo-Saxon Attitudes*, accompanied by huge caricature illustrations in full colour, nearly put me off reading the book. The editor had picked out a plum, one of Mr Wilson's plummiest and most exaggerated baroque inventions: Mrs Salad, charwoman and former lavatory attendant.

Angus Wilson's fans know well that he excels at oddities, dotty old women, criminal spivs and guilt-ridden intellectuals; the danger is, perhaps, that he might allow the richness and strangeness of his imagination to over-decorate his writing so that it became like a dinner of marrow bones and chocolate truffles.

In fact, however, Mrs Salad's place in this novel is a minor one, no greater than Mrs Gummidge's in *David Copperfield*. (If Angus Wilson reminds us of Dickens, and he does, it is of a Dickens who has read Freud and lost interest in reform.)

Among the crowd of personages my favourite monster is the Danish woman, Inge Middleton. Here she is with the village children whom she has taught to sing German, French and English carols at Christmas:

And now it was a little Jutland peasant song that the children were to sing, and Ingeborg led them with a deep contralto, her well-supported pastel-blue bosom heaving, her grey eyes round with surprise. 'Ole Dole, din, din,' she sang, or that, at any rate, was what it sounded like to the smaller children, who, thus reminded that they were hungry, began to cry.

'And now little Maurice Gardner will sing a verse of Holy Night and we shall sing the choruses. Little Maurice is a very shy, special little boy,' she said to the audience, 'so we must all help him.' When no sound came from his terror-struck mouth, she bent down from the heavens above and placing her huge doll's

355

face close to his, she asked, 'What is the matter, Maurice? Have the trolls bewitched your tongue?' so creating a deep psychic trauma that was to cause him to be court-martialled for cowardice many years later in World War III.

No wonder her clever, rich, attractive husband (a professor of medieval history) left her; he comes back each year to join the family, children and grandchildren, for a frightful Christmas to which the foregoing scene is prelude. He dislikes most his son John, Inge's favourite child, a homosexual Labour ex-MP who earns large sums on TV fighting the battles of the little man.

Anglo-Saxon Attitudes is the best novel I have read for a very long time. Among its many merits, it has a plot of extreme fascination; was the indecent fertility idol found by archeologists in the Anglo-Saxon bishop's coffin buried with him or was it planted there by a cynical practical joker? But the title has another meaning besides, for the book is a portrait of some of the less agreeable attitudes of present-day Anglo-Saxons.

Anglo-Saxon Attitudes, Wilson, A. (1956)

Encyclopaedia Of Britain

The omniscient Bamber Gascoigne has long since taken all general knowledge to be his province, and he says he wrote this enormous book because he needed it on his shelves. As his métier is asking questions on television he probably does need it, though for most people, like the game Trivial Pursuits, it may be more entertaining than useful.

The dust jacket, with its incredible muddle of people and places, gives a fair idea of what is inside. The Cheshire Cat and Laurence Olivier, a pop star in full cry and Shakespeare, Kitchener and London buses, Queen Elizabeth smothered in jewels and the Jarrow hunger marchers in their painful misery, bracing Skegness and Winston

Churchill, W.G. Grace and Winnie the Pooh are jammed together higgledy piggledy, and there'll be a thumbnail sketch of everyone. Do they add up to 'Britain'? Rather a grim thought. They are displayed against a sunset. Symbolic? Or just a bit more technicolour?

The book is heavy, all art paper with coloured illustrations, excellently done. Probably 'history' suffers most from thumbnail treatment, though biography runs it close. The brevity makes them tendentious, how could it not? The reader is constantly reminded of how much Britain loved interfering in the affairs of Europe and indeed the world, and how completely it has not lost the will or the power to interfere. The decline, and the speed of the decline, are surprising.

The encyclopedia is politically correct, warning that many popular hymns and nursery rhymes have become unacceptable: All thing bright and beautiful, eeny meeny miny mo and part of the National Anthem among them. Librarians in public libraries ban Noddy, but he remains a best seller; since he cannot be borrowed he is bought, which must have made a fortune for Enid Blyton.

The Bisto Kids, 1919 version, are here, a tragic picture of ragged and undernourished children longing for what looks like typically nasty British food. It induces many questions. Why were people so poor, in the 'richest country in the world'?

Why do the British put up with British Railways, is a question often pondered on the line between Dover and London by incoming tourists. Why so squeamish about a nursery rhyme but so tolerant of the filthy London underground? The encyclopedia tells us the underground dates from 1890, it has accumulated grime for more than a century, and nobody seems to mind. St Paul's Cathedral being hidden by office blocks? Not enough to do something. Is British tolerance a virtue or a vice?

Yeats is excluded for being Irish. Terry Wogan is in, described as an Irish broadcaster. This is probably just as it should be, although Britain's greatest gift to the world is the English language, used by Yeats with such admirable virtuosity.

A final question: what would Sir Francis Bacon think of this book?

Rather insular perhaps. But that is the object of the enterprise.

The Encyclopedia of Britain, Gascoigne, B., *Evening Standard* (1993)

In a Groove

'All the king's horses, and all the king's men, couldn't put Caitlin Thomas together again.' These words, the last in the book, are doubtless true. The only person who conceivably could pull her together would be Mrs Thomas herself, and she may very likely consider that the heavy task is not worth the trouble. That she is capable of doing it is proved by the fact that she was capable of the sustained effort and concentration required to produce the piercing, high-pitched, long-drawn-out wail which is *Leftover Life to Kill*.

A few months after she brought her husband's body back to Wales from America Mrs Thomas went with her youngest child to a Mediterranean island, where she spent a wretched, cold winter in a cheap hotel. She describes various sad little adventures, and even managed to fall in love in a rather mild way with an Italian miner aged eighteen. The inhabitants, according to her account, were relieved when she finally left their shores, although they did not, like her Welsh neighbours, go so far as to wish to tar and feather her and put her on a bonfire. She has a good many complaints to make about them, chief of these their drinking habits. She says they never wanted to drink with her at what they considered the wrong times, and she was never able to find out when was the right time. Unlike Wales, where, of course, the right time was opening time. The island and the island loves, hates and quarrels are really padding, however; for the point of the book is that it tells once again the story of Dylan Thomas the poet, whose death has left his wife at the bottom of a pit of despair in which she attempts to kill time; until life, which has become for her a useless misery, shall finally come to an end.

Here is one of her descriptions of her husband: 'He was never his proper self until there was something wrong with him; and, if ever there was a danger of him becoming 'whole', which was very remote, he would crack another of his chicken bones, without delay, and wander happily round in his sling, piling up plates with cucumber, pickled onions, tins of cod's roe, boiled sweets; to push into his mouth with an unseeing hand, as they carne, while he went on solidly reading his trash. His passion for lies was congenital: more a practice in invention than a lie. He would tell quite unnecessary ones, which did not in any way improve his situation: such as, when he had been to one cinema, saying it was another, and the obvious ones, that only his mother pretended not to see through, like being carted off the bus into his home, and saying he had been having coffee, in a café, with a friend.' He and Mrs Thomas fought and nagged and annoyed one another, but she misses him 'and pines, as keenly as a sick cow for its calf just removed.'

Jung says that perhaps we owe everything to our neuroses. We probably owe Dylan Thomas's saga to his neurotic desire to escape from the stifling petty-bourgeois Welsh atmosphere in which he had been brought up. 'No blue-blooded gentleman was a quarter as gentlemanly as Dylan's father. And, though Dylan imagined himself to be completely emancipated from his family background, there was a very strong puritanical streak in him, that his friends never suspected; but of which I got the disapproving benefit.' (He made Mrs Thomas wear gloves to go to Carmarthen market.)

This book confirms the horrible accounts already published of the poet's sordid life and death. To what do we owe its appearance? Did Mrs Thomas feel that if she unburdened herself, told all, held back no private details, she could be cured of her bitterness (which she describes as 'solid as a Christmas cake'), put away the past, start life anew? Apparently not. 'They say confession is a great relief, as liberating and loosening as a flood of tears, to the confessor. I don't agree— I find it unmitigatedly painful,' she says. Possibly she wrote the book to earn money. Thomas had an enormous success in America, and perhaps on the whole Mrs Thomas, who loathes such unalike places in Europe as Wales and Italy with an equal loathing, would be better off in, say, Greenwich Village, where she would presumably find plenty of hard liquor at all hours of the day and night and where the cracked Dylan Thomas gramophone record might be put on over and over again for a delighted audience of fans.

Leftover Life to Kill, Thomas, C. (1957)

✳

How Dear Is Life

Mr Henry Williamson's saga, or series of novels describing, generation by generation, a suburban English family, has now reached the beginning of the First World War. So cleverly has he reconstructed the period that we feel as though we were living in the pages of the *Illustrated London News* of 1914. The first half of the book is about Philip Maddison as a junior clerk in an insurance office; the second, his experiences as a private in the 'contemptible little army' of territorials who went through such hard fighting alongside regular soldiers in the autumn of 1914. Not the least of the book's merits is that the author pauses in his narrative from time to time to point out an historical truth; for instance, that the Kaiser never called the English army contemptible, (he may have called it little), but that the expression was invented by a zealot called General Maurice, who rightly imagined that it would whip up English hatred of Germany.

The war in Flanders is vividly and terribly described. Mud, blood, agony, terror, brutality and filth are dwelt upon by Mr Williamson, who has used his famous descriptive powers to bring before the reader war in all its frightfulness, as it seemed to a young, sensitive, rather lonely and friendless man, who has found himself transplanted from his insurance office into the midst of an inferno with terrifying suddenness. Like Fabrice at Waterloo, he is in the battle of Ypres without realising it. But, unlike Fabrice, Philip is not a sympathetic character, and this is the weakness of a brave book (brave because it must have cost a great effort to write, to force the memory to search for details which time had nearly obliterated, to re-live so many dreadful hours from long ago).

Presumably Philip is meant to represent *l'homme moyen sensuel*; but in his anxiety to portray the little man Mr Williamson has made him so little that he can hardly be said to exist. He and his dull, rather disagreeable father and his even duller though pathetic mother are altogether too dim; we cannot mind very much what happens to them, or feel involved in any way with their fate.

This leaves what might be called the *Illustrated London News* side of the book, and very brilliant and evocative it is. Probably no other writer alive could have done it so well. The dying English soldiers crying Mother! or Water!, the dying German soldiers crying *Mutter!* or *Wasser!*—the mad wickedness of European war is emphasised, as well as its useless stupidity. When the scene changes to Philip's suburban street, and the telegraph boy stopping at a gate can freeze every heart in terror; when the woman next door loses her three sons in as many days, it reminds us of the doomed generation, decimated, almost lost; and it seems unbelievable that Europeans should have been willing to start these miseries all over again in 1939. But this will, no doubt, be dealt with by Mr Williamson as his saga slowly progresses towards our own times.

How Dear is Life, Williamson, H.

Terrifying Cows

There are two sorts of children's books: those they like to read themselves and those written about them for old people to recapture the past.

Great Meadow belongs to the second category; it is supposed, throughout, to be by a little boy describing his life, but the reader knows quite well that Dirk Bogarde's evocation is not the work of a child. For one thing, the repetitive slang of the style is unlike a boy's way of writing. (More realistic is the way Daisy Ashford wrote *The*

Young Visiters.) Books loved by people of all ages, by Edward Lear, Hilaire Belloc, Lewis Carroll for example, never suffer from what Dirk Bogarde describes as his 'deliberately restricted vocabulary'. Children want a story, or jokes. *Great Meadow* is for adults only.

It follows a pattern the author has used with great success before, and is an autobiography starting at an earlier age than his previous volumes of memoirs, supposedly written when he was a child, living with his sister and a nanny in a cottage in Sussex. His age at the time is rather a puzzle. He appears from photographs to have been about 12 in 1934, yet he sounds like a child of six. He is not a country boy like Laurie Lee in *Cider with Rosie*; he is a London boy in a country cottage.

The nanny—to whom the book is dedicated—is not a countrywoman either; she is terrified of cows and indeed of all animals. She is rather unkind to her charges, not only sarcastic but rough, boxing their ears and cuffing them at the drop of a hat. She also gives them unsuitable tasks to perform, such as digging a deep hole and emptying into it the dread contents of the bucket in the earth closet, their only lavatory. This would hardly be possible for a six-year-old, yet if the boy is twelve he seems unusually backward. Would he put up with having his ears boxed by a nanny? To dig a deep hole once a week in the hard summer earth, or the frosty winter earth, takes some doing.

We can picture how much old people will enjoy hearing about the young Dirk Bogarde losing his white mice, or the tortoise, or the cat; he was unlucky with pets. Then there is fetching the milk in a can, or the water in a pail, or buying food in the village. His parents (a journalist and a former actress) sometimes appeared for a day or two and then disappear back to London where they belong.

The bitter cold and primitive discomfort of the cottage are part of a golden memory, and now turned to good account. Although the slang is rather improbable, and the deliberately restricted vocabulary a little sad, *Great Meadow* is restful, undemanding and a nice change. No four-letter words, no sex, a minimum of violence.

Great Meadow: an Evocation, Bogarde, D., *Evening Standard* (1992)

❉

How Britain Went to Market

In the beginning was the Coal and Steel Community. The merging of
French and German heavy industry made the new Europe possible. It
is the post-war miracle, and the well-publicised embraces of de Gaulle
and Adenauer were symbolic of a reality. Invited to join, Britain
declined. Jean Monnet said: 'There is one thing you British will never
understand: an idea. And there is one thing you are supremely good at
grasping: a hard fact. We will have to build Europe without you; but
then you will come in and join us.' Prophetic words.

How Britain Joined the Common Market is one of those books like *The
Making of the President*, where everyone knows the dénouement and yet
the suspense and drama of political struggle keep the interest up to
fever pitch until the very last page. In other words, it is skilfully written; Uwe Kitzinger says it will be a quarry for future historians, and it
is that and more besides.

The question in the mind of the reader remains—how DID Britain
succeed in joining Europe? English enthusiasm for the idea cooled
through the 60s as veto followed veto from France. By the time serious negotiations began, opinion polls showed that it had dwindled to
between 30 and 40 per cent in favour. Quite a lot of space is devoted
to opinion polls, although the author admits they defy analysis and it is
not easy to read in the tealeaves. There are one or two constants;
women, for example, have throughout been more hostile to joining
Europe than men. This is predictable; women are conservative
guardians of the hearth and against radical adventure. It is hard to
imagine a boat-load of Pilgrim Mothers.

The negotiations in Brussels were a nightmare. With so many people present it was hopeless to expect secrecy; hovering journalists discovered within minutes what had gone on in the conference room. The
unfortunate Mr Rippon* had the dilemma that if he started with a low
bid and gradually came up to a level acceptable to the Six he was jibed

in England for having been outwitted by them, while if he put in a real-istic bid from the start he was said to have given everything away with-out even trying. But the crucial battle was in Parliament itself. It swung to and fro, and in spite of the famous victory of October 28, 1971, when there was a majority of 112 for entry, there were anxious times throughout the passing of the consequential legislation. At Westminster, as in Brussels, there were all-night sittings and frayed nerves. There was a notable amount of arm-twisting used by both par-ties on their 'rebels'—Labour members who had remained faithful to the European idea after Wilson's about-turn, and Conservative diehards. Extremes met, the rigid right joining forces with the old-fash-ioned left (Enoch Powell and Michael Foot), while outside the House both blimps and communists were virulent in their anti-European atti-tudes.

The Press was mostly in favour of entry, including all the 'serious' papers: *Financial Times, Guardian, Daily Telegraph* and *Times*, as well as the multi-million circulation *Daily Mirror* and the *Sun*. Against were the huge *Daily Express* and the tiny *Morning Star*. Television coverage was vast, and tried to be fair to both sides, and with all this bombardment the campaign never came alive, the man in the street seemed bored with the whole subject; he looked with a jaundiced eye at the promised thrills, great opportunities, exciting challenges and so forth. The Trade Unions seemed to mutter, like the Sphinxes in Goethe's *Faust*: '*im heili-gen Sitz, lassen wir uns nicht stören*' [we won't be disturbed].

All in all, Mr Kitzinger demonstrates that it was a few men at the summit of affairs who brought this great event to pass. One only has to think of de Gaulle and Anthony Eden, and compare them with Pompidou and Heath, to see what might have been. Eden 'felt in his bones' that we should not join a united Europe. Heath felt with his whole being that we should, and must, and could. Mr Kitzinger empha-sises that the English Europeans have only won the first round—There are many powerful wreckers waiting to pounce. The UK econo-my, with its poor industrial relations, flourishing inflation and distress-ing unemployment, is in a bad way. From now on the Labour Party will see to it that every failure, every deficiency, is attributed to Heath's European policy. Mr Callaghan made the position clear when he said his object was 'to make sure they (the Tories) would have to carry the can all the way.' To what extent the lukewarm public will accept this myth remains to be seen; probably it will reject it, since it is what the French call sewn with white thread. The vital thing is that England should 'grasp the hard fact', as Jean Monnet said.

* The British minister who negotiated the entry into the Common Market.

Diplomacy and Persuasion:-How Britain Joined the Common Market, Kitzinger, U.,

Books and Bookmen (1973)

Violet Markham

This autobiography is a dull book about a dull life. It was reviewed in one of the left-wing weeklies under the title 'A Great Lady.' Opinions may differ as to what exactly constitutes a great lady, but one thing is clear: Miss Violet Markham has been a considerable busy-body. Hardly a day of her long life seems to have passed which did not find her sitting on some committee, interfering more or less with the lives of other people, or presiding as a large frog in some very small puddle. The description of her varied activities does not make exhilarating reading. Sometimes she is sweeping crippled and defective children into a class at Chesterfield Settlement; sometimes at work in the Anti-Suffrage League; between the wars serving on the hated Unemployment Assistance Board; during the last war running a canteen which (get ready to laugh) she called Topsy because it just 'growed.' She is an almost professional good works enthusiast (almost, because her independent income preserves her amateur status) and others of the breed are her chosen friends. Study the index—hardly one of the dreary crew of self-appointed goody-goodies is missing. No wonder she eyes with misgiving the replacement of well-meaning and more or less charitable individuals by the Welfare State. Perhaps if one were a 'defective,' or an immoral A.S. girl, or the unemployed father of a family being questioned by her with a view to application of the Means Test, one might feel that, sad though it may be to force the Miss Markhams of life into the ranks of the workless, yet it is for the greatest good of the greatest number.

She travelled a good deal; and it was obviously agony for her when she saw things of which she disapproved, and which badly needed investigation, not to be able to set to work immediately with a strong committee of maiden ladies. She could hardly, figuratively speaking, keep her hands off the Sultan of Java. 'I came away thoroughly disgusted by this passing sight of Javanese royalty and all it revealed in idleness, sloth and sensuality.' He appears, from her account, to have been a singularly harmless old man, who left the government of his country in the hands of the Dutch Resident while he lived quietly in his palace, surrounded by his numerous family of wives and children.

Oddly enough, in spite of her addiction to public and near-public life, Miss Markham joined the Anti-Suffrage League, formed to stop women getting the vote. In this matter she certainly shows her less attractive side, for she is insensitive enough to write: 'I am sure the suffragette movement was huge fun, and that they enjoyed themselves immensely. Smashing windows, being arrested and bailed out by distracted relatives, slapping policemen and heckling Ministers must have been a great change from many a placid life in town or country, varied only by conventional amusements.' Yes, indeed; and huge fun too, to be held down by six wardresses in Holloway Prison while a tube was thrust up your nose and you were forcibly fed, a rather unconventional amusement indulged in by the Home Office of those days.

Perhaps Miss Markham agrees with those who consider that Parliament is not a place where women shine? Not at all. Strange to say, no sooner had the suffragettes won their victory than Miss M jumps on the band wagon. 'I was one of the little body of women… who stood for Parliament on the first occasion that women were qualified to vote and to offer themselves as candidates.' She was not elected, and did not stand again. No great loss, we may feel. From her own point of view, given her odd predilection for busy-bodying, she was much better off sitting on numberless committees and boards. She even found time to be married, but (presumably as an ardent feminist, famous in the committee world) she kept her maiden name.

Miss Markham was born at the right moment, and we can congratulate ourselves that we shall not see her like again. When unemployment returns there will be another UAB, and those serving on it may be gruffer, harder, more unsympathetic than she; but at least what they are doing will be their work, done for a wage, not just for the fun of interfering in the old Now-my-good-man-where-is-your-self-respect way. She and a few like-minded and right-minded female enthusiasts may still be able to form committees to see to the morals of fallen women or study the reasons for the breakdown of family life; or they might get taken on as prison visitors, though here there is a danger that the prisoners might complain that it was not part of their sentence. But, by and large, their day is done. Whenever we feel inclined to abuse the Welfare State we should force ourselves to read a chapter of Miss Markham's autobiography.

Laying it down with, it must be admitted, a sigh of relief, we feel there is something missing. Of course—Dame Violet! How has she escaped it? We must pin our faith to the New Year Honours, and hope they will make good this curious omission.

Return Passage: The Autobiography of Violet Markham, Markham, V., (1953)

Unshocking Gems

This small and pretty book is a gift to the givers of gifts. It is guaranteed not to shock or annoy the recipient; no explicit sex, no violence, no sleaze (whatever that may mean, there's certainly none of it).

The Murrays, generation after generation, have been publishers, ever since their best-selling author in Byron's day. They can be relied upon for decent type and paper, and bindings that last. In recent years they have produced tiny gems, like John Betjeman's *A Nip in the Air*, as well as long, well-written biographies such as David Gilmour's triumph, *Curzon*.

The present John Murray's father, known as Jock, kept a commonplace book. It contains the usual Chinese proverbs; he who eats his towel gets a dry mouth. Confucius, or some other sage; no matter. All sorts of little jokes and oddities are here, illustrated by Osbert Lancaster and others. Hardly any Goethe, probably too deep, and perhaps too anti-clerical; no La Rochefoucauld, too bitterly cynical and worldly no doubt. The French quoted are, on the whole, bitter. Balzac says every great fortune is founded on great crime, and Voltaire, about biography: 'We must respect the living but the truth is good enough for the dead.' What is truth, the victim might ask.

Dr Johnson figures, and Byron of course, and there are reminders of the best-sellers of our own times: Betjeman, James Lees-Milne, Patrick Leigh Fermor. When a book by the latter was published a queue to 50 Albemarle Street stretched halfway down Piccadilly.

We were invited to comment on attributions. 'How do I know what I think till I hear what I say?'—Lord Hugh Cecil, I have been told.

A Gentleman Publisher's Commonplace Book, Murray, J.G. *Evening Standard* (1996)

Rebel Hearts

Not quite the moment, perhaps, to publish a book which is simply a résumé of all the newspaper stories of the last decades concerning the tragedy in Northern Ireland, just when it is possible to hope for better times. Anyone interested knows it by heart already, it has been television fare night after night for so many years.

Kevin Toulis lives in Edinburgh, but his ancestors were Irish and from childhood he has been familiar with 'the old sod'. As a journalist he went over to see for himself.

It is so readily imagined that we hardly need him to describe the agony of sorrow suffered by the parents of an only son, an innocent bystander, blown to bits by a bomb at Harrods. (Those not politically involved are called 'innocent'.)

In Ireland Toulis found, among nationalists and among Loyalists, heroes and saints and murderers and martyrs. 'Great hatred, Little Room,' as Yeats wrote of Ireland. But now that Britain and the Irish Republic are members of the European Community there is in fact plenty of room for hatred and dislike to be contained without violence.

Sometimes it seemed as if the IRA was the Loyalists' secret weapon. The sight of a hooded gunman was a boon to extremists. In the Republic it is noteworthy how few vote for Sinn Féin. Most people prefer to live and let live.

The numbers of dead are not to be compared with those suffered in natural disasters, earthquakes, floods, or even with road accidents. But the killing is deliberate. There may be a target, often it is haphazard, sometimes all the victims are 'innocent'.

Kevin Toulis talked to everyone and saw both sides and prudently went back to Edinburgh. He may have been a wiser man, except that he must have known it all long since. Perhaps he will go to the Balkans now, for a glimpse of something worse still.

Rebel Hearts: Journeys within the IRA's Soul, Toulis, K., *Evening Standard* (1995)

A Case of Myopia on a Grand Scale

However many histories, biographies and autobiographies one reads about the first quarter of the twentieth century, it is a period which never fails to interest and amuse; and as escapist literature for those whose minds are darkened by the thought that this third quarter of the century may be mankind's last, and that Conservatives and Liberals alike may be blown up into infinitesimal particles of the final giant mushroom, they have a special value, even though reading about the politicians of the past is not particularly reassuring. Hypnotised by events of small importance, like Home Rule or Tariff Reform, they floundered almost without noticing what was happening into the Great War, not one of them having the faintest notion of what the results would be.

Although Bonar Law was only Prime Minister for a few months, he was at the heart of affairs from 1911. Mr Blake says he was an ambitious man in those days; he also seems to have been a modest man, with plenty to be modest about. Lord Derby's description of him in a letter to the King when he became Leader summed up his character perfectly:

'He has all the qualities of a great leader except one—and that is he has no personal magnetism and can inspire no man to real enthusiasm.'

He was honest and people trusted him. 'The difference between Bonar Law and me' Lloyd George told Baldwin, was that 'poor Bonar can't bear being called a liar. Now I don't mind.'

Lloyd George relied on him throughout the years when they were in coalition; he was a loyal and hardworking colleague. But he was an extremely limited man; art, literature (except for Gibbon and Carlyle) and music bored him to death; food he did not care about, he drank milk and ginger beer; he hated society and yet was miserable in the country. His amusements were bridge, chess and golf. 'He was an adding-machine', said a man I spoke with who had sat in Parliament with him; 'but he was, also, the finest speaker to wind up a debate I ever heard.'

That this Scotch Canadian Nonconformist teetotaller should have led the Conservative Party is just as strange, in its way, as that Disraeli should have done so a generation earlier.

He only allowed himself to indulge in his quiet pleasures when he had plenty of time to spare, and he was deeply shocked when, visiting Asquith on a Monday morning in the middle of a political crisis during the war, he found him playing bridge with three ladies. 'Fond of bridge as he was himself' says Mr Blake, 'he regarded it as wrong that the leader of a nation engaged in a struggle for its existence should be playing cards on a Monday morning, and should oblige one of his principal colleagues to put off all arrangements in order to visit him at his country house fifty miles away from London.'

This biography is extremely well done, and all the old stories—the Irish dispute, the Marconi scandal, Pemberton Billing's Black Book (supposed to contain the names of 47,000 prominent men and women who were homosexuals)—are told with skill and freshness. New facts are added, notably to the curious story of how Baldwin became Bonar Law's successor when the latter had to retire because of ill-health.

Nothing can exceed the strangeness of the men who controlled the armed forces at the beginning of the 1914 war. Lord Kitchener, who said to Carson: 'I don't know Europe, I don't know England, and I don't know the British Army', and, on the subject of reporting to the Cabinet, 'It is repugnant to me to reveal military secrets to twenty three gentlemen with whom I am barely acquainted'. And Admiral Fisher, the First Sea Lord, who so detested Winston Churchill, then First Lord of the Admiralty, that he bombarded Bonar Law with letters: 'I am absolutely unable to remain with W.C. He's a real danger', he wrote, underlining the words three times. Bonar Law was of the same opinion, and had he lived, Churchill would not have been made Chancellor of the Exchequer in the 20s, but would have been out of office for a generation.

The Unknown Prime Minister: The Life and Times of Andrew Bonar Law, Blake, R. (1955)

'Stop a bit.'

Admirers of Lord David Cecil's book *The Young Melbourne,* published in 1939, will be delighted by its sequel, *Lord M,* which deals with the last twenty years of Lord Melbourne's life, during seven of which he was Prime Minister. Lord David has not set out to write a history of the time, but a biography of the man; and so wonderfully well has he succeeded, that after reading these two books Lord Melbourne seems to be an intimate friend whom we have known always.

Born ten years before the French Revolution, when he died Queen Victoria had been eleven years on the throne; his life thus spanned a period of great change, reflected even in the fashionable Whig society where he belonged. William Lamb was the son of the famous Lady Melbourne and of George Wyndham, Lord Egremont, one of her aristocratic lovers. When his elder brother died and he became heir, Lord Melbourne refused to give him the £5000 a year Peniston Lamb had enjoyed; he knew William was not his son, and to punish him for it reduced the allowance to £2000. However, William was now considered eligible to marry Lady Caroline Ponsonby, one of 'the Devonshire House girls' with whom he was in love.

In his unfortunate marriage, the future Lord Melbourne showed his great qualities: tolerance, humour, loyalty and affection. All were needed; first in dealing with Caroline's extravagantly public love affair with Lord Byron, later with the other manifestations of hysteria, madness and exhibitionism which made life with her so trying. After the publication of her novel *Glenarvon* in which she described herself, William, Byron and all their friends and relations in what, in those days, was considered an unforgivable way, Caroline was an outcast from society. But though he suffered deeply, William behaved with exemplary loyalty; the novel, indeed, which had seemed to be the last straw, brought them together again. How could he abandon her, just when all her old friends were cutting her? One of his political colleagues once said to him 'I will support you as long as you are in the right'. 'That is no use at all,' he replied, 'what I want is men who will support me when I am in the wrong.' In his married life he lived up to this maxim in generous fashion.

Rich, handsome, self-indulgent, well dressed, amusing, Melbourne was also clever in an intellectual way. In politics he would never have made a good party man, for he saw both sides of a question, was undogmatic about everything and never felt very strongly except perhaps about the uselessness of reform. 'Whenever you meddle with these ancient rights and jurisdictions it appears to me that for the sake of remedying comparatively insignificant abuses you create new ones and always produce considerable discontent' he said (about the administration of the Duchy of Cornwall). "'Delay" and "postpone" were still his favourite words' writes Lord David. He did not believe in any progressive measures; he thought public education a mistake: 'You may fill a person's head with nonsense which may be impossible ever to get out again,' he said. He thought England was better governed by gentlemen that it would be by merchants and business men, and the repeal of the Corn Laws would ruin the former class. Also, as Lord David says: 'It was the sort of practical subject that bored him to tears. Absent-minded and indifferent, he sat through one Cabinet meeting after another while his colleagues wrangled interminably about fixed duties and sliding scales. At last they came to an agreement and took their leave. As they went down-stairs they heard the Prime Minister's voice calling to them: looking up they saw him learning over the banisters: "Stop a bit," he said, "what did we decide? Is it to lower the price of bread, or isn't it? It doesn't matter which, but we must all say the same thing."'

Mrs Norton, beautiful, talented, 'not quite a lady,' was certainly more trouble than she was worth to Lord Melbourne. He was in the habit of paying her a visit nearly every day, and when her loutish husband decided to divorce her he picked on the Prime Minister, for blackmailing reasons, as co-respondent. Norton lost the case, but it had been extremely unpleasant for Melbourne. It was his last indiscretion. 'She's a passionate, giddy, dangerous, imprudent woman,' he said of her some years later.

By the time Queen Victoria came to the throne he was already an anachronism, his gaiety, cynicism, indolence and tolerance contrasting strangely with the new, priggish, strenuous earnestness. The Queen loved him; and he loved her, and teaching her from his store of wordly wisdom and political experience, but they were a strange pair: it was a case of the attraction of opposites.

When the Tories came in, in 1841, he had the sorrow of parting from Queen Victoria. 'For four years I have seen you daily and liked it better every day,' he said sadly. Though she lived so near by, as leader of the opposition he could no longer visit her, except very occasionally. The description of his last years, old, ill and rather lonely, is very sad. He was a great family man, and should have had his children and grandchildren about him at Brocket. He and Caroline had had an only son, Augustus, who never developed beyond the mental age of seven. He had died in 1836, when he was 29; his father had always been kind and gentle with him, and had hoped in vain that he might become normal.

Melbourne died in 1848, and was buried near Caroline. To the Queen, now completely absorbed in Prince Albert and their children, dear Lord M was a figure from the past. *The Times* obituary was spiteful. 'I never read so disagreeably toned an article as that on Lord Melbourne' wrote Lady Stanley of Alderley to Lord Stanley. 'It is evidently written by a Tory and will be very painful to his friends. I never liked Lord Melbourne myself, I thought him so selfish and heartless in his opinions of people, still he is one of that bright circle we met so often at Holland House and they are fast disappearing.' The nineteenth century was already half gone, yet some remnants of the eighteenth century had lingered on in England.

※

Heroines and Saints

Florence Nightingale was born in 1820, Edith Cavell in 1865. Both became nurses, and both are chiefly remembered in connection with wars: the Crimean War and the First World War. There the resemblance ends, for they could not have been more unlike.

Florence Nightingale was an overwhelming personality and a fighter with a will of iron. Although she was an invalid for her last fifty years she organised and directed, through politicians of both parties, a revolution in nursing, hospitals and the treatment of health in the army without leaving her sofa. Her energy and determination, her perseverance and unremitting work were extraordinary. Lytton Strachey says she was possessed by a demon, and Elspeth Huxley says that she heard God's voice speaking to her and urging her to his service. She had a talent for making important political and royal friends to further her cause. Politicians she drove and bullied, royal personages she seems to have treated in the way to which they were accustomed. '*Sie ist sehr bescheiden*', wrote the Prince Consort. Nobody else was ever found who could dream of describing Florence Nightingale as 'modest'.

Needless to say, she had most of the doctors, conservative and obscurantist, against her; yet she won the day.

Her first and perhaps her hardest fight was with her own parents, so hostile were they to the idea of their daughter going into any hospital, where she would certainly see dreadful sights unfitting for a lady's eyes. Nurses in those days were 'slatterns, more interested in the bottle than in their patients', or else prostitutes, according to Mrs Huxley. Florence finally overcame their objections, and she was in her early thirties when the Crimean War began. Lurid despatches from *The Times* correspondent which described the sufferings of the wounded and the fatal lack of organisation made a great stir, and Florence Nightingale with a group of nurses sailed for Scutari to help as best she could.

The conditions for the wounded soldiers were indescribably awful, and the general muddle a disgrace. In the filthy, crowded and unsanitary hospitals they died like flies of cholera. Florence made superhuman efforts to reorganise the hospitals, in the teeth of opposition from the army doctors, and mortality declined dramatically. Here again she made friends in high places, and the Commander in Chief, Lord Raglan, was her devoted admirer. He was a charming though absentminded man who had fought at Waterloo and was apt to refer to the enemy as 'the French'. The Crimea made Florence Nightingale into a celebrity and national heroine. Although broken in health her fame and authority were such that she was able to pursue her admirable work from her bed. Prime Ministers and Viceroys queued up to do her bidding. Elspeth Huxley has written a brilliant short biography, somewhere between Cecil Woodham-Smith's and Lytton

Strachey's essay in *Eminent Victorians*. Beautifully illustrated, it is a model of its genre.

Florence herself wrote voluminous memoranda and several books, the best known being her *Notes on Nursing*, which Strachey says is 'drawn up with the detailed acrimony, the vindictive relish, of a Swift'. Be that as it may, she laid down rules which should be the ABC of nursing, for example 'unnecessary noise is the most cruel absence of care which can be inflicted' and 'never allow a patient to be waked intentionally is a sine qua non of all good nursing'. Patients to this day are often wakened, usually to be washed. (A friend of mine, lying in a Paris hospital, may have been thinking of this habit when he said: 'Always be operated on in France, where there's no damned nonsense about washing.')

Edith Cavell's career would have been unthinkable but for Florence Nightingale's reforms. By the time she came upon the scene even the respectable daughters of clergymen became nurses. She trained at the London Hospital from 1896 until 1901. In 1907 she went to Brussels as matron of a school of nurses in charge of a clinic. When war broke out she never considered going back to England; she imagined the clinic would be filled with wounded soldiers. In fact, it was half empty; Brussels was occupied by the Germans.

English soldiers from the Flanders battlefields, some wounded and others not, turned up at the clinic from time to time. Those who were not wounded were hidden in the attics, and Nurse Cavell gave them civilian clothing and helped them to escape across the Dutch frontier, whence they shipped to England and got back into the war. When this activity was discovered by the occupying power Nurse Cavell and some of her Belgian helpers were arrested in August 1915. Ten weeks later they were tried, found guilty, and shot next morning. Presumably this was done 'to encourage the others', for afterwards Brussels was plastered with posters threatening the death penalty for harbouring enemy soldiers.

Edith Cavell's execution was a cruel and very stupid act from the German point of view. It was considered a German atrocity, she was said to have been murdered. The Military Governor of Brussels, von Bissing, was away at the time. The Spanish Ambassador who, urged on by the nurses from the clinic, did his best with the German authorities, wrote that 'had von Bissing been in command the outcome would have been very different'.

Yet Duff Cooper is quoted, from a speech he made years later to army officers: 'If ever a woman was justly executed according to the rules of warfare Nurse Cavell was.' Bernard Shaw hit the nail on the head as usual when he wrote: 'Such recent trials as those of Edith Cavell by a German tribunal and Roger Casement by an English one could never seem fair; the accused should have been tried by neutrals.'

Shaw added that 'Edith, like Joan of Arc, was an arch heretic: in the middle of the war she declared to the world that "patriotism is not enough".'

Mr Ryder's book leaves a number of questions unanswered; probably nobody is now alive who could answer them. One gets a strong impression that Nurse Cavell herself hardly realised the grave risk she was running. Did Colonel Boger, one of her first escapers and the highest in rank, explain to her 'the rules of warfare'? She did a number of unnecessarily rash things, like taking notes about her activities and stuffing them into a cushion. They were not discovered by the Germans, but they easily could have been. The 'Tommies' when they got bored with waiting in the attics for her to give them their disguises shouted and sang 'It's a long way to Tipperary' so that passers-by in the street heard them. Did they know the 'rules of warfare', and that their thoughtless behaviour was putting their benefactress in mortal danger? During her trial Nurse Cavell herself envisaged being sentenced to a term of imprisonment in Germany.

Mr Ryder writes in an artless way which at times comes near to boring the reader. Research into the childhood and youth of a Norfolk vicar's daughter a century ago must have been uphill work; the results are meagre. Here is Edith having a summer holiday: 'During these holidays Edith Cavell's favourite occupation included, at first, building sand castles with bucket and spade, shrimping expeditions with Eddy, and paddling with her sisters. The days of paddling over, Edith turned her attention to swimming.' There are descriptions of her appearance with special reference to her 'clear-cut East Anglian profile', whatever that may mean. By its very artlessness, however, the book builds up a picture of a simple, good, brave and truthful woman. It was typical of her that at her trial she spoke the whole truth; she was incapable of the prevarication usual with accused persons.

During her life she never laughed and seldom smiled, according to her friends. This admirable imperturbability served her well at the terrible climax, when she faced the firing squad with calm courage. Her sybilline pronouncement 'patriotism is not enough' remains mysterious. What exactly did she mean by it? Rowland Ryder describes her tragedy well; it is the tragedy of a very ordinary person who is yet extraordinary in her self-control and her bravery.

Both Florence Nightingale and Edith Cavell were heroines, and perhaps they were also saints. It is probably as well that they never met. The Lady with the Lamp had a fairly low opinion of other women. Queen Victoria wrote to the Duke of Cambridge, Commander in Chief, 'I wish we had her at the War Office,' but Florence herself could not even find a woman fit to be her secretary. 'They don't know the names of the Cabinet Ministers, they don't know which of the Churches has Bishops and which not' she complained. All the same, her axiom 'To be a good nurse one must be a good woman' fitted Nurse Cavell perfectly.

Edith Cavell, Ryder, R., *Florence Nightingale,* Huxley, E., *Books and Bookmen* (1975)

A Tendency to Disgust

Early in the nineteenth century, a missionary fervour and fever seized Europeans and North Americans, and in particular the Nonconformist youth of England and Scotland. The object of their concern was enormous: the whole non Christian world, no less. From the benighted heathen of the African bush to the highly civilised Moslem or Hindu sages and princes of India, and the philosophers and mandarins of China, nobody was to escape their ministrations, exhortations, prayers and sermons. They were convinced that they had but to make known the Good News of the Gospels for the multitudes to flock to them. They dreamed of mass baptisms, of Christianity triumphant from Pole to Pole.

The courage of these pioneers of the Faith was exemplary physical courage, and moral courage. They endured all the hardships of intrepid explorers at the mercy of flood, fire, famine and disease, and also the hostility of those whose souls they had hoped to save. Sometimes a dangerous hostility, always incomprehension; occasionally they were cooked and eaten, more often ignored or made fun of.

The Moffats chose Africa as the field of their mission. Robert Moffat left England in 1816 and Mary followed three years later; they were married in Cape Town. The journey out was daunting. For three months the ship was alternately buffeted and becalmed, the wretched passengers, who became very quarrelsome, suffered from seasickness and the sickness that came from eating the ship's fare. They endured tropical heat for weeks on end, stifling in airless cabins or going up to find the sailors had amused themselves by killing sharks so that the decks were awash with blood and the stench unendurable. When the future Mrs Moffat opened her porthole she was drenched in sea water; she was also bitten from top to toe by the bugs which infested the ship's timbers. All this time she was buoyed up by the thought that together, she and Robert Moffat, would convert the heathen in droves. It was a heady prospect, to be taking the Good News of man's salvation to countless millions in central Africa who had never before set eyes on a white man.

This life of Mary Moffat is a catalogue of disasters and hardships described by Mary in her letters home. The Moffats went from the Cape by ox-wagon hundreds of miles north, and settled at Kuruman among the Bechuana people. Sometimes they had to flee for their lives, when murderous hordes swept down, killing and maiming the peaceful Bechuana and driving away their cattle. The Bechuana them-selves, though not killers, were the source of endless frustrations to the missionaries. Robert Moffat complained of their 'deplorable want of mental energy.' The fact that they never asked a question was more depressing than their thieving ways, though less shocking than their nakedness.

Robert spent months digging a trench from a river to the mission station in order to induce crops to grow there (he had been an under-gardener until he got the Call). When the Bechuana noticed that in fact the crops flourished, they never stopped cutting the channel so that water flowed into their own land. This was rather intelligent, but Moffat spent his time toiling back to see where to mend his trench when he felt he should have been about the Lord's work spreading the Gospel, and he became understandably depressed.

The great work of his life was translating the Scriptures into 'Sechuana', a language he learnt with the utmost difficulty. At one stage in his gargantuan task he was told of a Mr Elliot who had devoted his entire life to translating the Bible into a rare language which meantime had become extinct, but Moffat was not to be put off. He thought he had but to teach the Bechuana to read, then put his Bible into their hands, in order to change them at a stroke into God-fearing and right-eous Christians. How he squared this notion with the fact that wicked Europeans had had the benefit of the Bible for hundreds of years without becoming one jot less wicked there is no means of knowing. As he laboured year after year at the Pentateuch and the Prophets and the Gospels, putting them into pidgin-Sechuana, no doubts as to the supreme value of the work crept into his mind.

Despite some bad frights when murder and slaughter approached to the very edge of the oasis they had created, none of the mission-aries was killed by the natives in this part of Africa, though one of them, a son-in-law of the Moffats, was blown to smithereens by a drunken English trader called Nelson. The Moffats had nine chil-dren, most of whom survived.

The missionaries hated the Boers, who were moving north to

escape from English rule and found a republic to their own taste. The dislike was heartily reciprocated because the missionaries gave guns to the natives, something the Boers never did. The most annoying thing about the Boers, from the missionaries' point of view, was that they were Christians too, and not only Christians but, Protestants of the same low variety as themselves. It was tiresome beyond words to see that the Bible was part of the stock in trade of these Dutchmen and Huguenots who had made Africa their home for a couple of centuries already. They interpreted the Bible in a different way, getting it wrong from beginning to end. One wonders whether Moffat sometimes had a suspicion that the Bechuana too might seize the wrong end of the stick. How interesting it would be to read their side of the story; what did they think of the English, the Scotch and the Boers? Did they enjoy the sermons? Did they like covering their oily bodies with Manchester cotton? Or did some of them run off into the bush just to get away from the Moffats?

Mary Moffat was not too enthusiastic about them: 'It is not conferring with flesh and blood to live among these people', she wrote. 'In the natives of South Africa there is nothing naturally engaging; their extreme selfishness, filthiness, obstinate stupidity, and want of sensibility, have a tendency to disgust....' She spent her life trying to turn them into dainty housewives and it was up-hill work. Robert Moffat too was disappointed, for after he had told prospective converts that they would have to abandon all their wives but one, keeping only unto her, they were not for it. When a young Scotch missionary, David Livingstone, came to Kuruman, there had not been a convert for five years.

Livingstone married the Moffats' eldest daughter, but he found Kuruman very tame and soon went further north. His mother-in-law disapproved, because she quickly realised that in him the missionary was secondary to the explorer and geographer. Elspeth Huxley's short life of Livingstone is a model of excellence. She describes his journeys, from East Africa to the west coast, up and down the Zambesi discovering huge lakes and rivers, swamps and jungles, as well as healthy flowering highlands, and his suffering of untold misery from chronic dysentery, heat, hunger, insect stings and the bites of wild animals, year after year, which makes the Moffats' tribulations seem like pin-pricks. All his stores and belongings, including his precious medicine chest and yet more precious notebooks, were stolen from time to time by the men he hired to carry them.

Livingstone had a touch of genius; the maps he made in these unpromising conditions were astonishingly accurate; and, however ill, he kept his notebooks written up. He was the grandson of crofters from the Hebrides, and he started work in a cotton mill at the age of ten. Before going to Africa he became a clergyman and took a medical degree. Although the Portuguese and the Arabs were the people who befriended him, and in fact often saved his life, he attacked them ferociously for being implicated in the slave trade. This vile traffic, which the Anglo-Saxons had given up in west Africa a generation before, still flourished in the east, and Livingstone awakened the conscience of Europe to what he called 'the sore of the world.' When he went to England he was lionised, met all the grandees and wrote a bestseller about his adventures.

However, he soon went back. He had moments of great joy in Africa, such as his first sight of the glorious Victoria Falls, but he also had endless disappointments. The Word fell on stony ground, and a ruined Portuguese monastery showed that white men had already tried it out, albeit in a rather mispronounced version, with no result. He thought that to open up Africa, and to persuade Englishmen to settle there, was the best way to serve the Lord. As we now know, this was a wicked idea for which Livingstone would be in deep trouble with the race relations industry were he alive today.

Elspeth Huxley succeeds in making the reader almost love Livingstone, while feeling profoundly thankful not to have been led by him on an expedition into central Africa. It would be instructive to have an account by the Portuguese who were so good to him. What did they think of this man of God, his emaciated body covered in sores, who was always ready and even longing to go back for another frightful wild goose chase into the vast interior of the dark continent? Who, accepting their proffered help, denounced them as devilish slave traders?

Meanwhile at Kuruman what is described as 'a great stone church' went up. It was for all the world like any Victorian parish church in Surrey, and bore not the faintest resemblance to the splendid baroque cathedrals, truly to be called great, with which the Spanish and Portuguese adorned Central and South America. The Bechuana dozed off during the sermons, and when one fell over, asleep, the others annoyingly screamed with laughter.

These two books give a lively picture of the missionaries in southern Africa. They complement each other. Mora Dickson's is interesting; Elspeth Huxley's brilliant, and illustrated with dozens of contemporary photographs and sketches. Undoubtedly the subject of her book is one of the world's strangest and bravest heroes.

Beloved Partner: Mary Moffat of Kuruman, Dickson, M., *Livingstone and His African Journeys*,

Huxley, E., *Books and Bookmen* (1974)

Literature of War

About ten years after the end of the First World War two books were published which for the first time described the war truthfully, and enabled people who had not fought in it to understand what it had been like. They were *Goodbye to All That* by Robert Graves, and *Her Privates We*, whose author concealed his identity by putting only his regimental number on the title page, 'Private 19022'. Nothing written before or since can touch the extraordinary and bitter realism of these books, one written by a great poet and the other by Frederic Manning, described by his publisher Peter Davies as 'an intellectual of intellectuals—poet, classical scholar… delicate in health and fastidious almost to the point of foppishness…' who had felt it his duty to enlist in the ranks.

Another writer, R.H. Tawney, also quoted in *The Literature of War*, complained of the stereotype of the 'Tommy' as a 'merry assassin, invariably cheerful, revelling in the excitement of war, rejoicing in the opportunity of a 'scrap' in which we know that half our friends will be maimed or killed', whereas in reality war is for most soldiers 'a load that they carry with aching bones, hating it... hoping dimly that in shouldering it now, they will save others from it in the future'. The poets who had rejoiced in the opportunity for a 'scrap'—Rupert Brooke and Julian Grenfell—had the luck to die before the terrible reality of war could make a mockery of their romantic, boy-scout-like attitude towards it. The poets who came after them, Wilfred Owen and Siegfried Sassoon, evoke the pity and horror. Out of all the millions engaged in the fighting a handful of writers of outstanding talent survived long enough to impress their view upon succeeding generations, and the First World War is familiar to us all because of them.

Letters from France are the letters to his mother of a very courageous soldier; he was awarded the MC and bar, and the DSO. They are extraordinarily brave letters simply because they hardly touch Lancelot Spicer's actual experiences. He fought in the front line on and off for years and almost all his friends were killed, but apart from an occasional grumble about water filling the trenches, and sometimes the mention of the abomination of desolation which was no man's land with its dead and dying, he spares his family as much as he possibly can. He never fails to pretend to be 'cheery', and even when he is wounded he feels perfectly well. He makes the very most of days 'resting' behind the lines in a cottage or farmhouse, though he is not particularly kind about '*les chers alliés*'. Understatement to this degree shows courage and thoughtfulness of a high order.

One of the vilest scourges of war in the trenches was the plague of rats which gorged on unburied corpses. There is a fearful description of them in Alistair Horne's history of Verdun, *The Price of Glory*. Lancelot Spicer never mentions them, except that as well as asking his mother to send a cake for the men he also asks for a tin of rat poison. His letters are a brave attempt to spare his mother and his family so that they might go on believing in 'Tommy' as 'a character like a nice big fighting pet bear with an incurable yearning and whining for cheap cigarettes' in Charles Sorley's words. Possibly he partly succeeded.

The Hungry Ones is a book by another brave young officer who also survived Ypres, Loos and the Somme: C.P. Clayton. It is described as his 'edited diaries', the editor being his son, born after the war. If it was indeed written as a diary it is a pity that it could not have been published as such, which would have given it much greater interest and immediacy. Whether it was C.P. Clayton or his editor son who wrote in the historic present, it is a tiresome way of writing. This rather shapeless account of the ghastly war will appeal to those who enjoy reading about war, and as publishers' lists bear witness, there are plenty of them.

Strangely enough both Lancelot Spicer and C.P. Clayton describe having white feathers pinned on them by mad old ladies in London; Clayton just after being decorated at Buckingham Palace when he had changed into civilian clothes to go on to a play. These pestilential women patriots did not re-emerge during the second war.

The Literature of War is very well done; it begins with Kipling and ends with John Le Carré's cold war spies. Only English writers are discussed, there is no Tolstoy, no Stendhal, no Solzhenitsyn. Andrew Rutherford is an admirer of Evelyn Waugh's three novels, *Sword of Honour*, far the most brilliant book to come out of the Second World War. There is a chapter on T.E. Lawrence and *Seven Pillars of Wisdom*, once so extravagantly praised. Mr Rutherford seems to accept Lawrence's book as a truthful account of his part in the 'revolt in the desert'. Not that it greatly matters whether it was true. It made a contrast with Flanders mud, and as such it was acclaimed. Lawrence's description of how he killed a 'mutineer', quoted by Andrew Rutherford, is not very attractive, but then like so much that he wrote the episode was most likely a figment of his imagination; whether that makes it any more attractive is for the reader to judge. In any case the literature of war is not necessarily the history of war.

The Literature of War, Rutherford, A., London (1978); *Letters From France 1915-18*,

Diana Mosley

Spicer, L.D., *The Hungry Ones,* Clayton, C.P., ed. Clayton, M., *Books and Bookmen* (1979)

The Adorable Duchesses

Beautiful, charming, high-spirited and affectionate, a loving sister and a perfect friend, Georgiana, Duchess of Devonshire, was not a perfect wife. She was a compulsive gambler, her debts multiplied year by year until their burden crushed her. She never dared tell the Duke how much she owed, so that though from time to time he paid up, or partly paid up, she was never free from debt. Mr Coutts the banker was dazzled by her charm and prestige, but although he had three daughters to marry and saw what a help it would be if the Duchess would give them a little push, even he jibbed at the size of the loans she asked him for and the fact that the Duke brushed aside his requests that at least the interest on the loans should be paid.

In another way, too, the Duchess seemed as if she might fail as a wife, though this was not her fault. The Devonshires were married in 1774 when the Duke was 25 and Lady Georgiana Spencer 16. Eight years later she had had a couple of miscarriages but no child.

In 1782 Lady Elizabeth Foster came into their lives. The daughter of Lord Bristol, Bishop of Derry, she had left Mr Foster by whom she had two sons; she was on her own and very short of money. For the Devonshires it was the *coup de foudre.* The Duke, hitherto considered rather cold and lethargic, became a new man. He flirted with Lady Elizabeth, he made jokes and was agreeable to everyone. Georgiana loved her not only for herself but because through her the Duke had become approachable. With Lady Liz as go-between life was in every way easier for the Duchess.

Inevitably there was gossip about grand people who lived in a goldfish bowl, and when the Duchess became pregnant it was thought wise that Lady Liz should go abroad for a while. She took the Duke's natural daughter by a Miss Spencer, a little girl of seven, with her, and she also took letters of introduction to Queen Marie Antoinette and Mme de Polignac. The Devonshires and Lady Elizabeth corresponded, and she kept a diary, which is why so much is known about 'Canis' the Duke, 'Mrs Rat' the Duchess and 'Racoon', or Bess, Lady Elizabeth Foster. The Duchess wrote to her: 'God bless you my angel love, I adore and love you beyond description, Canis sends a thousand loves'.

Lady Liz was a fatal charmer, adored and courted, and she did not waste her journey. Kings and Queens, at Versailles, Turin and Naples, received her with kindness, and she had a devoted admirer in Count Axel Fersen. She was having such a lovely time that she lingered in Naples long after the Duchess's daughter was born. Canis implored her to return. He had gone back to Bath for his gout.

'This place has been very unpleasant to me compared with what it was a year and a half ago. For then I had the Rat and Bess and good health and fine weather, and now I have none of them till a day or two ago the Rat and her young one came down here.'

Three months later Georgiana wrote, saying: 'As much as I long to see you it is not for me I write. I am certain poor Canis's health and spirits depend upon your soothing friendship'. Could Bess not spend the summer with them at Chatsworth? She could go abroad again for the winter. The Racoon gave in; she left Naples, and in Switzerland on her way home Gibbon described her in a letter to Lady Sheffield as 'poorly in health but still adorable.'

Did anyone dislike Lady Liz? Lady Spencer abominated her; she feared for her daughter's marriage. Many years later, Georgiana's daughters disliked her, and they said she was affected. This was obviously jealousy, both their parents being besotted by her. On the other hand Georgiana's sister, Lady Bessborough, loved her all her life.

Next time the Duchess became pregnant Lady Elizabeth did so too. Their daughters were born within a month of each other, but the circumstances were very different. Appearances had to be kept up, and the unfortunate Lady Liz had to hide herself and her baby. She went to a frightful flea-ridden hole in southern Italy for the birth, helped by her brother, Lord Hervey. She called the child Caroline St Jules and put it out to nurse. Thenceforward her one idea was to get little Caro into the Devonshire House nursery to be brought up with the Duke's legitimate children. Lady Elizabeth also had a son by the Duke; they called him Augustus Clifford and he became a distinguished Admiral. It was odd to give him the name Augustus since one of Lady Liz's sons by Foster had that name already.

When the Duchess was expecting her third child she was afraid her money worries might make her miscarry, so she fell in with Bess's idea that the baby should be born abroad. Undeterred by the French Revolution, which had begun in July 1789, the Devonshires, their daughters, the Duchess's sister and brother-in-law, accompanied of course by Lady Elizabeth Foster, all gathered at Spa, and Brussels, and finally went to Paris, where in May 1790 Georgiana gave birth to a son, Lord Hartington, always called Hart.

Back in England after this triumph, she was faced once more with her creditors. She totted up her debts, they came to £61,000. Worse still, she fell in love with a younger man, Charles Grey, future Lord Grey of the Reform Bill. Soon she was expecting his baby. The Duke was furious, and insisted that she leave England. On her way to the coast she was forbidden to stay at Devonshire House or at Chiswick. This makes it clear that had she produced a boy the Duke would have divorced her. He would have considered it dishonest to his brother that in the event of Hartington dying childless, Grey's son should inherit everything. Considerations of this sort did not prevent the ladies, Georgiana, her sister and mother, and Lady Elizabeth, who had all gone to France to be with her during this difficult time, from reviling the Duke. Bess said he was a brute and a beast. Fortunately the child, born at Montpellier, was a girl, 'Eliza Courtney'; the Greys adopted her.

When Georgiana returned to England from her two years exile little Hart did not recognise her at first, but he soon grew to love her. Lady Liz brought Caro St Jules with her, she was supposed to be a French refugee. Aristocrats were flocking to England; in 1793 France was gripped by the Terror. The Duke adored Caro St Jules, who was the prettiest little girl ever seen, and once, when the news was grim and he thought she might be in danger from the Paris mob, he had openly wept.

There were now huge house parties at Chatsworth, and great celebrations for the wedding of the elder daughter, but from this time on beautiful, generous Georgiana was never quite well. She had blinding headaches, she lost the sight of one eye, she suffered agonies from stone in the kidney. The treatment of illness in those days involved frightful barbarities from the doctors, which the Duchess endured with great courage.

She died in 1806, and fairly soon afterwards the Duke married Lady Elizabeth. She outlived him for many years, and when in 1824 she was dying in Rome the devoted Hart, now sixth Duke of Devonshire, hurried out from England and knelt at her bedside. Hart combined his mother's loving, generous nature with his father's cool intelligence. Known to history as the Bachelor Duke, it is possible to imagine that he had seen too much of the vagaries of married people to wish to marry himself.

The complicated loves and the children, legitimate and illegitimate, of the Devonshire House circles are described in detail by Arthur Calder-Marshall. His theory, that but for Lady Elizabeth Foster the Duchess would have remained childless, may be true.

Politics (except for the famous Westminster election in which Georgiana and her sister canvassed so boldly for Charles James Fox) are not much mentioned. As Whigs, the Devonshires were inclined to view the French Revolution in an almost indulgent way, although they had been well received at Versailles by Marie Antoinette, Mrs Brown as they called her. A friend of theirs writing to Georgina described the Queen: '... she is one of the most disagreeable looking women in the world, as I always imagined her one of the worst.' Compare this with Edmund Burke who also saw her: 'Surely never lighted on this orb, which she hardly seemed to touch, a more delightful vision... glittering like the morning star, full of life, and splendour, and joy.' Notabilities are never seen by their contemporaries except through the eyes of political prejudice.

Revolution or no revolution, when a love child was to be born they went to France. Georgiana's daughter by Grey was born in 1793, the year when the King of France was beheaded. (One of those who voted for his death was Philippe Egalité, Duke of Orleans. Mr Calder-Marshall says he was the King's brother, which makes him even more odious than he was. In fact he was the King's fourth cousin once removed.)

It is not correct to refer to Georgiana as the fifth Duchess of Devonshire. Supposing four dukes in a row each married twice (and many a modern duke has had three wives) would the second wife of the fourth duke be the eighth duchess? Of course not. She would be the second wife of the fourth duke. Such details do not detract from the interest and amusement of *The Two Duchesses*. Both ladies were legends in their own lifetime, exceptional in their beauty and charm, as all can see in their portraits by Reynolds, Gainsborough, Angelica Kaufmann and other artists. There is a picture of Georgiana as the moon goddess by Marie Cosway in which her face is much finer and lovelier than in the more famous Reynolds. Hart said this was the best likeness of his mother ever painted.

When he was quite old, Lord Melbourne, prime minister, describing what a great character his mother, the celebrated Lady Melbourne, had been, added: 'But she was not chaste'! He might have said the same of his mother-in-law Lady Bessborough, and of her sister Georgiana, and of their bosom friend Lady Elizabeth, second wife of the fifth Duke of Devonshire.

The Two Duchesses, Calder-Marshall, A., *Books and Bookmen* (1978)

The Lives of Others

Joe Kennedy

This is a hatchet job on the father of President Kennedy, but the axe falls on America itself. Is the story true? Who knows.

Joe is lunching with Cardinal Spellman: 'I just bought a horse for $75,000, and for another $75,000 I put Jack on the cover of *Time*.' The Cardinal's comment, if any, is not recorded. His nephew was present, and told the author. Joe Kennedy was very ambitious, and at one time hoped to be President himself, but Roosevelt appointed him ambassador to Great Britain, to get him out of Washington. He hoped at the same time to annoy, by sending such a very Irish American to England, but in fact Joe Kennedy became a popular figure in pre-war London, with his charming smile and large family.

He firmly believed money is power, and he amassed a huge fortune. He was clever about money, selling all his stocks and shares just before the crash in 1929, to buy back later.

If he could not be President himself, he determined his sons should succeed. In Jack he had a perfect candidate, handsome, charming, and a war hero. He organized the campaign in detail, but never appeared with his son in public. The 'image' is so important, and by 1960 Joe's image was not the brightest. He is supposed to have said, 'I'll pay for a win but not for a landslide,' and a narrow win is what he got.

After his well-known affair with the actress Gloria Swanson, Janet Des Rosiers was Joe's mistress for nine years. She speaks well of him: affectionate, thoughtful, generous, according to her, and she probably knew him better than anyone. He was clever, energetic, untiring and devoted to his family.

After his great triumph of getting his son into the White House things went desperately wrong for Joe Kennedy. He had a stroke which left him speechless until he died. Two of his favourite children had been killed long before in aeroplane crashes; now he had to endure the assassination of first Jack, then Bobby. Each time he was told the terrible news he sat in bed, tears streaming down his cheeks. He must have been in an agony of frustration as well as sorrow; the only word he could say was a loud 'no' whenever his wife Rose appeared in the doorway of his room, and he waved her away.

For such an executive man, accustomed to running manifold businesses, as well as everything connected with his children, loss of the faculty of speech must have been enough purgatory to cancel out any number of sins.

The Sins of The Father: Joseph Kennedy and the Dynasty He Founded,

Kessler, R. *Evening Standard*

❋

A Riot Of Fun

'I think you're the most American American I've ever met,' said the Foreign Minister to Ethel Merman in *Call Me Madam*; and the same could very well have been said to William Randolph Hearst. He was the European's idea of an American—not the typical American, because to be the multi-millionaire owner of the world's biggest chain of newspapers could not be said to be typical of anything, but rather the personification of what, presumably, the typical American aspires to be.

Business, success, money; with a glorious background of swimming pools, film actresses, Gothic banqueting halls, Arabian Nights palaces stocked with the Best Art that Money Can Buy, (this reverence for Art is a very touching American trait); it was glamour, glamour all the way.

What else can money buy? Why, power of course. It is no fun possessing more displaced Spanish monasteries, more square miles of California, more tapestries, silver, wild animals, Old Masters, Cadillacs, Tanagra figures and apartment buildings than anyone else if you cannot influence affairs and mould history.

Here is where the newspapers were supposed to come in. Hearst's genius for knowing what the public wants to read—sex, crime and comic strips—gained his papers their vast circulation and made him richer year by year. Money is power, and newspapers form public opinion.

Hearst was ambitious. He wanted to be Governor of New York and he hoped to be President; he also had causes he wished to promote (crusades as he called them). He spent millions of dollars, the presses poured out millions of gallons of printers' ink, on these crusades and on recommending W.R. to an ever-growing number of his fellow citizens. What a shop-window! America's biggest—the world's biggest. Everything about him the biggest in the world. And his political campaigns the world's biggest flop. Not only could he not put himself over, even his backing was fatal. To be supported by his newspapers was a disaster dreaded by politicians both Republican and Democratic. 'The professionals... wanted no more to do with him, since his touch was fatal to a candidate,' his biographer writes. His political power was a minus quantity.

For, incomprehensible though it must have been to him, even though x million families bought his papers daily through the length and breadth of the States and thoroughly enjoyed the comic strips and stories of sex and violence, and even (possibly) spared a glance for the carefully chosen political news and the inspired leaders composed with words of one syllable in sentences of not more than five words, this did not mean that x million men and women paid the least attention to what they had read (or skipped) when the time came for them to cast a vote. It almost seemed as though the mere fact of being invited to vote one way, the invitation cunningly sandwiched between a delectable rape and a coloured comic strip, was enough to make them do the opposite. It was very perverse of them. Could it have been that they distinguished what was serious and important to them from what it amused them to look at as they travelled to work?

'The Chief is gone, the man we all called Boss; Colossus of an age that changed the world; The galleons of his genius knew their course, his finger-tips around the cosmos curled', wrote Nick Kenny, the Hearst papers' poet laureate, when W.R. died. And that must be one of the most American verses ever penned in English.

The Life and Good Times of William Randolph Hearst, Tebbel, J. (1953)

Eleanor Roosevelt

Born in 1884 to a family ravaged by alcoholism, Eleanor Roosevelt was an orphan when she was ten. Her father died of drink, and her maternal uncles all succumbed to the demon. Brought up by her grandmother, nobody bothered to get a clever American dentist to do something about her unfortunate teeth.

All her relations were what Americans call aristocrats, descended from passengers in the Mayflower or a similar Dutch ship. Her father's brother was President Theodore Roosevelt.

Eleanor was sent to Allenswood, a school near London run by an intelligent head mistress, Mlle Souvestre. It was a positive nest of lesbians; one mistress was Lytton Strachey's sister Dorothy who wrote *Olivia by Olivia*, a lesbian love story. Natalie Barney had been a pupil. Mlle Souvestre had favourites, of whom Eleanor was one, and they went all over Europe together.

Back home, she married her distant cousin Franklin, and had to live with her detestable mother-in-law for years. With no say in running the house, she had six children and became thoroughly bored. A redoubtable prig, she longed to do good in the world but until Franklin went into politics she only joined a few 'leagues' and committees for this or that good cause. When she discovered he had a love affair 'the bottom dropped out of her life'; she moped for a few months, but then rediscovered her love of feminists and civil rights enthusiasts. Roosevelt did nothing to discourage her, busy with his career. But she was mocked by her sons.

Her good causes really were good, and she and her lesbian friends were worthy in the extreme. Two with whom she shared a cottage gradually came to consider Franklin more important than Eleanor, a sin she could never forgive. She dropped them, and went galumphing dressed in knickerbockers with two others, who had the words 'TOUJOURS GAI' painted on their house.

Franklin nearly died of polio, and Eleanor nursed him devotedly, but during his long convalescence in Florida she stayed in New York, teaching at a school she bought, chairing endless committees and working as a journalist and speaker all over the country. She was careful to keep her private life out of the newspapers because of Franklin's career.

He was elected President in 1932 and Eleanor could hardly conceal her dismay. She loathed the idea of living in the White House as first lady, unable to dash about serving her causes. Fortunately at this juncture she fell deeply in love with a woman journalist sent by AP to cover the new President's wife. Both ladies were about fifty; the passionate letters Eleanor wrote have survived.

The book ends with Roosevelt's inauguration in the depth of the slump. Bans failing, businesses bankrupt, the stability of the country was threatened.

Seen from outside, American presidential elections are still exhausting and crazy. But as with Eleanor's middle aged liaison, it's their business, not ours. Written in American, this biography is instructive and occasionally comic. I look forward to the next volume.

Eleanor Roosevelt, Cook, B.W., *Evening Standard* (1993)

Hollywood

It is highly interesting to try to discover how a cinema star of the 30s and 40s became President of the United States for eight years, succeeding finally in ending the Cold War and helping to bring about the collapse of communism. It is such an unlikely story.

Ronald Reagan was a convinced anti-communist even when he supported 'liberal' causes in his youth. His history is the classic rags-to-riches so popular in America. Born in 1911 in the mid-western town of Dixon, he went to Hollywood to seek his fortune. He found it, and by the time he was 30 was a star and a box-office success.

He worked for Warner Brothers, first generation immigrant Jews

who had fled from pogroms in Russian Poland. The Warners discovered him not only as an actor who excelled in out of door roles as the
good guy, but also as a speaker and committee man who was adept at
defending the motion picture industry when it was under attack, as it
rather frequently was.

The Warners were naturally very pro-war, and from 1939 urged US
involvement in every way they could, making anti-German films and
propaganda for recruiting, particularly in the glamorous Airforce.

Reagan's film career did not prosper after the war, but his politics
and his anti-communism did. He knew America was now the most
powerful nation on earth, and he gloried in it. Freedom and power
together could, he was convinced, bring to an end the 'evil empire', as
he called it, or Soviet Russia.

What was his secret? Probably his touching belief in the American
dream, his unquestioning conviction that America must lead the world
to prosperity and freedom. He was not clever, or even ambitious, but
he was certain of the righteousness of his cause and he convinced the
electors. Possibly Ronald Reagan was the only completely disinterested
President America has ever had.

Vaughn's book is far from hagiographical, and is very carefully anno-
tated. He seems to have told everything known about Reagan's
Hollywood years. Just as the parts he played in his films were in fact himself, so when he became President he went on being Ronald Reagan. Is
it possible to get to the top of the greasy pole without intrigue, or guile?
It almost seems as if in this case the answer may be yes.

With its ugly type face and garish cover the book is not a credit to
the Cambridge University Press.

Ronald Reagan in Hollywood, Vaughn, S., *Evening Standard* (1994)

Paul Mellon

This beautifully produced book is the autobiography of a man who has everything; he is very handsome, clever, perceptive, kind, enormously rich and incredibly generous.

As in all human affairs, there have been clashing personalities to deal with, soothed and smoothed by Paul Mellon, who must occasionally have wondered why he took so much trouble and spent so much for education, science, university scholarships and similar good works. His own passions were horses, the countryside and works of art.

Paul Mellon's childhood was saddened by the acrimonious divorce of his parents. He and his sister lived with them both in turns. His father was a genius at money making, only taking time off to rush to Europe with Mr Frick and buy old masters. These splendid pictures were then hung in the hideous, plush-curtained rooms of his house at Pittsburgh, then a grimy, foggy centre of heavy industry. His mother, who was English, also had a house at Pittsburgh, and a garden full of flowers. Love was in short supply.

Life only began to be enjoyable for Paul Mellon in 1925 when, aged eighteen, he went to Yale, and then to Cambridge (both showered with money later on). He loved hunting, in England and Virginia. He started breeding race horses, finally to reach the pinnacle of success with Mill Reef, which won the Derby and the Prix de l'Arc de Triomphe in 1971.

His father disapproved. He thought hunting dangerous, and racing plain silly, as everybody knows one horse can run faster than another. The aesthetic side of it, (Mill Reef 'walking like a ballet dancer') which meant so much to Paul Mellon, passed him by.

His father had amassed great wealth, and at President Harding's request, he went to Washington and served as Secretary of the Treasury for eleven years. The National Gallery was his munificent gift to his country; he left it all his pictures. Paul Mellon was twice psychoanalysed, first by Jung in person, and later, in Washington, he went to a Freudian analyst, who successfully swept away the shadows of childhood.

His wife died and he married a lady who, like him, loved pictures. They collected English eighteenth century and French impressionists, and built a new block for his father's National Gallery, now one of the great collections of the world.

The reader gets a strong image of Paul Mellon as a near-saint, untroubled by politics and religion, loved and loving. Even his war service, though frustrating and uncomfortable, he can joke about. This memoir was very well worth writing. To think of him buying miles of coast and thousands of acres to save them forever from developers, restores faith in human nature.

Though possessing more than one lovely oasis in the ugly desert mankind is making of the planet, he unselfishly spent millions so that at least part of the United States could keep its pristine natural beauty for future generations. He sails through the eye of a needle with ease.

Reflections in a Silver Spoon: A Memoir, Melon, P., *Evening Standard* (1992)

Leo and Gertrude Stein

Leo and Gertrude Stein were both educated at Harvard. She planned to be a doctor but failed to graduate, and in 1901 she 'chucked the whole thing into the waste paper basket' and decided to be a New Woman, and change America.

Her brother left Baltimore for Europe; he was an aesthete excited above all by the paintings of Mantegna. He came back for Gertrude and they set up house in Paris, inseparable. With enough money to live simply, they could just afford to buy pictures. Leo chose the pictures and they shared the expense. He bought Japanese prints, paintings by Cézanne, Renoir, Toulouse-Lautrec, Picasso and Matisse. Cézanne died in 1906, and by then their flat in the rue de Fleurus was papered from floor to ceiling with masterpieces.

Every summer they went to Tuscany, where they met the Berensons. Bernard Berenson enjoyed talking about pictures with Leo. Mary Berenson described them: 'a fearful apparition, a round waddling mass and a tall blaze of bright brown beside it. These queer things turned out to be Gertrude Stein and her brother, she fatter than ever (but fairly clean). They simply hurt one's eyes.' Another friend of Gertrude's wrote: 'she rather got on my nerves by her habit of not bathing and wearing the same clothes all the time'.

Gertrude, in Baltimore, Paris or Tuscany, was surrounded by a group of American friends whom she harnessed to her chariot, Lesbians who worked hard to get her books published. She wrote the whole time; her cupboards were stuffed with MSS returned by unwilling publishers. Sometimes the friends went too far, suggesting she might be less repetitious, or do some cutting or re-writing. She angrily rejected advice: convinced she was a genius there was to be no compromise.

Meanwhile Leo had a block and could not write at all. He took to painting, but was dissatisfied with the result, unlike his sister who loved her own work. He talked brilliantly to visitors when he showed his collection, but he worried about his health and digestion.

Alice Toklas came to Paris from California, and after a while moved into the rue de Fleurus. She typed, worshipped, did the housework and remained Gertrude's devoted slave for thirty five years. Leo was quite pleased to have her there, she took his sister off his hands after a lifetime together. He was attached to Nina of Montparnasse, a failed singer and *fille de joie* [prostitute] whom he loved and who loved him.

The catalyst of the Steins' separation seems to have been Picasso. Leo had bought his work for years, but after Les Demoiselles d'Avignon he never bought again. When Leo and Gertrude parted they divided the treasures without much quarrelling, and thence forth Gertrude bought Picasso and Francis Rose. Leo went to Tuscany with fifteen Renoirs and Cézanne's apples, and hung them in a villa he owned. He also had his Picasso drawings.

Gertrude's breakthrough to fame and fortune came after an exhibition of post-impressionist art in New York. In London a sensation, in New York it was a cultural earthquake. Nobody dared admit to being puzzled or startled, and Gertrude Stein was the woman who knew the wild men from Paris and had been their friend and collector for years. The woman who had been painted by Picasso, and whose prose, like his painting, might be difficult but must be admired. Her novels and stories and *Portraits* found publishers, her books were in every drawing-room, her lecture tour a sell-out.

The Autobiography of Alice B Toklas, written in ordinary prose which everyone could understand, was a bestseller. In it she pretended it was she who recognized the greatness of the post-impressionists at the beginning of the century. Leo was never mentioned.

Gertrude died one year before Leo. They had never spoken since they parted; she and Alice lived through the second war in France, Leo and Nina survived in Italy. At the end he wrote the book on aesthetics he had wanted to write all his life. It was a great success. But he had committed the unforgivable treachery. He had implied that the emperor might have no clothes.

Brenda Wineapple has told the story of the Stein siblings in fascinating detail. She admires Gertrude's inexorable will, and understands her desire for fame. As to Leo, at last given his due, he charms the reader.

Sister And Brother: Gertrude And Leo Stein, Wineapple, B. *Evening Standard* (1996)

Harriet Beecher Stowe

The author of *Uncle Tom's Cabin* was born in 1811 and lived to be 85. Her collected works filled twenty five volumes, but most people would be hard put to it to name more than one. She kept her family in relative affluence with her writings.

Her father, husband and brothers were all nonconformist clergymen, pillars of temperance, scourges of the infidels, though their fiercest hatred was reserved for the Scarlet Beast (sic) of Rome and popery. The whole family moved from New England to the Middle West to do God's work there, and come to grips with this dread opponent, flooding into America: The Irish escaping the potato famine and Poles fleeing Russian persecution.

Cincinnati in Ohio was the hog capital of America. Thousand of hogs were herded in daily from the countryside to the abattoirs, eating the garbage in the streets (there were no drains) making an indescribable mess and stink, and polluting the Ohio River. A quarter of a million a year were 'processed' and sent in river boats all over the US.

It was to this hell on earth that the Beecher clergymen came to preach about the other hell, awaiting everyone but the strictest Calvinist after death.

Harriet Beecher married a Mr Calvin Stowe, and henceforward is called by the author 'Stowe', which is fashionable but apt to lead to muddle unless Stowe himself is to be known as Calvin, which he often is. It is by way of being demeaning for a woman to be called by her first name, but if not Harriet, 'Beecher' might have been a better choice since it was her own name.

Poor Harriet, or Stowe, had an appalling life with Calvin. Frequent pregnancies and miscarriages were her lot, as well as dire poverty. Calvin was a learned theologian earning very little, and scolding when his children made a noise. Stowe never felt well, and the prescriptions of her ignorant doctor made her worse. She supplemented their meagre income by writing homely little notes and sketches for magazines. Sometimes she taught in a school run by her unmarried sister, and she planned to write a manual on how to bring up Christian children. Luckily she postponed this venture until her seven were gown up, because as it turned out one was an alcoholic, one a morphine addict, and her twin girls frivolous spinsters. Her favourite baby died of cholera, which not surprisingly swept through filthy Cincinnati like the black death. Not allowed wine, the family had only dirty water to drink. After years enduring these miseries, and having failed to wean the Catholics from their errors, the family moved back to the healthy East.

Cincinnati was a frontier town, divided from Kentucky, a slave-owning state by the broad Ohio. Stowe heard many lurid tales from escaping slaves, who were free once they managed to get across the river. In 1850 a new law was enacted making it a crime to harbour a runaway salve, who must be handed back to the owner. This outraged not only the growing number of abolitionists, but all right-thinking people like

Stowe. In furious protest she wrote *Uncle Tom's Cabin*, became a world celebrity and made a large fortune. The book was translated into every language, and if it has now dwindled from a long Victorian novel to a short book for children, nevertheless everyone knows the story of dear old Uncle Tom, angelic Eva and cruel McGree. She followed it up with *A Key to Uncle Tom's Cabin*, giving authentic accounts of slavery so that no one could say she had made it all up. Stowe had, in fact, never been to the Deep South when she wrote *Uncle Tom*.

Stowe and her family went to Europe and she was lionized by prominent liberals like Lord Shaftesbury and Lord Carlisle. Back in America she built herself two houses and gave her girls silk dresses. She had to keep on writing—her family was big and demanding.

Harrowed by the Civil War, in which half a million died, Stowe was received at the White House by Abraham Lincoln, who called her the little woman who had made the great war. Undoubtedly her book affected people deeply, though perhaps according to modern ideas she was not quite sound on class, gender, or even race.

Joan Hedrick has made the very most of Stowe and her entourage, their sufferings and their triumphs. If anyone wishes to know about them, this is the book to read.

Harriet Beecher Stowe: A Life, Hedrick, J. *Evening Standard* (1994)

Henrik Ibsen

When Ibsen's father lost all his money he sent Henrik away from home to work as a chemist's assistant. Henrik earned a tiny wage and shared a bedroom. Only in the shop, between customers, was he alone for a few moments. Yet he studied, borrowing books.

He fathered an illegitimate son and had to pay maintenance to the mother from his minute salary. Ibsen knew real poverty, even hunger, and was threatened with prison if he fell behind with the payments. He dreaded the scandal. He took Latin lessons given in the shop at odd times. He, who so loved solitude could never be alone except for long walks on Sundays.

His ambition was boundless; he knew he was a genius. His miserable, thwarted adolescence made him into a bitter, angry man.

The Latin lessons bore fruit: his first play, *Catiline*. Rejected by the Christiania theatre, it was published and admired, enabling him to escape from the pharmacy.

Ibsen was well-treated by his native Norway, he was the recipient for the rest of his life of a small income from the state. He had friends to back him up, young poets and journalists, and in his twenties was made director of the Bergen theatre, which sent him abroad to learn stagecraft in Copenhagen and Dresden.

For Ibsen this was a miniature Grand Tour. In Dresden's picture gallery he became aware of European art: Italian, Spanish, French and German masterpieces opened his eyes to Europe's culture. In Norway he had to pretend to a Norwegian nationalism he never felt. Despite early plays about Vikings, he knew he belonged to the world and to what he called the great Germanic tribe.

In 1858, at the age of 30, he married a perfect wife, Suzannah Thoresen, who had but one ambition, to see Ibsen's genius recognised and rewarded. Ibsen went to Rome, where Suzannah and their son joined him, and where they lived for four years.

He wrote *Brand* and *Peer Gynt* in Rome, a paradise in those days, ruled by the pope, before it became the capital of united Italy. Robert Ferguson considers these Ibsen's greatest plays… there were to be no more poetic dramas.

Ibsen's breakthrough came when his plays were translated into German and acted to enthusiastic audiences. The Ibsens lived in Dresden and Munich for many years where he wrote dramas and tragedies which had enormous success in Germany and England. They have never dated; the themes were love, jealousy, hypocrisy, incest, corruption, murder and suicide.

Ibsen furiously denied being a socialist, or a feminist. He was simply an artist, reflecting the world in a pessimistic way.

All the great actresses of the time wanted to play his heroines, Eleanora Duse, Mrs Patrick Campbell, Janet Achurch. Shaw said Duse 'knew Nora [*A Doll's House*] more intimately than Nora herself did.'

A solitary figure, fuelled by anger and mistrust, Ibsen sought honours and decorations. He loved to pin stars and ribbons and medals on the formal black coat he always wore. He liked kings and princes because they could bestow baubles, the outward and visible sign of success.

Apart from his wife and son he never saw members of his family, or even answered their letters, and he only went back to Norway at the end of his life, to be fêted as its greatest son. With his bushy whiskers, formal attire and regular walks each day, he became a tourist attraction. If a fan was bold enough to accost him a furious snub was the reward.

Like Hilda in *The Master Builder*, the younger generation came knocking at his door. He wrote love letters to several young women, who were flattered by the attentions of such a famous man. Suzannah loved Norway and stayed there while he flirted during holidays in Tyrol. His last mysterious play, *When We Dead Awaken*, was a tribute to her.

Hedda Gabler, Rosmersholm. The Wild Duck, Ghosts, enthral audiences as they did Shaw a century ago. This excellent biography perhaps fails to emphasise what wonderful 'theatre' they all are. Robert Ferguson, fluent in Norwegian, compares *Peer Gynt* with *Faust II*; Language is the barrier to appreciating poetry.

Henrik Ibsen, Ferguson, R., *Evening Standard* (1996)

Filthy!!!

Dr Wertham, an American psychiatrist who specialises in the treatment of children, became aware during the course of his work that horror comics have a bad influence on his patients' minds and behaviour. In his efforts to get these comics suppressed he collided with an enormous vested interest. *Crime does not pay,* perhaps, but horror comics do. Sales are astronomical; the Association of Comics Magazines Publishers estimates them at 80 millions a month, and '... the names of the firms publishing crime comic books are almost as elusive as the titles. They change, and quite a number of concerns function under different names for different comic books'—a difficult adversary to pin down, obviously.

Dr Wertham gives endless examples of the torture, sex and brutality which fill the *comic* pages, and a number of disgusting pictures of people having their eyes gouged or their tongues cut out, being shot, bashed, hanged or bound, balloons coming out of their mouths with 'Lousy!!! Filthy!!! I'll tear ya...' all chosen from these so-called comic magazines. They certainly make his case for him. After reading his book I asked a boy who was formerly an avid comic reader what effect they had had on him, he replied 'Well, I think they make you feel inclined to sock somebody'.

But Dr Wertham exaggerates; he cannot be taken seriously when he objects to Superman flying through the air, stopping aero-planes, lifting houses, on the grounds that children will get a wrong idea of basic physical laws. Even Peter Pan could fly. And when Super Duck terrorises a family of rabbits and we are invited to be scandalised, the shade of Mr Macgregor rises before us.

It is not only children who read comics, as the figure of 80 millions a month shows, and as anyone who has ever seen an American soldier knows. But lately 'The Pacific Fleet Command has banned the sale of most war comic books in ships' stores on the grounds that they are too gory for the American sailor'. Military authorities consider that they go 'beyond the line of decency'. So a beginning has been made; though, as Dr Wertham points out, it is odd to forbid soldiers and sailors what is permitted to children of six and seven.

Seduction of the Innocent, Wertham, F. (1954)

407

❋

The Last Tsar

When Harold Nicolson wrote his biography of George V he was disappointed by the King's diary, concerned entirely with weather. Nicholas II, first cousin and double of George V kept a diary hardly more interesting, at last available one of the sources used in this rather tiresomely-written translation.

The well-known cast takes the stage once more: Nicky and Alix, the Grand Duchesses and Baby, Anya, 'Our Friend', all except Anya to meet violent death. The murderers were themselves murdered late on by Stalin; only Lenin died in his bed.

The tragedy that the heir, Alexei, was haemophiliac led to other tragedies. Rasputin became 'Our Friend', and powerful, because of some magic healing power for the suffering boy; he was indispensable to the Tsaritsa. Yet with his orgies and disgraceful behaviour he was loathed and his power resented; he was murdered by aristocrats in 1916.

The war gave a respite from politics for a while, uniting the country behind the Tsar. But with the defeat at Tannenberg and the millions of casualties discontent grew, and the demand for a Constitution and an end to autocracy was louder than ever.

When Alexei was well enough the Tsar took him to Headquarters, and the Tsaritsa showered letters of advice. Baby must not be allowed to throw bread rolls in the Mess she wrote, and urged the Tsar to make himself feared by his critics, to show his iron fist and will of steel. Though unsuccessful, since it was not in his nature, she nevertheless made everything harder for him with her unwise advice. He always gave in to commonsense too late, though ever since 1905 the country had seethed with discontent. Disregarding compromise, in 1917 he was forced to abdicate, and kept prisoner with his family, first at the palace, then Tobolsk, and finally Ekaterinburg in the Urals, ferociously red.

The Grand Duchesses remained at Tobolsk for a time, and their mother wrote they must be sure to bring the medicines with them. The 'medicines,' diamonds and other gems they sewed into their bodices. They still hoped for England, where their cousin reigned, or rescue. But no thousands of swords leapt from their scabbards. Nobody lifted a finger.

Civil war raged, and as the fight approached Ekaterinburg in July 1918 it was decided to kill the family without delay. Their circumstances were miserable, the house overcrowded, the windows painted over. At dead of night they were wakened and ordered downstairs. Baby, now nearly 14, had bruised himself and was too ill to walk. The Tsar carried him in his arms. Seven in the Royal Family, Dr Botkine and three other faithful retainers were herded into the cellar room, and shot by Bolsheviks with pistols and rifles. After ghastly minutes the Grand Duchesses died of bayonet wounds, the bullets repelled by the jewels concealed in their underclothes. The bleeding bodies were loaded into a lorry and driven to a partly flooded mine. The men had petrol and sulphuric acid, but to get rid of eleven bodies is difficult. The remains were thrown in the mine, and found by the white army, soon to be overcome by the reds. Only nine skeletons were found, mysteries remain. Radzinsky interviewed many old people, still half afraid to speak, and the story is told over and over again. Perhaps the strange thing is we already know it so well.

The Last Tsar: The Life and Death of Nicholas II, Radzinsky, E., *Evening Standard* (1992)

Magical Ties

The conquest of Mexico is the most extraordinary adventure story imaginable. That four hundred men should have conquered, by force of arms, a large, rich, highly civilised country, inhabited by a race of fearless fighters, seems too fantastic to be believed; yet it happened. That it did so can be attributed in almost equal measure to two things: the incredible hardihood, courage and intelligence of the Spaniards, and the fact that Montezuma and the Mexicans, knew, through their magic, that they were coming, and that they would be victorious.

It had long been magically known to the priests that in 1519 a god would come to their shores from the East, and that he was destined to rule Mexico. It was even known that he would have a white face, a black beard and a high hat. When he heard that Cortes had landed, therefore, Montezuma at first offered him no resistance, but sent him presents of gold and hoped he might go away again. It was by no means certain that the other gods would welcome his arrival, and war between the gods was a contingency dreaded by Montezuma. Cortes sent the golden treasures back to Spain to the Emperor Charles V; they were seen, and admired, by Albrecht Dürer.

Mexico was a theocracy, and Montezuma, the ruler, was also high priest. The gods required unending human sacrifices; and when the Mexicans fought neighbouring tribes they were careful not to kill their enemies; prisoners were valuable, they were fattened up, lain on the stone of sacrifice, and the priest (sometimes Montezuma himself) cut the heart from the living body and offered it to the god. Afterwards the arms and legs of the victims were ritually eaten. Many of the Spaniards were to die in this way.

The curious thing is that the magic worked; all religions indulge in a certain amount of prophesy, but seldom with such accuracy as that of the faithful worshippers of Smoking Mirror, Humming Bird, and the other cruel divinities of the Mexicans.

After burning his boats to make retreat impossible, Cortes led his men across the arid, snowy mountain range towards Mexico City. They carried not only their armour, ammunition and arquebusses, but also a supply of crosses and images of the Virgin, and were accompanied by priests. Their aim was first and foremost to enrich themselves with the legendary gold of El Dorado, and secondly to convert the population to Christianity. When they reached the summit, after bloody battles and unspeakable hardships, they beheld, spread out before them, the rich plains and the distant lake upon which was built fabulous Mexico City, fated to be conquered and destroyed by them.

The character of Cortes typifies the striving, thrusting European of the age of the Conquistadores: brave, religious yet practical, greedy for gold, chivalrous and courteous, ruthless and cruel, subtle and intelligent; Montezuma on the other hand, was rigid, defeatist, rich and doomed.

A short review can give no idea of the fascination of Mr Maurice Collis's book.

Cortes and Montezuma, Collis, M.

The Fate of the Elephant

Douglas Chadwick worries about the fate of the elephant in its wild state. Africa and Asia are experiencing population explosions, jungle and bush are shrinking rapidly as man invades them with agriculture, forests are being destroyed and suitable habitat for elephants will soon be non-existent, except in wild-life parks. In the last few decades thousands of elephants have been killed with revolting cruelty by poachers who sold their tusks for enormous sums. This threat is dwindling since trade in ivory is banned, and the elephant listed as an endangered species; but it still goes on, poachers using powerful weapons and working in gangs.

On the positive side, ranchers in East Africa realize they can make much more money from wild animals than from farming. Sportsmen will pay thousands of dollars to be allowed to shoot an elephant or a lion, the creatures feed on each other and are less trouble than cattle. The elephant, a terrible enemy of farming which will eat and trample crops by the square mile, has turned into a money spinner. This fact is a gleam of light in a fascinating but gloomy book by a knowledgeable elephant-fanatic. He will endure any amount of danger and discomfort in order to have the joy of watching them. His time in the Congo jungle forest matches Conrad's *Heart of Darkness*, which most people would do anything to avoid. Eaten alive by swarms of pestilential insects, threatened by snakes, annoyed by sub-human bureaucrats, the odd glimpse of forest elephants compensates. Even charged by a bull elephant and within an ace of death, his love did not grow less. He says elephants talk to each other and can communicate from a distance, and gives convincing proof. But what do they say? Probably soon their 'words' will be picked up by some instrument and we shall know. They do very well in wild-life parks and become so numerous that they have to be 'culled'(murdered) for the sake of their well-being. They probably talk a lot about this, and may have difficulty distinguishing between cullers, sportsmen and poachers.

Elephants have been tamed for thousands of years, used in battle, for heavy work and for carrying kings, priests and children. They perform in circuses and are miserably imprisoned in zoos. They are unpredictable, and sometimes kill their keepers.

We are told elephants are smart, and so they are when dressed for a procession in India. But in American smart means clever. Men are even smarter, but they must make an effort and be smart enough to curtail their breeding. Over-population is by far the worst plague in our planet, beside which other plagues are relatively easily contained. 1 Chadwick's clever book makes this all too plain.

The Fate of the Elephant, Chadwick, D.H. *Evening Standard* (1993)

Portraits

EVELYN WAUGH, VIOLET HAMMERSLEY, LYTTON STRACHEY

Evelyn Waugh

Evelyn Waugh has been called the greatest English novelist of his day; high praise. He has also been attacked as a man, and is said to have been disagreeable, rude, drunken and snobbish. To take the last accusation first; in my experience of Evelyn, it is nonsense. His friends came from different walks of life and were never chosen on account of their rank, or worldly position. Such a criterion would never have occurred to him, although he was obviously aware, as any observant person must be, of its curious importance in England. He liked people, as I suppose most of us do, because they amused him, or he was fond of them, or he found them stimulating; sometimes he sought their company because of some oddity which delighted the novelist in him. He disliked those who bored or irritated him, and needless to say they, too, were all sorts of men and women and, as bores are perhaps in a majority, he confined his true friendship to a fairly narrow circle.

To give but one example, a very great friend of his at the time of which I write, 1929-30, was Tom Driberg, who had been at school and at Oxford with him. A journalist who wrote a gossip column in the *Daily Express,* he was a wonderfully funny man, though one might not have guessed it from his lugubrious aspect, nor from his journalism; his column contained few jokes. He was also a madly rash homosexual, at a time when the activities he indulged in could easily lead to prison. His employer, Lord Beaverbrook, got him out of several scrapes, and the old Fleet Street rule 'dog don't eat dog' worked, so that other gossip writers never gave him away.

Evelyn and he laughed together. In their political views they were at opposite poles—Driberg a Communist and Evelyn excessively right-wing—but they shared a deep interest in religion. Driberg was certainly not the sort of man a snob would choose as his boon companion. He subsequently rose to a high position in the Labour Party and was made a life peer, but he would have been shunned by any self-respecting snob. Perhaps this could be said of the majority of life peers, but it is nonetheless true. It was with Driberg that Evelyn went to midnight mass (high Anglican) on Christmas Eve 1929, and Driberg was the only friend whom Evelyn invited when he was received into the Catholic Church.

The last time I myself saw Driberg was in about 1972. He said he had got lost in the Paris Métro and had been helped by a Frenchman, with whom he fell into conversation; As this man got out of the train, and just before it rushed on, he turned to Driberg and said: 'And I *so* much admire your Mr 'Eat.' The idea of Mr Heath being *his* quite upset Driberg; almost as much as, one imagines, it might have annoyed Mr Heath to have to own him as an adherent. When Driberg told me this my thoughts flew to Evelyn, who would have enjoyed it very much.

The more I think about Evelyn the less snobbish does he seem. Not that snobbishness is a grave fault, and it may not be without significance that three great twentieth-century novelists. Henry James, Proust and Evelyn Waugh, have all been accused of it. Proust was fascinated by Paris society as an outsider looking in, but his portrait of Jupien is as grotesque as that of M de Charlus, and Françoise is as memorable as the Duchesse de Guermantes. In between is the whole range of middle-class characters: the narrator's grandmother, Mme Verdurin, Odette, Bloch and the rest. He appeared snobbish to the Guermantes because of the effort he made to get into what was in those days a closed circle, but he had to do it in order to understand the whole human comedy, the subject of his novel. For Evelyn, who came upon the scene after the First World War, there was never any question of trying to get to know grandees. The boot was on the other foot.

My deep friendship with him lasted for one year only. When extracts from his diary were published in the *Observer* in 1973 I rather naturally wondered, as the date of our first meeting approached, what he was going to say about me. The *Observer* had carefully selected the nastiest pages (as was discovered later on, when the diary was published as an enormous book). The extracts showed Evelyn in a lurid light; he had something sarcastic to say about nearly all his friends, and probably the *Observer's* choice of diary entries still colours many people's view of their author. I felt angry to think that this brilliant and delightful man might be judged by a new generation, who had never known him, by his exaggerated self-caricature. 'Don't worry,' said my son Alexander, 'we've got the books.'

I suppose I was partly relieved and partly sorry when it transpired that there was a gap of about a year in the diary, 1929-30, after the break-up of his marriage to Evelyn Gardner. It was exactly that year during which I saw him so often. Evelyn was lonely when his wife left him, but I am not at all sure that he was sad, though admittedly he wrote to Harold Acton and said he was unhappy. Of course, it is perfectly possible to be sad and at the same time full of the wonderful spontaneous gaiety which he epitomized. And yet... Pretty and charming though Evelyn Gardner was, Evelyn must have known that she could never have been his life's companion. I often thought there was a large measure of relief, mixed no doubt with a certain amount of wounded pride, in him at that time. He knew he had made a mistake, and he was thankful that the result of it had been relatively painlessly set aside. After he had found in Laura Herbert his ideal wife, the short and rather tiresome episode which is all that his first marriage amounted to seemed erased from his mind as though it had never been.

When we met I was just 19 and he was 25. I had been married for six months—to my first husband, Bryan Guinness—and I was pregnant. As usual with a first pregnancy, the nine months seemed like nine years; not in the least nine years of misery and pain, for I was in perfect health and surrounded by love and by delightfully amusing friends, but a seemingly endless time of physical and mental change and development.

Like many of our brilliant but penniless contemporaries, when he left Oxford Evelyn had become a schoolmaster at a private school, where his wages kept body and soul together, just. The great point about being a schoolmaster was that there were endless holidays, so that however deadly the company of the other masters, however tiresome the children, there was plenty of time for one's own activities. When, however, John Betjeman got a job on the *Architectural Review* and told him he was going to escape from being a schoolmaster, Evelyn said he was making a great mistake. 'You will never laugh so much again,' he warned. John agreed that his school, like Evelyn's, was wonderfully funny, but all the same he took the more congenial work he had been offered. Perhaps the joke had palled.

Most of the schools were in Hertfordshire, and there was always a wild rush after dinner to catch the last train. Evelyn's name for the home counties was Metroland, and there is such a thing as spending too much of one's life in suburban trains.

The school in *Decline and Fall* was far from Metroland, in wildest Wales; by the time I met him, Evelyn had transmuted his experiences into this perfect book, as funny today as it was half a century ago. He had published a life of Rossetti, which had a modest success, but *Decline and Fall* had ecstatic admirers and he then decided he could make his living as a writer. He also contracted his hasty and disastrous marriage.

His next novel was *Vile Bodies,* about what the newspapers called the Bright Young People. Evelyn himself was never a bright young person; his opinion of the group was unflattering, but he thought their antics were funny enough to make a novel. Bitter undertones have been discerned in *Vile Bodies* which are absent from the hilarious *Decline and Fall,* and this has been put down to bitterness within Evelyn resulting from his failed marriage. The betrayed husband is a recurring theme in his novels, but I am inclined to think that if he had loved his first wife enough to feel deep bitterness at her desertion of him he would also have suffered from jealousy, and there was little sign of this. Quite impossible, for example, to imagine him with the pain endured by Swann, waiting for hours outside the loved one's house to see who went in. Evelyn would have been too proud to nag. He walked out. It was my great good fortune that he walked into our house. He had been an Oxford acquaintance of Bryan's.

In London, Evelyn lived with his parents in Hampstead, but he spent his days at our little house in Buckingham Street. *Vile Bodies* was in the process of being published, and he dedicated it to us. We had a joke exhibition that summer of paintings by Brian Howard, an Oxford contemporary, assisted by John Banting; we pretended they were the work of a German genius whom we had discovered. Evelyn wrote a preface to the catalogue and we invited all the art critics to see the masterpieces. Nobody was taken in, but for some reason there was massive publicity. On the strength of this we too became, for a moment, bright and young, according to the gossip columns. They called the Bruno Hat show 'the art hoax of the year', as though, as Evelyn said, art hoaxes were a frequent occurrence.

No sooner had he finished *Vile Bodies* than he was obliged to start another book. Novelists with private means can probably hardly imagine the strain that need imposes. He never for one moment contemplated writing a novel which would not satisfy his own high standards, and therefore settled for a pot-boiler, *Labels,* a travel book for which he used various journeys he had made. He came with us to Ireland, and then in the autumn of 1929 he stayed with us at a flat belonging to my parents-in-law in Paris, but all his life Evelyn required solitude when he was writing, and we lent him an ugly villa called Pool Place almost on the beach in Sussex. He seemed indifferent to its hideous aspect, and to the freezing winds and noisy sea of the English Channel in autumn and winter. There was a cook, he was fairly comfortable, and when he felt the need for friends he came back to London, where I made him waste hours and hours at Buckingham Street, talking. He was the best company imaginable; as to disagreeable, never was there a more agreeable man. He had a very deep laugh, about an octave lower than his voice, and we laughed all the time.

At Pool Place Evelyn was fascinated by work going on in the near-by fields, where my mother-in-law, Lady Evelyn Guinness, was building a 'medieval' house. She wanted gnarled old trees for it to nestle in, and these were brought from afar, carefully replanted in the best soil, bound round in straitjackets of thick straw, and tied down with great cables and pegs as if they had been marquees which might blow away; and indeed it was the windswept nature of the site which had hitherto prevented trees from growing there as they normally do in the country. Evelyn loved eccentricity, and the sight of the armies of men, lorries and cranes required for the trees was a great amusement to him. According to him, Mr Phillips, Lady Evelyn's architect, had also imported squirrels and field mice to make the trees feel at home, and to impart an ancient, tapestry-like atmosphere to the surroundings of the 'old' house. Stones from demolished barns and cottages were used for the building of Bailiffscourt, as the place was called, and it did look old when it was finished, with its arrow-slit windows and half-timbered gatehouse. I went back there fifty years later (it is now a small, expensive hotel). Half a century had left no mark upon it. In fact it looked strangely new and had gathered no moss. Bailiffscourt reminded me of the song 'You're getting younger every day'. As to the trees, they had all died.

If ever we were with Evelyn at Pool Place he insisted on being motored over to Bramber, to see the 'museum' made by a disgusting clergyman, who had killed and stuffed tiny creatures and made them perform unlikely tasks: a kitten pushing a guineapig in a pram, for example, and put them in glass cases round a room. It made me feel sick, but Evelyn cherished the oddity of the mind which had conceived it, and Bramber, in its way, charmed him almost as much as Bailiffscourt.

In Paris he made a beeline for the Musée Grévin, which in those days was like Madame Tussaud's Chamber of Horrors only much more horrible. There was a particularly dreadful tableau of Christians and lions, and although even then Evelyn was a keen Christian, he was obviously sympathetic to the lions. There was sometimes menace in his brilliant eyes. He strongly disapproved of the French motto: *Liberté, Egalité, Fraternité*; he could understand that it was written on town halls, but that it should also appear on churches outraged him. He was shortly to become a Roman Catholic, but I sometimes thought he might have been at home as a Calvinist, subscribing to the doctrine of the elect. Equality, in particular, seemed to him a patently nonsensical idea. Letters from this period of his life are almost as non-existent as his diary, but he wrote to Henry Yorke from our Paris flat in the Rue de Poitiers and told him, among other things: 'We saw a magnificent Czech film called *Erotikon*. Also innumerable dress shows. And I have eaten a lot of nice food.'

Another solitary refuge he used when he was writing was the Spread Eagle at Thame; we once stayed with him there. The inn-keeper was a 'character' called John Fothergill, who was apt to stand by the table of favoured clients at dinner, talking. He made it clear that his bugbear was any motorists who came into the hall 'and used the place as a hotel', as he put it angrily. In other words, they had been to the lavatory. There were dreaded *'spécialités de la maison'*, such as cheese made out of reindeers' milk. Probably Mr Fothergill had been indulgent to Evelyn and his friends when they were undergraduates at Oxford. Now it was Evelyn's turn to be indulgent, and he made us swallow the reindeer cheese for fear of an outburst of disapproval from the choleric Mr Fothergill.

A very good portrait of him by Henry Lamb dates from this time. The artist has caught his fierce, unrelenting stare. It is probably fortunate that he suffered rather, staying with the Lambs at their cottage at Coombe Bissett. Lamb was on the edge of the Bloomsbury Group, through Lady Ottoline Morrell and Lytton Strachey, both of whom had been in love with him before the First World War. His portrait, in the Tate, of Lytton Strachey is masterly, and so is his portrait of Evelyn Waugh: the first langorous, the second pugnacious, two brilliant subjects for a painter. There was an element of low living and high thinking at the cottage, very much in the Bloomsbury tradition. Discomfort they scorned to notice. Evelyn disliked this, and Lamb perhaps saw a more discontented and more typical Evelyn than my kind, amusing companion; he painted what he saw. Evelyn wrote to me:

> I have to sit for my picture for nearly six hours a day and that is too much particularly when I have work of my own I must get done. Yesterday some visitors came over from Wilton whom I have heard you speak of but whether with approbation or not I can't remember. David Herbert, Michael Duff (this youth is awful) and his mother. I was quite glad to see a little company particularly when Lady Juliet asked me, had Mr Lamb any pictures in that big exhibition at Burlington House. But Lamb was so enraged by the invasion that he went to bed at nine o'clock.

The Royal Academy was so much despised in the art world in those days that to ask a painter whether he exhibited there was considered insulting to the last degree. However, some years later Lamb himself became an R.A. The letter went on:

> The pity of living with such fastidious people as these [the Lambs] is that it makes one think so much vulgar. I am now convinced that *Vile Bodies* is very vulgar and I am sorry for dedicating it to you but I will write many more exalted works and dedicate them to you. May I? Mrs Augustus John (wife of well-known painter and fornicator. Tell Nancy.) has just arrived for dinner.

In the same letter he says: 'I am signing a contract for a life of Swift and shall settle in Dublin I think for the early spring… Do recuperate from Baby G. at Knockmaroon and then we would have fun.' This projected life of Swift, which unfortunately was never written, gave us the idea of Jonathan as a name for Baby G. As Swift was Irish, it seemed a good compromise between English and Gaelic.

Evelyn often put enclosures in his letters if he thought they would amuse. One that has survived, and which, unlike his own letters in those days, is dated (1 March 1930), is headed *Vile Bodies*:

Sir.

I have read the above drivel, and strongly recommend you to take a course in English Prose. I am the possessor of two text-books which, I think, might promote your literary maturity. On receipt of an answer, I shall be happy to give more details.

This letter, which got a rapturous welcome, was from a Mr Fletcher, possibly a schoolmaster. He goes on to mention Evelyn's 'infantile view-point and inept mind'.

The birth of Baby G. was now imminent, and Evelyn wrote from Pool Place to describe an evening at Oxford, where he had been invited to speak at a dinner of a literary society.

Dearest Diana

I am back again in your house after my visit to Oxford. That was worse than I thought possible. I arrived very tired and miserable and went to Lincoln College where I had never been before and for a long time I stood in the porch being stared at by Indians. Then the president of that society I had to address came up and he looked like Matthew Ponsonby[*] and talked like Heygate[**].I don't think you would like any of the bucks at Lincoln because they are poorer than me and lower born. [N.B. for the literal-minded: this was a JOKE.] Then I had no evening clothes. You see I had been very ingenious as I told you about a 'rook sack' [sic] and all my plans depended on Mrs W. sending my evening clothes by post and all she sent was evening shoes. So I rang up James Alexander Wedderburn St Clair Ham [Hamish Erskine, friend of my sister Nancy] to borrow his but he ws out so I said I didn't mind coming in ordinary clothes but the bucks all looked shocked and said but we do so they borrowed a suit from a buck who was too low even to come to that dinner. Well I don't want to sound snobbish but it was made by a tailor in Leeds. So I put on that suit and it was not very becoming. Then there was dinner, very nasty things to eat and drink. I sat next to a homosexual international footballer. He was the second best guest of honour. He made a speech and everyone interrupted so he said fuck off you buggers and that was a great success. Oh how bad my speech was! So then the literary society ran out into the quadrangle and broke all the windows of a man called Weinberg so I said why and they said he's a Jew and I said so am I didn't you know and that sobered them a bit. Then the worst thing of all happened which was a theatrical entertainment. Two hideous youths dressed up in women's clothes and acted a scene from Noel Coward's 'Fallen Angels' and they acted worse than I spoke. Then we drank whisky punch and I stood in a corner and relays of tipsy bucks came up to me in turn and said oh Mr Waugh you are so different from what I expected and went on to say how much they liked my books. Rather rude I thought. Next day I had breakfast with that footballer I spoke of and did some shopping—I am rich suddenly—and I had luncheon with Basil*** and caught some trains back.

Are you and Bryan very excited about the Sharky-Scott boxing match. Wenborne [The gardener] and I are. At least W. is. I try to induce him to see the humorous side of it but his patriotism and sense of fair play are too strong. He says we haven't heard the last of it not by a long way. I think he expects us to declare war on the US.

I don't know what to say about the imminence of Baby G. Dear Diana it seems all wrong that you should ever have to be at all ill or have a pain.

Talking of boxing I think that what with my skipping rope and high-minded [two words illegible] all think I am a bantam weight in training.

I have put *Pastors and Masters* back in your shelves here or shall

I send it to you in London?

Here is a picture of the new cottage Mr Phillips has just built. I think it is one of his best don't you or don't you... Has Mrs Spearmint [Mrs Alexander Spearman] said how nice I am or anything like that no I suppose not or you would have told me.

Boast I was asked for my autograph by one of the assistants at Blackwells... I will write again almost at once.

[*] Second Lord Ponsonby, a very untidy person.

[**] Sir John Heygate, Bart. co-respondent in Evelyn Waugh's divorce.

[***] Basil Blackwood, Earl of Ava, afterwards Marquis of Dufferin and Ava.

I have tried to transcribe this letter correctly; Evelyn did not bother with punctuation. But I am not certain about the word 'buck'. If it is in fact buck, it must have been a reference to some forgotten joke of the moment.

My great friendship with Evelyn did not long survive the birth of Baby G. As a godparent he met Randolph Churchill at the font for the first time. The stormy friendship they then began went on until death parted them. Thirty six years later I wrote to ask him whether he could remember why, quite suddenly. we had almost stopped seeing one another. I was considering writing memoirs, I did so a decade later [‡ *A Life of Contrasts*]. He replied on 9 March 1966:

Dearest Diana

It was a delight to hear from you and to hear that you sometimes think of me... You ask why our friendship petered out. The explanation is very discreditable to me. Pure jealousy. You (and Bryan) were immensely kind to me at a time when I greatly needed kindness, after my desertion by my first wife. I was infatuated with you. Not of course that I aspired to your bed but I wanted you to myself as especial confidante and comrade. After Jonathan's birth you began to enlarge your circle. I felt lower in your affections than Harold Acton and Robert Byron and I couldn't compete or take a humbler place. That is the sad and sordid truth… I have become very old in the last two years. Not diseased but enfeebled. There is nowhere I want to go and nothing I want to do and I am conscious of being an utter bore. The Vatican Council has knocked the guts out of me. But you would find most of your English friends in a bad way. Bright young Henry Yorke I hear is quite decrepit… All you Mitfords seem to have great stamina.

All love, Evelyn

This generous letter was, needless to say, not really the whole story. At the time our friendship 'petered out' I was 20, and after the long winter of my pregnancy I no longer wished to dine in bed nearly every night with a table set up in my bedroom for the guests. Evelyn had usually come when he was in London, and it was extremely cosy and agreeable. But now although I looked upon him as my 'especial confidant and comrade' there were parties every night, and they were not the sort of parties Evelyn liked. He had no desire to put on a white tie for a grand ball, nor yet to disguise himself in fancy dress as the more bohemian of our friends loved to do. Doubtless I was taken up with frivolity, but he too had 'enlarged his circle'. He fell in love with Baby Jungman, a fascinating girl who attracted many suitors. He was already sought by hostesses who saw in him a potential lion, and he was bothered by innumerable fans. *Vile Bodies* was a bestseller. It was not a boast if he was asked for his autograph, because it happened the whole time.

In May we still saw each other nearly every day. At the end of the month we went, after lunching with Eddie Marsh, to look at a life-mask of me. According to Evelyn it was by 'the German invented by Harold Nicolson. It is very lovely and accurate. She has promised me a copy in white and gold plaster.' I had allowed myself to be talked into having it done, a disagreeable proceeding and the result dead and mechanical. Oddly enough, it came in handy a few years later. Its measurements were used by the surgeon Sir Harold Gillies when he restored my nose after a motor smash. He said everyone ought to have a life-mask, it would facilitate his work. The copy for Evelyn was never made.

From now on there is a change in his diary entries. For my twenti-eth birthday. in June, he gave me a tall. slender umbrella with an ebony crook handle and my name engraved on a gold band. He wrote:

Dearest Diana

Many happy returns of today. Here is an umbrella and Mr Brigg said oh how old-fashioned it will be interesting for my men to make one like that. Well I think it will go with your plumed hat.

I went to a cocktail party and Randolph insulted a young lady by throwing gin in her eye.

Fondest love, Evelyn

In his diary he says he gave me a Brigg umbrella which I broke next day. This is untrue; I treasured it for many years, until it was stolen. Perhaps the entry about the broken umbrella shows something of his state of mind when he wrote it. He was highly critical of me, sudden-ly. It would not be too much to say that he carped.

We invited him to stay with us in Ireland during August, but he refused. Yet only three months before he had written that if we were all at Knockmaroon 'we would have fun'. He seemed not to approve the list of guests, all great friends of his: Nancy, Hamish, the Lambs, the Yorkes. But there was also Lytton Strachey, whom he admired. but who was a 'new' friend, and disapproved of as such.

He came down to Pool Place, and he says in his diary that we 'quar-relled at luncheon and at dinner' and he left. We may have argued, but we did not quarrel. He remained a great friend of Nancy's, and they teased each other by post when, after the war, she went to live in France. When his collected letters were published, the best of all were to her.

Shortly after this rather disastrous visit to Pool Place, Evelyn noted in his diary that we met at a party and I looked reproachfully at him. He says he wrote me a letter, explaining 'it was my fault I did not like her, not hers. I don't suppose she will understand.' This letter has survived:

> Dearest Diana
>
> When I got back last night I wrote you two long letters and tore them up. All I tried to say was that I must have seemed unfriendly lately and I am sorry. Please believe it is only because I am puzzled and ill at ease with myself. Much later everything will be all right.
>
> Don't bother to answer, E.

This was on 17 July 1930. A week before, he had been to see Father d'Arcy, S.J. 'Blue chin and fine, slippery mind,' was his comment. It was the beginning of something much more important to Evelyn than any friendship.

In August he went to stay with the Yorkes at Forthampton, and he says in his diary: 'Henry and Dig left for Knockmaroon protesting their detestation of Bryan and Diana.' Despite the detestation their visit was a success, because Lytton Strachey, a fellow guest, was so greatly appreciated by Henry. That is about all. From time to time he wrote to me; in one letter he says: am a papist now, and quite different.' Fortunately the statement about being different, like the one about the broken umbrella, was untrue. He was the same witty writer and delightful, funny companion, but his companionship was bestowed on others. He usually sent me his books (not *Campion,* nor *Helena)* as they came out; they have disappeared over the years, taken by bibliophiles. I always remained his devoted admirer.

I should not have written to ask Evelyn what he remembered about the events of 1930 if I had remembered the letters quoted above, or seen the entries in the diary which he began again just then. They answer my question as clearly as possible, but I only discovered them fifteen years after our exchange of letters in 1966, and his diaries were not yet published. I should have reminded him of his own legion of new acquaintances, and of the fact that he had fallen in love, but my memory of all this was vague, and I cast around for something to say in reply.

During the war he had published an unfinished novel, *Work Suspended.* The heroine was a very dull girl, Lucy Simmonds, who was pregnant, and a young man who was fond of her took her to the Zoo in order to divert her in an appropriately unexciting way. This episode, rather similar to the sort of things Evelyn and I did in the winter of 1929-30, put me in mind of that time, so different from the circumstances I was in when I received his book. I was in Holloway Prison, and to this abominable dwelling he had addressed his gift. Twenty five years later I remembered Lucy and the scene at the Zoo and, with the idea of attack being a good means of defence, I answered with some reference to *Work Suspended.* I hope I shall not sound too conceited if I say that except for the pregnancy, and the Zoo (I disliked the Zoo almost as much as Bramber), I never for one moment thought Lucy was meant to be a cruel portrait of me. If I had been like her Evelyn would not have wished to spend his leisure hours with me. Had I realized how ill and depressed he was, I should not have written the letter. He replied by return of post. dated 30 March 1966 from Combe Florey House in Somerset:

Dearest Diana,

Beware of writing to me. I always answer. It is part of my great boringness, never going out or telephoning. An inherited weakness. My father spent the last 20 years of his life writing letters. If someone thanked him for a wedding present, he thanked them for thanking him and there was no end to the exchange but death. Nancy pretended she was going blind to choke me off.

But I must not leave you with the delusion that *Work Suspended* was a cruel portrait of you. It was perhaps to some extent a portrait of me in love with you, but there is not a single point in common between you and the heroine except pregnancy. Yours was the first pregnancy I observed.

I sent you a copy when you were in jug. Surely you remember me well enough to know I should not have done such a thing at such a time if I thought it a 'cruel portrait'?

You speak kindly of my war books. Do you possess them all in a single, final version? If not, I should like to send it to you as an Easter present in case you ever thought of looking at it again. It is not much different but slightly pulled together.

Easter used to mean so much to me. Before Pope John and his Council—they destroyed the beauty of the liturgy. I have not yet soaked myself in petrol and gone up in flames, but I now cling to the Faith doggedly without joy. Church going is a pure duty parade. I shall not live to see it restored. It is worse in many countries. Please don't answer, unless to say you would like the *Sword of Honour* omnibus.

All love. Evelyn

This sad letter appears to have been the last Evelyn ever wrote. He died of a heart attack on Easter Day, 10 April 1966, after hearing Mass said in Latin according to the ancient rite he regretted so bitterly. When I heard the news I went over to see Nancy, who lived not far away in Versailles. We were both very sad. We came to the conclusion that he had had enough. He hated what the world had become; even his Church, which he had always regarded as the last bastion of civilization, had failed him. The Greeks said, 'All death is good provided it is sudden'; this is not a Christian idea, but Evelyn died, from a Christian point of view, at a perfect moment, immediately after Mass. One of his aphorisms, printed at the end of his *Diaries,* is 'All fates are "worse than death".' He dreaded the thought that he might have to live for twenty more years.

Although I hardly knew her I wrote to Laura Waugh, just to say how fond I had always been of Evelyn, and she replied: 'Thank you very much for your letter. Evelyn had been talking so much about you the [last] few weeks. And I know how fond he was of you even tho you had met so rarely of late years. He was most distressed that you should have in any way connected yourself with Lucy Simmonds and said there had never been any connection between you at all.'

It was now my turn to be distressed. If he had been quite well he would have laughed at my letter, and it never occurred to me that he would give it another thought.

Among his supposed defects, listed at the beginning, I put rudeness and drunkenness. The two are linked; drunkards are habitually rude. It so happens that, during our year together, he drank very little. Perhaps the Evelyn I knew was not typical. Be that as it may, he was a perfect friend.

Violet Hammersley

Mrs Hammersley was a great friend and near contemporary of my mother, and for this reason we never called her Violet. To us as children she was Mrs Hammersley, and remained so, although when I grew up I had friends older than she whom I called by their first names. My brother-in-law, Andrew Devonshire, so much younger than I am, who like the whole of our family found her irresistible, firmly called her Violet.

Mrs Hammersley's mother, Mrs Williams-Freeman, was the wife of a diplomat, and Violet was born in Paris in 1877 at a flat in the Avenue d'Iéna. Later the family moved to the Avenue de l'Alma (now George V) where they lived until Violet was grown up.

She often spoke of her Parisian childhood. She and her brother played in the Tuileries gardens, still a children's playground a hundred years later, with sweet stalls and donkeys to ride and a pond for sailing toy boats. One of her companions was Somerset Maugham, 'Willie', who was to be a lifelong friend.

Even as a little girl she had a love of self-dramatization. She managed to impress her governess with her dramatics, and one day when she was playing the piano and her mother came into the schoolroom she heard the governess say in a low voice: 'Vous *savez, Madame, cette enfant m'inquiète. Elle a des idées de suicide!'* [Madame, this child troubles me, she thinks of suicide.] Violet heard, and she played very softly, hoping for an interesting reaction from Mrs Williams-Freeman. At the very least she expected to he folded in her mother's arms and comforted. But all she got was a box on the ears. Although she told us this story as a joke, it is nevertheless true that in after life she was quite often the victim of irrational fears and nervous depression. Perhaps her *idées de suicide* as a little girl were the forerunners of nervous breakdowns still in the distant future, one of which I was myself to witness.

Violet's mother had a very rich and fascinating French friend: M Aubry-Vitet. When he was coming to dinner there were important preparations in the kitchen, and the butler polished the silver for hours. *'Monsieur A.V. vient diner ce soir,'* he told Violet mysteriously when she visited him in the pantry. Until she was much older she imagined her mother's friend's name was Harvey, or Ave as in Ave Maria. M Aubry-Vitet had a little daughter Jeanne, who looked much more like Violet than did her own sister Agnes.

When Violet was eight there was a children's party at the Embassy. She and her brother Ralph were sitting side by side for the sumptuous tea. The huge table, covered with a white damask linen cloth, was decorated with bright crackers and in the warm dining room there was the scent of angelica and crystallized cherries and little iced cakes. There were twenty beautifully dressed children, the little girls in frills and lace, the boys in dark velvet with silk stockings and buckled shoes. The door opened and the butler announced: 'Mrs Gladstone'.

'Under the table, quick!' said Violet's brother seizing her hand, and they slid down and hid beneath the long tablecloth.

After a minute or two their absence was noticed. 'Where are the Freeman children?' asked the ambassadress, and out they had to come. 'Why did you hide?'

'Well,' said Violet's brother, 'we know *Mr* Gladstone is a murderer, and I thought Mrs Gladstone might be one too!'

'Home politics!' said the unfortunate hostess. It was 1885, and every Conservative, including Queen Victoria, firmly believed that the death of General Gordon at Khartoum had been entirely Gladstone's fault for not sending the relief expedition up the Nile much sooner, in time to save him.

A few years after Mr Williams-Freeman died, the family left Paris and went to live in London. Mrs Williams-Freeman was remembered by my mother as a friend of her own Frenchified father, Gibson Bowles, at the turn of the century.

Doubtless influenced by M Aubry-Vitet, she had become a Roman Catholic, and so had Violet and Agnes; this, added to the fact that they had always lived in Paris, made them seem quite foreign. Violet was one of my mother's greatest friends before either was married, and she sometimes stayed on board Mr Bowles's little yacht at some French port, usually Trouville. 'We shan't want any tea,' my mother called down to the galley, but Violet hurried to call firmly, '*I* shall.' She was always a demanding guest, but so clever and amusing that my grandfather was pleased by her company.

When she was 24 she married a rich widower, twice her age; he had grown-up children. Mr Hammersley loved hunting and shooting, and for him the best moment of the year was August in Scotland. He was also a great gardener. Although I never knew him, for he died in 1913, I can well imagine him from a portrait by Henry Tonks, a well-built blond man with a cheerful, rubicund face under a straw hat, the picture was like an Impressionist's version of a seedsman's catalogue, so sunny and bright, with so many flowers. Nothing, neither the man nor the scene, could have been more unlike Mrs Hammersley. Theirs must indeed have been the attraction of opposites.

She was rather small and very dark, with black hair and huge dark eyes, and she had an expression of deep gloom. She had a rather low, hollow voice, and although she often laughed it was as if unwillingly. Her garden, at least the only garden of hers I ever saw, was a discreet green. When I first knew her she was already a widow, and widow's weeds became her. To the end of her life she was swathed in black scarves and shawls and veils; in later years not exactly in mourning, because many of her clothes were dark brown, but the whole effect had something more Spanish than French about it. Once when she was slightly annoying my sister Nancy, who used the powder and lipstick universal among our generation, by saying: *'Painters* don't admire make-up *at all,'* Nancy retorted: 'Oh well Mrs Ham you know it's all very well for you, but we can't al I look like El Greco's mistress.' Mrs Hammersley gave her hollow, unwilling laugh.

She had the most beautiful, delicately made hands, and she was a talented pianist. Her long drawing room had a grand piano at each end and she loved to play duets with musical friends. On one slender, ivory finger she wore a diamond and emerald ring shaped like a *fleur de lys*. We all craved it, and I am sorry to say we never hesitated, as children, to exclaim, 'Oh Mrs Ham! Your ring! You are *so* lucky,' or even, 'Mrs Ham, when you die will you leave me your ring? *Please* do.' At a very early age we discovered the potency of the word 'lucky' when applied to Mrs Hammersley. She considered herself the unluckiest person alive, and reacted accordingly to our reiterated cries.

She had perfect taste, and no doubt the London house with the two pianos must have been delightful. I never saw it, but she told me that when it was finished she took her butler all over it. Clean and shining, with whatever labour-saving devices existed in those days, it was convenient, bright and beautiful. The butler said nothing; she had hoped for a word of praise. When every corner had been visited, he spoke: 'No boot hole,' was his only comment.

The Hammersleys had three children, Christopher, David and Monica. Mr Hammersley (like Mr Williams-Freeman) was a Protestant, but he said his wife could bring the children up as Catholics provided the boys went to Eton, and this is what happened. The sons were aged ten and eight when their father died of Bright's disease. They were all the world to Mrs Hammersley, handsome and intelligent.

She paid much less attention to Monica. The nanny reported that Monica had no appetite, she would hardly eat, and seemed unable to swallow. The nanny coaxed her; but everything appeared to be too much—even a teaspoon was too enormous to go into her little mouth, the smallest ever seen. Finally a mustard spoon was used, but hardly an ounce of Benger's Food a day could Monica eat. When Mrs Hammersley told us this, years later, she was able to laugh about it because the story ended in such an unexpected way. The whole family went for their annual visit to Fontaine-les-Nonnes, the farm near Meaux where Jeanne Aubry-Vitet, now Comtesse Carl Costa de Beauregard, lived with her son and daughter. Monica was brought into the dining room and sat at the end of the table with the other children and without her nanny. When her mother glanced down the table to see how she was getting on, Monica was polishing off a plate of *rognons au vin blanc,* after which she had some cheese and then *oeuf à la neige.* The whole mustard spoon episode was supposed to have been the fault of the nanny, who had in some way made Monica believe that to eat was beyond her powers, but although Mrs Hammersley herself obviously never thought of it, I have sometimes wondered whether the little girl might have been in the early stages of anorexia nervosa, and that the welcome company of other children combined with the delicious Fontaine food brought to an end a potentially dangerous situation. Monica was a friend of my sisters and myself and often stayed with us at Asthall, but by then the mustard spoon was a tale of long ago.

My parents had many friends and relations to stay; Mrs Hammersley was our favourite. I remember her first when I was seven and my sister Unity three. Unity had a familiar called 'Madam' whom she blamed for all her sins, such as scribbling with coloured chalks on the wall near her bed. My son Alexander, also at the age of three, had exactly the same excuse; his familiar was called the Dackerman. Once he got hold of some scissors and snipped his cot sheets to ribbons. When I reproached him he said: 'But the Dackerman did it. I *saw* him do it.' Unity also *saw* Madam at work.

Mrs Hammersley was fascinated by Madam. 'Tell me, Unity,' she said, 'what is Madam *like?*'

'She's got black hair, and a black dress, and a white shawl,' said Unity very slowly, gazing at her interlocutor.

'*Oh!* Am I Madam?' cried Mrs Hammersley. There was no reply.

The fact that she listened to us and seemed to be interested in us was very unusual and flattering, for in those days children were seen and not heard. Sometimes she was almost too interested. A cousin of ours who was having an unsatisfactory love affair told us that Mrs Hammersley padded along to her room late one night, and opened the conversation by saying: '*Tell*, me Phyllis. Are you *happy?*'

Phyllis replied untruthfully: 'Oh yes, thank you, Mrs Hammersley. *Very* happy.'

I think it was my father and uncles who called her 'the widow' in our hearing, and we adopted the name, which suited her wonderfully well; not only her dress, but her whole demeanour and expression were those of a widow. Her gloom acquired a new dimension when financial disaster overwhelmed her. Mr Hammersley had left her quite rich, but nearly all the money was in Cox's Bank of which he had been a partner, and the bank went into liquidation in 1923, leaving Mrs Hammersley if not exactly poor, at least very much less well off than she was accustomed to be. I remember my mother opening a letter at breakfast one morning and saying, 'Oh, poor Violet, Cox's Bank has failed,' and then, sorry though she was, laughing, because the letter announcing this terrible news was written on the back of a crumpled bill, as if to demonstrate that henceforward writing paper would be beyond the means of her old friend.

Many years later she did the same thing to me; someone had forged her signature on a cheque. The bank reimbursed her, but in telling me of it she wrote on a scrap of waste paper.

The big London house with the two pianos and no boot hole now had to be sold, and she moved to a charming little house in St Leonard's Terrace in Chelsea. Christopher was at Christ Church, but David when he left Eton had to earn his living instead of going to Oxford. She minded all this quite desperately, and made no attempt whatsoever to hide her despair, let alone count her blessings.

She never seemed poor to us because her possessions were so lovely. I knew St Leonard's Terrace well; my parents often took it for the summer when my sisters were out dancing every night. Furniture, pictures, china, all were perfect. But she certainly felt poor, and was more and more disinclined to spend money out of her purse. When she dined with us in London my father always stood on the doorstep with half a crown at the ready to pay her taxi. 'Oh no, David,' she used to say, rather pleased by his little joke. There was invariably a scene before dinner, whether in London or the country.

'Violet, what would you like to drink?'

With a hollow laugh resembling a groan, Mrs Hammersley said with great emphasis, 'You know. David, there's only *one* thing I *really* like.'

'Oh, what is it? Claret? Cider?' He never gave in until she had uttered the word *champagne,* although the bottle was waiting on the ice.

She was one of those rare persons who are equally good as hostess or guest; she was well worth the trouble she caused. Her luncheons and dinners were highly enjoyable, and possibly one of the reasons why she so resented the loss of her money was that she knew she had a great talent which she was now unable to use except in a modest way. Sybil Colefax was an old friend of hers, and it exasperated her to hear of endless luncheons at Argyle House, while she, so much cleverer and more fascinating in every way than Lady Colefax could ever be, was inhibited by lack of means from filling her house as she would, perhaps, have liked to do. In fact, however, she was far from having the robust health, stamina and energy required by anyone who aspires to the role of 'hostess', and she probably realized this, and was just complaining for the fun of it.

The Hammersleys' country house on the river at Bourne End where they had a gondola and a Venetian gondolier, was also sold. I never saw it, but heard much about 'My *friends,* the *Lehmanns'* who were her neighbours there. John Lehmann was Mrs Hammersley's godson, and she was devoted to his talented sisters, Beatrix, who became a famous actress, and Rosamond, whose first novel, *Dusty Answer,* was a best-seller in England and was also acclaimed in France. We felt very envious of the Lehmanns. Mrs Hammersley made all her friends sound thrilling in exactly the way we most admired as adolescents. We were very conscious of being country bumpkins, and she was a link with a glittering world of 'clever' people. She also loved to travel to outlandish places, and stayed with various High Commissioners in the outposts of Empire, returning with tales of adventure among the crocodiles. Once she told us she was going to Rome. 'Oh,' said Unity, 'isn't Mrs Ham *lucky!* She's going to *roam*. Where are you going roam *to?*' However, it was not her roaming, it was her clever friends we longed for.

As soon as I was grown up I acquired dozens of clever friends, and no doubt they are the salt of the earth. What they lack in good nature they make up for over and over again in the amusement and interest they provide. Mrs Hammersley was extremely clever and the best of good company, and it is curious that with so many friends who were writers she produced so little herself. I think it had to do with her character and her physique. She was not strong. and she certainly made the most of her various illnesses and was probably too engrossed in them to force herself to write. The French say '*il ne faut pas trop s'écouter*'; Mrs Hammersley listened to herself to a rather disastrous extent.

During a journey in North Africa with the Sitwells she fell ill, and Osbert Sitwell wrote a short story about her called '… that Flesh is Heir to'. The theme was that Mrs Hammersley (easily recognizable) was a carrier of every disease that flesh is heir to, and her bag stuffed with germs. When this was published she was, rather naturally, furious. With the brashness of extreme youth I invited them both to a dinner party on the same night. There was a moment of hesitation, and then they fell into each other's arms and Osbert was forgiven.

St Leonard's Terrace had now been sold, and she lived nearby in Sargent's old studio in Tite Street. She also had a charming little house, Wilmington, at Tolland Bay on the Isle of Wight. Not long after this she suffered a nervous breakdown; she sent a message, would I go round. I found her lying on a chaise longue in the drawing room at Tite Street; she looked desperate. Her face was yellow, I suppose from jaundice; her eyes were tightly shut and tears were flowing. She seized my hand and clutched it, murmuring: 'Child! Tell me something to make me better. Tell me that we are going on a journey together. Say you are going to drive me to *Cornwall.*' I fell in with her request as best I could.

She wanted to be convinced, she wanted to be able to say: 'I am far too ill to go to Cornwall,' and for me to reassure her by persuading her that this was not so, 'Oh no, Mrs Ham, you'll soon he well enough and I will take care of you.' I cannot remember how long she remained thus. I visited her several times. Cornwall faded from her mind as she painfully climbed out of the pit of despair. This depression had not, so far as I know, been brought on by any particular worry or sorrow. It came, and it went.

Nearly all her letters are complaints about ill health, or unlucky accidents that had befallen her; sometimes she fell back on the weather if there was nothing much else to complain of. But she had sympathy, too, for friends. In 1937 Kit, speaking in the open air in a street in Liverpool, standing on the roof of a van, was struck by a brick thrown at his head by an opponent. Unconscious, he was taken off to hospital. Mrs Hammersley read of it in the papers and wrote at once.

Darling child.

I am so grieved for you at your anxiety. Is it a serious injury? or only a slight one? Papers are so unreliable. Please write to me… I feel you so far over the hills and wish I could see you and have a long talk… I confess I am terribly anxious about international affairs.

Your loving old friend, V.H.

I was then living at Wootton in Staffordshire. I invited nobody to stay because Kit loved to be able to come at any time and guests bored him. Solitude was what he craved, for a few days or even hours in the whirl of his crowded, busy life, and that he found in the peace and beauty of Wootton. Our marriage was still unannounced, but naturally Mrs Hammersley knew very well that if I lived 'so far over the hills' it was for his sake. I made her an exception to my rule about no guests. Kit liked her company.

She used sometimes to be driven up to Staffordshire by Unity. After tea in the nursery we had wild games of racing demon. Unity and I each helped one of my little boys aged six and seven which enraged Mrs Hammersley because in spite of this drag on our speed she could never win. She tried to get us to help *her,* but we said she was much too old to need help. Part of her great attraction was that even nursery racing demon was taken so seriously by her.

She was very fond of Unity and visited her in Munich. Unity's love of everything German, and in particular everything Bavarian, was a passion she wanted others to share. She took Mrs Hammersley to Nymphenburg, and was delighted by the admiration evoked by the castle, the park, and the Amalienburg.

After a while, 'Child,' said Mrs Hammersley, 'is there anywhere here where I could *retire?'* *'Oh yes,* Mrs Ham,' was the enthusiastic reply, 'the whole Schloss is full of grace and favour flats with old princesses in them, oh *do* come!' She already envisaged the pleasure of having Mrs Hammersley as a permanent neighbour. But all Mrs Ham wanted was to be shown a lavatory.

Tite Street was a lovely house, and in the high drawing room, formerly Sargent's studio, her full-length portrait by Wilson Steer was shown to perfection. It is a masterpiece. She is sitting under a Gainsborough-like tree wearing a voluminous white satin dress. 'Oh, Mrs Ham, if you won't leave me your ring, *please* leave me the Steer!' we used to beg. Unfortunately this splendid picture, which should be in the Tate, was acquired by a gallery in Australia; when Tite Street was sold she had nowhere to put it.

She once took me to see Wilson Steer, who also lived in Chelsea near the river. After looking at his pictures we all walked rather slowly along the Embankment, as it was a fine spring day. Every now and again Steer stopped and put his hand inside his overcoat. Mrs Hammersley said that if he felt a bead of sweat on his chest he immediately returned home; he was a hypochondriac, and pneumonia was his favourite terror.

Once when I was lunching with her at Tite Street Mrs Hammersley began inveighing against the wretches who borrow one's books and fail to return them. A fellow guest, Logan Pearsall Smith, [Brother-in-law of Bertrand Russell and author of *Trivia*], got up from the table and opened a glass-fronted bookcase. He took out three volumes at random, and each had somebody else's name on the fly leaf. She was unabashed.

Not only an inveterate borrower, she never hesitated to ask for something if she happened to want it. After I grew up there was the reiterated cry of 'Child! Will you *céder* me that dress?'

The answer was usually: 'Oh Mrs Ham, I wish I could, but you see it's the only one I've got.'

She made me take her to Harrods because I refused to *céder* her a rather cheap coat I could not spare. The department where it was to be found was called Junior Miss, which seemed almost incredibly inappropriate for El Greco's widow: nevertheless she found what she wanted.

She knew we called her Mrs Ham, and in fact generally signed her letters 'Fond love always, Mrs Ham.' 'Wid' was another matter, and I am not sure whether she knew we generally referred to her thus among ourselves; certainly to my mother she was always Violet. However, one day Muv, very vague, answered the telephone, and we heard her say: 'Hello. Who? Oh, is it you, Wid?' There was a long pause, and then Mrs Hammersley said firmly, *'Yes. Fem.'* Fem (short for female) was the cheeky name my younger sisters had given our mother years before.

Poor Mrs Ham! Life, in the inexorable way it has, gave her many blows; quite enough to justify any amount of gloom. The worst by far was the death of her son David. Christopher lived far away, in the West Indies, so that she saw him rarely. Only Monica, with four children, remained, and she was too busy to have much time to spare for her mother, who now lived mostly in the Isle of Wight. Mrs Hammersley added a garden room to Wilmington and showed us the architect's plans. In one corner was the word 'German'. 'Oh Mrs Ham, you *are* lucky to have a German in the corner!' said Unity. It was where she intended to put a china wood-burning stove.

Our own tragedies were overwhelming, and Mrs Hammersley was full of sympathy. When my brother Tom was killed, at the end of the

Second World War, she wrote to me:

> I feel I must write one line to tell you how grieved I am about
> Tom. I always looked upon you as his special sister, but perhaps
> I was wrong about this and that he meant a great deal to all his
> sisters. Nevertheless that is how it did strike me in old days…
> Tom had so much charm, Byronic charm, was so handsome and
> clever, and I suppose he should have married long ago.
>
> I am ill again…

Now that the war was over, she gradually became slightly more cheerful. Working on a book, Nancy went to stay with her at Wilmington; rationing was still at its most stringent. Nancy wrote to me: 'The Widow performs the dance of the seven veils for the butcher, but he never gives us anything.' We had just killed a bull calf on the farm, and I wrote asking whether I should post them a few pounds of veal. A telegram handed in at Totland Bay arrived; it contained the one word: 'Yes'. Mrs Ham was famous for her short telegrams, sometimes they were so short as to be incomprehensible to the recipient, which necessitated a second telegram. Her only rival in this respect was a French friend of ours, Jean de Gaigneron, who, hearing of the death of an old lady in whose house he had lunched and dined times without number for fifty years, telegraphed her son: 'Navré and signed it with his surname.

During this visit Mrs Hammersley complained to Nancy that now the war was over she felt rather constricted by living entirely in the Isle of Wight and wished she had something in London. She missed her friends. She often stayed with the Julian Huxleys, but she wanted a place of her own. Monica had no spare room. The sort of hotel she could afford was rather wretched. Tite Street had fetched very little, much less than she had hoped it would. And so on and so forth. Nancy listened for several minutes and then said brightly: 'I know! Buy back Tite Street,' a remark which called forth a deluge of reproaches.

At this time we had a small publishing business. Euphorion Books, and we published *Thackeray's Daughter,* a memoir of Lady Ritchie written by Mrs Hammersley in collaboration with Lady Ritchie's daughter. It had a modest success; having taken the trouble to write it, Mrs Hammersley was anxious to see it in print, and we obliged. Later on, more ambitiously, a volume of her translation of a selection of Mme de Sévigné's letters appeared, and for this the publisher was Seeker & Warburg.

As I have said, she was a demanding guest. She was always welcome at Chatsworth, where Andrew and Debo could easily accommodate her desires, and where they and their friends delighted in her company. 'Come on Violet, think of the Pope!' Andrew used to say when urging her to get up out of a deep sofa. She also stayed with them at Lismore Castle in Ireland; we had a house not far away and Debo took Mrs Hammersley to see it.

She wrote to me:

Darling,

I've seen your house! It's delightful, and could be no-one's but yours, white, gold, light. O the bed in the window!!! I wonder you ever leave. It's been 'heaven' here, but alas! the ghastly journey looms ahead on Thursday. I'm glad I was brave enough to come. If only I could have a young, competent, strong Courrier, permanently attached! In fact an unpaid gigolo.

Much love, Mrs Ham.

When Nancy got her flat in Paris at 7 Rue Monsieur, where I sometimes stayed during the years before we bought the Temple at Orsay, she made me promise not to tell Mrs Hammersley that there was a bed in the dining room. We lunched and dined in the big drawing room, and the fact that there was a dining room with a bed in it was supposed to be a secret from Mrs Ham, who was never left alone in the flat for fear she might open the door of Bluebeard's chamber. Nancy thought to have her to stay would make too much work for the *bonne à tout faire,* Marie.

In any case, just then the annual visits to Mme Costa at Fontaine-les-Nonnes were resumed. They were a tradition for Mrs Hammersley ever since the days of her youth, interrupted only by the two wars. She introduced Nancy to Mme Costa and they took to each other immediately. Nancy was invited to stay at Fontaine, and these autumn visits had nothing in common with the two hurried days of a weekend in the country followed by an endless wait in a queue of cars returning to Paris on Sunday evening. They were more like visits in the eighteenth century and lasted for weeks, the golden weeks of September and October. Some of Nancy's happiest days, perhaps the happiest of her whole life, were spent at Fontaine with Mme Costa, Mrs Hammersley and a few chosen guests. They gossiped, played cards, and went for long walks across the vast stubble fields of Seine et Marne from which an abundant harvest had recently been cut.

Although so fond of her, Nancy could never resist teasing Mrs Hammersley; she was an ideal victim because she always rose so satisfactorily to the bait. Nancy's teasing was usually on the same lines: 'While I slave away writing books, you live comfortably on your *rentes*. Oh to be rich like you!' Nothing could be calculated to annoy Mrs Hammersley more, because in fact it was now Nancy who was rather rich. In any case Mrs Hammersley's poverty, dating from 1923, had grown to be an integral part of her, not to be doubted, much less made fun of. Mme Costa was very rich and, according to Mrs Hammersley, hardly a day passed without nuns calling at Fontaine, where they knew Mme Costa was a 'soft touch'; her own daughter had taken the veil. Their conversations with Mme Costa seemed to last an eternity, the sacred hour for luncheon came and went, the hungry guests grew impatient. Then there was a sound of crackling bank notes, and the nuns went on their way. Once Mme Costa came looking for pen and ink, and infuriated Mrs Hammersley afterwards by saying the nuns had been good-natured enough to accept a cheque, as she had run out of cash. This definition of good nature was altogether too much to be borne.

Very often a *curé* came to luncheon; there was a little chapel in the park where Mme Costa spent hours on her knees, praying. She confessed and communicated daily. The *curé* was such a friend that one day after a copious luncheon they boldly asked him: 'What on earth does Mme Costa find to tell you in the way of sins?' Good, kind old lady that she was, always shelling out money for church charities and praying half the day. The *curé* replied: 'Oh, *c'est toujours la même chose. J'ai été odieuse avec les invités*' [I have been odious to my guests].

Although this was untrue, there is no doubt that she sometimes joined forces with Nancy in teasing Mrs Hammersley. 'Jeanne and Nancy flatter each other outrageously,' she once wrote rather crossly. There may even have been moments when she regretted having brought them together. On the whole, however, the autumns at Fontaine-les-Nonnes were an idyll.

Mme Costa's grandchildren, Jean and Marie-Zéphyre, spent most of their holidays there. One day, when M l'Abbé, headmaster of Jean's school, came to talk to his grandmother, Jean guessed (rightly) that he would be the subject of their conversation, and he made arrangements accordingly. At 3.00 a.m. a lady guest who was crossing the passage to her bathroom was astonished to hear Mme Costa's voice, and then a man's voice, coming loud and clear from the attic. It was Jean's tape recorder, an invention which has proved a boon to eavesdroppers.

Kit and I often went over to Fontaine for luncheon, and he used to say, 'Try and make it a Friday.' Naturally in such a pious household Friday was fish day, and the fishes and sauces Mme Costa provided were, if possible, even more delicious than the fare on the other six days when there was no fasting.

Besides the money tease, Nancy had another way of annoying Mrs Hammersley. It was connected with politics. As usual, the world was in turmoil. In the 50s, the war in Indo-China, then the war in Algeria, were painful for nearly every French family, and yet the *bien-pensant* denizens of Fontaine wanted at all costs to cling to this 'French department' as Algeria was called. Nancy made sorties to Paris from time to time, and usually saw Gaston Palewski, or Gladwyn Jebb [the English embassador], or somebody who might be supposed to be in the know or at any rate to provide titbits not found in the newspapers. Mrs

Hammersley waited impatiently for her return; she longed to hear what was being said in political circles. 'What does Gaston *think* of the situation?' (It might be war, or strikes, or a threatened devaluation; whatever it was Mrs Hammersley herself could be guaranteed to take the most pessimistic view.) Nancy's answer was always the same: 'Oh, he thinks everything's *perfect*. He screamed with laughter,' and so forth. However familiar Mrs Hammersley became with this particular tease, however aware that of course Nancy's account of what she had heard in Paris was very far from the truth, it never failed in its object. 'Nancy has been her wicked little self,' she wrote to me. They loved each other, but Nancy could never resist the temptation to plant a dart. After a groan or two, however, they settled down to their bridge, looking forward to dinner.

Sometimes Mrs Hammersley came to us for a few days at the Temple in Orsay; Kit was always pleased to see her, just as he had been at Wootton twenty five years before. She and I, as always, discussed our friends and relations at length, each in turn. The agonized anxieties once lavished upon her children were now transferred to her grandchildren, though she could find little to worry about in Monica's large and thriving family. She was interested in every detail of the lives of friends, or the children of friends. She was getting deaf, and wore an 'aid' on a ribbon round her neck; it had a wheel which she twirled frantically if she thought something spicy might be coming up. Bad news she relished, and once when a friend of ours married a young man who was clever, rich, and handsome, she asked how they were getting on. 'Oh, very well,' was greeted with silence. Then she said, with great emphasis: 'Somehow one had *hoped* they'd be *so* unhappy!' Her hope was realized; there was a divorce soon after. The words 'somehow one had hoped' passed into our language, and also into hers. I found a letter in which, referring to a royal marriage, she says: 'We mustn't say Somehow one'd *hoped.*' Perhaps she was mellowing with age.

I see from her letters that Nancy was not the only one who teased Mrs Hammersley. After the war, when the English 'intellectuals' hurried over to Paris in droves, they seem to have bored their French counterparts with excessive adulation. There was a story at the time that Jean Cocteau had turned on Raymond Mortimer, saying: *'Allez-vous-en, affreuse bergère.'* [On your way, horrible shepherdess.] Raymond, a good critic and agreeable man, had a rather absurd side, one could very well imagine his unfortunate curls under the bonnet of a shepherdess. He was a friend of Mrs Ham's and I must have passed on this tale; at least I can think of no other reason for the letter I received. She wrote:

> Darling Diana,
>
> Long have I feared I was nourishing a viper in my desiccated bosom. But a nest of vipers!!! So sweet and charming, so lovely and benign *seemingly*. 'How charming Lady Mosley is, I wish I could have stayed' said Mrs Oglander*. A nest of vipers; the Mitford sisters.
>
> * Mrs Aspinall Oglander, a great friend and neighbour of
> Mrs Hammersley in the Isle of Wight.

She goes on:

> I dearly wish you were sitting here for a chat, though I suppose it would have ended with a back chat and scoffing....

Sometimes she referred to us as 'the horror sisters', and once she wrote:

> Darling:
>
> You tell Nancy I've dropped you. Have I ever dropped you? I tell Nancy that you and she have come full turn to being one— in politics, you sisters love dictators. I don't. Anyhow I'm much too feeble just now to hold anyone so I can't drop them. They can drop me. Please don't. I still sit cramped in my chair staring at the snow and the dying birds.

She heartily disliked and disapproved of de Gaulle, a cause of friction with Nancy, and wrote triumphantly of a bishop she met at Mme Costa's who told her he was the devil incarnate.

Much as I loved her, I sometimes dodged Mrs Hammersley. Unless one had plenty of time to spare, it was worse than useless to get in touch with her. She wrote at the end of 1961:

> Where is Debo? *Silence de glace a mon égard.* Have you joined the Horror Sisters? *Et tu Brute?* All the promises of a visit, all come to nought. You creep silently over from Paris, and hope I shall not get to know. But you betrayed yourself in the *Daily Tel…* [how? a letter perhaps]. Well well, I don't much wonder considering the floods and hurricanes and cold and wet.
>
> Did Muv tell you my friends have forced me to come to London Jan 1st for six weeks (they have not offered to pay) so I go to the Adria Hotel from Chatsworth (D.V.) on 1st. Now *don't* tell me you won't be in London. Fond love all the same,
>   Mrs Ham

We were in London during the winter of 1961; Mrs Hammersley was now 84. She wrote:

> Have you forgotten you said you'd come down for a few days? Or is the weather too daunting—too much like the end of the world, which I constantly think of, as the coast crumbles and erodes, trees are hurled down, my hedge breaks up and the heart sinks… I think *Sowing* [Leonard Woolf] the best of all those numberless autobiographies.

Another time she wrote: 'Please come here in the New Year, or will the bomb have fallen?'

It was not easy for me to get away, although I very much wanted to see her, and no doubt wrote saying: 'I *die* for you.' A postcard came: 'If you really died for me, or w'd my b, you'd come.' Elizabeth Winn, a great friend of Debo's and much loved by Mrs Ham, was once heard addressing her dog with the words: 'I worship your body.' This expression was taken on by Debo, and applied to people, animals and inanimate objects she happened to like. I once heard her say, 'Oh! that *chintz*! I worship its body.' Probably now that the liturgy has been changed and everything with the savour of the seventeenth century removed, young people will not recognize body-worshipping as having been part of the marriage service. In any case, Mrs Hammersley said if I really died for her and w'd her b, I would go down to the Isle of Wight. I went, and very delightful it was. Delicious food, pretty house, windy walks along what she insisted was the crumbling coast—rather unexpectedly, even in old age she was a great walker. And then the joys of the 'chat'.

My poor mother had Parkinson's disease, and Mrs Hammersley, though genuinely sorry, could not resist saying: 'What about the good body now?' Muv had been used to dismiss doctors in a rather airy way, saying the good body would cure itself. *She* would never have written: 'My health is precarious nowadays, despite Nancy's gibes, and I have to take care and not get tired. Fond love always, Mrs Ham.'

In one of her last letters, in January 1963, she says: 'If you love me at all, let alone W my B you will write to me again. Letters alone sustain me…'

There is no cure for old age, and my mother and Mrs Hammersley, friends for sixty five years, died within a few months of one another. Hers was the charm of sharp intelligence, wonderful elegance, and a real and deep interest in every aspect of the lives of her friends. This interest was also lavished upon small children, who loved her accordingly as she loved them. When Debo's son was three, Mrs Hammersley said: suppose you realize he's at the very *zenith* of his sweetness.' There was a song she had composed for her own children when they were little; she played and sang in her rather husky voice. The last line was: 'How I shall miss you, when you are grown!' She sang it to us, and then a generation later to my little boys. The poignancy and truth of the words only struck me, painfully, when I was myself old, and my children 'grown'.

Towards the end, Rosamond Lehmann had built a house near Mrs Hammersley at Totland Bay; having her, whom she had known as a child, nearby was a great comfort. Christopher says that for his mother Rosamond was, in every sense of the word, her closest friend during those last months. She died in her eighty seventh year.

Lytton Strachey and Carrington

I was 18 when I first met Lytton Strachey in 1929, and 21 when he died at the age of 51. To my present aged self 51 sounds quite young, and yet I always thought of him during our friendship as an old man. In the early days he complained in a letter to Roger Senhouse [his passion of the moment] that I was 'probably too young to provide any real sustenance'. However youth's a stuff will not endure, and partly because of him I grew up quickly.

He was a hero to our generation as author of the wittiest books. After his death he was scolded by his less brilliant successors in the art of biography for having made fun of great figures of the past. He was said to have 'de-bunked' them, and even to have twisted the truth in order to further his devilish denigrations. In fact, his eminent Victorians (for it is his essays about them which are the principal target of the anti-Strachey school) leave the reader with profound admiration for Cardinal Manning, Florence Nightingale, and General 'Chinese' Gordon. Dr Arnold is another matter. Had they met, he and Strachey would have loathed one another, and perhaps it is a mistake to write about someone so thoroughly disliked. As to Queen Victoria herself, she is an authentic heroine to Lytton Strachey, though (like Disraeli) he could not help seeing the comic side.

When Bertrand Russell read *Eminent Victorians* he was a prisoner in

Brixton Gaol; it was during the First World War. His screams of laughter were so loud that, he says, one of the turnkeys came to remonstrate with him and to remind him that prison was a place of punishment. Similarly, when Queen Victoria's great-grandson the Prince of Wales (Edward VIII) found, lying on a table at Philip Sassoon's, Lytton's book about his ancestress, he was convulsed with laughter the whole time he was reading it.

The oddities of the characters who make history are just as true and often as important as battles or Acts of Parliament or the ending of one reign and the beginning of the next. It is seldom, indeed, that even fairly solemn newspapers like *The Times* or the *Guardian* fail to provide subjects for laughter every day of the week, and so it has always been. The jokes and ironies in Strachey's books help to underline the pathos which is also part of truth. His own view of history is explicit. In his opinion it is not a science but an art. Faced with an unwieldy accumulation of facts, only an artist can convert 'this raw mass of grape juice into a subtle, splendid wine'.

Early in 1929 Emerald Cunard introduced me to him at the opera, where he was in her box, and at a supper party that she had afterwards we sat next to each other. I had longed to meet him, and having done so I clung to him tenaciously, inviting him to dinner, to luncheon, or for a chat by the fire in the afternoon. He always came, and enthralled us all by being so wonderfully, so exactly what we had imagined him to be: learned, rather intimidating, and brilliantly amusing.

By this time the Victorians and his teases were in the distant past, but the enormous success of the two books had changed his life because money was no longer a worry. He lived in modest comfort at Ham Spray, near Hungerford in Berkshire, and in London, and he could afford to go abroad from time to time. He reviewed when he chose to, and above all he could concentrate upon the period of history which puzzled and enthralled him: the sixteenth century. French literature was his passion. He was a natural teacher who liked to read aloud, which he did in the Strachey voice, but not with the shrieks and squeaks that added so much zest to his jokes in conversation.

Lytton had designed his own appearance. He was tall, lanky, delicate-looking, inclined to stoop, and he had an enormous nose. To balance the nose a moustache, which he grew as a young man, was inadequate; he decided upon a long and bushy beard, brown with reddish tints. Beards were much more uncommon in those days than they are now, or were in Victorian times. He could, therefore, never pass unnoticed in a crowd and was instantly recognized by nearly everyone. It is odd that such a fundamentally shy person should deliberately have drawn attention to himself in this way, but there is no doubt he transformed the curious physique bestowed upon him by nature into an artistic reconstruction of a patriarch or an early Christian saint. There is a mosaic in one of Constantinople's Byzantine churches which could be a portrait of Lytton Strachey, as exactly like him as Lamb's and Carrington's pictures. He was almost beautiful, but it was a strange beauty wholly without sexual attraction. Since he was beguiled by a succession of seductive young men he suffered agonizing disappointments, some of which we know about—like his despair when Duncan Grant preferred Maynard Keynes to him. Ignorant of these dramas, I nevertheless instinctively knew his life was in this way unsatisfactory; it was quite obvious.

In 1930 I invited him to stay with my husband Bryan Guinness and me in Ireland, which was bold to the point of rashness, because the long and disagreeable journey it was in those days entailed a sea crossing, nearly always rough, in a boat with few comforts, and had to be followed by a rather lengthy visit if it was going to be considered worthwhile. The whole outing started disastrously because, owing to a muddle 'owing to the incompetence of the idle rich' was Lytton's description in a letter to a friend), he was not met, and was obliged to get into an uncomfortable train and then take a taxi which got lost, 'the rain all the time pouring cats and dogs'.

It is dreadful to contemplate what Lytton's feelings must have been when no welcoming chauffeur appeared on the quayside at Dublin. I am sure I was contrite, but until I read his letter about it almost forty years later I had entirely forgotten that his visit began in this inauspicious way. His journey back was perfect. He took a cabin with no port-hole so that he could not see the rocking of the ship and arrived at Holyhead 'without a qualm', he wrote.

Lytton had bought a new suit for Ireland, a tweed of a rich marmalade colour which set off his beard to perfection. He had discussed his packing with Carrington and decided to take full evening dress as well as his dinner jacket; rather lucky, as I am sorry to say we dragged him to an evening party at Government House, as the Viceregal Lodge was then called. Carrington wrote to him: 'What wizards we are to have guessed there would be a Vice Regal Ball with white shirts!' I expect he hoped to get out of it, but this I refused to allow. He was worth his weight in gold on such occasions, his presence keeping boredom at bay in even the most unpromising surroundings.

The only time during the visit that he resolutely refused to do what I asked was when he was expected to go to a play at the Abbey Theatre. We had already been to one play there, and it had been very dull. As I could see that Lytton was suffering we all left after the first act. When the programme changed (the Abbey was a repertory theatre, but there was a dread sameness about the plays) he simply refused to go. He hid behind his beard and spectacles, but his thoughts were easy to guess.

Henry Lamb, the painter, with whom he had been in love twenty years before and subsequently had a rather uneasy, quarrelsome relationship, was also staying in the house. I think they were quite glad to find each other, old friends, even old enemies, of the same vintage in a crowd of the very young. Among the guests was the clever, saturnine Henry Yorke, [Henry Green, the novelist, then aged 24] who never forgot sitting next to Lytton at the deadly play, and how Lytton had whispered to him about one of the dreary characters: 'I'm feeling rather *low* about *Ignatius.*' When Strachey's biographer, Michael Holroyd, asked many years later what Henry Yorke's impression of him had been, he stressed his unfailing courtesy to us all. Naturally in his letters to friends a more critical, fiercer Lytton emerges, but he rather enjoyed the company of young people and basked in our admiration and our laughter at his jokes. He did not write, as he once did from Garsington, that he had been on the point of screaming from sheer despair. When one considers Lady Ottoline Morrell's hospitality had saved him from the boredom and discomfort of his life as a young man among the crowd of Stracheys at home in Lancaster Gate, this fact alone—of the relative mildness of his complaints—shows the enormous change in Lytton and the extent to which success had mellowed him.

Society made a lion of him, and although he laughed at his hostesses, he also enjoyed himself. There is a theory that he felt a little guilty about his excursions into the *beau monde*. I am sure this is not so. The outside world could never influence him—he was incorruptible and irreverent. But he was not a puritan; he liked good food and wine and comfort and beauty. He dreaded boredom, but he fled at the merest hint of that. It is hard to imagine a French writer who would refuse a delicious dinner because the host was one of the idle rich; on the contrary, if not invited he would censure the rich man for lacking the wit to realize that clever conversation is as essential to a good dinner as old wines and perfect cooking. Lytton's sorties into the fashionable world were severely rationed by his need for quiet to write, but he would regret that it is now an almost vanished world, into which writers and other artists can but seldom escape. In those days, for them, it was like a free journey into another, rather delightful, country.

Lytton's bread and butter letter was no doubt as insincere as such letters generally are. 'How, oh how, to say how much I enjoyed every moment of my visit, and how, how, oh how, to thank you for your angelic kindness? It was the greatest refreshment for me—a veritable experience too!—I dwell in memory upon every detail, every single one. [Including, I suppose my reprehensible incompetence.] What fun! I only hope my occasional vagaries didn't infuriate you. I imagine you at this moment in a nest of Sitwells.' There is a postscript to this letter. 'Oh! The fires of Knockmaroon. A subject for an Ode by Pindar.' It was August, but fires, if not a necessity, are at least a comfort in a damp climate.

While Lytton was with us I continually questioned Henry and Pansy Lamb about his life. I doted upon him. I particularly wanted to hear about Carrington, who was said to love him so dearly and to ask so little in return. People told one that Carrington's husband, Ralph Partridge, and his lover, Frances Marshall, lived with Lytton and Carrington and made a happy foursome; but the one who mattered to me was Carrington. Would she like me, or at any rate not dislike me too much? The Lambs were pessimistic: they said they couldn't imagine Carrington and me together; no, it would never do.

A month or two later Lytton invited Bryan and me to stay at Ham Spray. Besides Carrington, Ralph Partridge and Frances Marshall there were Raymond Mortimer and Roger Senhouse, a typical Ham Spray house party. Lytton's library, a well-proportioned room where he worked, was upstairs. Standing beside him in the window with its view of the Berkshire Downs, I saw Roger Senhouse crossing the lawn. 'Almost too charming, don't you think?' asked Lytton, in such a way that I realized Roger was his beloved.

I felt shy of Carrington, probably because I so much wanted to be liked by her. On Saturday evening Lytton read us an essay on Froude he had recently finished. Perhaps it was true that the Irish visit had been a refreshment to him, at any rate when he got home he began to write again, which he had not done for months. He liked reading aloud: he said it helped him to judge the flow of words.

On Sunday evening Carrington made us a rabbit pie for dinner. I had never tasted rabbit before—it is forbidden to the children of Israel, and we were brought up by my mother according to the laws of Moses. Why rabbit? Not to eat the dirty pig, the accursed one as my mother always called him, was probably wise for the inhabitants of hot countries like Jews and Moslems. But surely the rabbit with its clean vegetarian diet must be harmless? However, Moses was right, as I discovered that night. Like the oyster, it occasionally harbours a poisonous substance which has an appalling effect upon the human digestion. Carrington's was one of these terrible creatures. I was violently ill all night long; I thought I was going to die. The doctor had to be summoned in the small hours; he gave me something that sent me to sleep for a long time. When I woke up the house party had disappeared, except for Carrington who nursed me back to health. This accident of food poisoning was a short cut from mere acquaintance to great friendship, for henceforward I looked upon Carrington as a great friend.

I cannot remember what I said to Lytton in my bread and butter letter; nobody cares much for a guest who falls sick, and he with his long history of ill health probably minded a good deal. If he did, he soon forgave me, and we saw each other quite often in London. I hoped he was going to be bowled over by Harold Acton, the one friend of our own generation whom we revered as well as loved. I longed for them to appreciate each other as much as I appreciated both. After dining with us, 'a rather dreary dinner', he tells Carrington, 'once more Harold Acton figured. I feel myself falling under his sway little by little'.

A few months later, having acquired Biddesden, a house on the borders of Wiltshire and Berkshire, we became neighbours of Ham Spray and Carrington. She frequently came over, sometimes with Lytton and sometimes without. I imagined I knew her intimately, but this was mere illusion. Only many years later, from innumerable books about the Bloomsbury Group, did I learn that although obviously Lytton was her star, the irreplaceable focal point of her life without whose presence she preferred to die, yet she was simultaneously juggling with a number of lovers whom she kept throwing up in the air and catching and throwing again. Just occasionally one of them fell to earth with a crash but, though painful for him, it was of supreme unimportance to her. It was natural to her to dispose of the part of herself for which Lytton had no use in a rather cold-hearted way, and she made her lovers suffer because they all sensed her indifference, and that ultimately they meant nothing to her at all. Only Lytton counted.

Carrington wielded an extraordinarily powerful weapon which she used with unusual skill. It was flattery. Once caught by it the lovers probably found it indispensable. It was comforting, insidious flattery calming their sense of insecurity, an addictive drug they soon could hardly do without. Jealousy raged around her who always appeared to be so calm. She dwelt in the eye of the storm.

I suppose Lytton knew a good deal about it. In early days he certainly knew how violently jealous of him the painter Mark Gertler had been. Gertler attacked him physically in the street after a party of Augustus John's; Lytton was saved by Maynard Keynes, who managed to lead Gertler away. But Lytton had the selfishness of the true artist. Carrington adored him, made him comfortable and ensured quiet when he was working, and entertained his friends when he decided to invite them to the house. He would no more bother himself with her affairs than he would wish to hear whether she had found fish or lamb chops in the local shops for his dinner. That the 'happy foursome' at Ham Spray was not so happy as it might have been, and was, in fact, upon the point of breaking into fragments, was something he preferred not to think about.

I have said that Lytton seemed old to me. Carrington, in her thirties, did not seem young. She was a contemporary and great friend of an extremely beautiful and seductive woman, Phyllis de Janzé, who lived in a different world but who had been at the Slade School with Carrington before the First World War. Phyllis had left her French husband for a succession of lovers; at the time of which I write she was looking for a rich protector, for she was very short of cash. She confided in me, among others—she made free of her confidences. She used to telephone every morning to tell how she was getting on. One day she rang me up to say that Cartier's van had arrived with a parcel for her, a present from a multi-millionaire ducal admirer.

'Don't ring off while I unpack it, it's from the dumble,' she said. 'Is it light or heavy?' I asked.

'Heavy.'

That was a bad sign, and, the layers of tissue paper removed, it turned out to be an onyx paperweight with her initials in gold, not at all what was needed to pay the hills. However Phyllis was an optimist, and her beauty and charm did not long go unrewarded; the rich protector soon appeared. Carrington and I talked it all over—she loved Phyllis and admired her extravagantly. It seemed to me that if Phyllis could confide in me so could Carrington, and as she did not I naively assumed there was nothing to tell. If at the time I had been told that she and not Phyllis would be known to posterity as a famous lover, if not a *femme fatale,* I should have laughed in disbelief, as would Carrington herself; yet so it has turned out. Carrington wrote fascinating letters and diaries and her many talented friends did the same, and there are innumerable biographies and autobiographies about her circle. Above all. it is because of the depth of her love for Lytton and her tragic death that she is remembered.

In the early 60s there was a retrospective exhibition of Henry Lamb's drawings in London. All Bloomsbury was on the walls, and the survivors were there at the private view. Clive Bell, whom I knew slightly, came up and said: 'You knew Lytton, didn't you?' We talked for a few minutes, and went our ways. Some years later I got a letter from David Garnett, who was passing through Paris, inviting me to luncheon 'so that we can talk about Lytton'. We had met briefly years before when I was visiting Lytton in a London nursing home. The power of Strachey's personality was undimmed, he was someone whom those fortunate enough to have known him liked to remember and discuss. Of late years fewer people say, 'You knew Lytton Strachey.' It is more often, 'You knew Carrington. How fascinating she must have been!'

Yes, she was fascinating. To me, she looked like a little Beatrix Potter character in her unfashionable print cotton dresses, but Lady Ottoline Morrell describes her as a moorland pony. She had brown hair, cut straight and short with a fringe, as though she hoped to hide as much of her face as possible. It was no longer the 'golden bell' described by Aldous Huxley. Her deep-set eyes were blue, her hands worn with toil—gardening, cooking, working for her beloved Lytton. All summer she had bare legs, sunburnt, sandals and white socks. When she walked she turned her toes in, and her every gesture was that of a desperately shy and self-deprecating person. She was clever and perceptive and original; she had learnt a great deal from Lytton over the years. Gossip amused her, but she did not confide much to me. What else? There was the delightful flattery. I suppose she sensed just how much of this rich and delectable fare her companion of the moment could swallow.

Carrington was a talented artist, and it is sad that Ham Spray and the other houses where she lived with Lytton consumed so much of her time and energy. She loved painting, and creating objects like a rococo fantasy of shells she gave us; it was mounted on a painted wooden base which she said once belonged to a sewing machine. She made beautiful flower pictures out of crumpled silver paper—exuberant huge bright flowers with silvery green leaves. Far too modest about her work, to which she attached little importance, she painted because she loved painting; she was like a bird singing, all too easily interrupted.

In August 1931 Lytton went for his last visit to France. Roger Senhouse was to have gone with him, but finally went elsewhere. He probably felt remorse about this a few months later, but he need not have worried. The solitary journey in late summer seems to have been nearly perfect, with Lytton unaccountably calm and contented, not nervous as he usually was when he travelled.

While I was in London in September for the birth of my son Desmond, Carrington painted a surprise for me—a girl peeling an apple, watched by a cat—on a blank window at Biddesden. She said that Phyllis sat for the girl and Tiber (Lytton's cat Tiberius) for the cat. The picture was not quite finished when I came back, and I was kept away from the west side of the house so that it should be a complete surprise. She wrote to Lytton that she had got up early to go over and finish it, but the car refused to start and it was ten o'clock before she arrived at Biddesden.

> Then, typically as you would say, the moment I started to paint it came on to rain. So all my paints got mixed with water. My hair dripped into my eyes and my feet became icy cold.
>
> Diana was delighted. Bryan kept it a complete surprise from her till 3 o'clock. May [A parlourmaid] joined in the joke, and kept my presence dark all this morning and pretended I had walked over from Ham Spray as my car had to be hidden. Diana, of course, thought nothing of my walking over in the rain

[Twelve miles] and merely said 'But Carrington you ought to have let me send the car for you.' I had tea there and then came back.

This letter dated 29 October 1951 must be one of the last that Carrington wrote to Lytton about days she spent at Biddesden. He was in London, because 'Diana says Will you tell Mr oh indeed to remember the christening on Monday.' I called him 'oh indeed' because it was what he so often said during our conversations, and it is more than possible that on being told of the christening this may have been his rejoinder.

Once when she and Julia Strachey [Daughter of Oliver Strachey, and niece of Lytton] came for luncheon my younger sisters were there. Carrington wrote: 'The little sisters were ravishingly beautiful, and another of 16 very marvellous, and grecian [Unity]. I thought the mother was rather remarkable, very sensible and no upper classes graces. The little sister [Debo] was a great botanist and completely won me by her high spirits and charm.' She also told him that she and Julia 'had a long talk on rather painful topics and got rather gloomy. I do not know what to advise, for I have very little faith in there being any happiness for human beings on this earth.'

The painful topic was the imminent breakdown of the 'happy foursome', which was becoming unhappier all the time. One sensed a good deal of strain at Ham Spray, with Ralph Partridge torn between his love for Frances Marshall, his fondness for Carrington, and his deep affection and admiration for Lytton. Yet to me there was also a feeling of permanence, perhaps only because to the young the idea that the present is transient seldom occurs.

My great joy was their frequent visits; Carrington telephoned: 'Lytton says may we come over?' Sometimes, in that autumn of 1931, Lytton seemed rather quiet; there were fewer jokes, fewer shrieks; he was not well. But none of us, not even Carrington, who watched over him so lovingly, realized that he was mortally ill, that tragedy was looming and that quite soon the problem of the unhappy foursome was to be permanently solved.

Carrington was becoming very worried about him when she wrote to Rosamond Lehmann to tell her she had met Mrs Hammersley at Biddesden, 'and was fascinated by her. She talked a *great* deal about you.

She is so beautiful in a romantic Russian style I couldn't take my eyes off her… You are dear to write such cheering letters. I've been feeling in a black dungeon all this week. Nightmarish day and night.'

He became much worse; typhoid was diagnosed, he had a high temperature, which persisted. He had to have nurses, and all his friends and relations gathered round, some staying in the house, some at the Bear in Hungerford. I tried not to telephone too often, but during those weeks my thoughts were constantly with Lytton at Ham Spray, and with Carrington, distracted by worry and grief. On the telephone she always said he was a *little* better, but it was not true. He saw many grand doctors, but only after his death was it discovered that he had been suffering from cancer; inoperable cancer. He died in January.

When he was in a coma and there was no more hope, Carrington tried to kill herself. She waited until the milking machine at the farm near the garage started up at five thirty in the pitch-dark early morning, so that nobody in the house should hear the car engine running. Then she lay down and breathed in the fumes from the exhaust, and after a while lost consciousness. Unluckily for her she was found and brought painfully back to life. Life without Lytton, which she rejected.

In her diary she has set out, unanswerably, her reasons for wishing to die. Every single thing had lost its point for her since he was no longer there to share it: everything—art, nature, books, friends, jokes. Thus life could only be a burden and a bore. We who loved her and longed for her to live thought that if only a little time could go by her grief would become less sharp and painful and intense. But this was precisely what she most dreaded. The idea that she might become accustomed to life without Lytton was abhorrent. When she went to stay with Dorelia and Augustus John at Fryern Court in Wiltshire we hoped the change of scene and the fact of being surrounded by such old and dear friends might do her good, which was in fact what she herself feared. All the time she was thinking of ways and means of suicide.

Out riding at Biddesden her horse bolted; she hoped to fall and be killed. She did fall, but only got a few bruises: 'I who long for death find it so hard to meet him,' she says in her diary describing the incident.

From Fryern she wrote me a loving letter:

Darling Diana

It was lovely seeing you on Saturday... Diana, I wanted so much to give you something of Lytton's. He bought an 18th Cent waistcoat years ago and we never could think of anyone worthy of it because it was so beautiful. Now it will be yours. Perhaps you could alter it. I'd like to think of you wearing it.

Then a few words about Lytton, and 'we talked of you so often'. The waistcoat was thick silk embroidered with little flowers, pink and blue.

Not long after this, once again at Ham Spray, Carrington shot herself. I have never understood why she did not repeat her attempt of two months before and breathe in fumes from her car. As she was alone in the house, she would have been undisturbed. Perhaps this time she was determined to make absolutely sure.

Looking back, how strange it seems that I knew Lytton for barely three years and Carrington for less time still. They had become so closely woven into my life that their loss was extremely painful. This must have been generally realized, for I received many letters of condolence, almost as if they had been near relations.

When, a generation later, Lytton and Carrington were put under the microscope, I read the results with interest, but could hardly relate them to the people I knew and loved. Carrington in particular has been blown up into something quite unlike herself. Not that it much matters. Lytton lives in his books, and she in her pictures, her letters, and her diaries.

Acknowledgements

Articles written for the privately printed *European* have only the title of the book, author and date. The diary has its own section. The remaining articles were mainly written for the (defunct) *Books and Bookmen* and the *Evening Standard* (Diana was the catch-all reviewer for A.N. Wilson as literary editor). 'Paradise on Earth' is unpublished. The collection is thematic rather than chronological so that there is a coherence to the selection; to an extent the location arbitrary as essays can at times come under several different themes or subthemes. 'Large Huts', the portrait of Lady Evelyn Guinness is edited from *A Life of Contrasts*, and the 'Portraits' are from *Loved Ones*.

Index

467

Index

Index

Index

Index

Index

Index